A BOLD AND DANGEROUS FAMILY

Fortune's Hostages

Sidney Bernstein: A Biography

Freya Stark: A Biography

Over the Rim of the World: The Letters of Freya Stark (ed.)

Troublesome People

Betrayed: Children in Today's World (ed.)

Bertrand Russell: A Life

The Lost Treasures of Troy

Dunant's Dream: War, Switzerland and the History of the
Red Cross

Iris Origo: Marchesa of Val d'Orcia

Martha Gellhorn: A Life

Human Cargo: A Journey Among Refugees

The Letters of Martha Gellhorn (ed.)

Dancing to the Precipice: Lucie de la Tour du Pin and the
French Revolution

A Train in Winter: A Story of Resistance, Friendship and
Survival

Village of Secrets: Defying the Nazis in Vichy France

A BOLD AND DANGEROUS FAMILY

The Remarkable Story of an Italian Mother, Her Sons, and Their Fight Against Fascism

CAROLINE MOOREHEAD

Random House Canada

PUBLISHED BY RANDOM HOUSE CANADA

www.penguinrandomhouse.ca

Random House Canada and colophon are registered trademarks.

Library and Archives Canada Cataloguing in Publication

Moorehead, Caroline, author
A bold and dangerous family : the remarkable story of an Italian mother,
her sons, and their fight against fascism / Caroline Moorehead.

Includes bibliographical references.
Issued in print and electronic formats.

ISBN 978-0-345-81405-0
eBook ISBN 978-0-345-81407-4

1. Rosselli, Amelia. 2. Rosselli, Carlo, 1899–1937. 3. Rosselli, Nello,
1900–1937. 4. Rosselli family. 5. Intellectuals—Italy—Biography.
6. Fascism—Italy—History—20th century. 7. Anti-fascist movements—
Italy—History—20th century. 8. Italy—Politics and
government—1914–1945. I. Title.

DG575.R38M67 2017   945.091092'2   C2017-900798-X

Cover images: Jacket photographs: (front) © Getty Images;
(back) 50,000 Blackshirts saluting Mussolini at Littoriale Stadium,
Rome, 31st October, 1926 © akg-images/Mondadori Portfolio

Printed and bound in the United States of America

10 9 8 7 6 5 4 3 2 1

Penguin
Random House
RANDOM HOUSE CANADA

To Penny

Carlo and Nello

Contents

Principal Characters ix

Chronology xi

Preface xiii

Chapter 1   A Watery Childhood   1

Chapter 2   *Donne Emancipate*   19

Chapter 3   Defining *la Patria*   32

Chapter 4   Becoming a Man   51

Chapter 5   The Dark Seraphim   66

Chapter 6   Planting a Tree   89

Chapter 7   Moral Choices   109

Chapter 8   'Non Mollare'   127

Chapter 9   Breaking Free   152

Chapter 10   Defying the Barbarians   170

Chapter 11   *Il Confino*   188

Chapter 12   The Island of Winds   202

Chapter 13   Not Even the Flies Escape   221

Chapter 14   To Be an Exile   236

Chapter 15   Just One Heart   259

Chapter 16   Dancing for Liberty   278

Chapter 17   A World of Moral Richness   297

Chapter 18   A Free Man Again   328

Chapter 19   A Corneillian Tragedy   351

Postscript 373

Acknowledgements 375

List of Illustrations 377

Sources and Select Bibliography 379
Notes 389
Index 405

Principal Characters

The Family

Amelia Pincherle Rosselli, playwright
Joe Rosselli, musicologist
Aldo, their eldest son, known as 'Topinino', born in 1895
Carlo, born 1899
Nello, born 1900
Marion Cave, Carlo's wife
Their children, Giovanni ('Mirtillino'), Melina and Andrea
Maria Todesco, Nello's wife
Their children, Silvia, Paola, Aldo and Alberto
Gabriele Pincherle, Amelia's brother
Alberto Moravia, Amelia's nephew
Giulio and Giorgina Zabban, honorary uncle and aunt

Their anti-fascist circle

Giovanni Bassanesi, pilot
Riccardo Bauer, economist
Piero Calamandrei, jurist
Gina Lombroso, writer
Emilio Lussu, friend on Lipari
Francesco Fausto Nitti, friend on Lipari
Ferruccio Parri, journalist
Ernesto Rossi, teacher
Gaetano Salvemini, historian
Filippo Turati, socialist leader

Mussolini's Men

Italo Balbo, *ras* of Ferrara
Arturo Bocchini, head of police
Galeazzo Ciano, Mussolini's son-in-law and foreign minister
Carlo del Re, spy
Amerigo Dumini, fascist henchman
Dino Segre ('Pitigrilli'), spy
Tullio Tamburini, leader of *squadristi* in Florence

Chronology

1870	16 January	Amelia Pincherle born in Venice
1892	3 April	Marriage of Amelia to Joe Rosselli
1898	29 October	Premier of Amelia's first play, *Anima*
1903	October	Amelia Rosselli and her sons, Aldo, Carlo and Nello, arrive in Florence
1921	May	Mussolini wins thirty-five seats in parliament
1922	28 October	March on Rome, after which Mussolini becomes prime minister
1924	April	General elections give the fascists a majority
	10 June	Giacomo Matteotti kidnapped and murdered
1925	3 January	Mussolini's speech to parliament and start of his dictatorship
1926	5 November	Passing of the 'most fascist' laws: opposition parties dissolved, anti-fascist organisations closed

xi

		down, censorship increased, penalties for trying to leave the country illegally. Appointment of Arturo Bocchini as head of police
	25 November	A new law 'for the defence of the State' sets up the Special Tribunal with severe penalties – including death – for any opposition activity
1929	11 February	Concordat between the Italian state and the Vatican
1935	3 October	Italian invasion of Ethiopia
1936	5 May	Italian troops enter Addis Ababa
	9 May	Declaration of Italy's African empire; Victor Emmanuel III becomes Emperor of Ethiopia
	July	Start of the Spanish Civil War
1937	January	Italy leaves the League of Nations
1939	22 May	Mussolini and Hitler sign the Pact of Steel and become Axis partners
1940	10 June	Italy declares war on France and Britain
1943	25 July	Overthrow and imprisonment of Mussolini
	8 September	Armistice with the Allies announced
	23 September	Mussolini sets up the Repubblica Sociale Italiana in Salò
1945	27 April	Mussolini executed by Italian partisans

Preface

On 30 May 1924, a tall, elegant man in his late thirties, lean but not bony, with thinning, slightly curly hair, and very blue eyes set off by an equally blue sapphire on his watch chain, rose in the Chamber of Deputies in the Italian parliament in Rome and delivered an excoriating attack on Mussolini and the newly elected Fascist Party. His name was Giacomo Matteotti and he was a socialist from the Po Valley. He had recently brought out a book in which he analysed Mussolini's speeches, pointing out their inaccuracies and inconsistencies, and had devoted 42 pages to a list of some 2,000 separate assaults committed by Mussolini's fascists between November 1922 and October 1923 – murder, beatings, arson, destruction of the homes and offices of left-wing opponents, and the forcible administration of castor oil. He had come to the Chamber, he said, to denounce the voting irregularities of the recent elections, the atmosphere of intimidation in which they had been conducted, and to call for them to be declared invalid.

Matteotti spoke for two hours, against a background of jeers, threats, bullying and calls for his removal. He told the Chamber that he was preparing a dossier of fascist crimes which would include evidence of bribes accepted by the fascists from an American oil company in exchange for the right to control the distribution of petrol in Italy, in which Mussolini's brother Arnaldo was complicit; and that he would soon be presenting it to parliament. He spoke calmly, without hyperbole; but he was implacable and he loved spare, precise facts. In Italy's political world, where daily business had become a matter of obfuscation, deals, lies and evasions, and the many different opposition parties were weak and fighting among themselves, Matteotti was a rare honest man.

As he left the Chamber, he said to a colleague: 'Now you may prepare my funeral oration.'

Mussolini, sitting at the back, had kept largely silent while Matteotti spoke. Afterwards, bursting into the office of the secretary of the Fascist Party, he shouted: 'If you weren't all a pack of cowards, no one would have dared make that speech . . . People like Matteotti . . . should not be allowed to circulate.'

At 3.30 on the afternoon of 10 June, Matteotti left his home at 40 Via Pisanelli on the banks of the Tiber. It was very hot and the streets were almost deserted. A black Lancia pulled up alongside him. A small boy playing with friends reported later that he had seen a man hit in the face and carried, struggling, into a car. Matteotti disappeared. A few hours later, Amerigo Dumini, leader of a semi-official terror squad with a string of political murders to his name, appeared in Mussolini's office carrying a small piece of bloodstained upholstery from the Lancia.

Next day, 11 June, Mussolini publicly denied all knowledge of any crime, saying that since Matteotti had recently been given a passport, he had probably gone abroad – a claim vehemently denied by Matteotti's wife, Velia. On 12 June, while journalists gathered outside, Mussolini told parliament that though he still knew nothing, he was beginning to suspect foul play. He spoke of a 'diabolical outrage'.

Banks of flowers piled up on the spot where Matteotti had been kidnapped. A cross was painted on the wall in red. In the Piazza del Duomo in Milan cars, carts and buses stopped while people knelt to pray. To prevent further criticism and rumour, Mussolini prorogued parliament and visited the king to tender his resignation. The king refused it. The number of the Lancia was reported to the police by a vigilant caretaker, the car traced and found to be spattered with blood. Matteotti's bloodstained trousers were discovered in Dumini's briefcase; he and his associates were arrested.

On 17 August, a road mender inspecting pipes on the Via Flaminia, fifteen miles outside Rome, discovered a jacket. It was identified as belonging to Matteotti. Nearby, in a shallow ditch, was his body, decomposed and bearing clear stab marks. Isabella, Matteotti's mother, identified what remained of her son.

A sense of horror and disgust spread around Italy. The Italians had grown accustomed to daily violence, as fascist leaders despatched their black-shirted *squadristi* on punitive raids against editors and publishers, union representatives and uncorrupt lawyers and judges, beating those who opposed Mussolini into silence. But this cold-blooded murder was something different. Even previous supporters of the fascists expressed shame and indignation. No one could quite believe that Italians were capable of such a deed. Within fascist circles, there were accusations, counter-attacks, a feeling of panic.

Mussolini, with ruthlessness and great subtlety, survived. But no Italian ever forgot the moment when fascism itself seemed to stumble.

In 1924, having endured five years of strikes, impotent governments, street-fighting and the poverty that followed the First World War, the Italians were exhausted. Mussolini's opponents were weak and disorganised. In the wake of the Matteotti murder they met, they talked, they discussed setting up a broad-based coalition to challenge Mussolini; but no one gave the order to move and no one could agree on what to do. They had won a great moral victory; but they failed to translate it into a political one. Scattered in ones and twos around the country, however, in universities, lawyers' and editors' offices and publishing houses, were individuals for whom Matteotti's death was a defining moment, the start of twenty years of struggle inside Italy and abroad, conducted against overwhelmingly stronger forces, with many casualties along the way. Anti-fascist resistance was born and it would end only with Mussolini's death.

And for one Florentine family – ardent followers of Mazzini, hero of the Risorgimento, full of strong feelings about duty, responsibility and courage – the murder of Matteotti was the day their lives changed, and there would be no going back. It turned them into bold anti-fascists, heedless of their own safety, as uncompromising as Matteotti himself, a man they had revered and believed capable of saving Italy from violent, unprincipled rule. Their names were Amelia, Carlo and Nello Rosselli.

Amelia and her sons

CHAPTER ONE

A Watery Childhood

Venice 1870

Amelia Pincherle was born on the second floor of the Palazzo Boldù on the Grand Canal, Venice, between the Ca' d'Oro and the Rialto, on 16 January 1870, the year that saw the unification of Italy in the final act of the Risorgimento. All through her childhood she would sit on a step on the balcony, the sun shimmering on the grey water, watching the gondolas and the funeral barges with their biers of black and gold, and fittings in the shape of sea horses, harps and dolphins, making their way to the island of San Michele. As dusk fell, and the man arrived with his long pole to light the gas lamps, the Grand Canal turned red and the swallows appeared; from her stone step, still warm from the sun, she followed them as they circled and dipped. What she would remember later, when she came to write her memoirs, were the cries of the gulls, and in the winter, the rain against the window-panes, the sea that could be heard but not seen, with its dull, distant roar.

Amelia was the last of eight children, three of whom had died in infancy. Her mother, Emilia, was forty-two when she was born, already worn out and ailing from her repeated pregnancies and the blood-letting that followed. Her father, Giacomo Pincherle, was a businessman, and had added the name Moravia as a ges-ture to the uncle who had adopted him when his own parents died young. The marriage was considered a *mésalliance* by her family: she very beautiful, he heavily marked by smallpox caught during their engagement. When he recovered, he offered to break it off, but she refused, though appalled by his scarred face and the loss of his thick, fair hair, saying that it was her duty now to marry him. By the time Amelia was a small girl the Pincherle business had ceased to prosper. One of Amelia's first conscious memories was of being asked by one of their two maids, Giovanna, whom they had decided must go in order to save money, to intervene on her behalf. Giovanna was in tears. Amelia went to find her parents, but when she confronted them, their faces were forbidding, and she dared not speak. 'I felt as if I had failed in my duty,' she wrote later. 'I should have fought for her, but I wasn't brave enough.' Courage and duty: two messages learnt early.

Elena, the eldest Pincherle daughter, was twenty in 1870 and had already moved to Turin to marry. So little did Amelia know about this sister that when Elena came to Venice to visit them, she thought she was a stranger and addressed her as 'Signora'. Next came Gabriele, later to be Amelia's closest brother, a young man with deep-set eyes and narrow shoulders who was a law student at Padua university. Nearest to her in age was Carlo, seven years her senior, but he had friends with whom he wished to spend his time and, when obliged to take her with him, dragged her through the maze of crooked waterways and alleys at a terrifying pace.

The sister Amelia loved was Anna, thirteen when she was born, more mother to her than stern and worn Emilia, whose disapproval caused her constant misery. Anna, laughing and affectionate, was the centre of her life. She sat the little girl on her knee and read to her, and when Amelia had done her lessons, played to her on the piano, Mozart's Turkish March or Boccherini's Minuet, which made Amelia think of dancers, elegant and stately. Anna had a friend, as ugly as she herself was pretty, but of great charm and character. When the two girls sat whispering in the shuttered *salotto*, Amelia hid under the eighteenth-century console with its Sèvres tea set and listened.

The Pincherles were Jewish, descendants of the Sephardic families driven from Spain by Ferdinand and Isabella in 1492. By the nineteenth century, Venice's Jews had long since knocked down the walls of their ghetto. Liberated in 1797 by Napoleon, who at the same time ordered the removal of every winged lion in the city, they had fared better than Jews elsewhere in Italy, even after Venice and its hinterland had been ceded to the Austrian Empire.

Venetian-Jewish girls were educated, bookish; their parents owned property and worked for the city council. The Pincherles were no more than passingly religious, but they were mindful of the moral precepts of their faith; and they were patriots.

The popular unrest which had swept Europe twenty years before reached Venice in March 1848, when a lawyer called Daniele Manin led the Venetians in an uprising that expelled the Austrians from their city. A second Republic was set up. Among the men appointed to the provisional government was Leone Pincherle, Giacomo's uncle; Giacomo himself, newly married, fought with the Guardia Nazionale of Venice. The Austrians besieged the city, subjecting it to violent bombardments. Emilia was about to give birth to her first child. When the baby, a girl, arrived, she sent her with a wet-nurse to the Giudecca, and had herself rowed over by gondola each evening. But the baby did not thrive. The little girl was dead by the time the city, starving and full of cholera, capitulated to the Austrians on 23 August 1849. Among the men forced to flee was Leone Pincherle, who, with Manin, made his way to Paris. The events left the family with a profound hatred of the Austrians, but with great enthusiasm for the Risorgimento, the social and political movement of resurgence or rebirth, which would ultimately turn Italy into a single country.

When, in 1859, a new war between Austria and Piedmont broke out, many Venetians joined Giuseppe Garibaldi and his thousand volunteers, who landed in Sicily and conquered the Bourbon-ruled Kingdom of the Two Sicilies. On 17 March 1861 – nine years before Amelia's birth – the Kingdom of Italy, freed at last from foreign domination, long dreamt about by Dante, Petrarch, Machiavelli, Cavour, Mazzini and many others, was formally proclaimed. It included Parma, Modena, most of Lombardy, Tuscany, most of the Papal States and the Kingdom of the Two Sicilies, with a Piedmontese capital in Turin and a Piedmontese king. But it did not yet include Venice, which joined the new kingdom only in 1866. True unity came in 1870, the year of Amelia's birth. Italy was thereafter a single country, with many different languages, one of them Latin, many laws, many taxation systems and many currencies – in Piedmont the lira, in Naples the *ducati*, in the Papal States the *scudi*. So convoluted were the regulations that it was said that travellers descending the river Po had to cross twenty-two customs barriers and pay taxes at each one.

Among the Pincherles, Jewishness and *la patria* were both spoken of with reverence, but of these two religions, *la patria* was the one that counted. One day, opening a cupboard in her parents' bedroom, Amelia caught sight of something small and hard and grey. It was, her father told her, his most precious object: a piece of petrified bread saved from the days of the siege of Venice. In the same cupboard there was a torn and faded flag, which was suspended from the balcony on anniversaries, while in the dining room hung scenes of patriotic acts.

It was a lonely childhood. When Amelia was nine, her much loved sister Anna left to get married and moved to Bologna. This, Amelia wrote later in her memoirs, was 'a catastrophe, a black stone in my existence'; watching the betrothed pair from her hiding place under the table in the *salotto*, she regarded the tall young man with the huge black whiskers as a thief. With Anna gone and only Amelia and Carlo still at home, the house, kept shuttered and dark for much of the time, was silent and still except for the winter days when winds from the open sea howled and the candles flickered and went out. There was no electricity and no central heating, and the only stove that was kept permanently lit was in the room in which her parents sat. The winter of 1880 was the coldest on record; month after month rain fell. Amelia's feet never seemed to feel warm.

Spartan physically and obedient morally, she and Carlo were expected to follow the new Jaeger gymnastics recently introduced from Germany, which excluded all forms of weakness. Her nights were full of terrors and in the dark the heavy oak furniture took on menacing shapes. In the huge sombre rooms, with their high ceilings, she felt herself to be an echo. Her mother was unbending towards her fears; Teresa, the remaining maid, was indifferent. The Pincherles had trouble adjusting to the hard times that had hit them; in their long, dark clothes they seemed to belong to an earlier, more formal age.

Alone so much, Amelia lived a rich imaginary inner life. She turned the chairs in the *salotto* upside down and pretended that

4

they were gondolas, rowing across a marble lagoon. She formed a desire to make others happy, since she could not be happy herself, and revelled in the bitter pleasure of their happiness. Excessive altruism became her mask, colouring much of her childhood and adolescence, and leaving her with a taste of shame and duplicity.

But she had a cat, wary as were all Venetian cats of the numerous rats that infested the city, and she was not totally without friends to play with. Amelia went on walks with her younger cousin Augusto Levi along the lagoon to the Veneta Marina, near the station, where old steam engines and carriages were left to rust, perfect for hiding and make-believe journeys. The Levis were the Venetian-Jewish aristocracy. Augusto's mother, Zia Nina, was a fierce woman, her face permanently clouded with anger, her lips clenched together, ruling over her mild, bearded husband and her ten children as if she were a general in command of an army.

What Amelia enjoyed least were the long walks to the public gardens – where an elephant was to be found – with a cousin of her mother's, Emma Grassini, a tall, fair-haired martinet who lectured Amelia and her own four children along the way, her conversation unremittingly erudite and bossy. Her children were obliged to speak a different language every day, and neighbours learnt to tell the days of the week simply by listening to them talk. Amelia, who spoke only the Venetian dialect, felt, as she wrote later, *nuda*, exposed, inadequate. Of Emma's children, the one closest in age to Amelia was the clever and fanciful Lina, who wanted to be a boy and called herself Colombo. The two girls became friends. Lina had a much younger sister, Margherita, already pretty and forceful, who would later, as Margherita Sarfatti, become a popular journalist and Mussolini's mistress. Though there was no respite from instruction at the Grassinis', where even charades were used as occasions in which to impart more knowledge, Amelia loved the noise and the constant chatter and she dreaded returning to the muffled silence of her own home.

She was terrified of their thin-lipped neighbour from downstairs, another Levi relation, always dressed in black, and her small ugly husband in his tight-fitting suit and beret who forced her to answer in Latin when he gave her a chocolate. But once a year the Levis' Florentine relations, the Orvietos, came to stay

and then Amelia would be sent down, in a starched white pina-
fore, to play with their young sons, Angiolo and Adolfo, and
though they teased her, and she felt ashamed of her uncouth
Venetian dialect, she saw in their warmth and wildness something
deeply enticing.

Every Wednesday, women friends of Emilia's gathered for tea,
the only social event of the week, when Teresa would polish the
brass handles until they glowed, and the dust covers were removed
from the pale-blue silk furnishings. Then there were weekly visits
from a forester who looked after the family's woods outside the
city. A child of largely tree-less Venice, Amelia loved to hear him
talk about the different species and the birds which nested in
them. But she was much distressed when he brought her a chaf-
finch, blinded in order to make it sing more sweetly.

In the autumn of 1881, when Amelia was eleven, the first
vaporetto, the *Regina Margherita*, was launched on the Grand
Canal. Standing on the balcony with her father, Amelia watched
as the large unfamiliar boat rounded the bend by the Rialto, with
smoke rising from its funnel. Loud whistles scattered the gondolas
in its path. Her immediate feeling, she wrote later, was one of
delight: at last a sign of real life on 'those dead waters'.

Though D. H. Lawrence would call Venice 'abhorrent, green,
slippery' and Ruskin railed against the 'canals choked with human
dung', the city was still, as Amelia grew up, the high point of the
European tour. Despite the decay, despite the depredations of the Austrians as they pulled out, tearing up parquet flooring to make boxes
for their loot, despite Napoleon's own frenzied plunder, Venice itself
remained magnificent, a place of frescoed churches and public buildings full of masterpieces of the Venetian Renaissance. The launch
of the first vaporetto had been timed for the Geographical Congress
of 1882. The king and queen of the new Italy, along with invited
European nobility, arrived to find silk carpets and flags hanging
from the balconies along the Grand Canal, a pageant, a regatta,
gondoliers in fifteenth- and sixteenth-century costumes, and a procession of decorated boats, in one of which the crew were dressed
as polar bears, while a walrus lay crouched in the bows and on the
stern was a pyramid of ice. That night, the Piazza San Marco was
illuminated by myriad tiny lamps, whose flames seemed to waver
in a great sheet of living fire.

Venice remained a city of music, where Vivaldi was born, Monteverdi was for many years *maestro di cappella* of St Mark's, and where Wagner worked on *Tristan and Isolde*. Venetians enjoyed their feast days, their processions, their clergy robed in vestments, and there was no city in Italy so in love with customs, the rituals of food, the separate identities of its different quarters. Nor a city so superstitious: ants, said the Venetians, were harbingers of death, oleanders were deeply unlucky and centipedes the bearers of good fortune.

A regular line had recently been started from the United States to Italy, and Venice made a terminus for the Indian mail steamers. The many new visitors were advised to spend five days in Venice – fifteen in Naples, thirty in Rome – to sit drinking in Florian's and to visit Murano to watch the glassmakers. In the summer months, tourists took the steamer to the Lido, where Byron had once galloped his horses along the beach, and where bathing establishments, restaurants and concert rooms now opened. Venice, observed Browning, was 'gaily international, though somewhat provincial'.

Foreigners, however, played very little part in Amelia's closeted life. For her, Venice was a place of sea and sky, the water constantly changing to different shades of green and grey, pure and silvery under the moon, while beyond lay the lagoon, which the low spring tides transformed into a meadow of long pale sea-green grass. In winter the storms turned the courtyards into lakes, soaking basements and the stores of wood for the stoves. And what she carried away with her when, in her fifteenth year, her father suddenly died and she and Emilia moved to Rome, was a memory of her watery childhood, along with a strong sense of discipline, integrity and justice, a conviction that one had to distribute what one had not out of charity but as a duty, and that fortitude was not a matter of choice – all beliefs handed down to her by her intensely moral parents. Years later she would feel grateful for the strength they gave her.

Rome 1886

In 1872, the year that Amelia was two, Rome had been made the capital of the new united Italy. King Victor Emmanuel II, a small, squat man with little grey eyes and thick legs, voracious for food and women, installed his court in the Quirinale. By the mid-1880s, when Amelia arrived, this city of fountains and gardens, green marble and pink travertine, of monasteries, convents and seminaries, was in a fever of construction. The ill-planned new buildings were causing more harm, noted the writer Augustus Hare, than all the invasions of Goths and Visigoths.

As a capital city, however, Rome was curiously old-fashioned. There was no stock exchange, and very little industry, though Pius IX had installed electricity and been a generous patron of the arts. Teams of oxen pulling carts brought in fruit every day from the countryside. Rome was an immense farm, where cows and goats grazed, in the middle of a great plain of wheat. When the cardinals went walking on the Pincio, their black soutanes revealed flashes of scarlet stocking. In summer, mock sea battles were fought in the flooded Piazza Navona, where at Christmas shepherds descended from the Abruzzo to play their bagpipes.

Amelia and her mother moved in with her brother Gabriele, now a respected jurist and working in the Ministry of Justice. Though the apartment in Via Nazionale had few rooms, these were grand, with high ceilings. The formal drawing room had Biedermeier furniture and Bokhara rugs on the polished parquet floors. Amelia settled into her new home and excelled at her studies. Italian had replaced Venetian as her main language. She had grown closer to Emilia, who had become softer and less judgemental. And Amelia was turning into a striking young woman, with thick hair piled high on her head, arresting blue eyes and a long thin nose. The soft white muslin dresses of the day suited her. In character she was strong, tenacious, shrewd, and she liked to be right; insecure and uncertain, she could appear inflexible. But she was also loving and anxious to please, intelligent and profoundly honest.

Sometime in 1889, when she was nineteen, Amelia met Giuseppe Rosselli, a near neighbour in Via Nazionale. Joe, as he was known,

Amelia Pincherle at the time of her marriage

was a natty dresser, sporting flowery cravats and a cane with a silver handle. He was broad-shouldered, with a soft full beard and straight black hair. To satisfy his father, he had taken a degree in law, but his real love was musicology. He sent Amelia snowdrops and violets, and a sheet of music written especially for her. She was delighted with his elegance and his enthusiasms. Soon he was writing: 'I love you. I don't know what else to say: I say it over and over again, to you, to myself, to your letters, to your hair, to your dear little face, to the songs on the piano, to the air, in my dreams, always ...'

The Rossellis too were Jews, equally cosmopolitan, polyglot and secular, Roman citizens who had moved to Livorno, with its large Sephardic Jewish community, in the early nineteenth century to escape the Pope's anti-semitic laws and to extend their commercial activities. From Livorno's free port, four Rosselli brothers – Sabatino, Pellegrino, Raffaelo and Angiolo – had set up banking and business links with London, where they had opened a money-changing office near Fenchurch Street. They traded and prospered on exports of oil, coffee, coral, ostrich feathers, fezzes, lace and embroidery.

Joe was born in Livorno on 10 August 1867, the son of Sabatino Rosselli and his wife Henrietta Nathan, whose own mother, Sara or Sarina, was the matriarch of the Nathan family. The Rossellis and the Nathans were joined by a series of marriages between brothers and cousins. To his father, as a small boy, Joe wrote in English, letters often seeking forgiveness for misdemeanours. 'My dear Papa, my mother says I have been a little better lately, will you write to me?' and 'Will you try to forget my faults?' Joe did well in oral exams, especially in Greek and Italian literature, but said that all sciences were 'odious' to him.

Like the Pincherles, the Nathans were also patriots for whom *la patria* mattered more than religious observance. They felt grateful to the Risorgimento which had brought them freedom both from the Austrians and from the papal authorities. In the 1830s in London, both the Rossellis and the Nathans had met Giuseppe Mazzini, the Genoan visionary journalist and pamphleteer who, along with Cavour and Garibaldi, would be one of the founders of the united kingdom of Italy. A good-looking man, with soft feline grace and a long, mournful, oval face, Mazzini had an uncompromising, even religious sense of patriotism. He had spent his life organising one insurrection after another, calling for a new Rome for all the Italian people, based on morality and duty. He believed that if only countries were given the frontiers that God had intended for them, then peace and goodwill would surely follow, and that the unification of Italy would be just one step towards the unification of all Europe. He thought of himself as a 'missionary of a religion of progress and fraternity'. Others saw him either as the principal theorist of patriotic movements in nineteenth-century Europe, or as a dangerous radical.

At the age of twenty-six, having narrowly escaped execution, he went into exile, to spend most of the remaining years of his life abroad, dedicating himself to the cause of political and social revolution. He reached London after expulsion by the Swiss. He lived and dressed plainly and was appalled by the cost of everything, though he had a taste for scent and expensive writing paper. He thought the English unusually prone to drunkenness and complained about the bed bugs in his cheap lodgings, but he enjoyed pale ale, saying that it was far healthier than the London water, which was full of worms and bugs. Mazzini loved music. He had not been in London long when he met Sarina Nathan, and together they played in ensembles of chamber music. Money was always short, but the Nathans were happy to provide it. In the evenings, in Sarina's house, there was much talk of suffrage, education, poverty, and how Karl Marx and communism would not work in a liberal, united Italy. Mazzini had great charm but paid little attention when urged to shave off his moustache, which friends said gave him the look of a wild revolutionary. Sarina and her husband Mayer Moses, whose father was rumoured to be a Rothschild, helped Mazzini send coded messages into Italy in the form of trading exchanges: Purchase '50 *sacchi della solita merce*' – 50 sacks of the usual goods – meant buy guns.

To win Rome and make it Italy's capital had always been Mazzini's great ambition. In the summer of 1868, he slipped back into Switzerland and crossed secretly into Italy. It was too soon. Arrested and imprisoned in Naples, he was in jail while the military conquest of Rome took place. When freed, he returned to exile in London, spending a few days on the way with the Rosselli brothers in Livorno, then a further two months on Lake Lugano, where Sarina, by now a rich widow, had a house. All twelve of her children had turned out satisfactorily *Mazziniani*. Three years later Mazzini himself was back, having crossed the St Gotthard pass in a horse-drawn sledge, once again staying with Sarina as he launched the last of his twenty newspapers, *La Roma del Popolo*; he sent her son Ernesto to Rome to run it. February 1872 found him in Pisa, calling himself Dr Brown and staying with Sarina's daughter Gianetta, wife of Pellegrino Rosselli, who nursed him through asthma and bronchitis. A month later, shortly before his sixty-seventh birthday, he died. When he was buried in Genoa, the ships at anchor in the bay lowered their flags.

Mazzini's story, his patriotism, his hatred of xenophobia and imperialism, his honesty and moral clarity, were all crucial to the Rossellis' view of themselves and the world they lived in – all things greatly pleasing to Amelia and her family, whose attachment to the recent heroes of the Risorgimento was no less fervent than the Nathans', and for whom Mazzini had long been their champion.

In 1891, Amelia Pincherle and Joe Rosselli became engaged. When he was away in Florence or Livorno they exchanged letters every day, later pasting them into an album decorated with flowers. Their tone evokes their courtship: urgent, unexpectedly amorous, even sensual, sometimes apologetic on his side; reassuring, almost maternal, on hers. He called her '*Miliettina cara*'; she called him '*Mio adorato Joe*' and occasionally '*Joino*'. 'We will always love each other as we do now,' she wrote towards the end of April. 'And, like now, I will feel the need to kiss you and sense your dear lips on mine.' And, three days later, 'Happy, happy in a superhuman way. I feel within myself this great fire, and I ask myself: who can say if Joe feels this way too? who can say ... I feel that my heart, my soul, everything in me is absorbed in you, I am yours in the most complete meaning of the word.'

Whether Joe felt as strongly, whether, indeed, he was capable of such intensity, is not clear. He wrote to her about his new piano, about how when they were married she would sit on his

Amelia and her husband Joe Rosselli

knee while he worked, and they would kiss, not once, not twice, but a hundred times; he told her of his difficulties composing music; he warned her about his bad moods, his doubts, his days of sadness. She told him that she did not mind. 'Come here, my poor little boy, come here to me and I will cover you with kisses, and hug you very tightly, tell you such loving things that it will cure your sadness.' Even so, her letters could be firm: she intended to be taken seriously. 'I want you to get used to the idea of a woman capable of understanding you, comforting you, and raising you up, earnestly and serenely.'

When he sent her rare flowers, or those out of season, she scolded him for his extravagance. Just very occasionally, in one of their many letters, they seemed to be moving tentatively towards the idea that they were perhaps not really made for each other, that the whole edifice of their love was without solid foundation, that his easy-going, conciliatory, light-heartedness was not altogether suited to her strong will and moral clarity. But then they shied away. The fulsome, adoring messages resumed. On 3 April 1892, in a synagogue in Rome, they were married. The night before, Joe wrote to Amelia to record that this was his last letter 'before I am happy'.

Letter-writing was in Amelia's blood. Their honeymoon took them to Naples, Nice, Monte Carlo, Spain, Portugal, North Africa, France and England. From all these places letters and postcards showered down on Via Nazionale in Rome, where Emilia said they kept her company. Amelia wrote in a neat, flowing hand; Joe scrawled messages along the side of the page. In London they visited Madame Tussaud's with Joe's cousins and Amelia marvelled at the elegance of the Londoners. In Bordeaux they stood on the riverside and watched the boats bound for the United States and the East Indies. They went to the races in Seville and visited Fez and Tétouan. Sometimes there was so much to say that Amelia wrote first one way and then another, so that the letter looked more like tapestry than writing. Emilia wrote no less often. On 15 May, when Joe and Amelia reached Madrid, they found fourteen letters waiting for them. The honeymoon lasted nearly three months.

Vienna 1892

By the late 1870s, Vienna had been the musical capital of the western world for over a hundred years. Even if the musical world was riven with a deep and acrimonious gulf between Wagnerians and Brahmians, the first loving and the second despising emotional depths, there was music everywhere, all the time, in the magnificent new Opera House, in concert halls, in private houses and even in the parks. When Joe proposed to Amelia that they settle in Vienna, in order for him to pursue his musical career, she was pleased. For Amelia it meant theatre – in which she was growing more interested – art, culture, an escape from the formality of Italian domestic life.

They arrived in August 1892 and took a flat at 3 Amalien-strasse; Joe enrolled at the Conservatoire to take lessons from Mahler's teacher, Robert Fuchs. Vienna was an agreeable city, surrounded by vineyards, meadows and the beech woods made famous by the waltzes of Johann Strauss, with the river Wien curving away across the plain towards Hungary. Emperor Franz Joseph was living in Olympian isolation from his people, complaining that Mozart's 'Seraglio' had too many notes, and presiding over an aristocracy of sixty-five archdukes and -duchesses. Sisi, the frantically dieting empress, who lived on bouillons of venison and eggs whipped up in port, spent much time travelling abroad and was not popular. But a new constitution had brought civil rights to the emperor's subjects, and prosperity had caused an unrivalled flowering not only of music but of all the arts and sciences.

Led by Klimt, Carl Moll and Otto Wagner, the future young secessionist artists were beginning to replace the carved and inlaid furniture, the fringed tablecloths and heavy dark hangings, the bric-a-brac and peacock feathers, with a sparer, more austere look. The Impressionist painters were arriving; the heavy, declamatory style of theatre was evolving into a swifter, lighter form; trotting races had never been more popular, and before Lent each year, Vienna saw fifty balls held on a single night.

Coffee houses were central to the intellectual life of the city. Open all day and for most of the night, they came in all sizes and forms, and provided food, beer, newspapers and billiard tables. Chess-players met in the Café Central; the Café Griendsteidl was home to musicians and writers. Many of these cafés had been decorated to look like richly gilded drawing rooms, with oil paintings, carpets, stuccoed vaulting, chandeliers and swirls of marble, malachite and alabaster. The best were positioned on street corners, with bay windows on both sides, allowing people to see and to be seen. For the gregarious Joe, who loved to talk, these cafés were extremely alluring. They had little to offer Amelia, for women were not made welcome, and went instead to Demerol's, the imperial confectioner, where they drank hot chocolate and ate creamy cakes. With time on her hands, Amelia went to the many packed theatres, to light comedies and verse plays, and to Schnitzler's sketches about modishly melancholic Austrian youth. She was a good linguist, and in any case Vienna was multilingual, from the days when the Austro-Hungarian empire stretched across swathes of Europe. Joe kept the household accounts meticulously, noting down expenditure on wood, concert tickets, ties, blankets, newspapers and tips to porters. He also recorded his gambling wins and his debts, which grew steadily.

Behind all the exuberance and magnificence, however, was a vague sense of impending collapse. Anti-semitism was stirring, fed by disparaging references to the *goût Juif* – the modernity many disliked – and to the *haute Juiverie*, the prominent Jewish bankers and industrialists.

But there was something else happening in Vienna, and it became of great interest to Amelia. Not wanted in the cafés, banned from the faculties of medicine and philosophy at the university, Austrian women were turning to politics. Adelheid Popp, the first woman public speaker for the Social Democratic Workers Party, was writing and campaigning for the rights of the many badly paid and overworked women in industry. All over Vienna, feminist movements were taking shape. They found an echo in *The Doll's House*, Ibsen's play about a woman who leaves her husband and children. Its theme, that women were living in a world made and ruled by men, intrigued Amelia, as did Freud's work on the unconscious, which she had recently discovered. She turned her thoughts to a play of her own, working quickly, as if, she said later, by instinct, seeing the scenes appear before her, hearing the voices and conversations of her characters in her head. In three months the play was written.

Even in iconoclastic and experimental Vienna, *Anima – Soul –* was a bold play. Amelia's heroine Olga is an artist, a free, independent woman from a good Italian family, who is known to paint nudes and receive gentlemen in her studio. One day she falls in love with the respectable and conventional Silvio. Just before they marry, she tells him that when she was fifteen she was raped. Silvio breaks off their engagement and marries a pure, dull woman, with whom he has nothing in common. Amelia's verdict is harsh. Olga finds, marries and is happy with another man. Silvio shoots himself. Implicit is the idea that men lack moral understanding, that they cannot distinguish between the 'virginity of the body' and the 'virginity of the mind', and that in any case their only concern is a trivial one, that of the chasteness of women.

For the time being, Amelia did nothing with her three-act play. Her first son, Aldo, known to the family as 'Topinino', was born on 21 July 1895. But unlike her heroine Olga, Amelia was far from happy. Joe's eye was wandering. His small talent had not flourished in Vienna's exuberant but hard-working musical world, and there was too much else to distract him. In the summer of 1896, having been away four years, they returned to Rome, to a flat in the Palazzo Marignoli, not far from Piazza San Silvestro.

Rome 1896

In the years that Amelia and Joe had been away, the rulers of the new united Italy had been floundering. Public debt, corruption and bribery were rampant. Francesco Crispi, a self-important former Garibaldino who had been prime minister on and off for the past decade, presided over a parliament in which votes were bartered for favours, and the word '*trasformismo*' had been coined to denote the hanging on to parliamentary majority through alliances with often incompatible partners. Unification had happened too fast, seven states moulded into one in under two years; there seemed to have been no time to think through a credible modern democracy.

On top of this, Crispi dreamt of military conquest. He longed for Italian men to become martial, and for Italy to acquire colonies. Smarting from a humiliating defeat by Ethiopian troops at Dogali in 1887, Crispi had despatched a force to overthrow the Emperor Menelik. Shortly before Amelia, Joe and Aldo returned to Rome, these soldiers too had been humiliatingly defeated at Adowa, with the loss of more than 6,000 lives and many men taken prisoner. With the Treaty of Addis Ababa, Italy was obliged to recognise Ethiopia as an independent state. Only Eritrea and Somaliland, seized in a punitive raid unleashed against what Crispi called the 'barbarians', remained Italian. Crispi, now in his seventies, was forced to retire. As prime minister he had been quarrelsome and embarrassing; and he had won few friends by declaring that Italians had been injected 'with the morphine of cowardice'.

Amelia's brother Gabriele had become a professor in jurisprudence and was engaged on redrafting the constitution; her second brother, Carlo, was working as an architect and engineer. Important in all their lives was the presence in Rome of her uncle by marriage Ernesto Nathan, the man sent by Mazzini to Rome to run his newspaper, and who had recently become Grand Master of the Roman Masonic lodge. Ernesto, who still spoke Italian with an English accent from his childhood in London, had a formidably austere and intransigent wife, Virginia Mieli, as republican in her views as her husband: in Roman circles they were considered the perfect Mazzini couple.

Joe now sought out the Roman musical world, in which Verdi, '*il maestro della rivoluzione italiana*', had replaced Donizetti as the most popular composer. Amelia turned back to her play. Conscious that *Anima*'s story of rape and disregard for social conventions was little suited to Catholic, family-minded Italy, she entered it with no expectations for a national theatre competition in Turin. Others – Verga – had written on such topics, but they were men. *Anima* reached the final shortlist of three, the winner to be selected after a performance by the prestigious Teatro dell'Arte. And there, on 29 October 1898, it was declared the unanimous favourite. Amelia gave 500 of the 2,000 lira prize to the association of Italian playwrights.

Anima was taken up and produced in other cities, and she was soon being referred to as the 'foremost woman playwright of

Italy'. Many years later, looking back over her life, she would write in her memoirs: 'Perhaps the day on which I was first recognised as a playwright was also – unbeknownst to me – the day on which my happiness as a woman ended.'

She now sat down to write a novella, *Felicità Perduta*, 'Lost Happiness', once again a desolate tale of the fissures between men and women, passion and love, work and domesticity. For Amelia, happiness could come only from equality and truthfulness. When Luisa, the young wife in her story, asks her husband Giulio, who has reluctantly admitted to an earlier affair, what would happen if a wife set out to inspire passion rather than conjugal love in her husband, Giulio replies: 'Any woman who felt this way ... would not be an honest woman, nor a desirable wife.' For Luisa, consumed with jealousy, the marriage has died.

Amelia and Joe's second son, Carlo, was born on 16 November 1899; Sabatino, their third boy, always known as Nello, followed a year later on 29 November 1900. Shortly before Nello's birth, Joe's father died, leaving him a substantial fortune. But Joe, always somewhat reckless, entrusted it all to an unscrupulous lawyer, who invested it unwisely. Within two years, the money was gone; Joe, ever gambling, ever losing, was forced to sell everything to pay his debts.

These financial calamities shook Amelia. But she was far more shaken when she learnt that Joe had formed an attachment to an opera singer he had met in the casino at Monte Carlo. The moral code in which she so passionately believed had been breached and, like Luisa in *Felicità Perduta*, she was not forgiving. Joe had dug an 'abyss' between them with 'his own two hands', and there was no going back. It was not that she had ceased to love him; on the contrary, she 'loved him beyond everything'. But they would have to part.

CHAPTER TWO

Donne Emancipate

The Florentines loved their city. They loved the way that every street and every house gave a sense of past harmony and measure. For them, its magic lay not in the greatness of its artists but in the fact that, in the thirteenth and fourteenth centuries, it had been a city of bankers and merchants, modest and parsimonious men who spent their fortunes on architecture and paintings and built palaces filled with frescoes and books, surrounding them with cypress trees. They liked the way that artists called their studios *botteghe*, shops, and thought of themselves as artisans. It was in Florence, they said, that perspective was invented, along with clocks that rang the hour, and art in which reason dominated over fantasy. There was a word – *fiorentinità* – for what the citizens felt about themselves. It meant not just intense pleasure in their surroundings – in the scent of the orange blossom, the lilac and wisteria, and the light, yellow by day, violet at dusk – but a certain dry wit, discretion, irreverence and an instinct for non-conformity. And also a kind of heaviness, an ever-present consciousness of passing time, so that in some houses they built a small door, the size of a coffin, called '*la porta della morte*'.

It is in Florence that the story of Amelia Rosselli and her three sons really begins.

They arrived in 1903, Amelia having decided to leave Joe and embark, as she put it, 'on my life as a woman alone'. Joe, she would write, was an exceptionally intelligent man, possessed of great charm, but his intelligence was too eclectic and his will too weak. She was not, of course, a woman alone. She had Aldo, now aged eight, Carlo, four, and Nello, three, to whom she explained that their father had stayed behind in Rome to look after his affairs and would be joining them. She had been forced to leave behind Emmy, an English nanny the children loved and who had been with them since the birth of Aldo. In the boys' heartbroken reaction to the loss of Emmy, Amelia thought she perceived her sons' future characters: Aldo said nothing and disappeared; Carlo raged; Nello looked confused and miserable.

Of all the cities in Italy, Florence was the most sensible choice for Amelia. Joe's uncle Pellegrino, a tall, magisterial figure with a full white flowing beard, lived in the city, and Amelia was much attached to his clever, feisty wife Gianetta, who was also a good pianist. Gianetta lamented the deaths of Mazzini and his heroic companions and bewailed the banality of her contemporaries, 'small men . . . not worth frequenting'. Italy, she said, had become a duller and flatter country since they died, and Florence a less romantic city: in the last fifteen years alone, one of the most famous city centres in the world had been stripped down – 26 old streets destroyed, along with 40 piazzas – in the name of modernity and hygiene. Amelia took a flat in Via Cherubini, not far from the Duomo and the central station. It was in an imposing eighteenth-century villa and rather dark, and on the grey, rainy days of the Florentine winters, damp and cold seeped through the walls. But she was short of money.

There was another excellent reason for choosing Florence. Amelia's success with *Anima* had brought her fame in literary circles, and Florence was Italy's cultural heart. Here, she could earn a living, writing more plays and short stories, and here she would find friends. Very conscious of herself as a separated woman, in a country in which the Catholic Church frowned upon such things, and suffering from what she described as '*esaurimento nervoso*', nervous exhaustion, she took stock, and thought long and hard about how she should raise her sons to understand about duty and generosity of spirit. She was not sorry that they had so little money: it would teach them that the real riches of life lay with the spirit.

Topinino, the title taken from her name for Aldo as a baby, was the first of her children's books, read aloud to Aldo, chapter by chapter, when he went to bed. It says everything about her state of mind. Topinino is a small boy who has a grey cat, Baffino, and a large white dog, Nadir. His mother – illustrated in the book by a slender, elegant woman, with the nipped-in waist and long dresses of the day – takes him shopping for a sailor suit, in which he preens himself as he walks along, complaining loudly that no one is admiring him. She reproves him: 'what has he done to earn admiration?' With the help of a family of flies, Topinino, defying his mother's orders, sets out on a series of adventures. These involve ocean liners, the newly installed telegraph system and many other educational things besides. But the message in each chapter is clear: small children needed to be obedient, think of others, not steal and always help 'the weak and the oppressed'. 'What is the point', observes the narrator, 'in being sorry when it is too late?' Amelia dedicated the book to her 'little birds'.

From time to time, Joe came to Florence to see the boys. The visits were affectionate, but brief and uneasy, with Joe miserably saying that he was 'not worthy'. In his absence – for the three boys were growing up to regard the writing of letters as a natural part of life – Aldo sent him reports. 'Charley and Nino have grown very tall', he told his father, 'and Charley is very fat.' The younger boys added their names in careful large letters. Amelia invented excuses for his few appearances. She spoke of him with respect to the children, and had resolved to say nothing of the true reason for their separation – or indeed that they had separated at all – until they were much older.

There was another Florence, one that Amelia observed but for the moment played little part in. Since the early nineteenth century, the city had been, as the Goncourt brothers noted, '*une ville toute Anglaise*'. Home to some 3,000 English residents – writers, retired diplomats, pensioned-off governesses and teachers, referred to by the diarist Lady Walburga Paget as 'a galaxy of spirits on this small plot of land' – it was also a stopping point for many others who came to look at the art and enjoy the pleasant life. Browning and Henry James both passed through, as did Edward Lear, who spoke of Florence as 'plum pudding, treacle, wedding cake, sugar, barley sugar, sugar candy, raisins and peppermint drops all at once'. Marmalade, digestive biscuits and seed cake were to be found in Via Tornabuoni. There was an English chemist, Roberts & Co, an American doctor, Dr Lewis Jones, an Anglo-Italian boys' school, an English-language bookshop and lending library, as well as a group of English nursing sisters on

Via Ferrucci. In the tea rooms, couples tangoed. Steam-driven trams ran along the Lungarno, where the mosquitoes were said to be fearsome, and little horse-drawn omnibuses, with six people inside and two on top, toiled their way up to Fiesole, San Domenico or Settignano, where many of the foreigners had their villas.

What delighted the romantic novelist Ouida was that she could buy anenomes in March and lilies in April in the very places in which Ghirlandaio as a boy had played among those sculpted in gold by his father. Standing on their terraces above the city, visitors remarked on the last moment of light over Florence, spread out along the valley of the Arno below them, when every contour, every tree and leaf seemed to be picked out in sharp intensity. As Arnold Bennett noted, it was a city without hurry and with very little ambition but where 'there is a great deal more happiness than in England'. For these foreigners, Florence was Arcadia, a dream landscape, in which the Italians were often little more than picturesque components. Of the remarkably rich Italian cultural world of music, literature, clubs, magazines and associations that was flourishing all about them, they knew very little. Just as they knew nothing of the political tensions which by now were simmering around the city. It was perhaps not surprising that it would be some time before Amelia made friends among them.

Not long after reaching Florence, Amelia renewed her friendship with Angiolo and Adolfo Orvieto, whom she had last seen in Venice when they were children and envied the warmth and humour of their lives. Both had become good-looking, well-educated men, Adolfo clean-shaven and bowler-hatted, a bibliophile and author of satirical verse, Angiolo a poet and journalist, thin and very dark, with black eyes and a thick black moustache which curled at the tips. In 1889, while still in their early twenties, the two brothers had founded a magazine, to which the already celebrated poet Gabriele D'Annunzio had contributed a number of provocative articles. Though it closed two years later, Angiolo and Adolfo had gone on to start a second magazine, intending to make it more analytical and irreverent. D'Annunzio proposed the title: *Il Marzocco*, from the Florentine lion immortalised by Donatello in the Piazza della Signoria. Contributors met in the Café Giacosa in Via Tornabuoni, or in the Cascine, the park on the right bank of the Arno where the fashionable Florentines walked under the trees, and where Angiolo rode his pure-blood Arab horse. Pirandello sent in articles; when funds ran low, the Orvietos put in more money.

Having travelled around the world for half a year, Angiolo, the elder and the more extrovert of the two Orvieto brothers, had married his third cousin, Laura Cantoni. She was a small, fair-haired woman with sapphire eyes who looked frail and diaphanous but was in fact both capricious and obstinate. As a student in London, Laura had met Dickens and dreamt of working in the slums. Though Angiolo and Laura had done up a house in the centre of Florence, their real home was a white mansion in the hills, surrounded by olive trees, the Villa del Poggiolino. The Orvietos had two young childen, Leonfrancesco and Annalia, much the same age as Carlo and Nello, and the Rossellis were invited to their large family gatherings, with several generations sitting at one long table, the meals often followed by plays written by the visitors and performed in the *limonaia*, the lemon house. Laura took to Amelia immediately, noting that she was intelligent, understanding, fascinating, exceedingly elegant and that 'even when suffering herself, is always ready to take pleasure in the happiness of others'. Not much, it seemed, had changed in Amelia since her guarded Venetian days. Whenever she was troubled, Laura went to see Amelia, whom she regarded as more reliable and grown-up than herself, and though firm, 'never hard or combative'.

It was at Villa del Poggiolino that Angiolo and Laura dreamt up the idea of starting a new club, the Società Leonardo da Vinci, where scientists and men of letters could meet and devise ways of shaking up the staid and sleepy Florentines. It was to be elegant, but not 'social', a counterpoint to the Club dell'Unione, where the old Florentine aristocracy gathered, or the more raffish Casino Borghese, where the '*ceto medio*', the middle classes, met. Foreigners and university professors went to Doney's, painters and writers to the Café Michelangelo.

Some five years earlier, Gabriele D'Annunzio had rented a fifteenth-century villa in Settignano, where he lived 'like a great Renaissance lord' among his dogs and horses, enjoying an exquisitely aesthetic life, writing his cycle of poems, *Laudi* – 'Praises' – and very occasionally descending regally into Florence, where he would be recognised and admired. D'Annunzio, whose support of *Il Marzocco* ensured that it had a steady number of readers, was a man of exceptional vanity, who gloried in his beautiful neat ears and flat stomach, and loved to shock with tales of incest and satanism. Since 1895, he had been having an affair with the humourless but extremely successful actress Eleonora Duse, who had added his plays to her repertoire and reluctantly put up with his notorious promiscuity. With their shared, self-consciously precious, behaviour, each extracting all that was most beautiful from their surroundings, they seemed to make a perfect couple.

Eleonora Duse, a woman who alternated periods of great affection with silence and rejection, was a regular guest at the Villa del Poggiolino. Laura, herself restless and prone to intensity and melodrama, had become infatuated with the actress, to the point of neglecting Angiolo, her children and her friends. Amelia, emotionally very orderly herself, worried about Laura's capacity for sowing disorder, and wrote to her friend, referring to Duse as '*la grande Donna*', and saying that whatever she touched acquired a strange 'vibration'. 'When you receive a letter or a visit from the Duse, then you hate me. I didn't at first understand why, but now I do: it's because she is important while I am not. It's a mistake to allow yourself to be totally consumed by another human being. It shows a lack of personality.' It never occurred to Amelia to be any less honest with others than she was with herself. But Laura was not to be deflected. 'I would have liked to have lived just for her', she replied, 'and to have been able to provide for all her dreams.'

The day came when Amelia and Eleonora Duse were at the Villa del Poggiolino at the same time. The actress was enduring a temporary estrangement from her compulsively unfaithful lover, who, she declared, had 'squeezed me like a lemon and then thrown me away'. The two women should have liked one another: *The Doll's House* was a regular part of Duse's repertory and both belonged, after all, to the world of theatre. But their encounter was a painful affair. Politely, Amelia asked *la grande Donna* whether she preferred contemporary or earlier plays. Duse was snappy. 'If you are going to set me an exam,' she replied, 'well then I shall leave!' Since it was perfectly clear that Duse had no interest of any kind in Amelia herself, Amelia hazarded a second more general question. This time Duse did not even reply; she covered her eyes wearily with her hands. Amelia crept away, went upstairs and burst into tears.

For a while, Laura and Amelia's close friendship suffered. But Angiolo grew angry and the strange passion for Duse faded; Amelia, Aldo, Carlo and Nello were again guests at the Villa del Poggiolino. Better still, Amelia had been introduced to Giulio Zabban, a man of wide interests and prodigious memory who would later become vice president of a large Florentine insurance company, and Giorgina, his well-dressed and no less intelligent translator wife, author of biographies of Elizabeth Barrett Browning and Florence Nightingale. Amelia soon thought of Giorgina as her sister, saying that they agreed on almost every topic. Being childless, the Zabbans quickly took on the role of honorary uncle and aunt to the three boys, calling themselves Zio Giù and Zia Gì. Villa Il Frassine, their house at Rignano sull'Arno, surrounded by groves of olive trees and a walled kitchen garden, became the Rossellis' second home. Zia Gì was famous for her tea parties and exquisite anchovy-butter sandwiches. The Zabbans, said Amelia, were an incomparable gift from Providence.

Il Marzocco was part of a wider, more ambitious cultural movement. By the turn of the twentieth century, Florence alone boasted eighty-three magazines, all aspiring, one way or another, to influence and shape post-Risorgimento Italy. It was here that the European avant-garde was taking root. Writers dreamt of breaking out of the isolation in which they considered themselves to be still living and of offering what they described as a spiritual alternative to the modernising forces of science, commerce and industry. In all of this, *Il Marzocco*, with its elegant typeface and its heraldic lion, saw itself as paving the way, defending art for art's sake, harking back to the glories of the Renaissance, and attacking the ills of modern life, the smoking factories and the ugly mechanical innovations. In 1903 came a rival, the *Leonardo*, started by two journalists, Giovanni Papini and Giuseppe Prezzolini, who professed themselves 'intoxicated with idealism', ready to lead the lost Italians out of the dark and towards a new 'spiritual virility'. All these magazines were prone to schisms, defections and intense rivalry. But for Amelia they represented a source of work. On one occasion she asked the Orvietos if she might reply to a piece in *Il Marzocco*, in which the novelist Neera had argued that, since men and women were different physiologically, it must follow that their rights and duties were also different, and there was therefore no reason why women should be allowed to take men's work. Amelia's reply was crisp, forceful. Whether or not the future would prove Neera's assumptions to be valid, she wrote, what was important now was to provide all women with autonomy and recognition. And as for those who chose to be mothers, that role too was vital in imparting the ideas of justice and morality to the young; it was a job like any other and needed to be recognised as such. As a polemicist, Amelia was turning out to have a fearless and distinctive voice.

Before leaving Rome, Amelia had worked with the upright, implacably good Virginia Mieli for various philanthropic causes, and had helped put on an exhibition of women's art and work. Its aim, to obtain social recognition and fair pay for women workers, had stayed with Amelia. She had been involved with the Industrie Femminili, an organisation promoting women at work, and they now asked her to become their Florence representative. Since the needle-workers were short of designs, she went to look for ideas in the city's frescoes and paintings.

She was also finishing work on a collection of short stories, *Gente Oscura*, 'Humble People', taking her characters from among the working classes, the 'vagabonds and the disinherited'. When it was published, the left-wing newspaper *Avanti!* praised her for being 'without a doubt a socialist'. This she immediately refuted, announcing that it was more that she felt great sympathy for women who did not have the fortune to belong to 'so-called good society', and that she remained profoundly influenced by Mazzini's democratic principles and by her conviction that society needed to help those who were less well off. A new play, *Illusione*, had been taken by the Carignano theatre in Turin, with one of Italy's best-known actresses, Teresa Mariani, in the lead. Once more a tale of emotional inequality, turmoil and lack of forgiveness, it revolved around the story of a man who, betrayed by his young wife, nonetheless takes her back and says that he still loves her. To start all over, however, could only be an illusion; once again it is Amelia's female character, braver than her husband, who makes the decision herself to leave.

Critics compared Amelia to Ibsen, but also noted that the language was too literary, not dramatic enough. After the enormous success of *Anima*, the reaction by audiences to the new play was muted. Laura Orvieto observed that her friend's writings never quite did her justice. They lacked her particular voice and style, one which was robust, full of sudden insights and eclectic memories, and at once humorous and profound. Clever, poignant, with characters easy to admire or pity, the plays were somehow too wordy.

At home, Amelia was having trouble with Aldo. Though he did well at school and showed signs of being artistic, he seemed to her to have become boastful and arrogant, and his manner towards the very people about whom Amelia wrote had become 'distastefully superior'. The real Topinino had clearly not listened closely enough to her teachings and she feared his influence on her younger boys. With Laura protesting that she was sometimes too hard on her three children, and Amelia replying that she abhorred what she called 'moral disorder' and was determined that her three sons should acquire 'strength of will', Amelia took a most unusual step. She asked a local carpenter whether he would take Aldo as a perfectly ordinary apprentice, after school, making no allowances for him.

Thus, three afternoons a week, dressed in rough clothes and an overall, Aldo was to be found sweeping up, running errands, being bossed around by the genuine apprentices. Carlo and Nello enjoyed gazing through the shop window at their embarrassed elder brother, in his huge blue apron, his blond hair cut like that of a thirteenth-century pageboy. And Amelia, for whom writing, life, family and duty formed one continuous whole, sat down and wrote *Topinino, Garzone di Bottega* – 'The Shop Boy' – in which her hero, now a teenager, refuses to study and is boastful and proud, until his father takes him out of school and sends him to live and work with a local carpenter. Topinino's hair is cropped short, he is scolded and made to work very hard, and he learns not just about poverty and hunger, but about humility. 'I had always thought that the world I saw from my window was the real world,' he remarks, 'never realising that there was another one, once you chose to see it.' His character reformed, Topinino resolves to become a doctor or a lawyer, in order to look after the poor. This time, Topinino's adventures were read aloud to all three boys before they went to sleep. Amelia dedicated the book to the ever-supportive Zia Gì, and in due course Aldo, in words almost identical to those of his father to his own parents, wrote to Amelia: 'I will be good so as to make you happy.'

Some of Amelia's acquaintances were shocked by her treatment of Aldo, but she had no regrets. To reinforce her message, she told the boys that the will was like a piece of steel, which, unless constantly burnished, grew rusty. She drew a picture of three steel bars with their names underneath and hung it over their beds. When one of the boys demonstrated what she considered lack of will power, she drew fuzzy lines to suggest a patch of rust. At the end of the month, the child with the least rust was declared the winner. It was a true Mazzini gesture.

Both *Topinino* books sold well; Amelia's moral overtones suited the mood of social-minded Florence, and she was an accomplished story-teller. Laura was also writing children's books, and making a name for herself on *Il Marzocco*, where she wrote a fashion piece under the pseudonym Mrs El.

Slowly, Amelia was making her way in Florence's literary world. She was finding friends, writing short stories for magazines, and planning new plays. In her memoirs she recalls first falling in love with the theatre when, as a small child in Venice, she had listened to her sister Anna's stories and seen herself as a spy, overhearing the conversation of people who did not know that she was there. Never had the city seemed so lively; people talked about a new Renaissance. Amelia delighted, both for herself and for the boys, in its openness to newcomers, and the way it seemed so alive to influences from all over Europe. The theatres and concert halls played to large audiences. Amelia's friends, like herself, read widely in different languages and met to discuss the issues of the day. Though she doubted that her young sons were old enough to take in much of it, she felt that they were absorbing the atmosphere, acquiring, as she wrote, a very 'elevated impression of life', just as she felt satisfied that she was providing the boys with the model of a mother who worked hard, staying at her desk all the time that they were at school.

When Amelia visited Rome, she stayed with her uncle Ernesto who, despite being half-English, Jewish, a *Mazziniano*, a Freemason and an anti-papist, had been elected mayor. Much as she enjoyed these trips, she was pleased that she had exchanged luxury in Rome for her modest but intellectual Florentine life. Amelia and the boys had moved to Via Gianbologna, to a larger flat in another solid eighteenth-century house, with gardens where the boys could play under the oak trees. The wider family remained very important to them all, and both Gabriele, now at work on revising Italy's legal code, and her much-loved sister Anna came to stay. Gabriele, more father to her than brother, would ask her whether she was still reading Dante, which made her think of a doctor, taking her intellectual pulse.

The three boys were turning out very different from each other. Aldo was dark, and like Joe in looks; Carlo and Nello had fair hair. In character, Aldo was reserved, almost secretive; it was clear that he felt deeply about things but did not choose to show it.

Carlo, as a boy in Florence

In appearance, Carlo looked strong and sturdy, but he had a tendency to plumpness, and fell ill easily; when he cut or scratched himself, the wound quickly went septic. He ate too fast and too much, and was fidgety and impatient when he had to wait for the others. Of the three, he was the most openly affectionate and high-spirited. Nello, who Amelia sometimes called 'Ninnolino' or *Pinguino* – Penguin – on account of his roundness, was quieter and more steady, and looked the most like her. Both the younger boys shared a certain stubbornness, a refusal to accept defeat, but while Carlo reacted by taking action, fighting back, trying to think up ways to make things work his way, Nello withdrew into himself and reflected. For all her severity, Amelia was the most affectionate and devoted of mothers. When she was away, the boys wrote her urgent, loving letters, all on the same page, with Assunta, the housekeeper, adding a note along the edge. Aldo took his duties as eldest child seriously: 'Nello stayed up until 11 last night. Is it true that he shouldn't always do this?'

Amelia had never shied away from bold subjects, and nor was she about to. In *L'idea Fissa*, 'The Fixed Idea', written in 1906, a doctor's advice to his neurotic, possibly psychotic, patient that he should do his best to get over his obsessions, made it clear that she was reading Freud, and that the inner conflicts of men and women, tortured and remorseless, trying to come to terms with a fast-changing world, were what interested her the most. She had long championed writers who used local dialects as the best way to express their feelings, and now, thinking to refute her critics and that she might sound less stilted if she returned to the language of her childhood, she embarked on two plays in Venetian dialect. Once again, they touch on the clash between men and women, courage and cowardice, the domestic, cautious, safe life versus the new spirit of revolt and independence, personified by *donne emancipate*, women braving the new world. She was fortunate that Carlo Goldoni had paved the way by writing in Venetian, and that a company of celebrated Venetian actors, the Compagnia Italo-Veneziana, was in its golden age. *El rèfolo* – 'The Whim' – and *El socio del papá* – 'The Father's Associate' – were both accepted and staged.

Standing in the wings for the first night of *El rèfolo* in Rome, Amelia feared that the critics' verdict would be 'inexorable and harsh'. She need not have worried. They loved it, praised her lively dialogue, the poetry of her language and her 'astute' understanding of psychology, remarking only that she seemed at her best as a playwright when her characters were *gente oscura*, humble people, and that it was when she made them upper class that her plays came across as somewhat lifeless. Amelia had proved, wrote a notably difficult theatre critic, that women were not, after all, incapable of writing 'theatrical poetry'. *El rèfolo* was translated into French and put on at L'Odéon in Paris. When Amelia went off to attend first nights of her plays, the boys stayed behind in Florence with Assunta, watched over by Zio Giù and Zia Gì. Carlo wrote to his mother: 'Who knows how much money you will earn! Plays are so beautiful!' At the bottom of the letter, Assunta added: '*Brava, brava, la mia signora.*'

For all her success, Amelia felt alone. On one of her trips away, she wrote to Aldo, in a surprisingly adult tone: 'I am a little sad, because I still can't get used to going about the world so alone.' Her friend Laura remarked on it too. Though Amelia was now at the centre of a group of friends who loved and admired her, she gave off a feeling of being ever more solitary, 'always taller and straighter, like a blade of steel in a velvet sheath'. A new friend made around this time, a novelist and children's writer called Maria Bianca Viviani della Robbia, visited her and admired the way that her drawing room seemed more like a study, full of books and flowers and very stylish. She described Amelia as somewhat pale, with regular features and eyes the 'indefinite colour of deep water', and her manner as friendly and measured. But, she added, Amelia had a sad expression.

CHAPTER THREE

Defining *la Patria*

That the Florentines were independent-minded, even combative, was a fact long known inside Italy. The city had been the site of the first general strike in the country's short history when, in August 1902, twenty-two workmen were sacked from the Pignone metalworks, and railway-workers, train-drivers, dustmen and even tailors came out in sympathy. To the surprise and consternation of the middle classes and the employers, Florence stopped. There were lock-outs and military cordons and much talk about the need to 'tame these wild animals'. *La Nazione*, Florence's right-wing paper, referred to the strikers as the 'new barbarians'.

For all its art-loving foreign visitors and wealthy landowners, Florence was a city with many poor inhabitants, some of them forced from their homes during the building upheavals which accompanied its short spell as Italy's capital. Some 59,000 families were officially registered as '*miserabili*', extremely poor, and among these was to be found a considerable number of anarchists and revolutionary socialists, angry at the vast gaps in income and for the most part fiercely anti-clerical. The anarchists had a long history in Italian politics and it had been in Italy that early anarchist attempts at revolution had taken place. There were many to be found among the Florentine artisans, the majolica-, lace-, leather- and tapestry-workers, the carpenters, clockmakers and potters, and particularly among the straw-weavers, who made hats and containers for Chianti, Tuscany's most important wine trade. Many of them were highly literate and united in small, tight-knit associations. Florence, it was said, had become the capital of Italy's anarchist movement.

Since the turn of the century, Florence had been ruled by liberal monarchists with strong ties to the Risorgimento, many of them belonging to the city's 400 leading families. But Tuscany, where the trade-union movement was increasingly powerful, also had a long tradition of socialism and in 1907, after years of control by aristocratic families, a junta of socialists, radicals and republicans was elected to the city council. On the cover of the socialist *L'Avanti! della Domenica* was a bare-chested man with an anvil, and a woman with an olive branch.

Most of Florence's political turmoils were a mirror of what was happening in Rome, where a pragmatic liberal called Giovanni Giolitti, a man of sober manners and a flourishing moustache, had been in power on and off since 1892. Under Giolitti, who was more interested in economic reform than in political turbulence, national income had risen sharply, mortality rates had dropped, and in the north at least – the south remained backward and neglected – a steady process of industrialisation was under way.

Since 1895, when the Italian Workers Party had renamed itself the Italian Socialist Party, socialism had spread rapidly among academics, students and the educated middle classes. Its leader, Filippo Turati, a genial lawyer with a round face, wispy beard and protruding eyes, had proved skilful at holding together a party often riven by ideological disputes. With his lover, Anna Kuliscioff, a Russian exile and one of the first women to graduate in medicine in Italy, Turati had started the most influential journal of the left, *Critica Sociale*. The two of them had done more than anyone to spread Marxist theory in Italy, and to transform Italian socialism from a small anarchical group to a broad socio-political movement. Their salon in a palazzo by the Duomo in Milan had become the epicentre of the intellectual left, and the blonde-haired, handsome Kuliscioff, smoking ceaselessly and invariably dressed in a long black skirt and white shirt, was a figure of fascination to young Italian politicians and journalists. Giolitti had made overtures to these socialists, improved conditions in the factories and reduced taxes on food, and the moderates among them were willing to cooperate.

But Italy was awash with controversy, discontent, opposing ideas, dreamers and revolutionaries, reformers and reactionaries, and the schisms that would mark Italian politics for the next twenty years – and far beyond – were already at play. Every shade of political opinion, every nuance of left or right, found expression in a chaotic and shifting mix of parties and associations. Giolitti, for all the prosperity he had brought, was unpopular with the right for his desire to make Italy economically sound rather than great. As the poet Carducci put it, Giolitti's Italy was a 'busy little farce of ponderous clowns'. Nor was he liked by the left, some of whom aspired to nothing less than revolution, and who accused his government of opportunism, his ministers of incompetence and his elections of corruption. Giolitti, they said, was nothing but a dictator, the master of *trasformismo*, holding on to power through deals and bribery.

Some measure of stability might have been provided by the monarchy. But Victor Emmanuel III, who had become king after the assassination of his father Umberto in 1900, was a singularly retiring man, more interested in military history than affairs of state. He was exceptionally short – just over five feet tall – and looked even smaller when standing by his statuesque Montenegrin wife, Queen Elena, particularly when she wore the vast hats of the day. By nature weak and vacillating, the small king – nicknamed *Sciaboletta*, little sabre, by his people – had been struggling, but largely failing, to establish the monarchy as a strong symbol of the new nation. People who met him remarked on his watery blue eyes, which tended to flicker and dart about when he was nervous. His third cousin, Prince Amadeo, Duke d'Aosta, was by contrast exceptionally tall, a foot and a half taller than the king, and made a popular and martial figure on ceremonial occasions.

Among Giolitti's most outspoken critics was a man who was about to become inextricably bound up with the Rosselli family. His name was Gaetano Salvemini and he was a senator from the south and a historian. Giolittian politics, said Salvemini, were 'dead, dull and morally reprehensible'.

Born in Molfetta in Apulia, Salvemini was one of nine children; his grandfather was a fisherman. His mother Emanuela was ambitious for this clever son and much interested in politics. Having taught him to read and write and how to be a *gentiluomo*, she sent him to a seminary for eight years, then to the prestigious Institute for Higher Studies in Florence on a scholarship. After this, saying that he had been turned into a socialist by the disastrous Ethiopian wars, Salvemini embarked on a career as a historian and a teacher. He promised himself that his life's work would be a search for the truth and that he would give his students 'a key to open locks, a compass to direct them across a sea of facts, to guard them against improbable or false assertions, and to teach them to think for themselves'. Salvemini had no patience with rhetoric. He claimed that one reason for Italy's backwardness lay in the fatal preference among Italians for discussing general theories rather than practical solutions.

In 1897, Salvemini married a girl from Molfetta and became professor of history at Messina university; they had five children very quickly and moved into a house on the seafront. On the night of 28 December 1908, an earthquake struck the Straits of Messina; it was followed by a tidal wave. Salvemini was thrown from a window by the quake, but his fall was broken by an architrave. His wife, five children and sister were swallowed up. Salvemini groped in vain among the ruins. Eventually, he found all the bodies except for those of his wife Maria and his youngest son, Ughetto. Between a quarter and a third of the inhabitants of the coastal cities of Reggio Calabria and Messina, some 80–100,000 people died that night. What tormented Salvemini was the thought that Ughetto, too small to explain who he was, might have been saved and taken away on one of the rescue ships. For days and weeks he searched the makeshift orphanages. 'I made a mistake', he wrote later, 'in not killing myself on the first day.'

For the despairing Salvemini, the loss of his family served to give shape to what had until now been mostly a spiritual inclination. He was fired with the conviction that he had to devote his life to the problems of the undeveloped south – for southern Italy remained for most Italians an alien land, magnificently beautiful but lawless and extremely poor – and that he would henceforth no longer talk, reflect, analyse, but act. What brought him back from a profound wish to die was his determination to work for 'these people, who must and can rise up again'.

By the time he arrived in Florence in 1909, Salvemini was thirty-six, balding, with a large head, small, kindly and intelligent eyes, a snub nose, a 'great fence of teeth' and a pointed beard. He had a pleasant, wry manner, tended to be impetuous and usually wore a black hat. His tread was heavy and his friends spoke of him affectionately as a 'man from the fields, not the literary salons'. He had been taken on to teach at the university and had already contributed articles to Turati's *Critica Sociale*. He was soon drawn in as elder statesman to a new magazine started by Prezzolini and Papini to take over from the *Leonardo*. It was called *La Voce* and consisted of four folio pages of dense print, unrelieved by pictures. Maintaining that only a reinvigorated and educated public could hope to solve the current ills of illiteracy, divisive regional aspirations and lawlessness, it fed its readers an austere diet of articles on suffrage, European art and good governance.

Salvemini's involvement took *La Voce* into a closer interest in politics and particularly in class struggle, the south, and international justice. What he shared with his young colleagues was a loathing for Giolitti and a conviction that, if Italy were to become a truly united and great nation, the Italians themselves needed to change their habits and their way of thinking. Never greatly concerned with his own reputation or place in Italian academia, Salvemini became a fervent critic of Italy's most revered intellectual thinker, the idealistic Benedetto Croce, who had turned his pen to history, philosophy and ascetics and was having a considerable influence on his contemporaries, whether from the right or the left. Salvemini complained that Croce was merely misleading people with his rhetorical abstractions, and thus preventing them from addressing the burning question of how to make Italy a truly liberated and civilised country.

One of *La Voce*'s contributors was Giovanni Amendola, a handsome, liberal-minded journalist with very black hair and a sombre look, widely regarded as a rising political star.

Another was a blacksmith's son from the Apennine foothills of Emilia-Romagna, a pallid, thick-set young socialist, anti-clerical teacher and journalist called Benito Mussolini. Although, like Amendola, still in his twenties, Mussolini was already a man much drawn to power, uncouth and rough in manner, writing fiery articles and prone to outbursts of fury and glaring looks. He was about to become editor of the socialist *Avanti!*, in whose pages he waged virulent warfare against his opponents, whether on the left or the right, displaying all the volatility and inconsistency that made his own politics so hard to pin down. But he was all in favour of *La Voce*'s crusading message. As he wrote to Prezzolini in the autumn of 1909: 'To create the "Italian" soul is a superb mission.'

Mussolini was living with, but not yet married to, Rachele, born in the same village of Predappio in Romagna as himself, a small and buxom girl he described as 'an attractive wench, coarse-mannered but inviting'. Their first child, Edda, was born in 1910, but this did not prevent him from carrying on with any number of women, to whom he could be brutal. One of these was Amelia's childhood friend Margherita Grassini, now married to a lawyer called Sarfatti, who had just inherited a fortune. Margherita was beautiful, fascinated by politics and deeply ambitious, and she tried to teach the dishevelled and belligerent Mussolini how to dress and behave.

Nineteenth-century Italy had not held women in high regard. Two doctors in Lombardy, investigating the high rate of women with pellagra, a disease of hunger, described how local farming families, having only a single cow, gave the milk to the men, or made butter which the men ate or sold. The men also ate all the eggs. The doctors concluded that these women were simply perceived to have *minori bisogni*, 'lesser needs'.

But as the century approached its end there had been a sudden rise in interest in the bettering of women's lives, and in its wake came a flowering of feminist groups. People began to talk about the *elevazione della donna*. Some concerned themselves with suffrage, others with factory conditions and infant mortality. In Florence, in 1897, a Lega Femminile had met to discuss ways in which to confer rights on school teachers and the new telephonists. Not long after Ernesto Nathan became mayor of Rome, the first National Congress of Italian Women was held in the capital, organised by feminists from the left. Though ruthlessly appropriated by the right, and some of the more ambitious goals deleted from the agenda, its message about improving the lives of ordinary women did not go unheard. Amelia, already active in a number of Florentine associations, went as a delegate. Mindful that the new social-welfare laws making their way through parliament had omitted to mention domestic servants, she was at work drawing up proposals for sick pay and pensions, outlining her ideas in a long article for *Il Marzocco*. With her customary lack of sentimentality, she praised the 'common sense' of Italian women who, she said, were quick to ridicule the more theatrical aspects of feminism.

Florence, with its many clubs and associations, was a natural home for these women campaigners. In 1904, a talented young British feminist called Constance Smedley, a novelist, playwright and creator of pageants, had founded the first Lyceum Club, in London, with the aim of getting women out of their domestic settings and into public life. Branches had since opened in Paris and Berlin, and in 1908 Amelia became a founder member of the Florentine chapter. Exclusively for women – men could be guests but had no voting rights – the Lyceum started ambitious classes in languages, journalism and international affairs. Amelia immediately proposed lower dues for the 'less fortunate sisters', women just as refined, well-educated and upper class as the founders, but obliged through straitened circumstances to earn their own living. Though this went through, there were already tensions among the more patrician Florentine ladies, who spoke of the need for exclusivity, and they blocked her second suggestion, the setting up of rural libraries. On the surface, the debates remained exquisitely courteous. After a performance of Amelia's *El rèfolo*, the ladies offered a tea in her honour.

Around this time Amelia made another important friend. In Turin for an early performance of *Anima*, Amelia had been introduced to Guglielmo Ferrero, a distinguished historian of Roman antiquity, and his wife Gina Lombroso. Gina was a successful writer on the psychology of women and professed herself interested in the 'essence' of men and women. The Ferreros had a son, Leo, a little younger than Nello, on whom Gina doted. She devoted a special book to his deeds, saying that he had 'moral sensibilities', a great feeling for justice and that he possessed a 'refined aesthetic' sense. Leo was indeed a little prodigy, and also a budding poet. When the Ferreros moved to Florence in 1910, to a house near the Boboli Gardens, Amelia introduced Gina into the Lyceum Club. Though distinctly eccentric in her dress, with a penchant for long Grecian tunics, Gina was soon befriended by Laura Orvieto and Zia Gì. These four women – all Jewish, all very well educated, all determined to make other women under-stand that work and a degree of independence led to greater happiness – became a formidable quartet.

Leo's reputation as a child prodigy was much discussed in clever Florentine circles. Both Carlo and Nello somewhat dreaded meeting him, imagining a tall, imposing boy so clever that he would put them to shame. In the event, Leo turned out to be short, like a little shrimp, and rather silent. None of this, however, could disguise the fact that he excelled at school, while Aldo and Carlo were both struggling. With Aldo, Amelia decided, it was once again a question of behaviour, with Carlo a combination of laziness and lack of intelligence. She was not a woman to let things slip. The rather tubby Carlo had had a long bout of ill-health. First appendicitis then phlebitis had kept him in bed on and off for almost a year, and he had used his ailments as an excuse not to study but to play the piano instead. He was argu-mentative, and refused to learn from the tutors brought in to help him. Scolding made little difference. Amelia now took another step, as radical and unpopular with her friends as the sending of Aldo to a carpenter. Both Carlo and Nello were in Florence's most prestigious private classical Gimnasio, the Michelangiolo, to which the brightest Florentine boys were sent. In the middle of the year, Amelia abruptly removed Carlo and sent him to the local tech-nical school, widely considered inferior, where he continued with his maths but abandoned Greek and Latin. Humiliating as this was, he was given no chance to object.

For Amelia, her Jewishness as yet played very little part in her life. But a forceful new rabbi, Samuel Hirsch Margulies, had recently arrived in Florence, started an association called Pro Cultura, and begun to attract some of the younger Jews in the city, among whom were spreading ideas about Zionism and a *rinascita idealista*, a renewal of their Jewish faith. Somewhat to Amelia's discomfort, Carlo suddenly asked to be taken to the synagogue, and she worried that she had made a mistake in imposing her lack of religion on her sons. For her there was no debate: the *italianità* of Italian Jews was something precious, to be jealously guarded. She had no time for Zionism, fearing that it might damage the position of assimilated Italian Jews. For her, Judaism was 'a religion and not a race'. There was just one *patria*,

Italy, and they were Italian first and Jews second. To her relief, Carlo rapidly lost interest. The visits to the synagogue were abandoned.

All three boys were turning out to be musical. Aldo and Carlo played the piano, Nello the cello: Amelia said that music was something that could take the place of religion in 'elevating the soul'. Deaf to her appeals, Aldo continued to waste his time and neglect the Mazzini principles she had sought so hard to instil: absolute clarity between right and wrong, the necessity of personal sacrifice and the practice of virtue towards others. Finally, Amelia removed him from his day school in Florence and sent him as a boarder to the Catholic, semi-military Collegio Tolomei in Siena, where he rose at six, spent eight hours a day at his books and had his lights out by nine. Punishments consisted of long periods of total silence, sometimes lasting several days. There were hot baths only on Sundays.

When Amelia had news that Aldo's marks were good, she wrote to him as 'Aldolino' and signed herself 'Mammina'. When they were bad, or there were complaints about his manners, she was implacable. Could he come home for the four-day break over *Carnevale*? No, he could not. 'When you understand, for once and for all, that by behaving badly you are harming yourself, then you will behave better.' Aldo's handwriting, she pointed out, had become very sloppy, and 'character and handwriting go hand in hand'. Unless things changed, he would not be coming home for the Easter holidays either. For his part, Aldo was remarkably uncomplaining. His letters were full of references to his desire to earn her approval. 'I must now do everything I can in order to merit being allowed to come home for ever.' As one Christmas holiday approached, Amelia wrote: 'If in the next 20 days your behaviour does not improve . . . then you can give up all hopes of coming home.'

Even with Carlo, as his letters show, Amelia could be brutal. 'I promise to be better,' he wrote to her one day. 'You'll see that I won't make you cross again. I am older and I understand that it causes you much unhappiness.' Yet Amelia loved her sons and thought about them constantly, even obsessively, and she missed Aldo painfully. It was as if she was terrified that Joe's weak and vacillating nature might have been handed down to the boys, and that only by the most ferocious vigilance could she hope to turn them into the kind of Mazzini characters she longed for.

Joe had never lost touch with Amelia and his sons, though his letters to them were often wistful. In April 1910, thanking the boys for their birthday wishes, he noted sorrowfully: 'Your life interests me a great deal more than my own ... which is fuller of pain than happiness.' Nello, who, unlike his brothers, was a diligent student, wrote to tell his father that he had come first in his class of sixty-six pupils. 'When', he asked, 'will you come to live with us properly?'

It might have happened. In the nine years they had been apart Amelia had formed no other attachments, while Joe seemed genuinely to have shed his irresponsible ways. There was talk of him moving to Florence. But early in 1911 he fell ill and when he failed to get better the doctors recommended a stay in a specialist nursing home at Capodimonte in Naples. Leaving the boys with Assunta and Zia Gì, Amelia went south to look after him. Nello wrote to her: 'My longing to be with you is gigantic.' On the same piece of paper, sending messages of love, Carlo signed his name with a great flourish: '*Carlo Alberto Rosselli*'. In another letter, Nello drew a picture of a tall, elegant woman in a long dress, a suitcase by her side, clasping two small boys tightly to her, while an older one in a large hat stands alongside. From his boarding school, Aldo wrote to suggest that his father might recover more quickly were he to come home to live with them. But Joe was past recovery. On 9 September he died. He was forty-four.

Amelia was devastated. It was as if, paralysed by her sense of moral rectitude and duty, she had been completely unable to accept or forget the past, and now that he was dead she felt bitterly all she had lost. She put on black, and it would be many months before her friends were able to persuade her to take it off.

Florence was gradually turning into a modern city. Trains now linked it to Rome, Arezzo, Faenza, Pistoia and Livorno. Typewriters and gramophones were to be found on sale in Via Tornabuoni, and in *La Nazione* a motorist wrote of his 'most agreeable ride' in a car with pneumatic tyres. The desire of the Florentine intellectuals to link their city to the currents of progress sweeping across Europe received a further boost when, in 1908, the Grenoble Centre for Italian Studies opened an annex in the city. Its first director, Julien Luchaire, spoke of Florence as 'one of the most intellectual cities in the world', an 'Italian Athens', and declared his intention of rivalling the strong German and British presence. This was particularly pleasing to those Florentines who considered Paris to be the heart of all that was most avant-garde.

On the surface, this cultural fervour was all about freeing the Italians from the leaden weight of what they called '*passatismo*', a cult of the past, and getting them to embrace modernity. But it had a darker side, one which glorified war and was seduced by the idea of violence and conquest. The Futurist Movement was launched in *Le Figaro* in Paris in 1909 with an essay by the journalist and poet Filippo Tommaso Marinetti, an exhibitionist, flâneur and experimenter in literary forms, who had a moustache with pointed ends and loved to shock. Marinetti had spent the early years of the century moving between Rome, Turin and Milan preaching novelty and a hatred of historical nostalgia. In 'A Manifesto of Futurism', he spoke rapturously of the beauty of mechanical objects, and particularly of planes and cars, conjuring up an intoxicating vision of automobiles racing through a hail of bullets. It was important, he wrote, to liberate Italy from 'its smelly gangrene of professors, archaeologists, Ciceroni and antiquarians. We mean to free her from the numberless museums that cover her like so many graveyards.' And, he added, 'we will glorify war ... the world's only hygiene' and 'scorn ... women'. Language, sculpture, art, poetry, the theatre, all were ripe for Futurist reappraisal. At his Futurist evenings, the audience was encouraged to throw vegetables.

Closely linked to the Futurists by their taste for violence were the Italian Nationalists, who, in 1910, formed themselves into a party in Rome. Instead of looking forwards, the Nationalists looked back with longing on the days of Roman antiquity. Futurists and Nationalists now joined forces and called for the conquest of Cyrenaica and Tripolitania, the Ottoman provinces in Libya, whose own territorial claims were guaranteed by the recent Hague Conventions, to which Italy was a signatory. They called these lands 'Italy's fourth shore'. Getting them back – for were they not once part of the Roman Empire? – would make Italy richer and more important in the world and compensate for its humiliating defeat by the Ethiopians in 1896. It would yield a fortune in minerals and the Turkish garrisons were known to be weak. The fact that such a war meant breaking a treaty made the whole thing more of an adventure.

Their passion paid off, and Italy resounded to martial speeches. Neither Giolitti nor Victor Emmanuel III wanted war, the former because he had not been fooled into believing that any real benefits would come from such an undertaking, the latter because he was such an irresolute man. Nor did the young Benito Mussolini. Though currently imprisoned for fomenting disorder, damaging railway and telegraph lines and resisting police orders, Mussolini called for a general strike against this 'unjust, imperial, colonial war' and an end to Giolitti's chaotic government.

In September 1911, Giolitti succumbed to pressure and sent the navy to bomb Tripoli. In Florence, tricolour flags festooned the streets. The socialists protested and called on the Florentines to strike, but few people listened. In the days that followed passions for and against the war flared up into brawls. Though it took a year, the Ottoman Empire, needing its soldiers for wars in the Balkans, capitulated and signed an agreement in which Italy was recognised as the de facto ruler of Libya. The Florentines, stirred to heights of bellicose fervour, celebrated wildly.

But it was all somewhat misleading. Libya's Arab population was not prepared to yield up their lands so readily to Italian colonists. For the next three years, skirmishes and attacks were followed by harsh reprisals, and the war simmered on until only a handful of towns along the coast remained in Italian hands. Since Giolitti could ill afford a costly military failure, the defeats were recast as victories, campaign medals were handed out and streets across Italy given new names of Libyan triumphs. Liberal Italy's treatment of its conquered people was harsh: hundreds of Libyan families who had dared to protest against occupation were sent off to the Tremiti Islands, where children and the elderly quickly died of malnutrition, cholera and typhus.

The war in Libya served to harden political positions. Salvemini had from the start felt that the war was an insane waste of Italy's few resources. Having got hold of documents purporting to be accounts of happy colonists on their new Libyan farms and shown them to be forgeries, he now founded a paper of his own, a weekly he called *L'Unità*, with the subtitle 'Problems of Italian Life'. Writing many of the articles himself under different names, he embarked on a crusade to educate the young, sort out trade barriers and improve conditions in the south. His tone was confrontational, a mixture of Mazzini militancy and ideas for a modern, western democratic future.

As a member of the Lyceum and a regular contributor to *Il Marzocco*, Amelia was much caught up with the political tensions swirling around Florence. Salvemini had now entered her life and was instantly drawn into the Rosselli family circle. The boys called him Father Bear.

Five of Amelia's articles for *Il Marzocco* had been on the subject of education, and she and Laura Orvieto, who was writing history books for children, agreed that teaching was best done through enjoyment. Laura, who was a natural story-teller, had produced her own version of *Topinino*, with her own two children as the main characters. *Leo and Lia* has two Italian children asking their English governess a number of questions, to which she gives serious and proper answers. Both women were impatient with the hypocrisy, evasions and distortions which seemed to them to fill not only the texts but the illustrations of children's books. Children, they agreed, had to live in the real world, 'the world of today, its vastness and complexity', and parents should be reading the new books on education, science and medicine. The fanciful Laura and the down-to-earth Amelia had become very attached to each other, Laura writing one day: 'Dearest, don't you think our friendship is wonderful? I am so fond of you. I was thinking about this just now, and I wanted to tell you.'

For Amelia, the liberation of children was closely bound up with that of women. She had become increasingly involved with the suffrage debates being pushed by reformers such as Salvemini and the socialist feminists, but insisted that suffrage itself was not enough: women had to be educated, to learn to express themselves, to demand not so much sexual equality as their rights, which themselves carried duties. 'I deny women the right to isolate themselves', she wrote sternly, 'and not to participate in the life of the country.' She had become president of the literature section of the Lyceum, which put her on its board, and organised, to the delight of Carlo and Nello, a talk by the popular writer of fairy stories, Térésah. At last, she was emerging from her cocoon of grief over Joe's death. She stopped wearing black and began to invite friends and their children to the house. Salvemini was a frequent visitor, as were the Ferreros and their son Leo, ever cleverer and more precocious, and the Orvietos and their son Leonfrancesco. Always close to the Orvietos, Amelia became involved in their efforts to excavate and restore the old Roman theatre in Fiesole, where, with Eleonora Duse's encouragement, some of the Greek tragedies were staged. She would look back on these years as 'bathed by a marvellous light', in which so much was happy, intimate and rich in friendship and affection.

Some time in 1912, Amelia started work on a new play. Once again it was a portrait of a society in the throes of change, and written in Venetian. But this time, urged on by the Orvietos, she decided to set it in her own family past, during Venice's heroic resistance to the Austrians in 1848. *San Marco*, told through a series of domestic scenes, charts the rift between two generations. The play was to have its premier in Venice, but Amelia soon fell out with the director, saying that he was too parsimonious with his crowd scenes, and that the power of the crowd was what *San Marco* was all about.

Even so, it might still have come on, but for its timing. Italy was filled with anti-Austrian feelings and there were fears of riots. The government ruled that unless she toned down the fierce attacks on Austria in the play, it would be banned in Venice. She refused, but since there had been protests and much publicity, *San Marco* was picked up by the Manzoni theatre in Milan. There, to Amelia's dismay, the influential critic of the *Corriere della Sera* dismissed it as a 'play of little value and somewhat insipid'. Though restaged in Rome to better reviews – Roman critics tended to praise what Milan had slammed – Amelia was downcast. 'Alas,' she wrote, 'it's so very difficult and rare to pull off perfect harmony between heart and pen.'

When in Rome, where Ernesto Nathan was busy modernising the city, she always stayed with Gabriele, on whom, since Joe's death, she had become very dependent. She was ill-at-ease with their brother Carlo, who used the name 'Moravia', and whose son, Alberto, was suffering from TB of the bones and had to spend months in bed.

The years 1911 and 1912 marked something of a watershed for Giolitti's liberal Italy. Although extreme poverty continued to drive desperate southerners to emigrate – just under 1 million people in 1912 – even the socialist Turati was forced to agree that the country had seen considerable progress. But as a nation Italy remained profoundly divided, full of unruly dissident political forces, none willing to make compromises. The hope of melding the socialists of different persuasions, the Nationalists, the Futurists, the liberals, Catholics, republicans, syndicalists and anarchists into a united country without resorting to violence or dictatorship seemed more distant than ever.

The elections of 1913, the first to see universal male suffrage, brought large gains for the socialists. In Florence, 52.3 per cent of the vote went to socialists, and it was quickly dubbed 'the reddest city in Italy'. But many Catholics had abstained from voting altogether, the liberals were bitterly divided, and all over Italy there was beginning to be a longing for a leader to cut through the confusion and the rampant corruption.

Then, on 7 June 1914, police fired on and killed three demonstrators at a socialist rally in Ancona, and wounded thirty-one others. In what became known as 'Red Week', churches were attacked, red flags hoisted over town halls and the villas of rich landowners looted. There was talk of civil war. Florence and Rome were the cities most affected. At a Futurist *grande serata Fiorentina* in the Piazza Santa Croce, pandemonium broke out. Barricades were set up and defended by strikers throwing stones and bottles. After a carabinieri officer was beaten up, police on horseback charged the demonstrators. There were many casualties. All over Italy, telegraph lines were cut, trains halted and fires lit. Salvemini, who had stood for parliament for Apulia, was shot at by an opponent, but not injured.

The strutting and boastful Mussolini was one of the principal instigators of Red Week. As editor of the socialist *Avanti!* he had quadrupled its readers and won admiration for his forceful rhetoric and irrepressible ambition. At the Socialist Party Congress, held in Ancona that April, he had secured his dominance over the revolutionary wing of the party. In many ways, Red Week had been a successful tactic, effectively proving that it was possible to paralyse the country; but it had also shown that, without the backing of the police and the army, it was impossible to confront guns with stones.

When the schools closed for the summer, Amelia decided on the advice of doctors to send Carlo to Viareggio, where the sea air would do him good, and where a tutor could be found to coach him. Carlo was now fourteen, a somewhat overweight boy apparently not greatly interested in the world around him and showing disturbing signs, she thought, of 'superficiality' and 'impulsiveness', though always loving and exuberantly affectionate. In one of their many letters, when Amelia had been absent from Florence, Carlo wrote: 'Last night I kissed your portrait, I thought about you and tears came to my eyes.' Sometimes, now, he signed himself 'Charley'.

Having seen Carlo off for Viareggio in the company of a spinster cousin, Amelia took Aldo and Nello to the alpine resort of Macugnaga, near Monte Rosa. To her considerable surprise, the letters that arrived from Viareggio were anything but childish; over many pages, they raised urgent questions about the Balkans, and about the worsening international situation. Pleased as she was to receive them, she scolded him for sending them by expensive express post: 'You know perfectly well that when I tell you not to do something, I mean it.' From friends in Viareggio, Amelia heard that at dinner in his pensione, Carlo impressed the other guests with his adult conversation and the maturity of his views. The only sour note came from the spinster cousin, who reported that Carlo always insisted on doing things his own way.

Amelia was still at Macugnaga when news came on 28 June 1914 of the assassination of Archduke Franz Ferdinand, followed within weeks by Austria-Hungary's declaration of war on Serbia. On 4 August part of Europe went to war. Carlo's letters were now about the duties of Italy under various treaties, whether Italy should remain neutral or join the war, and in which case, on what side. He told his mother that when the newspapers arrived in the pensione, the guests fought over them 'like wild animals'. Amelia was beginning to regret her former enthusiasm for war. 'I have become convinced of something,' she wrote, 'and that is that I have a horror of fighting. The beautiful war predicted by the Nationalists does not exist: or rather, it exists only in a single situation, that of a true war of independence ... I am ashamed at the levity with which I said that war was something necessary in people's lives. It is a horrible lie.'

Two months later, the family gathered together again at Il Frassine, the Zabbans' house outside Florence. Amelia would never forget, she wrote later, the moment that Carlo first entered her room. She had seen off to the seaside a boy, pale, stout and unhealthy. The young man who walked in was taller and much thinner, with his face and broad shoulders brown from the sun and his eyes gleaming with good health. He was, she wrote, '*bellissimo*, with the beauty of a man'.

Though Aldo, now eighteen and a medical student, continued to tease his younger brothers and call them '*i bimbi*', the little boys, they admired his dashing clothes and hair worn fashionably long. Since his return from college, to Amelia's immense relief and pleasure, Aldo had once again become extremely close to her. Carlo and Nello were inseparable and went to learn fencing together. The house rang to their shouts and laughter and was often filled with their friends. Carlo, the most adventurous and high-spirited of them all, was their ring-leader. When the moment came to pick the grapes, the boys went to work in the vineyard, and in their spare time gave lessons in reading and writing to local children. The household had never seemed happier or more secure.

At the outbreak of war, Italy was caught between its membership, with Austria-Hungary and Germany, of the Triple Alliance, and its traditional friendship and ties to Britain and France which, with Russia, formed the Triple Entente. On 3 August 1914, it opted for neutrality. Though a clear majority of Italians wanted to remain neutral, there were strong forces ranged against them. War against Austria was tempting, as Austria-Hungary held the '*terre irredente*', the 'unredeemed' Italian-speaking city of Trento and part-Italian city of Trieste. The '*irredentisti*' claimed that the retaking of these places would finally fulfil the goals of the Risorgimento. And there were the 'interventionists', backed by a powerful assortment of intellectuals. Among them were Salvemini, the Orvietos, the Zabbans, the Ferreros and the Rossellis, all harking back to Mazzini's belief in a new Europe born of a revolution against the aristocracy, and regarding the war as a moral struggle between the reactionary forces of Austria-Hungary and Germany, and those of liberal, democratic France and Britain. For his part, Marinetti and his Futurists maintained that a 'blood bath' would serve to 'purify' the nation.

As Venetians, the Pincherles had always been anti-Austrian, and they had Jewish relations in Trieste. Not even memories of her creative and happy years in Vienna in the 1890s, or her instinctive distaste for war, lessened Amelia's conviction that Italy should join Britain and France and go to war. She hated the Austrians in her bones.

In October 1914 a pro-interventionist demonstration took place in Piazza Vittorio in Florence. Aldo marched with fellow students. Six weeks later, a 'Revolutionary Interventionist Florentine Fascio' was formed to coordinate their various forces, taking the word *fascio* from the *fasces*, the bundle of sticks carried by lictors in Roman times; a series of inflammatory war poems became their anthem. Those socialists who remained opposed to the war were becoming increasingly gloomy and despairing.

So quick to judge and to harbour grudges, Mussolini was usually slow to develop policies, preferring to react and respond to those of others. But now he moved quickly. Challenged to clarify his own socialist position, he abandoned his former neutrality, resigned from *Avanti!* and started his own daily paper, *Il Popolo d'Italia* – this with funds from the government, from industry, and from the British and French secret services – and announced that it would be far better for the future of Italian socialism if Italy fought. Attracting pro-war intellectuals to write for his paper, his own style was fierce and declamatory. Neutralists were castigated as cowards: neutrality implied passivity, while intervention spelt dynamism. Other zealous crusaders for the cause of intervention included a fanatically anti-clerical railway-worker called Roberto Farinacci, who excoriated the feeble socialists still clinging to neutrality. Observing the hesitations of the government, Mussolini advocated 'the shooting, I say shooting, in the back of a dozen deputies . . .' Parliament, he declared, was a 'pestiferous pustule poisoning the blood of the nation'.

On 26 April 1915, having haggled, toyed with and finally rejected offers from Austria and Germany in exchange for remaining neutral, the Italians signed the secret Treaty of London. In return for the promise of Trentino, Trieste, Istria, much of Dalmatia, the upper Adriatic and Valona in Albania, Italy committed its troops to the war, though for the moment only against Austria and not Germany. In what was named a 'Radiant May' of joyful preparations, many newspapers celebrated what they called a triumphant 'resurrection against traitors to the *patria*'. In Florence, the bells in the Palazzo Vecchio rang out and 'patriotic vigour . . . broke out in every heart like an aria from Verdi'. Little heed was paid to the new Pope, Benedict XV, who refused to sanction what he considered an unjust war, or to the misgivings of the unwarlike king, or to the fact that 60,000 Italian soldiers remained in as yet unpacified Libya, or indeed to the military unpreparedness of a country that remained in many areas remote, backward, unmodernised and profoundly illiterate.

In the Rosselli house, there was much rejoicing, and much excited talk of liberating Trieste and Trento. 'What I do or don't do now is of no importance,' wrote Amelia. 'The individual does not count . . . at a time of national crisis we must all rise to small personal contributions.' Coming home one evening from a student rally, Aldo insisted that they hang a flag from the window. Watching her three sons, Carlo and Nello already in their pyjamas, scrambling over each other to secure the flag from a hook in the wall, Amelia remembered herself as a child watching her father hanging out his tattered, faded flag from their window on the Grand Canal to mark every anniversary of the Austrian defeat of 1849.

CHAPTER FOUR

Becoming a Man

On 23 May 1915, after thirty years as allies, Italy formally declared war on Austria-Hungary. Within a few days, soldiers began to leave for the front in the Dolomites. The chief of staff, General Cadorna, spoke of reaching Vienna by Christmas. But he was already in his mid-sixties, a stubborn man whose military ideas were formed in an earlier age. Furthermore, Italy's army was the weakest of any of the great powers, top heavy with administration and red tape and weighed down by useless ancillary units. As many as half the soldiers were illiterate. Jumbled together in brigades, men from different regions shared no common language. The front to which these men were now despatched by their commanding officers was one of high mountains and tree-less plateaux, swept by gusting winds coming from the north-east, and with fissures of limestone so tough that trenches were little better than shallow scrapings or holes in the rocks. Even in August, the cold at night was ferocious. All the soldiers, in their letters home, spoke of the *muraglie massicce*, the massive walls of mountain, the incessant booming of enemy bombardments against the rocks, and above all of the rain, mud and water, in which they advanced, retreated, fought and slept. But when occasionally the sun shone, they discovered a vast panorama of peaks, in shades of grey and brown and purple, stretching around them in every direction, and air that was crisp and thin and very bright.

For the first few days, the Italians advanced, encountering little opposition. But the Austrians had simply pulled back their men to better positions. On 23 June Cadorna ordered the first major offensive; despite the lessons of the Western Front, he had decided on frontal attacks by infantry along the Isonzo river, and a defensive line through the Trentino, paying little heed to the artillery which had proved so vital in northern France, or to the carnage caused there by barbed wire and machine guns. The Italian soldiers, ill-equipped and ill-led, often with no helmets or bayonets and in boots which had wooden soles and cardboard uppers, found themselves faced by serried rows of wire and guns. The cutters they had been issued with were little better than garden secateurs. Soon, the few metres they had taken and then lost again were covered in corpses. By 7 July, when orders came to cease the advance, the Italians had lost 15,000 men.

In Florence, Amelia had just finished a new play about Lady Hamilton called *Emma Liona*. She put it to one side. She had briefly fallen out with some of the Lyceum's ruling council when, shortly before the declaration of war, she had arranged for a talk by a writer from Trieste, Haydée – the pen name of the novelist and journalist Ida Finzi – and had been told that this might be offensive to Austria, as her irredentist views were well known. Amelia had threatened to resign, but the quarrel had blown over, and now that the Austrians had become the enemy, the talk was reinstated, though the council urged a 'tacit reserve' by members when it came to political matters. The next and final talk arranged by Amelia before cultural events were suspended and the society's premises handed over to the Red Cross, was by Margherita Sarfatti, Mussolini's mistress and now a successful journalist.

For his part, Angiolo Orvieto was anxious to turn the Leonardo da Vinci Society into a centre for '*l'italianità fiorentina*', where Jews, always wary about their standing, could prove themselves 'ardent and useful Italian citizens'. He had taken over rooms in the Palazzo Vecchio and had started an information service for the families of men at the front, with a section given over to weighing, packing and despatching woollen garments to the cold Dolomites. Fifteen-year-old Carlo, who came after school to help, was much fêted by the ladies. He told his mother that he thought he might eventually make an excellent businessman, which depressed her, though she admired what she saw as his 'insatiable desire to do things'. Laura had set up a training scheme for volunteer nurses and her twelve-year-old daughter Annalia gathered together her school friends to knit for soldiers. Amelia herself was working in Angiolo's information office. Sometimes, as they transcribed the lists, news would come of husbands, sons and brothers fallen in battle. Then the room would fill with terrible cries of anguish.

Amelia had made one of the rooms in their flat into a studio for Aldo, where he could receive his friends. He was now nineteen, dark, with even features; photographs show an elegant, even dapper, figure in a dark coat and hat, with a round face and ears that stick out a little. Like his father, Aldo had many talents and was undecided about which to pursue. He had enrolled at the university to study archaeology, but Amelia, fearing that he would squander his life on artistic pursuits, persuaded him to join the medical faculty, saying that it would instil 'self-discipline'. Intrigued by the idea of anatomy and the drawings it would entail, Aldo willingly agreed, and his early studies went well. As a medical student and the eldest son of a widowed mother, he was not liable to the ordinary draft. 'We mothers, what should we do with our sons?' Amelia wrote to Laura. 'Turn them into men of action or men of thought? ... This is hell, of the most immediate kind.'

Both her uncle, Ernesto Nathan, and Salvemini, despite their ages, had volunteered, but while seventy-year-old Ernesto was able to join the elite Alpini corps as a junior lieutenant with the job of looking after foreign visitors, the doctors sent Salvemini home to Florence after discovering that he had traces of TB. Even now, seven years after the earthquake that had destroyed his family, he continued to hope for news of his small son Ughetto, and waited each day until after the second post before paying his calls, in case it brought him a letter.

Then the day came when Aldo appeared in Amelia's room and told her that he had decided to join up. Her immediate instinct was to try to dissuade him. But Aldo took her hand and asked her how, having demonstrated through the streets of Florence in support of the war, he could now sit by while his friends left for the front. 'Would it', he asked her, 'be fair?' Aloud, Amelia said: 'Yes, yes, I understand.' But inside, as she wrote later, she could only think: 'I can't bear it. I can't stand to see you leave. I love you so much, I don't want you to be hurt. I don't want to be fair ... no, no, I don't want this.'

Two months later, Aldo left for officer training at the military

Amelia and Aldo, in military uniform

college in Modena, and after this was posted as second lieutenant to the 145th Infantry Regiment at Carnia, where most of his men were Sicilians. Before leaving, he went to the Orvietos' villa to say goodbye, and while he was there carved his initials in the trunk of a lime tree in the courtyard where he and his younger brothers had so often played. Amelia noted with pleasure that Aldo had become 'very straight and idealistic'. His great friend Giacomo Morpurgo, the son of the director of Florence's national library, left for the army with him. When Amelia went to visit Aldo soon after, Carlo wrote to her: 'I am certain that Aldo will be so happy to see you so proud of him.'

In November, when the men on the front line were sleeping on wet straw or in the mud, and their uniforms had been turned to parchment by sweat, dust and rain, Aldo came down with pleurisy and was sent home for a month to convalesce. Not long after he returned to his base at Tolmezzo, he wrote to Amelia to tell her that he longed to see action and so had asked to be transferred to an alpine regiment at the front. He was now with the Alpini on the Pal Grande, conveying weapons up from the plains by mule, under enemy fire. His letters were cheerful and uncomplaining; he told her that his trench was so close to the enemy that he could hear the Austrian soldiers speak, and that he was happy. Two weeks later he was granted a short leave and Amelia and Carlo travelled up to Udine to meet him. They found him ruddy from the mountain air. They climbed to the keep of a castle and Aldo pointed out the front lines at Carnia, Pal Grande and Pal Piccolo. In the distance they could hear the thud of shells.

Back at the hotel, they found a telegram recalling Aldo to duty. Before he left, Amelia sat on his bed and stroked his dark hair. She was touched when Carlo told her that Aldo had resisted buying a special officer's beret that he badly wanted, remembering her feelings about extravagance. On their way home to Florence, Amelia and Carlo stopped in Verona, where Zio Giù, with the rank of colonel, was training young officers. Verona had become a garrison town, and sacking covered the ancient monuments. When they reached Florence, they found a long line of women outside the Palazzo Vecchio, waiting for news of their men. One evening, over dinner with a cousin, Amelia said: 'If I were told that Aldo would not come back, I don't think that the sun would ever shine for me again.'

As deep winter settled over the Dolomites, orders went out to keep up the skirmishes and tie down the enemy, but not to tire the troops. The men dug trenches under the snow and tied canvas across the openings to caves, inside which they crouched in their sodden greatcoats, trying not to freeze to death. Aldo wrote to say that the snow was piling up all around them and that the strong winds blowing from the north were arctic, but that he was content with his companions. He wrote to Amelia almost every day, and she wrote back, anxious, loving. On 26 December, he reported: 'Yesterday was the saddest of Christmases: rain and fog all day.' But he had been given leave to descend the mountain and eat in a hotel, where he had had an excellent meal, and had laughed and joked with his fellow officers.

Early in January, Aldo went briefly on leave to Udine, where, observing officers wearing greatcoats lined with fur, he bought one for himself. '*È molto bellino*', he wrote, but he worried that it might be a bit short in the sleeves. Away from the front line, shelters had been set up with stoves, food and water; the larger ones had baths and ovens. Even so, a senior medical officer sent early in January 1916 to report on conditions, described clothing torn and encrusted with mud, frostbitten feet and 'psychological disturbances'. Lives were being lost, he noted, because the men had not been given elementary training in how to keep warm, and were so careless about latrines that the surroundings had become 'literally a field of filth'. There was typhoid and cholera.

Aldo was keeping a diary, with entries on training, expenses and the different phases of the campaign. Twenty-four new Italian infantry regiments had been formed, plus thirty-one companies of Alpini, and conditions were said to be very slowly improving, with a delivery of hobnailed leather boots and iron helmets. Stints on the front line had been shortened. Amelia wrote to him: 'Remember, do everything you have to do, but be prudent.' On 20 February, Aldo spent the day doing a round of the trenches and took some photographs; he had a cough, but assured her that it was getting better. On the 23rd, a 'furious tempest' cut off his platoon and they received no letters or supplies; he put his men to clearing paths and in the evening gathered with his fellow officers. There were rockfalls, howling winds and hailstones the size of walnuts. On the night of the 26th, he was in the mess, writing in pencil by candlelight: he told Amelia that he had marched five kilometres through the snow. Then came news that the Alpini might be moved, and there was a chance he would be allowed to go on leave. On 5 March, he sent her a card: 'Weather still appalling: snow and yet more snow!' Orders came for further forays, to tie down the enemy, confuse them. There were avalanches almost every day and casualties were mounting. And still it kept snowing.

At two in the morning on 26 March, the Austrians, taking advantage of the dark night and thick fog, attacked on Pal Grande. The Italian gunners responded strongly and the Austrians withdrew. A second Austrian assault was launched on Pal Piccolo, and the Italian commanding officers, fearing that the whole mountain might fall to the enemy, despatched more troops. Aldo and his friend Giacomo were among them. At 5.30 on the morning of the 27th, after a night of heavy shelling by the Austrians, the Alpini were sent to take the peak. The Austrians exploded bombs with poisonous gas. The Italians retook their lost positions. In just two days they had seen fourteen of their officers killed and nineteen wounded.

In Florence, Amelia was working grimly in the Palazzo Vecchio. She had heard about the heavy fighting on the Pal Piccolo. On 29 March, she wrote to Aldo: 'I am very worried about you. I have had no news since the 25th ... I hope that tonight's post will bring me something.' Next day she wrote again: 'Nothing today either. Why haven't you thought to send me a telegram? You must always do this, send me a telegram when there is fighting in your area.' On 31 March: 'Yet another day without a line from you. How long can this go on? ... I kiss you, my dearest, with all my love.' On 2 April: 'My Aldo, where are you? How can these days pass, one after the other, with no news of you? ... I hug you very close to my heart.'

On the tenth day of silence, Amelia went to a meeting in Angiolo's information office; as she entered the room she saw two women exchange glances. Nothing was said. She got home to find a cousin, Mary Nathan, waiting for her. Very carefully, Mary told her that Aldo was missing.

Amelia's reaction was to embark on a 'fever of activity'. She sent telegrams, contacted the Red Cross, got in touch with friends at the front. Ugo Ojetti, a family friend serving not far from Pal Piccolo, cabled back: 'About Rosselli, remain calm. Tomorrow will have more precise news'. There was a rumour that Aldo had been wounded in the head. Amelia sent a telegram to her brother Gabriele, who had been instrumental in having Aldo moved to the Alpini: 'First news reassuring'.

Three days of silence followed. No news came. The house fell quiet. Carlo and Nello tiptoed around, whispering. Amelia kept thinking that she could keep Aldo alive, providing she willed it enough. She took to her bed and lay in the dark. If she let the light in everything would fall to pieces. She listened to her neighbour, who had recently lost her son, opening and shutting her door to let mourners in.

Then came the morning that she woke to find Gabriele sitting at the end of her bed. Speaking calmly, he told her what she already knew: that Aldo was dead, killed on 27 March during the battle for Pal Piccolo. His friend Giacomo had died with him. Gabriele was firm: she had to accept it, if not for her sake, then for the sake of Carlo and Nello. She had no choice. And so, she wrote later, 'A great black shadow descended' but 'I obeyed. And the house, as if waking from an appalling nightmare, began once again to move.'

Time did move again. But Amelia was inconsolable. A death notice for Aldo appeared in the *Giornale d'Italia*, in the name of the family and of Zia Gì and Zio Giù, asking for no visits and no contact. For this profoundly literate woman, who had spent her whole life exploring language and meaning, trying to make sense of the world and the people in it through talk and books, words at this moment could do nothing. She wrote to Laura that she was suffering 'indescribably' and that the pain never let up. 'I am living two parallel lives,' she wrote, as so many others in her position have written. 'I speak, I laugh, I move about, and behind that person is another ... I live suspended between these two conflicting states, somewhere in the clouds.' What she found so unbearable, she said, was not being able to tell Aldo how proud she felt of him, knowing how very pleased he would have been to hear her say so.

She found no comfort in Carlo and Nello; indeed, their physical presence caused her more agony, with its constant reminder of what she had lost. She sat at meals in silence, counting: one, two, but never again three. What terrified her was the idea that the war would end, and everything would return to normal, 'when nothing can ever be normal again'. She felt as if the madness of grief had 'shattered the mechanism of my mind'. Many years later she would write that she had known how 'shut away, savage, even cruel' she had been to the two boys; and later, too, they would say that her rejection of them had been terrible to bear.

What at last brought Amelia back to life was the idea of setting up, in Aldo's name, a home for children of serving soldiers whose mothers were dead or unable to look after them. Every day, after school, desperate to do something to counter his mother's grief, Carlo rode around the countryside on his bicycle looking for a suitable place. One day he came home to say that he had seen a one-storey building, attached to a farmhouse, on the road between Bagno a Ripoli and Grassina. Amelia rented it, called it La Casina di Aldo, and threw herself into finding furniture and books. Zia Gì provided linen; Laura sent a grandfather clock. Assunta, who had been looking after the boys for the past thirteen years, offered to run the home; she was firm, capable and loving. By the summer of 1916, the Casina had twelve children living there.

Towards the end of the year, Nello wrote to his uncle Gabriele to tell him that he was thinking of starting a magazine, 'not a trivial one, but a serious paper in which to discuss good ideas'. His co-editor would be Gualtiero Cividalli, a friend from the Liceo Michelangiolo, who came from an observant Florentine-Jewish family. The two boys, whose fervour and patriotism knew no bounds, decided to call it *Noi Giovani* – 'We Young'; its motto alone was proof of its extreme highmindedness: *'Purezza, Forza, Amore'*, Purity, Strength, Love. Saying that they did not wish to 'exalt themselves', they wrote under pseudonyms. Nello became 'Nero' or 'Juventus', Gualtiero took 'Il Direttore', Carlo was 'Civis', and Leo Ferrero signed his poems with two asterisks. Jean Luchaire, the son of the director of the French Institute, joined them, as did Leonfrancesco Orvieto.

The boys met in the Rosselli house for long, intense debates. Six numbers came out, full of exhortations to young Italians to remain 'noble' and 'uncorrupted', both physically and morally. Nello contributed patriotic short stories, in which a florist or a maid lost her young man in the war. Carlo tackled politics. In the issue of 4 April 1917, he wrote a paean of praise to the recent Russian Revolution: 'It is as if we were waking from a deep sleep ... What has happened is so beautiful, so magnificent, so extraordinary that it is still impossible to believe it.' In June, Gualtiero was called up and the magazine closed. But in its few issues, Carlo and Nello had put down extremely clear markers. It was up to their generation, they wrote, to prepare for the future, with firmness and conviction and a 'true concept of Good and Evil ... an ideal of justice and liberty for all mankind'.

The winter of 1916 was bitterly cold. In Florence it rained steadily for three months, then snowed. Fuel was rationed, and in their dark and draughty old houses, all in stone and terracotta, people froze. Sugar was so scarce that it was sold in tiny twists of paper. In a hall attached to the church of Orsanmichele, under the flags of the guilds of medieval Italy, lessons were laid on by Florentine ladies in how to cook stews and bean soups by putting a casserole over a flame for just a few minutes, then packing it tightly in straw where it would simmer gently on. To counter the growing hostility towards the Allies, and particularly the British, Angiolo proposed starting an Anglo-Italian library. A loggia off Via Tornabuoni was rented; its ground floor, which had fluted columns and a magnificent carved and curling ceiling, was turned into a reading room. The grander and more affluent members of the Anglo-Florentine community who had decided to sit out the war in Italy – Bernard Berenson, Harold Acton, Janet Ross – gave books. Salvemini came to lecture on history.

In 1917, both Carlo and Nello left school; they had now reached military age. Carlo had wanted to volunteer earlier, but Amelia's frantic anxiety persuaded him not to. She missed Aldo no less keenly, but all her former love for her younger sons had returned, and with it her customary scolding. They were too extravagant, she said, too soft on themselves, too heedless of others. Characteristically, on what would have been Aldo's twenty-first birthday, she told them she would be sending to charity the money that she had set aside for the watch she had planned to give him; and she hoped that Carlo and Nello would make similar gestures, 'so we can almost create the illusion that our dear Aldo is still with us'. She and Zia Gì had started a small organisation to send sick and poor children to the seaside in his name, and, together with her friend Gina Lombroso, Amelia was setting up an association to 'encourage Italian women to take part in the scientific, social, political, philosophical development of the country'. Slowly, very slowly, her sense of duty was beginning to assert itself again.

In June, Carlo received his call-up papers and was sent to an artillery regiment stationed at La Spezia; in October he was enrolled in an officer school in Caserta, from where he wrote to his uncle Gabriele, in his rather childish round hand, that he had spent seven lire on gloves and another seven on shoes. When he wrote to Zio Giù however, asking for his help in getting him posted to a front-line unit, the answer was adamant: 'No, dear Carlo, I have already told you many times, and I will go on telling you ... you must not apply to join the Bombardieri.' There was no reason to put himself in any kind of danger, and it was morally wrong, 'whether out of ambition, whim or impatience', to cause his mother such pain.

Carlo was still in Caserta when, on 24 October 1917, the Austrian and German forces broke through at Caporetto and invaded Friuli and the Veneto. Cadorna had proved a terrible general, committing his exhausted, demoralised, underpaid, ill-equipped troops to a 300-kilometre front, where they had fought eleven battles against Austria for the control of the Isonzo valley. In one alpine area, 750 men had been allowed to freeze to death. Often, the courage of the soldiers had been heroic. The Italian defeat at Caporetto was overwhelming. Forty thousand men were killed or wounded; 280,000 taken prisoner; 150 kilometres of terrain lost. On 27 October Cadorna ordered a retreat. A river of men took to the road in a long trail of abandoned weapons, animals and cannons, burning villages as they went in order to leave nothing for the enemy but the mud and devastation of the land over which they had fought. '*Fare Caporetto*' came to mean 'run away quickly'.

General Cadorna, who had reacted to earlier defeats by dismissing his officers for incompetence and by having his soldiers executed for cowardice, was finally replaced by a more humane and abler man, Armando Diaz, who had no taste for sending men towards machine guns to be mown down in waves. Hearing of the catastrophe of Caporetto, Carlo wrote to Amelia: 'Italy's honour must be saved ... Today we retreat, but tomorrow ... there will be a magnificent resistance. I am sure of this. We have to be morally strong to win.'

Against a backdrop of recriminations and rancour, the right calling the soldiers *imboscati* – draft dodgers – and blaming them for 'revolutionary defeatism', Italian refugees from Austrian-occupied territory began to stream down through Italy. 'They are arriving in thousands and thousands,' Amelia wrote to her mother Emilia in Rome, saying that when she had been to meet the trains at the station she had almost been knocked over in the crush. 'You can nearly touch with your hands the reality of the invasion.'

The destitute families, many of whom had brought nothing at all with them, were taken to a carabinieri barracks near the station or to the cloisters of Santa Maria Novella, where, until mattresses were found, they slept on the ground. The more fortunate, usually the better-off families who had thought to escape with their jewels and some money, wound up in hotels on the Lungarno. Amelia spent her days taking down names, reuniting families and caring for the children, four of whom she entrusted to Assunta in Aldo's Casina. 'The more the days pass,' she wrote to Carlo, 'the more I see the enormity of the disaster that has hit us.' One day she bumped into Salvemini, wandering among the refugees; he was in tears. She wanted very much to visit Carlo, but the trains were too crowded. It was clear to her now, as it was to many who had so fervently supported the war, that many of the men sent to fight had not even known where they were going, or who their enemy was.

With Carlo in the army and Nello soon to depart, Amelia decided that she could not bear to stay on in Via Gianbologna, where she had once waited so desperately for news of Aldo, to find herself waiting once more for word of her two younger sons. 'I am still stunned by grief,' she told her mother. 'I can't think of the words to describe my state of mind.' She had discovered an empty flat in a beautiful if dark fifteenth-century palazzo, Stiozzi Ridolfi, on the other side of the Arno, in Via San Niccolò, a busy road that snaked its way in a long S parallel to the river. It had high ceilings and views across the countryside to San Miniato. Here she recreated 'Aldo's room', 'to keep him near and close to me'. From the open windows, she could hear the birds singing. She made herself a study and filled it with the furniture she loved: an eighteenth-century table, a silk screen, a bookcase. Here she sat in a striped blue blouse with a high white collar, writing at her desk in her tidy, legible hand.

In November, Nello – who had enrolled in the law faculty at Pisa university – volunteered but was told that the infantry was not taking recruits for the moment. While waiting, he decided to switch to a literature degree at the Istituto di Studi Superiori in Florence. The winter passed, slow and grim; Amelia was lonely and fretted ceaselessly about Carlo, who had been moved to various different barracks in the north. Postal services between serving men and their families had been greatly improved and the two of them exchanged letters almost daily, in which they discussed books, philosophy, religion, the inner life. They talked about Freemasonry, Carlo expressing interest and sympathy, Amelia saying that the Masons were an anachronism, and the Masonic ritual of stroking palms as a sign of recognition seemed to her 'like monkeys scratching their stomachs'. They agreed that Britain represented the 'greatest liberty and the greatest discipline'.

In April 1918, Nello was sent first to Vigevano, in Lombardy, for training, from where he reported that there were more pretty girls than flies, then to a military academy in Turin. Occasionally, when she heard nothing for more than two days, Amelia was reproachful: 'I am so alone; you have to know that I live for your letters.' Once they lost the habit of communicating every aspect of life, she warned her sons, they would never get it back. From a punishment cell in his military academy – to which he had been confined for ten days for talking during a period of compulsory silence – Nello sent a humorous note, including a drawing of a cell, barred windows and bread and water. He added 'very loving kisses' and signed himself *terribilmente gelato*', terribly frozen.

In mid-June 1918 the Austrians, this time not backed by the Germans, launched a major offensive against the Italians on the Piave, east of Venice. Supported by the Allies, the Italians held firm and then gradually pushed back, capturing Trieste and Trento. But then came the Spanish flu. In Bologna, Nello was put to work transporting the dead and the dying, and briefly became ill himself. Amelia now never left her flat in San Niccolò without meeting three or four funerals, and hardly a day passed without her having to write a letter of condolence.

She was staying with Zia Gì at Frassine when, on 4 November, the news came that the Austrians had surrendered. She stood outside, listening as the bells rang out from churches all round the Florentine hills. Though Carlo had been very slightly injured by a splinter of shrapnel, and though one of her nieces was very ill, her sense of relief was overwhelming. She felt light, weightless. Carlo and Nello had survived. On his nineteenth birthday she wrote to Carlo: 'This is the last of your birthdays we will ever spend apart.' She was planning to give him a raincoat she knew he coveted and she was thinking of him entering Trieste with his men: 'It's a solemn and great moment for an Italian, to see the frontiers of our country pushed back.' She had decided to set up a library in the elementary school in Timau, at the foot of Pal Piccolo, 'where my Aldo died fighting'.

Italy, however, was in disarray. The victory itself was ambiguous, with unclear gains and many losses. Five million Italian men had gone to war: 500,000 had been killed and perhaps double that number wounded. The soldiers who now came home were exhausted, disillusioned. Their complaints that they had been ill-led and ill looked after were only increased by the currents of political tension swirling around the country. After Caporetto, in order to keep enough soldiers at the front, the government had made extravagant promises about land reform. Those who returned to Florence found no signs that these promises would be kept, and a city whose economy had been devastated by four years without tourists. There was talk of 'internal enemies' and a 'moral disintegration of the political system'. Finding no work, these men vented their anger on those who had spent the war in factories, thereby avoiding the draft.

During the war years, there had been no one dominant leader, but rather power had been shared between successive politicians, military commanders, industrialists, Freemasons and land-owners. A monarchy ruled by a timid, irresolute king, the country was awash with the conflicting dreams of Nationalists, republicans, Futurists, liberals, socialists and Catholics, each competing for influence in a society still marked by profound social divisions, and all wrangling about the war, and what it meant for the future.

It would be early 1920 when Carlo and Nello finally arrived home. Neither had yet reached the age of twenty-one. Both boys had filled out, become self-contained, self-reliant, organised; they were sturdy, robust. Carlo was the more dominating, with a lively, argumentative manner and slightly myopic eyes which shone with an ironical and questioning gaze. He was, as Zia Gì said, 'a sauce-pan always on the boil'. Nello was quieter, more studious, with innocent, almost child-like, blue eyes. He had inherited Amelia's sweet smile and his look was '*luminoso*'. The brothers remained inseparable.

Both envisaged some kind of academic future, though Nello,

with his mind set firmly on history and literature, was the more decided. Carlo, still drifting between the social sciences, politics and the law, and needing extra qualifications to make up for what he had lacked at his technical college, enrolled to study economics at the Cesare Alfieri Institute in Florence. He told his mother that she had been wrong to relegate him to a second-class education, and called it a 'refuge for donkeys'. Both brothers spoke of having been profoundly changed by the war. They had met and become friends, for the first time, with men 'of the people', and said that it had given them a shared dream of a socialist world, and of forging bonds between the classes. 'I left as a boy,' Carlo would later say; 'I came back a man.' He told Zio Giù that a thousand ideas were racing through his head. 'I want to study in depth a great many things and I want to read and learn about everything.' His mind, he wrote, was alive with the '*tumultuosa rapidità*', the tumultuous speed, of the world awaiting him. Amelia told him: 'I see the sail of your boat not black ... but beautifully white, open to a wind which will carry it far, very far ...'

CHAPTER FIVE

The Dark Seraphim

Aldo and his friend Giacomo were just two of the 47,000 Tuscan soldiers – one for every six men sent to the war – who did not come home. Many who did were wounded. The trains from the north arriving at the station of Santa Maria Novella no longer brought refugees but angry, exhausted men who found little to please them in post-war Italy. As Salvemini would say, at the war's end the capitalists got the 'substance' and the soldiers the 'shadows'.

The Versailles Conference opened in January 1919 to set the peace terms for the defeated powers. The Italian delegation arrived full of expectations. Along with the other promises made to them at the Treaty of London in 1915 – the acquisition of parts of Dalmatia, territory from the Ottoman Empire and islands along the Adriatic – they hoped for Fiume and South Tyrol, which they called Alto Adige. But the United States was seeking self-determination for nations and few of the Allies had much liking for the Italians, whom they accused of not fighting hard enough in the war; they were quick to dismiss Vittorio Orlando, Italy's premier, as untrustworthy, and Italy as a land of 'sturdy beggars' who alternated whining with truculence. The young diplomat Harold Nicolson noted that Orlando was a 'white, weak, flabby man', while Curzon referred to the Italians as 'mere bagmen, who would sell either party'. No one paid much heed when Orlando warned that if the earlier promises were not honoured, there would be civil war.

By the time a crushed Orlando arrived home to be ousted from office and replaced by a professor of economics, Francesco Saverio Nitti, most concessions to Italy had been abandoned. Italy came away with almost nothing except for a permanent seat at the League of Nations, a share in German reparations and two small areas of Istria and South Tyrol. Not surprising, then, that Gabriele D'Annunzio, who despite his age had waged a heroic war, referred to the treaty as a 'mutilated peace', a phrase quickly repeated around Italy, and sometimes altered to 'mutilated victory'. The fact that Italy's old enemy, the Austrian-Hungarian Empire, was dismantled did little to assuage a widespread feeling among the Italians of being ill-used.

Fiume – the area of 28 kilometres which lay between the Kingdom of Italy and the Kingdom of Slovenia and which contained a large Italian population – now became a rallying cry among Italian nationalists. On 12 September 1919, the posturing, theatrical D'Annunzio, who had lost the sight in one eye as a result of his plane crashing in the war, led one thousand disbanded veterans into Fiume, forcing out the occupying Allied troops. Many of D'Annunzio's followers were *Arditi*, the shock troops who had led the attacks against the Austrians. From the balcony of the governor's palace, D'Annunzio proclaimed the annexation of Fiume; he called himself *duce* of the Regency of Carnaro, and his followers *legionari*. And there he remained, seducing visitors with his rituals and dramatic *mises en scène* until December 1920, when Giolitti, now nearly eighty and recently returned to power, ordered the *Andrea Doria* warship to bombard the governor's palace, and D'Annunzio's weird, flamboyant reign ended. His much-repeated promise – 'Either Fiume or death' – turned out to amount to very little. D'Annunzio opted for neither. He returned to Venice and eventually accepted the title of Principe di Montenevoso.

Many Italians, from all sides of the political spectrum, considered D'Annunzio absurd; but not Mussolini. The editor and proprietor of *Il Popolo d'Italia* was now thirty-six, the father of three illegitimate children, and finally married to Rachele, although this had not prevented his incessant womanising. He had observed D'Annunzio's antics with envy and admiration. But he had not been idle. Twisting and turning in the political chaos of the hour, ever ready to address a crowd, however small, he told the returning soldiers that they represented the 'admirable, bellicose youth of Italy' and that their daggers and grenades would 'wreak havoc on all the wretches who desire to hinder the advance of Italy towards greatness ... She is yours! You will defend her!' The cry of the *Arditi* – '*Me ne frego*', 'I don't give a damn' – found ready listeners among the three million demobilised men who had become accustomed to obeying orders and were drawn to uniforms, parades and jackboots. The Belgian poet Léon Kochnitzky, who was an admirer of D'Annunzio, called the *Arditi* the 'dark seraphim of another apocalypse'.

By February 1919, there were some twenty ex-servicemen's leagues, calling themselves Fasci di Combattimento, active everywhere from Messina to Venice. Though still not making it clear as to whether he favoured a monarchy or a republic, a clerical or lay state, Mussolini told them that the old political parties were 'like corpses you keep as relics'. On 23 March, he invited the *fasci* to a meeting in Milan. Though the numbers were not particularly high, this meeting, in a building overlooking Piazza San Sepolcro, would later be seen as the founding moment of fascism; some of the men who attended – Roberto Farinacci and the Futurist Filippo Tommaso Marinetti – would soon be fascist leaders. The *Arditi* who showed up came in their black shirts. By the summer of 1919, the *fasci* had 1,000 members calling for a 'patriotic revolution'. By then they had cut their teeth on attacking an anarchist rally in Milan, helped by 200 students from Bocconi University.

The first Florentine *fascio*, which had grown out of a group of Futurists, students and war veterans, all passionate anti-communists, was bent on defeating those they considered 'degenerates'. In the second week of October 1919, Mussolini – fresh from a flight to congratulate D'Annunzio on his seizure of Fiume, and dressed in a dirty flying suit and beret, goggles perched on the crown of his bald head – paid a visit to Florence. By now, *Il Popolo d'Italia* had dropped its claim to be socialist. It was aimed at 'soldiers and producers', at all the small shopkeepers, clerks and students who had come home to find no work and rising prices, and at the young who would rescue Italy from its decadent, fossilised leaders and make it virile once more. There was a large crowd to greet him in the Teatro Olimpia. Glaring at his audience with his near-set, intense dark eyes, he told them that he intended to make 'a clean sweep of the past' and that he needed followers 'energetic and ruthless' enough to help him to do so. Fascism, he declared, stood for the spirit of the trenches, for the wounded veterans who now paraded through the streets demanding their rights, and fascists were needed to act as a bulwark against Italy's 'internal enemies', the Bolsheviks and socialist 'eunuchs'. Leninism, he warned, entailed autocracy, bestiality, terror and chaos, and Bolsheviks were little better than murderers. Socialists, said Mussolini, were 'un-Italian'. His skills as an orator – by turn sentimental, brutal, rabble-rousing, confessional, philosophical – were dazzling.

For an all-too-brief but happy moment, the Rossellis stood apart from the turmoil. Amelia was filled with overwhelming relief that two of her sons had survived and she took slightly bitter pleasure in hearing that Aldo was to receive a silver medal for valour.

Her long years of worrying about money were brought to a sudden end when the mercury mine in which she had inherited shares from Joe, the Siele on Monte Amiato, was taken over by the government as part of their new monopoly on coal, oil and mercury. They were now rich. Amelia decided to leave the small, dark apartment in Via San Niccolò and they returned to the residential streets near the Duomo, buying an imposing eighteenth-century house in Via Giusti, close to Piazza Massimo d'Azeglio, where magnificent vast sycamores cast a deep, dense shade. The house had a large garden, a trellis of wisteria, a music room with a grand piano, and another with a billiard table. Just as Amelia was moving, she witnessed one of the first Florentine street attacks, when a group of local women, infuriated by the steep rise in the price of bread, ransacked the bakery opposite and made off with sacks of flour and loaves of bread. It was perilous, now, to be a shopkeeper suspected of hoarding.

Nello had settled on a future in the academic world, though he was still casting around for a subject for his thesis. Amelia was worried about Carlo, whose thoughts and interests seemed to her dangerously scattered and whose spirit appeared constantly 'elsewhere'. She told him that he had to find and become passionate about just one thing, and then study it in depth, 'looking only down that particular path' and nowhere else. Convinced that he had no talent for languages, literature or the law, she dreamt that he might choose something practical such as chemistry, or join one of the new industrial concerns where he would be able to explore their ethical and social implications. But Carlo hesitated. He and Nello talked and talked, often far into the night, though Nello complained that his brother's insistence on seeing every side to every problem could be wearying. '*Basta*!' he would say. 'I can't stand any more. You have overstuffed my head.' Even Carlo's friends were drawn into his doubts and quests. 'Enjoy yourself,' wrote one. 'Don't fret about the blackness you say that you see ahead, because it's rubbish. There is no future clearer or more rosy than yours ... You are intelligent, cultured, extremely hard-working, willing, and passionate about politics.'

Among the educated young officers returning from the front there was a hunger for knowledge, for poetry and literature, for spending time with friends and talking. Writers and artists had drifted back to their old haunts and cafés. Carlo and Nello were both on the editorial committee of *Vita*, a magazine that had been founded before the war by their friends Leo Ferrero and Jean Luchaire to debate politics. Leo, who was already producing his own plays and poetry, proposed starting a club for his friends to meet in cafés and discuss ideas. There was much talk about Henri Barbusse and Romain Rolland and their work for peace and solidarity among nations. In earnest articles, the young men expressed pious hopes that the war might at least have served to break down the barriers between social classes.

One evening, as Amelia was going to bed, Carlo and Nello came to suggest to her that they give away the fortune coming to them from Siele, and move to a cheaper part of the city. They loved their new house, they said, but they felt that it was morally wrong to own it. Sensibly, she demurred. As she pointed out, neither of them was earning any money, and nor was she, but she conceded that they might put aside a little to support the causes they believed in. Nello opened a small children's library in San Frediano, one of the poorer quarters, and asked various publishers and friends to donate books. He and Carlo took turns to run it. He was also planning to set up a summer colony for sick children in a house on the road to Vallombrosa. As Amelia said, Nello possessed a 'large and marvellous generosity of spirit'. Their cousin Alessandro Levi, a distinguished lawyer and lecturer at the university, had recently come into their lives; considerably older and more like an uncle to the boys, Levi too was a devoted Mazzinian. He was also a member of the reformist wing of the Socialist Party.

Observing the mixture of youthful idealism and intellectual uncertainty in which her sons and their friends seemed to spend their days, Amelia turned her hand to another of her highly auto-biographical novellas, this time on the theme of boys who had lost an older brother in the war and felt guilty at not having suffered enough. Many of the scenes in *Fratelli Minori*, 'Younger Brothers', come straight out of her own life; in places they read like a diary. There is a mother, distraught at the loss of her eldest son, and reduced 'in her pain to wordlessness', who had once witnessed her three boys laughing with happiness as they hung a flag from the window of their apartment to celebrate Italy's entry into the war. 'Upright, rigid, the mother stared with an unseeing eye ... But the mother thought: "It is right, oh Lord, to suffer for Italy."' The boys in the story are 'like children, despite having so much bitter knowledge'. *Fratelli Minori*'s style is staccato, haiku-like. 'Rancour. Unsaid. Unsayable. Against everyone and no one.' It carried a prescient warning. These young men, she concluded, were getting far too immersed in politics. Once 'too cerebral and obsessed with literature', they were now too cerebral and obsessed with politics. It was a form of sickness: *'pericoloso'*, dangerous.

In the immediate aftermath of the war it had seemed as if Italian women might be about to get the vote. A debate in parliament in the early twenties ended with 292 deputies in favour and 42 against. But over the next few days the deputies wavered and prevaricated until, having one by one changed their minds, they decided that it was far too soon, and that more time was needed in order to prepare the 'Italian female world spiritually for electoral battle'* Amelia was surprisingly unconcerned. For all her championing of the rights of women workers, she remained ambivalent, writing in *Fratelli Minori* that 'women create men but not ideas'. She tended to agree with her more emotional friend Laura Orvieto that women's existence was ultimately best defined

---

* It would be twenty-seven years before Italian women got the vote.

by domesticity and maternity, though both of them insisted that marriage should no longer be regarded as an 'absolute monarchy', but rather as a 'republic', lived with 'perfect equality'. Radical feminism sometimes seemed hysterical and absurd to Amelia, especially when indulged in by women of means. Gina Lombroso took a tougher line: giving the vote to women, she said, would only alienate them from family life and it was in the nature of women, 'powerless to attain happiness by their own means', to make 'others the centre of their desires'. When the three friends met, they pored over these matters. What had changed, they conceded, was that now, in the wake of the war, 'women were more exposed to the knocks of life, to its temptations, its dangers'.

No less than her sons, and soon to be fifty, Amelia was having trouble deciding what to do. She was still beautiful and elegant, with her thin, neat features, her thick hair piled up. But Aldo's death had caused a fracture in her own sense of herself and her future, and it seemed to her highly unlikely that she would ever write a play again. Amelia was translating Maeterlinck's *The Blue Bird* for a children's publisher, and now she agreed to become a judge in a competition for the best short story written by a woman and to edit a series of books 'aimed to widen the horizons of young girls – of all classes'.

Moving slowly back into her position with the Lyceum, she joined the National Union of Italian Women, which shared the Lyceum's offices in Via Ricasoli. One day its president, the Contessa Luisa Capponi, rang her to say that Florence's prefect had ordered her members on no account to fly the Italian flag from their windows on the anniversary of the Armistice. In the few months since the men had come home, the war had become so deeply unpopular that soldiers in uniform risked being spat on in the streets. But the Florentine ladies were not easily cowed. 'I believe I don't have to tell you, Signora Rosselli,' said the Countess, 'that it is our duty to disobey this shameful request.' Next day, Amelia's flag, along with those of the other Union women, fluttered in the sunshine. It took rather more courage when, having decided to fly a second flag from Aldo's Casina, Amelia not only had to brave a disapproving shopkeeper when she went to buy it, but run a gauntlet of jeers when she drove up the hill towards Bagno a Ripoli with it flapping merrily from her car window.

Salvemini, back at his old job teaching at Florence university, had got into the habit of inviting his favourite students to his apartment in Piazza Massimo d'Azeglio. He was now in his late forties, his manner as trenchant and blunt as ever, his mind bold and independent. As Anna Kuliscioff put it, Salvemini's intelligence was 'phosphorescent' and his thought totally devoid of clichés. In his huge black cloak, the same as that worn by the Florentine horse-cab drivers, with the sugarloaf hat of Apulian peasants perched on his head, he had become a familiar figure around the city. Loud in his attacks on Mussolini and the *fasci*, outspoken against D'Annunzio, whose Fiume adventure he considered a 'source of dishonour and ridicule', he was already making dangerous enemies. In the streets there were now calls of 'turncoat' and 'renegade' as he strode by. Early in 1919 Salvemini began warning that Italy was suffering from 'profound moral weakness', and that the young *Arditi* were nothing but '*scimmie urlatrici*', shrieking monkeys. Writing in *L'Unità*, he declared that a 'programme, a party, a group ... to stand up against disorder and arbitrariness' was needed, and asked: 'Are we too late?' That same year he organised a conference at which a League for the Renewal of National Unity was born, and introduced what he called '*problemismo*', the posing of political problems, to which concrete answers had to be sought.

Nello, still in uniform and still looking for a topic for his thesis, went to see Salvemini, and the older man was immediately struck by how young Nello looked, with 'something adolescent about him, with his rosy cheeks and eyes as blue as the skies of Florence'. They talked at length; by the time he left Nello had found his subject. He would write about Mazzini, the revolutionary thinker who was so vital to the history of the Rossellis and the Pincherles, and his battles with the Russian anarchist Bakunin. A few days later he returned, bringing Carlo with him. Carlo was about to finish his degree in social sciences and was writing his thesis on contemporary socialism. Salvemini never forgot the occasion. 'It was', he wrote many years later, 'one of those Florentine spring days when the air is as clear as crystal and when from Florence itself you can see every leaf on the olive trees on the slopes of Fiesole.' For all of them, it was a decisive moment. Carlo, concluded Salvemini, was obviously a young man of 'exuberant vitality'.

The visit was repeated. The brothers were now joined by a third young man, Ernesto Rossi, whose elder brother had also been killed with the Alpini, and who had himself been wounded in the stomach, and was partially deaf in one ear. Rossi was twenty, the same age as Nello, and a very clever, troubled boy whose father was notorious for once having shot his mother – but not killed her. He was thin and wiry, with neat features, heavy eyebrows, receding dark hair and a charming smile. Pragmatic and sceptical by nature, he was impatient when faced with stupidity. Immediately after the war, he had been drawn to Mussolini and had contributed articles to *Il Popolo d'Italia*, but one meeting with Salvemini had been enough to make him change his views. He was still in uniform when he happened to hear Salvemini lecture. 'It was', he wrote, 'as if someone had taken a cloth and wiped clear a windowpane shrouded in steam ... I learnt from him to beware of the lure of false ideas, to be rigorous, to love precise facts ... and to be intransigent over matters of truth and conscience.' About himself, Rossi would say that he had been born in the wrong century; he was in love with the British and French rationalists, and believed in a tiny luminous world created by rational men standing against the surrounding chaos.

Salvemini called his three young disciples '*la mia nuova gioventù*'; they made him feel young again.

After a while, they were joined by others, such as Piero Calamandrei, a somewhat older university professor and lawyer, but no less filled with a longing for change than the younger men; Carlo's study in Via Giusti, a great jumble of books and papers spilling over on to the floor, became a second meeting place. Salvemini saw himself as their Socrates, drawing out their thoughts. He would say that what he contributed was experience, but that these enthusiastic and naive young men brought 'courage and faith in these hours of darkness'. When it was clear that the meetings had become important in all their lives, they decided to turn them into something more formal. One day, in the offices of a lawyer-friend, Alfredo Niccoli, they constituted themselves into a Circolo di Cultura, an 'intellectual cooperative'. They agreed to meet every Saturday evening in one or other of their houses to discuss everything from the economy to European literature, without party political bias, but starting from two simple premises: that Italy had reached a moment of crisis, and that its existing parties were apparently unable to solve it. As Carlo saw it, there needed to be a revolt against this 'old, bloated world' among the new generation, who would introduce 'light, light, fresh air, youth, youth'. 'We must not be blinded', he declared, by a *'paura cretina'*, a stupid fear, of Bolshevism.

Neither Carlo nor Nello was yet quite ready to enter the political fray; but politics was moving inexorably towards them.

Mussolini and his supporters did very badly in the general elections of November 1919: they won no seat in parliament. Mussolini himself stood as a 'soldier wounded in action', portraying himself as dynamic and intent on modernising Italian political life, but it earned him few votes. The socialists, under Filippo Turati, became the biggest party. Giolitti's liberals lost many seats. Amelia had a particular dislike of Giolitti, saying that he was nothing but 'a sack of lies'. At this point, the socialists could have formed a government, either by entering into a coalition, or governing as a minority with outside support. Instead they bickered and splintered. 'We are witnessing painful times,' Amelia wrote to Carlo; 'the best people are resigning and the liberals ... can agree on nothing.' The new government was just a 'Russian salad ... made of many different vegetables, all concealed by mayonnaise'. In Florence the weather was unnaturally cold; it snowed. 'Even the seasons', she wrote, 'are in revolt.' Zia Gì told Carlo that the fig trees at Il Frassine looked like candelabra, every leaf picked out in snow. Salvemini stood once again in Apulia and was elected. When he accused Mussolini of collecting money in the United States to help D'Annunzio, Mussolini challenged him to a duel; but as Salvemini's seconds insisted on proof, Mussolini withdrew.

By now, it was becoming plain that Italy was sinking rapidly into precisely the kind of civil war that Orlando had warned the Allies about. And Italy was not alone: in Russia the Bolshevik

A post-war occupation of the factories in Piedmont

revolution had turned into civil war; in Germany an attempted uprising of revolutionary socialists had been savagely put down. Borders were unstable. Lines were being drawn, of a confused and confusing kind. Throughout Italy, landowners and employers were fiercely resisting reform. The workers from factories, industry and agriculture, were demanding higher wages and better conditions, and were supported by the war veterans, who had come home hoping for change but found only old parties, old institutions, old injustices. 'With all these heightened tensions,' wrote Amelia, 'something bad will happen. Where and how will it end?' Her tone was increasingly despairing: 'We need so badly to create something. To create it and then to believe in it.' In September 1920, workers at the Alfa Romeo plant in Milan occupied their factory; engineering workers in Turin and Genoa came out in support. What became known as the '*biennio rosso*', two 'red' years of occupation and strikes, had begun.

In Rome, the political leaders appeared to have sunk into what

Salvemini called "Buddhist apathy" paralysed by competing threats. Into this vacuum came the ever more powerful *fasci*, intent on dealing with those they called 'Bolsheviks' and winning growing support from landowners and industrialists. In the background, D'Annunzio remained a keen promoter of disorder. As were the Futurists, mystical warriors and apostles for *la patria*, whose cult of death, taste for danger and exaltation of physical courage found perfect expression in the new violence. All over Italy, bands of war veterans, petty criminals, resentful soldiers, excitable students – most of them people accustomed to solving problems with violence – embarked on *spedizioni punitive*, punitive expeditions against left-wing rallies, institutions, newspapers, and factories they considered 'nests of subversion'. They thought of themselves as hunting parties. The youngest members were no more than sixteen; these raids were exciting rites of passage. Some likened them to Siena's Palio, or medieval jousts with trophies. Their weapons were pistols and revolvers left over from the war, knuckledusters, cudgels and the famous *manganello*, a strong knotted stave with a lead tip, sometimes covered with leather.

Though the epicentre for these *squadristi* was usually a city, punitive expeditions were often despatched into the countryside to track down, intimidate and punish agricultural workers and their cooperatives. The *squadristi* travelled by bicycle, train, car, lorry or on foot. The Fiat 18 BL, once used to transport troops, was their preferred vehicle. In order not to be identified, they operated outside their own areas, or covered their faces with

A band of *squadristi*, off on a 'punitive raid'

masks. Wherever they encountered opposition, they set buildings on fire, lashed out with their *manganelli*, and forced those who refused to give in to drink castor oil.

For the most part, they met with little resistance, particularly after the police and the army, who sided with the *squadristi*, began surreptitiously to supply them with grenades and machine guns, which they were able to mount on to their trucks, though many of the targeted socialists fought back bravely with pitchforks and their fists. Equally the magistrates, asked to uphold law and order, became deaf and dumb. Some of the *squadristi* referred to their raids as 'propaganda', occasions on which to instil their anti-Bolshevik message; others spoke of themselves as *i puri*, and claimed that they were engaged in acts of 'national purification'. They gave their *squadre* the names of their 'martyrs', struck down in street-battles, and adopted popular slogans, such as that used by the *Arditi*, 'Me ne frego'. By March 1921 there were reported to be some 150,000 *squadristi* across the country, grouped into about a thousand local sections. In a little under a year, they killed 172 people and wounded many hundreds more; their own losses amounted to four dead. 'We want revenge,' they shouted; 'whoever is frightened, get out.'

In Rome, where successive governments formed and quickly fell, the mood was one of helplessness. In the absence of any concerted policy, plan or alternatives, landowners and industrialists continued to finance and arm the *squadre*. One of the clearest exponents of calm was the articulate young deputy, Giacomo Matteotti, whose speech to parliament on 31 January 1921 was a model of dignity. Do not react, he told the beleaguered socialists up and down the country; however angry, remain calm; even silence and inaction can be heroic. But the socialists were divided and on the run, and in the Chamber of Deputies their protests were weak and irresolute. Turati, the party leader, described what was happening as a revolution of blood against a revolution of words.

In Florence, the troubles began slowly but soon gathered pace: Tuscany, along with Emilia-Romagna, would before long become the scene of the fiercest fighting and the most violent punitive expeditions. At the time of the first fascist congress, held in Florence in October 1919, the local *fascio* had just sixty members.

But Tuscany was a region of large agricultural estates and successful industrial concerns – marble, chemicals, textiles and steel – and now, terrified by demands for reform, property and factory owners turned backwards, to a time when they had been all-powerful.

Spedizioni punitive were launched against radicals, democrats, social reformers, striking factory workers, rebellious peasants, newspaper offices, town halls and the homes of trade-union officials across the whole of Tuscany. In Florence the *squadristi* were nurtured and fanned by the fascists, preaching the menace of Bolshevism. Their crusade was bolstered by the arrival on the scene of an Italian-American called Amerigo Dumini, who had fought in the war and been much decorated, then drifted to Florence and worked his way up through the *squadrista* underworld. Dumini was a bland-faced young man, with neatly parted dark hair and ears that stuck out. He had a small, tidy moustache, but no beard. He was soon powerful enough to have his own *squadra*, the Disperata. Dumini's men were a mishmash of former soldiers and disaffected students, filled with pseudo-revolutionary ideas; recruits joined in such numbers that he was able to launch five raids each day. His enforcer was a cabinetmaker called Albino Volpi, renowned for his savagery. They had at their disposal one Fiat 18 BL, two slightly faster trucks and three sports cars. Dumini's headquarters were in Piazza Ottaviani and he held his meetings in the Teatro della Pergola, where, with the help of Marinetti and his Futurists, he orchestrated flamboyant parades and demonstrations.

Throughout Tuscany, the summer of 1920 was marked by agricultural strikes and labour disputes. On 10 August, an army ammunition dump was blown up: the socialists were blamed. On 29 August, 'tragic Sunday', a police chief was shot while trying to quell rioting which had left three people dead. For the whole of September, red flags flew over the factories in Pignone and Sesto Fiorentino.

Carlo and Nello were in Florence, studying hard; they were watching events, but not taking part. As Carlo wrote to his uncle Gabriele, he was filled with a passion to learn, to 'acquire culture', and he was reading Italian political historians, the French classics, Dostoevsky and Carlyle. He told his mother that at heart he felt 'very, but very different from all the other people of my age'. In their letters, Amelia and her sons say surprisingly little about the violent events unfolding around them. The brothers talked about their friends, about meals and the opera, about visits to their uncle Gabriele or to their young cousin Alberto Moravia. It is all like a last cocoon of childhood. Nello himself still had his *'riso da bambolino'*, his childish giggle, and his soft face looked cherubic and unformed.

On 15 January 1921 Carlo went to Livorno to take part in the Seventeenth National Congress of the Socialist Party, which had stumbled from crisis to crisis in recent years. He was just twenty-one, and it says much for his awakening interest in left-wing politics that he chose to attend. 'Today', he wrote to Amelia, 'I really felt a new man coming to life inside me.' Watching her son's passion taking shape, Amelia noted that he was a boy filled with 'specific ideas, grandiose ambitions, so that even the ocean is now beginning to look small to him'. In Livorno, Carlo was introduced to Turati, and for the next six days he watched and listened as Turati's 'reformist' wing, which believed in socialism through peaceful measures and alliances with other parties, battled it out with the *massimalisti*, who insisted on Marxism and social revolution by any means. By the time the delegates departed, after days of quarrelsome, agitated talk, the Italian Communist Party had been formed. But the splintered left had been severely weakened; all over the country the Fasci di Combattimento had been handed further ammunition for their rallying cry against communists and Bolsheviks.

All-out war was averted, and in May, the Italians were back voting once again; this general election, which saw 105 dead and 431 wounded in the violence that led up to it, resulted in yet another weak alliance. However, Mussolini won 35 seats and he was welcomed into parliament by Giolitti, who hoped thereby to draw the fascists' sting. Mussolini announced that he would sit on the right, and, in one of his customarily obscure pronouncements, that he would at one and the same time be 'conservative, progressive, reactionary and revolutionary, accepting the law and going beyond it'. He was determined, he declared, like the old soldier he was, to 'act rather than to talk'. Lina Waterfield, the correspondent for the London *Observer*, noted that in the Chamber the new fascist members behaved like conquerors, and that Mussolini had the expression of a circus trainer holding his whip.

Then, on the last Sunday of February 1921, a bomb was thrown into a procession of liberal students on their way to lay a wreath at a ceremony for those who had died in the war. That same day, a *squadrista* gunman shot dead a socialist union leader, after which fascists and carabinieri paraded together through the streets brandishing trophies looted from the homes of known socialists. Over the next few days, it looked as if Florence was on the edge of civil war. 'Fascism', as Amelia wrote later, was beginning to cast 'its vast menacing shadow'. Barricades went up, buildings were set on fire, fights broke out in the streets. The city became a tinderbox, the slightest spark enough to light a fire. When a young fascist was attacked by strikers as he cycled over the Ponte Sospeso, then beaten to death and his body thrown into the Arno, the army was called in: shops and restaurants were closed, trains stopped running and, for a while, the gas and electricity supplies were cut off.

At the congress of the Fasci di Combattimento in early November 1921, the National Fascist Party was born; it could already count on some 217,000 supporters. The word 'fascist' was now squarely in the vocabulary of the day, with its links to antiquity and *romanità*, and its symbol, the fasces, conferring on the bearer the solemnity of office and authority. A military tone was spreading. Writing to his mother from a short spell with the army as a reservist, Nello said that among his fellow officers there were many who seemed to 'aspire to a dictatorship'.

By July there were said to be some 6,300 Florentines enrolled in *squadre*, and the number was growing. The Marchese Dino Perrone Compagni, known as the *granduca* of Tuscan *squadrismo* and who personally coordinated raids and selected targets, was losing ground to a more Machiavellian adventurer, Tullio Tamburini, a decorated veteran and itinerant calligrapher from Prato, who, promoted by Dumini, was busy setting up his own Fascio Autonomo. Tamburini was wily, deeply corrupt and renowned for his cruelty; he was also fanatical in his devotion to Mussolini.

It was becoming clear that in Tuscany, perhaps more so than in any other part of the country, the *squadre* were not only supported by the police, army and judiciary – who saw the fascists as helpful protectors of private property – but that serving policemen and soldiers were taking part themselves in the punitive raids. Sometimes one would be sent from one town to another to help set up and run a *fascio*. The *fasci* were flush with agreeable amounts of money, and it was rare to find a *squadrista* without a good weapon of his own. The men travelled on trains without bothering to buy tickets and ate in restaurants without paying the bill. When they needed a car, they requisitioned one at gunpoint. Another characteristic of the Tuscan *fasci* was the presence of many members of the same family within each group: in Arezzo the *fascio* had forty-two members from twenty families. Tuscan *fasci*, however, were also subject to tempestuous schisms, and nowhere more so than in Florence itself.

By mid-1921, fascism of one version or another controlled vast swathes of Tuscany. The movement had become a safe haven for criminals, for whom membership of a *fascio* conferred immunity from punishment. Police and carabinieri regularly arrested and punished socialists, but magistrates, whether fascist themselves or fearful for their own safety, went to great lengths not to convict *squadristi*; trials were marked by procrastination, intimidation of witnesses and mislaid evidence. The Florentine *squadristi* were generally regarded as the leaders, and so numerous and powerful were they that they regularly sent men to export fascism to neighbouring Lazio and Umbria and even distant Apulia. When Dumini and Tamburini decided that the high price of food should be brought down, an energetic young fascist called Umberto Banchelli was despatched with his men to teach shopkeepers a lesson. Those who proved stubborn were dosed with castor oil and their shops closed down 'for theft'.

Then, on 29 June 1921, came a night of terrifying violence. The walled and gated town of Grosseto had shown itself to be uncooperative. Banchelli, who regarded himself as a 'true paladin', took twenty of his men under cover of darkness and, joined by other *squadristi* from Siena, Lucca and Arezzo, scaled the walls. That night, fifty-five people died; bookshops, lawyers' offices, clubs were all destroyed. Burning down left-wing newspaper offices not only gave the premises 'the aspect of a putrefying corpse' but had the added advantage of ensuring that no news was published.

Until now, Salvemini and his disciples had been safe, lying low, trying to escape notice, keeping their anger to themselves. The members of the Circolo di Cultura continued to meet, but discreetly. Writing later, Calamandrei noted that they all felt that they were 'witness to a miserable moral collapse of an entire people' but that 'first of all we needed to understand'. But the war was coming closer. On the night of 12 December 1921, Ernesto Rossi's house was attacked by a band of *squadristi* and carabinieri. He defended himself with a rifle, and in the ensuing chaos, one carabiniere was killed and two others wounded. Rossi was arrested but eventually released. He got home to find his house ransacked and most of its contents destroyed by fire. The culprits were 'unknown assailants'.

The violence continued. Faced with the impossibility of restoring calm, the new prime minister accepted Mussolini's proposal for a pact of reconciliation between the socialists and the fascists, but the plan was rejected by the communists, the anarchists and the former *Arditi*, and even the socialists seemed more intent on keeping their ideological purity than making peace. Mussolini, wary of the growing power of the fascist leaders in the provinces – men now known as *ras* after the Ethiopian word for local chieftains – was eager to disarm some of his more independent followers. The *ras* would not hear of it; they kept their weapons. It was not long before, in the *Popolo d'Italia*, the accord between socialists and fascists was described as 'dead and buried'. In its place came yet another proposal for reconciliation, with the intention of imposing some kind of structure on the disparate paramilitary forces. A pact was eventually signed, but it was never observed. It was all too little and it had come too late. Parliamentary democracy had failed to tame the fascists; on the contrary, it had given them legitimacy.

As the summer of 1922 approached, a new alliance of liberals, democrats and Catholics was sworn in, even feebler than its predecessors. Salvemini, blaming Giolitti for making Mussolini 'necessary', continued to hope that Mussolini would eventually destroy himself because '*è un clown*'. In October a general strike was called against 'the illegality of *squadrismo*'. Italy stopped. The fascists played their cards well. Orders went out to the different *fasci* to sit tight, do nothing other than fan fears of a Bolshevic takeover. A sense of menace and anarchy spread. Nello, with his reservists, was sent to guard a station. Turati called what was happening 'our Caporetto'.

When, after forty-eight hours, the *squadre* were ordered to attack the strikers, much of the country was with them. Police and carabinieri stood by while trade-union offices, cooperative buildings, left-wing political headquarters and the homes of the strikers were destroyed. After the offices of the socialist *Avanti!* were raided, Mussolini spoke of 'the great, the beautiful, the inexorable violence'. Two hundred and twenty-one local socialist offices were ransacked. *Squadristi* occupied buildings, took over the trains and buses. Formed into platoons and companies, armed with machine guns and with small cannons mounted on their trucks, they operated unopposed. In one place, a butcher and his *squadra* descended on a village with fifty litres of castor oil, rounded up 'suspects' and decreed how many glasses of oil each would be made to swallow. The socialist mayor was given three; a municipal councillor one. The butcher measured out the doses. They called it 'magic exorcism', purification by castor oil, after which the men could return cleansed to *la patria*.* Elsewhere, the *squadristi* painted the beards of their victims with the colours of the Italian flag.

One of their leaders was the young *ras* Italo Balbo, a showy, well-connected journalist, lawyer and Freemason, who had led a punitive march across the top of Italy and then declared war on left-wing Bologna, where an honest prefect, Cesare Mori, had succeeded in jailing some of the more violent fascist thugs. Mori, pursued by shouts of '*Mori, mori, tu devi morire*!' – 'You must die!' – was hounded out. Carlo had first come across Balbo at his institute in Florence, when he saw him thumping the table after failing an exam, demanding that the professor give him eighteen marks out of twenty. The professor said nothing and

---

* Twenty years later, partisans identified the butcher, took him to a pond and told him to eat a toad. If he failed to do so, they would kill him. He ate it.

fled, pursued by Balbo's shouts: 'Either you give me eighteen or it will end badly.' He got his marks.

Other cities fell to the fascists: Cremona, Viterbo, Novara, Rimini and Ravenna. In Carrara, the *ras*, Renato Ricci, put his *squadristi* to purging places of work. Milan, Ancona, Bari, Terni and Varese fell too. In September, Civitavecchia and Savona capitulated. And so it went on. Fascism had become a power, able to intimidate and get rid of hostile prefects, its mounting authority tacitly endorsed by the government in Rome. All over Italy, people were looking to Mussolini and to the provincial *ras*, now the effective heads of local government, having captured the state machinery from within. Dumini and his Disperata had never worked harder: Florence was now second only to Bologna as the leading urban centre of fascism.

From the calm of their house in Via Giusti, Amelia, Carlo and Nello looked on, appalled. For the first time they thought they detected signs of anti-semitism and Carlo warned that they should start thinking about possible attacks, 'before it is too late'.

Events were moving so fast that it was hard to see how they could be stopped. And yet, soon after the failed strike, something took place that showed that, had they been united and strong, the forces of democracy might have proved a match for the fascists. A punitive raid of *squadristi*, with Italo Balbo at its head, advanced on Parma. The *questore*, who until now had stood up to the fascists, said he did not have enough forces to counter such a raid, and ordered his carabinieri to remain in their barracks. However, the word went out, and the men of Parma, armed with sticks, pitchforks, hunting rifles, lengths of railway track and knives, and helped by the women and children, began to build barricades. By dawn, Parma looked like a battle zone. Look-outs were posted in church belfries. At nine the next morning, Balbo ordered his men to attack. The inhabitants stood firm. Next day, the *squadristi* appeared to be gaining ground. Singing 'The Red Flag' at the tops of their voices, the men of Parma swarmed over the barricades. Thinking that they were merely a vanguard and would be followed by many more, the fascists fell back. From the windows, the women hurled bowls filled with oil and petrol. This continued back and forth for five days. On the sixth day, at 7 o'clock in the morning, the fascists withdrew. From their vantage points, people watched and cheered as lorries, cars, trucks and bicycles were seen streaming out of the city. It was a rout.

But Italy was exhausted, its people cowed by the violence, fearful for their future; they longed for tranquility. In Rome, the government appeared to be paralysed. Some 2,500 people had died in street-fighting and punitive expeditions, and countless more had been injured. By the summer of 1922 the army of *squadristi* in their black shirts had swollen to around 300,000, and they were now dangerously fragmented and out of control. Against this background, Mussolini summoned to Rome the ten most prominent fascist leaders to discuss mounting a challenge against the ineffectual liberal government. At a second gathering in Milan, on 16 October, Mussolini announced that he had been tentatively offered two ministerial posts. He had refused: he wanted six or nothing.

Three days later, having made Perugia their headquarters, the fascist leaders divided Italy into twelve sectors and began to arrange an uprising. There was a dry run on the 24th, when thousands of *squadristi* attended a fascist congress and shouted 'Roma! Roma! Roma!' The new fascist hymn, 'Giovinezza', with its rousing call to fraternal courage and national salvation, was chanted, again and again. The atmosphere was jubilant, the

Mussolini and his followers, during the March on Rome

message plain. From Perugia, where the leaders continued to wait, an ultimatum was delivered: it demanded that Mussolini be appointed prime minister. Parliament dithered.

From different corners of the country, travelling by lorry, train, car and bicycle, fascist supporters began to converge on Rome. The weather was bright. Looking out from his embassy window, a French diplomat, François Charles-Roux, noted an 'extraordinary flowering of shirts', none of them white: the black of the fascists, the sky-blue of the Nationalists, the green of the agricultural workers, the grey 'from who knows what grouping', and just a few reds, worn by those who worshipped Garibaldi. In the cities where opposition was expected – Milan, Turin, Parma – the local fascists quietly, smoothly, took control. In Florence, Tamburini sent his men to occupy the telephone exchange and the main post office. Then he organised for 2,380 men to leave on a special train for Rome.

Mussolini, shrewdly, stayed in Milan and, ostentatiously, went to the theatre. On 29 October came a call from the king, asking him to form a government. That night, he boarded the sleeper for the capital, where a suite had been prepared for him at the Hotel Savoia. His manifesto was ready: it promised 'the glorious soldiers of the new Italy' a government worthy of *la patria*. The next day, wearing a black shirt under his formal suit, and spats and a bowler hat, he called on the recently elected prime minister, Luigi Facta. Outside, his *squadristi* prowled around the city, singing 'Giovinezza' and '*Eia! Eia! Eia! Alalà!*', D'Annunzio's battle cry, occasionally looting and brandishing their weapons; some were disgruntled that they had seen no action. They were instructed to remain calm. Rome was described as being in a 'fever of delight', and florists had run out of flowers.

Mussolini – the man who had led a rebellion against the state and whose followers continued to commit atrocities – was offered and accepted the post of prime minister, to which he added those of minister of the interior and of foreign affairs, both crucial for managing the secret areas of government. It was to be another coalition – but from which the communists and socialists were excluded. The socialists had in any case been further weakened when, at their Seventeenth Congress not long before, the reformist wing – and Turati – had been expelled. Outside Italy, the March on Rome received surprisingly little attention. As *The Times* in London remarked, mobs were part of the 'very pulse of this dramatic and theatrical nation'.

On 31 October 1922, at the age of thirty-nine, Mussolini became Italy's youngest ever prime minister.

Salvemini wrote to a friend in Paris that Italy was 'on the verge of madness'. Turati continued to call for a united front against the 'dictatorship', saying that he would happily gang up with the devil, 'if only fascism could be defeated'. Luigi Albertini's prestigious *Corriere della Sera*, which had written a sharp attack on the fascists, fell silent after its offices were invaded by *squadristi*: there was no point in writing, he said, if every thought would now be 'mutilated'. Not everyone shared their despair. There had been 86 ministers of education and 88 ministers of justice in just 61 years of liberal government: many found it easier to see events as yet one more government crisis, with its attendant change of cast.

It could, of course, have been otherwise. Against the estimated 25,000 Blackshirts, uncoordinated and often poorly led, stood a trained army of 28,000 regular soldiers ready to defend Rome. But the vacillating king, who had at first been persuaded to declare martial law, changed his mind and refused to sign the decree; both the powerful Duke d'Aosta, a popular and courageous soldier during the war, and the queen mother were on the side of the fascists; the new Pope, the Milanese Pius XI, was intent on strengthening the power and prestige of the Vatican; and the socialists and liberals had lost their way. With almost no violence and almost no opposition, a *coup d'état* had effectively taken place. Only much later would it be realised that the threat of a Bolshevik takeover, cleverly fanned by the fascists, had in fact been grossly exaggerated. Recalling an earlier assault on the city, a Catholic priest observed: 'We, in 1870, defended Rome far better.'

CHAPTER SIX

Planting a Tree

Salvemini's wish that Mussolini would rapidly destroy himself by his circus-like antics was soon disappointed. The Duce's initial moves were calm and shrewd. Only five ministries in his first cabinet went to fascists; the other nine were offered to friendly allies. The philosopher Giovanni Gentile, a man with an international reputation, was made minister for education. When Mussolini appeared in parliament on 16 November, boasting that he could well have turned this 'bleak assembly room into a bivouac for my platoons', and demanding 'full powers' to reform the state, only the communists and socialists opposed him. All five liberal former prime ministers – Giolitti, Salandra, Orlando, Bonomi and Facta – voted with the majority. In the senate, where there were no fascist senators, just twenty-six people voted against.

Mussolini could now govern without having to seek parliamentary approval. Clare Sheridan, the English journalist, sculptor and diarist to whom he gave an interview for the American press soon after his victory, noted that he had effectively browbeaten the deputies into submission, but that as a character he was less impressive than Kemal Atatürk or Lenin, both of whom she had also interviewed. *The Times* was more approving: here, they said, was a very possible heir to Garibaldi. Even the legendary editor of the *Observer*, J. L. Garvin, spoke of him as a 'volcano of a man'.

Settling briskly down to work with what even his enemies agreed was an impressive show of diligence and determination, Mussolini rose very early, exercised fiercely, ate a sparse breakfast and read several Italian and foreign newspapers before arriving in his office at 8 o'clock. Twice a week, he visited the indecisive and feeble Victor Emmanuel in the Quirinale. His previous threat to replace the king with the more energetic and martial Duke d'Aosta was not repeated, his earlier rantings against the monarchy and the Church forgotten.

Having moved the foreign ministry into the Palazzo Chigi, where there was a useful balcony overlooking a square, Mussolini set about making friends on the European stage. Sir Ronald Graham, the British ambassador, came away 'agreeably surprised and favourably impressed' from a first meeting. This was a man 'with whom one could do business', though he admitted that it was a bit strange that Mussolini drove about the streets of Rome with a lion cub perched at his side. 'The Italians seem to like this sort of thing.'

In private, even if some colleagues complained that he was humourless, fidgeted constantly and seemed boorish and ill-versed in the niceties of governance, Mussolini could also be charming. He was still a bit gauche, a 'sheep' in private conversation, but 'a lion in a crowd'. The *Daily Express* of New York compared him favourably to the Ku Klux Klan: both shared, it said, a mission to protect their countries from a decline in morals caused by corruption in the government and the judiciary, and by the presence of 'inferior races'.

Not everyone was impressed, especially when Mussolini started to travel abroad. At his first foreign meeting, in Lausanne in July 1923 to discuss the Turkish peace treaty, he turned up late, brought a bodyguard of *squadristi*, and seemed very ill at ease. A British delegate noted that he was a 'second-rate cinema actor', an 'absurd little man not destined to stay in power long'. In London, where he joined international leaders to discuss German reparations for the First World War, thirty Italian immigrant fascists who turned out to greet him at Victoria Station in their black shirts singing 'Giovinezza' had to be persuaded to leave their *manganelli* behind. Privately admitting that he had little patience with compromise or lengthy negotiations, he briskly demanded severity towards Germany. The British, who wanted to be lenient, referred to him as a 'dangerous rascal' and 'possibly slightly off his head'. But these were early days, and Mussolini was learning fast.

At home, his appearances were far surer. They needed to be,

as Italy's main cities remained lawless, with *squadristi* battling it out in internecine squabbles and continuing to run riot. The *ras* remained all-powerful. At the end of 1922, in an attempt to curb the power of local thugs and enforce his own central authority, Mussolini had announced that he was turning the *squadristi* into a national militia, the Milizia Volontaria per la Sicurezza Nazionale (the MVSN), responsible directly to him, to defend the 'revolution of October 1922' and to act as a political police force. The MVSN's leaders would be known as 'centurions' and 'consuls' and receive good salaries, and its members were to display military discipline and obey the Fascist Party. An amnesty was declared for *squadristi* previously charged with violent crimes; those who had been wounded in the 'civil war' were to receive pensions. He also set up the Grand Council of Fascism, to run alongside and counterbalance the cabinet, in order to formulate policy; to this were appointed senior fascist leaders who had not got ministerial positions.

Mussolini now brought the conservatives, monarchists and nationalists into a 'marriage of convenience', fusing the nationalist and fascist parties. He courted the Vatican, denouncing contraception and making swearing in public a crime against the state. In his years as a journalist he had loudly condemned the dangerous practice of censorship, but he now set about controlling and silencing the press. 'What can save our country now?' Kuliscioff

The socialist leader, Filippo Turati, with his lifelong companion,
Anna Kuliscioff

wrote to Turati. 'A revolution? a civil war? new elections?' October 1922 was made the '*anno primo*', and the Roman salute, an outstretched arm, became the official form of greeting. A fascist court uniform, a hybrid of diplomatic, military and naval dress, was designed. As Lina Waterfield shrewdly observed, Mussolini was enlivening 'national vanity'. By early 1923, the number of fascists had almost trebled to 780,000.

In May, George V and Queen Mary paid a state visit to Italy, travelling in the specially built Royal Saloon train carriage, which was kept in a little hut in Calais; it was hitched to Victor Emmanuel's royal train at the Italian border. The British royal couple gave Mussolini what he called the '*Gran Croce dell'ordine del Bagno*', which sounded absurd in Italian. To their embarrassment, they were greeted on their return to Victoria Station by a guard of honour of black-shirted Italian fascists.

Italy's constitution was intact, and, for the time being, was not being challenged, but Salvemini was not alone in changing his mind: Mussolini was not after all a clown, but fast on his way to becoming a dictator. 'The right has scored a clamorous triumph,' Carlo wrote to his mother. 'An enormous black plague has settled on the body of Italy.'

Fascism quickly spread its tentacles over the fabric of Italian life. The army, the aristocracy, the Church and industry, all were rallying to defend the rights of a usurper. Those who disapproved turned their backs and looked to their private lives; but not Salvemini. From the day of the March on Rome, he adopted a position of absolute moral intransigence towards the fascists; and he never abandoned it. There were to be no deals, no games, no concessions. What had been allowed to happen to Italy was a shameful betrayal and a terrible indictment of Italian intellectuals. In the Circolo di Cultura, wrote Ernesto Rossi later, Salvemini immediately 'gave us our orders. Our duty was no longer to obey laws, but to disobey them. We had just one goal: to eliminate Mussolini and his accomplices. Violence had to be met with violence. Intentions were useless unless they were accompanied by actions. We were not to concern ourselves with the likelihood of success, but with saving our souls.' Mussolini had to be proved utterly wrong when he spoke of the 'putrefying corpse of liberty'.

Salvemini's passion, his total contempt for the paltriness of Roman politics, expressed wittily, brusquely, with touches of a kind of peasant malice, were very attractive to his young disciples. As Rossi said, he was 'our perfect mentor'.

But he was not an optimistic one. In October, just a few weeks before the March on Rome, Turati, Matteotti and Claudio Treves, all three of them expelled from the Socialist Party, had founded a new party, the United Socialist Party, the PSU. But while whole-heartedly endorsing their views, and personally liking the men themselves, Salvemini had little faith in their ability to achieve much. In the Circolo, surrounded by Carlo, Nello, Rossi and Calamandrei, he would say that, much as he hated the fascists, there were times when he hated the opposition even more, for its reasonableness and compromises. 'The more I think about it,' he wrote to a friend, 'the more I am coming to think that Italy is a country which is not worthy to exist, and that it is condemned to decompose, to fall yet again under foreign servitude.' Carlo, whom the others were beginning to regard as Salvemini's spiritual son, was of another mind. He was ready for a fight. But he needed to distance himself, if only briefly, from his mentor, telling Rossi that he could no longer tell what was his own thinking and what was Salvemini's.

First, Carlo needed to complete his two university degrees. In December 1922 he went to Turin to search for a supervisor for his dissertation on economics from among the political philosophers who had made the city their home. Turin, with its sombre, imposing buildings and its vast open piazzas, its long straight streets built on a grid, and its neoclassical and baroque architecture, prided itself on being different from other Italian cities. Having played a decisive role in the unification of the country, its inhabitants regarded themselves as the nation's moral guides. The Piedmontese values of hard work, honesty and reason, they claimed, had created a city 'which works and which thinks'. Turin was home to heavy industry, to vast modern factories, to Fiat, to new working-class suburbs encircling the city, and to the Marxist theoretician Antonio Gramsci's newspaper, *L'Ordine Nuovo*, with its call for a working-class elite dedicated not solely to material well-being but to human dignity. Its inhabitants, who had participated in the most violent and protracted strikes of the *biennio*

The youthful Piero Gobetti, fierce critic of Mussolini

rosso, were very outspoken against the industrialists, whose profits were immense and who kept their workers on the bread-line. But Turin was also home to a collection of highly articulate liberals, communists, republicans and anarchists, all of them intent on challenging Mussolini. They were gathered around one of the most remarkable figures in the as yet very small world of anti-fascists.

Carlo had heard a great deal about Piero Gobetti. Born in Turin in 1901, and thus two years younger than Carlo, Gobetti was tall and very thin, with a pale, gentle, oval face, an attractive, sensual mouth, and long, unkempt reddish-brown hair which flopped over his forehead. His sight was poor and he wore glasses; he also smiled a great deal. Indifferent to what he wore and despising all forms of elegance, so that he looked like a scruffy student, Gobetti had bright and penetrating eyes which conveyed both utter cer-tainty and youthful power. People found his uncompromising gaze disconcerting, though no one left his company without feeling that they had met someone truly remarkable. He could be cen-sorious, even a little prudish, but the strength of his lively and inventive character, and the unshakable certainty of his convic-tions, were magnetic. When he spoke of being a '*sacerdote di se stesso*', a priest and master of his own conscience, and declared that people with 'elastic consciences' were evil, his friends listened. They also listened when he described his 'inexorable passion for liberty' and his contempt for the intellectuals who had gone over to the fascists. As a friend put it, Gobetti possessed a 'democratic aristocracy of values'.

94

Gobetti was not quite eighteen when he started a monthly magazine called *Energie Nuove*, aimed at infusing the 'tired' cultural life of his 'rancid and decrepit' city with fresh ideas. Drawn to the cross-currents of European literature, he would say of himself that he was not a theorist, but an 'organiser of culture'. By the time Carlo met him, however, Gobetti had abandoned his cultural review, largely as a result of listening to Gramsci on the struggles of the workers in Turin's immense factories; he had, he would say, grown up, matured, read a great deal. He had taken a degree in the philosophy of law and recently started a new magazine, *Rivoluzione Liberale*, in which he had begun to alert readers to the dangers of fascism. Unlike Salvemini, he had never believed that fascism would quickly exhaust itself. Fascism, he said, was part of Italy's 'autobiography', an expression of all that was lacking and all that had gone profoundly wrong in its history, and an indictment of the moral weakness of Italians. Youthful, enthusiastic fascism had been made possible precisely because of the authoritarian and elitist way in which the country had been governed since 1870, and because Italy had never had an Enlightenment.

Gobetti was running his magazine from his home in the heart of the old city, where he lived with his parents, and was about to marry Ada Prospero, a young woman no less remarkable than himself, with whom he had learnt Russian, and who also had a degree in the philosophy of law. Ada was nineteen. The two of them looked little older than children.

In Florence, in his cousin Alessandro Levi's house, Carlo had been introduced to Claudio Treves, the socialist leader and Turati's closest friend. In Turin, exploring his academic future, he met them both again. Levi considered Turati to be the 'giant' of Italian socialism. Everyone loved this soft-hearted, rumpled, quiet man, whom friends compared to 'a kindly faun' and who, as a small boy, had helped carry his school banner for Manzoni's funeral. Turati and Anna Kuliscioff lived on the fourth floor of a building on Piazza del Duomo in Milan, its high windows looking directly on to the cathedral. Their apartment had become the main meeting place for young Marxists and intellectuals from all over Italy. Kuliscioff was now an old lady, her hands twisted by arthritis, her small face heavily lined but smiling. Though she had lived in Italy for over forty years, she still spoke Italian with a foreign inflection; it bore, said a young friend, 'a quality of velvet'.

Carlo met Gobetti and Ada in their house in Via XX Settembre on his first visit to Turin, together with Carlo Levi, who was studying medicine. Levi had a long, serious face and a mass of dark curly hair; he, too, looked little more than a boy. Another frequent visitor was Giacomo Matteotti, the bold socialist deputy, whose wife Velia had recently given birth to their third child, a daughter called Isabella. Matteotti had already published his first, damning inquiry into fascist violence. Carlo was immediately struck by his seriousness, his obvious lack of egotism or self-aggrandisement. Matteotti exuded energy, he wrote, 'he never adopted gladiatorial poses and he laughed readily'. What all these new friends were preaching was the need for a new, freer society in which men were neither tyrants nor servants, but took responsibility, courageously, for their own actions. To them all, the austere, implacable Gobetti was fast turning into a myth, reminding his listeners of the young Saint-Just, the eighteenth-century French revolutionary. As Carlo Levi later put it, 'He seemed to me the most perfect man I had ever met.'

Carlo was not immediately drawn to Gobetti. He found him, he told Amelia, a little irritating; he was put off by his abrasive and dismissive attitude towards the Italian socialists, and his assertion that Mazzini's views were nebulous and romantic, while Marx's were 'realistic and workable'. But when Carlo returned to Turin in February 1923, he was drawn into Gobetti's inner circle and spent long hours in his house debating the Russian Revolution, liberal British politics and the way that industrialisation and urbanisation could transform not just politics, but how people thought. Gobetti, who refused to be pinned down to any one political credo, described his beliefs as 'revolutionary liberalism'; he, Ada and their friends were talking of starting a clandestine anti-fascist movement, which they planned to call L'Italia Libera. Soon the tone of *Rivoluzione Liberale* shifted to one of open hostility towards Mussolini and his despotic and corrupt government; soon, too, Carlo began to contribute articles on the working-class movement and liberal economics, carrying on his disagreements with Gobetti in the pages of the magazine. In the summer of 1923 he published his first outline of what would become his defining political statement, 'Socialismo Liberale'. Liberty, he said was something that had to be won, and once won, nurtured by people who remained constantly vigilant.

Gobetti's renown was spreading, finding followers in Rome, Florence and Milan, where another group of teachers, lawyers and university lecturers had been inspired to start a magazine of their own, *Il Caffè*. One of these was a level-headed, wary-looking, yet idealistic economist in his late twenties, Riccardo Bauer. Another was the slightly older Ferruccio Parri, a teacher, war hero and journalist, a tall, slender, very pale man with a shock of unruly dark hair.

On 6 February 1923, Gobetti was arrested as he returned from his honeymoon with Ada and charged with subversion, and for 'plotting against the state'. The house and library were ransacked and papers carried away. Gobetti's father was also taken briefly into custody. The prison in which they were held was bitterly cold.

The historian Gaetano Salvemini, 'Father Bear', mentor to Carlo and Nello

When Gobetti was released, two weeks later, after influential friends intervened, he started a new publishing venture to which he hoped to attract literary critics, essayists, poets – all of them hostile to fascism. He had no intention of being silenced. *Rivoluzione Liberale* was no longer an eclectic magazine of culture and ideas: it had become a 'battle unit' for a great range of people, some younger, some older, some to the right, some to the left, but who all shared a passionate belief that ethics, politics and culture had to go hand in hand and that they had to be fought for and protected. Carlo was turning into one of its most important voices.

Under Salvemini's socratic influence, the Circolo di Cultura in Florence was attracting many new members. When they could no longer cram into the Rossellis' house in Via Giusti, Carlo and Nello decided to use some of the money they received from the Siele shares to rent and furnish rooms on the second floor of a fifteenth-century palazzo at 27 Borgo Santi Apostoli. Carlo took exuberant pleasure in finding chairs and tables, hurrying around Florence in search of books for the library and arranging for subscriptions to ninety Italian, French and English papers and journals, including the *New Statesman*, the *Observer* and the *Times Educational Supplement*.

He and Nello thought of the Circolo as somewhat like a London club where like-minded acquaintances could meet, read and talk. There were large, comfortable armchairs. Some sixty members gathered every Saturday evening for debates that ranged from syndicalism, Marxism and European federalism to the problems of the south, a subject always dear to Salvemini's heart. Those who came were not all of the same political views, but they shared a deep revulsion towards the bullying behaviour of the *squadristi* who haunted Florence's streets. At all their meetings, it was Carlo who was the organiser, but Salvemini the driving force, 'a midwife' wrote Ernesto Rossi later, 'bringing the truth to light'. Salvemini was ruthless with those who spoke in abstracts or fell back on dogma and he criticised the 'timorous and the indifferent' for being complicit with the fascists. '*Concretismo*!', Be concrete! he kept repeating.

'He was planting a tree,' Nello explained later, 'in the hope that it would not be uprooted by the storm, and that one day men who came after him would rest in its shade.'

It was Salvemini who introduced one of the very few women into the circle. Marion Cave was English and, at twenty-seven, a little older than the Rosselli brothers. She was the granddaughter of a postman, and the fourth child of a self-educated Quaker. Her family, all of them strong and tall, came from Uxbridge near London, where her father, Ernest Cave, was headmaster of a progressive school. Recognised at a young age as very clever, Marion had been sent to St Paul's Girls' School in London, where she had been thwarted in her desire to study the sciences – not deemed suitable for young ladies – but excelled in languages, before going on to Bedford College in London to read Italian. She was a keen musician and passionate about Italian opera – she claimed to have been to *Madam Butterfly* eleven times – and she had come to Florence to write her thesis on the Paduan philosopher Antonio Conti. She had had a bad bout of rheumatic fever, but refused to let it hold her back. To keep herself, she offered to give English lessons at the British Institute, which is where she met Salvemini, who planned to learn English 'with the help of Miss Cave and her beautiful eyes'. Marion was both romantic and serious-minded; her Quaker father had brought her up in his own socialist mould. To prepare herself for her Italian adventure, she had conscientiously read *Avanti!* every day for six months.

Shortly after arriving, while staying in the American YMCA in the San Frediano district, Marion had witnessed a fierce battle between *squadristi* and a group of local men in the square below. Refusing to join the other lodgers in a safe inside room, she climbed up to the attic and watched the fighting through her opera glasses, until spotted and shouted at by a policeman, whereupon she slipped out into the streets to observe events more closely. She was standing near the river when she saw two lines of men, holding on to each other by either ends of their *manganelli*, drawing a cart: in it stood Mussolini, waving graciously. Marion had come to Italy, she told her friends later, because she believed in an imminent socialist revolution. She planned to 'die on the barricades', not to skulk in the background.

Marion was not exactly beautiful but her chestnut-brown hair was thick and curly, and her dark-grey eyes gleamed. Anna Kuliscioff called her a 'ray of sunshine' in the midst of Salvemini's intent, earnest young disciples, and soon they all took to calling her *Biancofiore*, white flower. Salvemini was much taken with her. Like the Rosselli boys, she too addressed him as Father Bear.

To demonstrate how open-minded they all were, the members of the Circolo decided to invite two local fascists to come one Saturday to debate with them. Alberto Luchini, who had followed D'Annunzio to Fiume, spoke at length about the need for a curb on free speech and tolerance and became very angry when contradicted. 'At that moment,' Marion said later, 'we understood . . . that there was an abyss between them and us, and that nothing would bring us together, not even language.' To his mother, Carlo wrote: 'The chains grow tighter, things are proceeding along their fatal course. We will see how, where and when they will halt.' Three days later, he wrote again, to say how pleased he was that the fascists were becoming visibly more authoritarian, since it would open the eyes of those who had been fooling themselves. In his letters, Carlo was often brisk, jaunty. Nello's letters were gentler, more ruminative.

Carlo and Nello completed their theses in the summer of 1923, having accomplished a remarkable amount in a very short time; both received the top marks, summa cum laude. It was clear that they were heading for impressive academic careers, though the direction each was taking reflected their very different natures: Nello, whose research into Mazzini had broken new ground in archival studies, was looking backwards, exploring history and the lessons it could teach. The more impatient Carlo, ever hungry for experience, was setting his sights forwards, to what could be done to shape a better Italian, and European, future. Both of them, along the way, had had bruising encounters with Salvemini, who returned the drafts of their theses covered with question marks and crossings out, repeatedly urging more intellectual rigour. Wherever Carlo used the words 'I think' or 'I believe', the margins were full of angry lines. Carlo, said Salvemini, was like a 'volcanic eruption' and lacked 'criticism, equilibrium and substance'. The two young men had felt crushed. Carlo slunk away, railed, spent a few days hating Salvemini, then got down to work; Nello licked his wounds and immediately started revising his text. In private, however, Salvemini was delighted with his two young friends. 'Carlo and Nello', he wrote, 'had their own characters. They were modest and they were honest. They knew how to listen and how to learn.' The future, for both of them, seemed wide and full of promise.

While in the north, Carlo had met Attilio Cabiati, a friend of Salvemini's and a distinguished economist working at Milan's Bocconi University. Cabiati now offered him a post as unpaid assistant for a few months in the Institute of Political Economy, which would give him time to explore his interest in monetary policy and syndicalism, after which he would receive a salary. A part-time lectureship was also coming up at the Istituto Superiore di Scienze Economiche e Commerciali in Genoa, and Carlo accepted both jobs. That spring, Salvemini had been invited to London to meet Labour politicians and give a series of lectures on Italian foreign policy at King's College. When Cabiati suggested to Carlo that he would do well to go to England to attend the Fabian summer school before taking up his posts in Milan and Genoa, it seemed an excellent idea that mentor and disciple should do so together. And Carlo was restless, looking for something new – not so much a new political order, but a return to fundamental values based on socialism and a 'doctrine of liberty', possibly, as he wrote to a friend, 'a truly enormous front capable in the long term of overthrowing every adversary'. He was in search of inspiration.

Carlo arrived in Paris, by overnight train from Turin, very early on a fine morning in late July 1923. He had never been to France. His immediate feeling was one of dislike. He hated the architecture, the tall grey buildings, the 'hideous' churches, though he was impressed by the speed of the cars whirling round the Place de la Concorde. But once he had visited the sights and been to the theatre and the opera, he began to experience a pleasing sense of the weight of history; and he felt very grateful to his mother, he wrote, for having made him learn French and for the long hours they had spent together reading French literature. He was expecting Salvemini to join him, but Mussolini had refused to grant him a passport – a new form of control over his opponents – and Salvemini was now somewhere on the border, trying to find a way to cross clandestinely.

When, by the 26th, Salvemini had still not turned up, Carlo caught a ferry across the Channel on his own. A room had been booked for him in a boarding house off Russell Square. London, as he immediately wrote to Amelia, was so 'immense, grandiose, vertiginous', so busy and bustling, that he felt 'stupid'. Though disconcerted by the formality and coldness of officials, he was charmed by the warmth of his new friends. The historian Professor Tawney took him off to meet George Cole, the political economist and exponent of the guild movement, and L. T. Hobhouse, author of *Liberalism*. When Salvemini finally arrived, having been helped out of Italy by a friend and a false passport acquired in Paris, teacher and disciple visited the House of Commons together. Carlo was particularly taken by the Underground, which now had eleven stops, and its escalators, which he described in detail to Amelia, marvelling at the men in their top hats and the women clutching packets and babies, as they sank down into the subterranean depths on these 'rolling carpets'. He was finding England expensive, and, in one of his few lapses of English, told Amelia that 'yesterday I expensed four shillings'. At twenty-three, Carlo was a strange mixture of boyish excitement and cool, critical reflection.

Neither Carlo nor Salvemini was at all eager to embroil himself in the political tensions simmering in London's large Italian community, though it was becoming increasingly difficult to avoid them altogether. The first Italians, pedlars, organ-grinders and jugglers, had arrived in London early in the eighteenth century, and settled in Clerkenwell, turning its narrow, modest streets into a little Italy, where few of the women spoke English. England had been welcoming to these exiles, as it was to the artisans, barbers, asphalters, carpenters, tool-makers, cooks and ice-cream makers who travelled up through France and across the Channel all through the nineteenth century. Arriving in Clerkenwell, they felt at home among the flowering window boxes and the sheets hanging from the windows. Some sold ice from the back of a horse and cart. Others opened boarding houses. Pasta was made at home, then hung from the washing line to dry. During their periods of exile in England, both Garibaldi and Mazzini had promoted the idea of Italian schools and written articles to sway public opinion in favour of the Risorgimento.

News of the violence in Italy, of the *squadristi* raids and the *manganello*, was initially greeted with revulsion. But by 1921 London had also become home to a sizeable number of Italian bankers and industrialists, along with hotel managers and the owners of shops, many of them in touch with the embassy, where a career diplomat and warm supporter of Mussolini, Giacomo De Martino, was ambassador. In June 1920, a weekly Italian paper called *La Cronaca* had been launched, financed by Fiat and Pirelli. In theory, it proclaimed itself to be above party politics, but since its views were shaped by the staff at the embassy, and by a group of pro-Mussolini lecturers in the Italian department at London university, its tone became gradually more bracing and nationalistic.

In the winter of 1921, a group of prosperous Italian Londoners – some of them war veterans with experience of fascism at home – together with their friends Sir Rennell Rodd, former British ambassador to Rome, and Camillo Pellizzi, a lecturer at London university, had met to establish the first foreign *fascio,* a 'nucleus of vibrant patriots of the purest Italian spirit', open to men over twenty-one and women over eighteen 'of excellent morality'. On hearing of its existence, Mussolini called it 'my first-born abroad'. It was proposed to pull together all existing Italian organisations in London, from the Ice Cream and Temperance Refreshment Federation to the Molinari Sporting Club, under the discipline of *squadre d'azione*, to '*tutelare*' the Italians in London in the true path of fascism. The general spirit of good cheer in which they seemed to be living had to be replaced by a more rigorous '*concordia fascista*', and schools set up for London's Italian children, since English ones, though good on moral and physical education, lacked a 'spiritual drive towards nationalism'. It was only a pity that the particularly slow pace of life in Britain, '*il metodo Londinese*', meant that nothing would happen very fast. At the *fascio*'s meetings in its new headquarters in Soho, and at its launch at a reception in the Savoy Hotel, many of the men wore black shirts. The *manganello* made its appearance on the streets of Clerkenwell. At first little interested, the British public took note when, after the March on Rome, a group of young *squadristi* laid a wreath in Westminster Abbey and raised their arms in the Roman salute.

In *La Cronaca*, along with advertisements for Chianti, Asti

Spumante, olive oil, alabaster, pearls from Venice, leather bags and the Barbetta Bakery – 'Specialists in Panettoni' – on the Hampstead Road were warnings about Bolshevism and how, without a firm hand, Italy could easily sink into 'Mexican or Balkan-style chaos'. Early in 1923, it reported on the great success of a 'Black Shirt Gala Ball', at which Italian and English guests alike had sung 'Giovinezza'. Socialists were described as a 'bunch of waiters', Salvemini as a man who, 'blind and deaf, denies the light of a truth he refuses to see'.

Not all the Italians in London were happy with this fascist onslaught. In July 1922, an anti-fascist paper, *Il Commento*, had been launched. It, too, professed to be truly 'independent of every group or vested interest', and said that it intended to inject a 'disinfecting current of ozone' into the over-heated Italian community. Soon, however, it began commenting unfavourably on the violence happening in Italy, and filled its pages with cartoons portraying the fascists as toads and flies. Mussolini's speeches were reported in mocking tones, and fascists referred to as 'Knights of the *manganello*'. When, in September, Mussolini announced that 'sporadic, individual, unintelligent, uncontrolled' violence had to stop, *Il Commento* asked: 'What, then, is intelligent, controlled violence? Is it instructive, kindly, evolved, well-mannered, knowing, perspicacious, courteous, genial?'

The Fabian Society conference was to be held in Hindhead in Surrey, where a boarding school, empty for the summer holidays, had been taken over. The Fabians were the oldest surviving social group in Britain; their 2,000 or so members, who saw themselves as practical reformers, spoke of reconstructing society 'in accordance with the highest moral possibilities'. Their motto was 'Educate, agitate, organise'. By the early 1920s, the Fabians had long been dominated by George Bernard Shaw and Sidney and Beatrice Webb, who lectured regularly on the state of the world. As Shaw had written, 'My hours that make my days, my days that make my years follow one another pellmell into the maw of socialism,' which was precisely what Carlo wanted to learn about. The summer school, now in its seventeenth year, was the highlight of the Fabian calendar.

On Friday 3 August, Carlo, Salvemini and Carlo Levi, who had joined them in London, caught a train for Hindhead. St Edmund's School sat on a low hill surrounded by heather and pine trees. It had a nearby tennis court, golf course and open-air swimming pool, as well as a large wooden hall, perfect for the Swedish drill laid on every morning for ladies in bloomers and tunics. Alcohol was forbidden, but glee singing, concerts, fancy-dress parties and excursions on foot, by bicycle and charabanc, were all regarded with as much seriousness as the lectures. The mood was friendly, polite, seldom confrontational; nothing happened in a hurry. It was a far cry from the turbulence and frenzy of Florence and, to the three Italians, a source of marvel and humour.

The weather was sunny and rather windy, much like Italy on a spring day, noted Carlo approvingly; he did not care for great heat. On Saturday, they joined a party of fifteen and walked to nearby Frensham Ponds for tea. That evening, Salvemini gave an impromptu talk on fascism: Carlo remarked, not without a certain smugness, that his English was 'improvised'. On Sunday, there was croquet, a discussion on the growth of public ownership, and dancing. Carlo was led round the dance floor by many 'dear and sympathetic Fabians', as he told Amelia later, charitably refraining from further comment. The visitors' book lists a housewife, a number of teachers, a couple of journalists, some civil servants, and a 'blouse manufacturer' among those present. Under 'Publications', the housewife has written 'two children'. On Tuesday, a Miss Hawkinson led a party 'into the wooded portion of the grounds', where they sang '"à la Wolf Cubs" until 11 pm'. Whether Salvemini and Carlo joined them is not recorded.

During the first week the weather remained dry and fine and lectures were held outside. Sidney Webb gave a talk called 'Is Civilisation Decaying?' There was much admiring chat about Mazzini. Carlo intervened in praise of the Bolsheviks, about whom his listeners seemed strangely ignorant. One day, he joined the swimmers: the water, he reported was 'freddissima'. He could not quite come to terms with the fact that while no one dreamt of mentioning any embarrassing physical ailment – though someone did once refer to what he called a 'tommy ache' – they seemed perfectly happy to go naked into the shower or swimming pool. He put it down to 'fascinating' puritanism.

The visitors' book records 'our Italian visitors again entering into the fun', though what the Fabians made of their exotic guests it does not say. At this point, Carlo, Salvemini and Levi were sharing a room, and for that night's fancy-dress carnival and ball they came down in their pyjamas, with chains around their wrists and ankles, as Italian prisoners of the fascists. Carlo felt himself drawn still more strongly to Salvemini, who had shown a side of himself Carlo had not seen before, full of unexpected subtlety and refinement. Thunder and the rain drumming on the wooden roof of the hall completely drowned out a lecture entitled 'Is International Anarchy Curable in a Capitalist Society?' but it had cleared in time for a farce, in which all joined, called 'Bananas on Trial Through the Looking Glass'. Italy and its concerns, Carlo told Amelia, had 'shrunk'. There was something in this mixture of high-mindedness and innocent, unworldly fun that delighted him.

The three Italians were not greatly impressed by the lecturers: their minds seemed 'ossified' and they depended too heavily on facts, though Carlo was struck by their pleasing lack of rhetoric and posturing. What they relished were the long conversations, held over scones and hot chocolate, in which Carlo explored the intricacies of the Anglo-Saxon mind, the 'very rich interior' that lay behind these rational, practical exteriors. His English improved dramatically and what he was learning about the guild

Salvemini, Carlo Levi, and Carlo at the Fabian summer school

movement – which called for workers' control of industry through a system of national guilds – and British Labour Party politics was making him rethink some of his own work on a non-Marxist approach to socialism. He decided to extend his stay, for another week of eurythmics, tennis, cabarets and talk about British parliamentarianism.

Levi and Salvemini stayed on too. One night, Salvemini came to a fancy-dress ball as Janus, with two faces, two stomachs and two pairs of spectacles. Carlo put on a voluminous gown and passed himself off as a 'formidable but courteous English lady'. He told Amelia that the three Italian friends had 'made these grave English people laugh'.

And then he left for Birmingham and the Midlands, to see what he called 'the real England, smoky, dirty, industrial, ugly, product-ive', as compared to the 'dead England' of the Home Counties, where the countryside, with the sunshine gone, seemed to him grey and sad and featureless. The only blight on the excellence of his Fabian weeks, he wrote to his mother, was the food. 'Here', he said, 'is the bad part ... I loathe English cooking, a mixture of spices, sauces, little sauces, big sauces, marmalade jams, fats, minced meat, barley, horrific combinations of still more horrific ingredients'; how people could survive on them for long he could not imagine. Only the brioches at tea were bearable. Salvemini felt the same way. 'If you but knew', he wrote to a friend, 'what an infernal thing is this English cooking!' But, as he wrote to Rossi, the three weeks had been 'magical', and Carlo 'had stirred up a storm among the ladies'. There had even been a comic occa-sion when he and Carlo, both taken by a Junoesque Irish lady, had gone walking in the woods, Carlo throwing himself into seduction 'with youthful high spirits, me limping along behind'. To both men's astonishment, the Irish lady chose Salvemini. Carlo left. 'What happened then,' wrote Salvemini, 'under the light of the moon, I cannot tell you: because nothing happened. English women are like Italy: nothing ever happens and nothing lasts.'

Before leaving England, Carlo paid a short visit to Oxford, where he fell in love with the colleges and their soft green velvet lawns. He was taken to the National Liberal Club in London, where the WC was so big, he wrote, that the Circolo di Cultura could easily have fitted into it. On reaching London, he had learnt of the assassination of General Tellini – sent to Corfu to arbitrate over a boundary dispute between Greece and Albania – and of Mussolini's decision to bomb the island, claiming insufficient apologies and indemnity. After terms exceedingly generous to Italy were negotiated, Mussolini agreed to withdraw his troops, but not before Harold Nicolson remarked dryly that he had not only succeeded in muzzling the League of Nations but also extracting money from Greece 'without evidence of guilt'. The weeks of innocent fun were sharply brought to an end. The Italian newspapers came out loudly in praise of Mussolini's firm stand. 'Do they not realise', Carlo asked his mother, 'into what a terrible, infernal volcano we are plunging our hands?'

CHAPTER SEVEN

Moral Choices

Carlo arrived home towards the end of October to find little had changed. The *squadristi* rampages had been somewhat curbed, but their violence was being more strategically directed at specific targets, those identified as opponents of Mussolini. Francesco Saverio Nitti, the former prime minister, had his house in Rome invaded, and his clothes, linen, silver and even his shoes and typewriter looted. Amendola, the principled former minister of culture who had become one of Mussolini's most persistent critics – though he insisted that he was not an 'enemy' but an 'adversary' – was being dealt a series of 'lessons' in the form of attacks in the street or when he went out in his car. When Salvemini got back to Florence after his lectures in London, he found posters all over the city with the words: 'The ape of Molfetta should not re-enter Italy'. Molfetta was Salvemini's home town. The stairs and corridors of the university were full of threatening young fascists; but his students, who loved and admired him, turned out in large numbers to protect him.

Nello had become the delighted owner of a motorcycle, and he was constantly setting out on excursions around the city. Despite the almost total absence of vehicles on the streets of Florence in the early 1920s, the day came when he managed to collide with a car and was knocked unconscious. The hospital discovered that he had broken his left femur and put him in plaster. Since he remained in considerable pain Amelia had him transferred to a specialist in Bologna, where the cast was removed and his leg put in traction. Unlike Carlo, Nello was a worrier. He lay in his hospital bed fretting that he would end up with one leg shorter than the other. The weeks of enforced idleness fed his constant sense of self-doubt; he brooded and grew depressed. Carlo was not unsympathetic; but his tone tended to be brisk.

Once Nello had recovered, Amelia, who had involved herself in every step of his treatment, was now able to turn her attentions to helping her nephew Alberto Moravia, whose tuberculosis in the bones of his legs was beginning to cause unmanageable discomfort. She happened to be visiting her brother Carlo in Rome when a doctor decided to put Alberto in a cast, but this proved extremely painful. In her researches for treatment for Nello's broken femur, Amelia had heard that there was a new cure for TB of the bones being tried out in a clinic in Cortina d'Ampezzo. Alberto's father was sceptical. While Amelia was trying to persuade him, the fifteen-year-old boy went to stay with the Rossellis in Via Giusti in Florence, where he was much impressed by the writers and professors who came to the house, some of whom, now very elderly, were able to tell him their memories of the exciting days of the Risorgimento. One afternoon, Alberto went to Via Tornabuoni and bought himself a copy of the newly published *Ulysses*. Carlo and Nello found their cousin unnervingly precocious and well read, but thought that he exuded loneliness. Amelia had become attached to this bookish nephew, with whom she had long conversations about writing. Once he left, she sent him subscriptions to magazines and membership of a lending library. Moravia would later say that while his aunt's house had a very particular 'liberal, socialist, Jewish' style, his own was like a windy port, into which 'swept everything, even fascism'.

Slowly, very slowly, Amelia was coming back to life, though every anniversary of Aldo's birth or death brought fresh pangs of sadness. She had not been able to find a theatre to take *Emma Liona*, her play about Lady Hamilton, and was planning to publish it in book form. She had also gone back on to the council of the Lyceum, and was made president of the prize-giving committee of the *Almanacco della Donna Italiana*.

Mussolini, at this stage, remained somewhat ambivalent about women's rights. In 1919 he had favoured extending the vote to women, but then in 1922 he told a reporter that 'I am a supporter of universal suffrage, but not female suffrage, especially since women always vote with their men.' In 1923, a bill to give women the right to vote in local elections got through parliament. But this was also the year in which fascism went on the attack against feminism. The fascist-run Consiglio Nazionale delle Donne, which had its offices in Florence in the Lyceum's building, scolded women for losing their way during the heady campaign for emancipation. They needed, the organisation claimed, to be 'moralised' and to rediscover themselves and their values in the 'real female job' of keeping house. The good fascist woman was one who accepted collective goals.

The Lyceum had asked Amelia to preside over their third International Congress, which took place in Florence in 1922. But by 1923 the uncertainties affecting Italian women generally had infected the members of the Florentine chapter. No one has ever been able to discover why Amelia and another vice president suddenly gave in their resignations, to be followed immediately by those of Zia Gì and Laura Orvieto. A 'heated' debate ensued, and the whole council resigned; but peace was brokered by the president and all returned to their posts. One possibility is anti-semitism. Both Amelia and the other vice president were Jewish, and there is a suggestion that a cabal formed against them. For those who chose to see it that way, a small drop of poison had been spilt, and over the next few years, one by one, Jewish members began to fall away.

For all their intense interest in politics, neither Carlo nor Nello had yet joined a party. They were watching, waiting. In any case, both were extremely busy. When Nello's leg healed, he went to work for the publishing house started by *La Voce*, in order to help produce what they called 'debates', short books on different aspects of current political and cultural life, rather on the model of the discussions conducted on Saturday evenings in the Circolo di Cultura. For this, he set aside four hours every afternoon. He was also working on an article about Mazzini, Bakunin and the Paris Commune for the respected academic journal *Nuova Rivista Storica*, and told Amelia that he was happily 'swallowing' books in the archives. Mazzini's 'admirable intransigence' fascinated him. Both he and Carlo loved what they called the 'defeated' intellectuals of history.

Soon after returning from England, Carlo went to Milan to take up his post at Bocconi University, where he was put to hearing the oral examinations for his students' theses. He was impressed by the generous funding given to the Bocconi, which lent it, he said, *'una larga signorilità'*, a feeling of space and refinement, but he did not immediately take to the much-respected economist Luigi Einaudi – whom he described to his mother as 'taciturn, small-minded, boring etc etc' – or to Milan itself. The city, he complained, was obsessed with money: 'Intellectually it is a real disaster.' In his letters home he sounded cheerful and overworked, spending long days at the university, long evenings with friends or at the opera, and seldom getting enough sleep. He worried that he was getting fat, and kept planning strict diets, *'niente vino, niente dolci'*, and was annoyed when his new shirts did not fit, sending them back to Florence to have their collars and sleeves altered. He was not without a certain endearing vanity. Later, Anna Kuliscioff would say that Carlo 'was like a spring wind, youthful, sane and intelligent, full of promise, his intellect robust and impressive'.

With time, Carlo, who was unsure of himself as a speaker and could not quite take himself seriously as a professor, began to feel more *'à mon aise'*, particularly as his classes were packed. A colleague teased him that he looked little older than his students and described him as 'a chubby, blond, myopic youth'. He was asked to give a series of ten lectures at the Università Proletaria on protectionism and free trade, and was reviewing Keynes's 'A Tract on Monetary Reform'. Then, early in 1924, his lectureship at the Bocconi University was confirmed for the following year. Things were going well. He was starting to make plans for the moment when the 'Fascist pressure has fallen' and the 'socialist movement rises again in full strength'. Salvemini kept urging him to stay away from active politics.

Fascist pressure, however, was not falling but rising. The subservient parliament had granted Mussolini a year with full emergency powers, and the Fiume crisis was satisfactorily concluded with a deal in which Yugoslavia recognised Italy's sovereignty over both the city and the port. Mussolini was also encouraged by the tacit support of the European powers: the London *Times* spoke admiringly of his firm hand and the way in which *'Fascismo* has abolished the game of parliamentary chess'. Within Italy, left-wing newspapers were cowed, devastated by

Mussolini addresses his supporters from a balcony in Rome

frequent visits from *squadristi*, while money was being poured into their right-wing rivals. Turati was fast losing hope that the combined forces of Giolitti and the communists might yet prevent the slide towards dictatorship: 'A train travelling at full speed', he wrote to a friend, 'is crushing us while we are tied to the rails.'

Even so, parliament remained a problem for Mussolini: he was still the leader of only thirty-five fascist deputies in the Chamber. What he needed was a far broader base. Giacomo Acerbo, his deputy minister in the prime-ministerial office, was instructed to revise the electoral laws. The new law he came up with proposed that any party obtaining at least a quarter of the total number of votes would automatically be assigned two-thirds of the seats in the Chamber, the remaining third to be distributed proportionally. In November 1923, the Acerbo Law was voted in by the supine, quiescent deputies. Though it was blatantly framed to ensure total control by the fascists, it was welcomed by the king, the Vatican and even by a number of liberals, who maintained that it would introduce a measure of stability. Parliament was dissolved and new elections called for 6 April 1924. The fascist ticket, appropriately enough, was called *il listone*, 'the big list'. Fascists all over Italy were urged to unite and become 'genuinely *Mussoliniani*'.

For all his calls for an orderly and peaceful election, Mussolini intended to use the militia and the *ras* to intimidate the opposition. In Genoa, Milan, Turin, Udine, Savona, Urbino and Rome, dissidents were attacked, along with prominent liberal-Catholic supporters. One socialist candidate was murdered. Early in 1924, Mussolini declared that governments in a state of transition needed 'certain illiberal branches to take care of their adversaries'. He summoned to Rome two notorious veterans of the punitive raids, Albino Volpi and Amerigo Dumini, and put them in charge of a band of *fedelissimi*, the most faithful, to menace the deputies. Dumini looked more school-masterly than martial, but was in fact vicious and quick-tempered and was known to have shot dead the mother and brother of a girl spotted wearing a red carnation – symbol of the socialists. Cesare Rossi, head of Mussolini's press and propaganda office, had been entrusted with overseeing Dumini and his *fedelissimi*; and Dumini had been promised by General Emilio de Bono, veteran of the March on Rome and now chief of police, protection from the legal consequences of any crimes committed.

With the journalists silenced, the opposition cowed, the ballot boxes a farce of irregularity and militiamen prowling the corridors of parliament, the election results were a foregone conclusion. Just the same, they represented a triumph for Mussolini. The *listone* took over half the seats in the north, 76 per cent in central Italy and 81.5 per cent in the south; the left, too divided to form an alliance, saw their vote cut to just 14.6 per cent. In the new Chamber, 374 of the 535 deputies owed their allegiance to Mussolini. It was the most resounding victory since 1861 and there had been no need for the Acerbo Law. The 'new politics', declared Mussolini, would give the Italian people 'five years of peace and fruitful work'. His spirits were high: he had proved himself a canny administrator, an able political force, and he had publicly distanced himself from the worst of the violence. Better than anyone, he had shown that he understood Italy's love of strong rhetoric.

Salvemini, who had refused to vote, was visited by five fascist thugs and threatened. Afterwards, he went with Carlo, Nello and Ernesto Rossi up to Fiesole, where they lay bleakly on the grass in the sunshine.

*

The last photograph taken of Giacomo Matteotti, shortly before his murder

Of all the many thorns in Mussolini's side, Matteotti was the most irksome. However often he was attacked – and he dealt with each attack with dignity and courage – he refused any notion of compromise. For the left, for Carlo and Nello, Salvemini, Gobetti and Rossi, Matteotti represented a symbol that democracy and honour had not quite died in Italy. Carlo called him a 'prosaic hero', admiring his gravitas and the way that he considered standing up to Mussolini a moral imperative. And he shared Matteotti's intolerance towards all ideological extremism, whether from the right or the left, and his fears that some of the socialists were drifting towards communism and the Bolsheviks.

In the late spring of 1924, Matteotti slipped secretly out of Italy and went to London, where he hoped to convince the Labour leader, Ramsay MacDonald, of Mussolini's violence and the dire state of the Italian economy. Just before he returned home he was asked by a reporter whether he was not afraid to go back to

Rome. 'My life is always in danger,' he replied. 'That is what I want you to understand.'

Then came the day when he stood up in parliament and called for the recent elections to be declared invalid; and soon after his kidnapping, murder and the discovery of his mutilated body in a shallow ditch on Via Flaminia. When his corpse was transported to his home at Fratta Polesine in the Veneto, the route was lined with people. At the moment the coffin appeared, someone shouted out '*Tutti in ginocchio*' and they all knelt. His mother, Isabella, howled 'like a wolf whose cubs had been killed'. She was dragged away, her cries resounding across the countryside. *Squadristi* were overheard to say: 'This is the first. There will be others.' Velia Matteotti was warned not to visit her husband's grave, 'for this could cost her her life'.

Whether this act might have provided the spark for radical action no one can say. The opposition leaders hesitated. Mussolini kept the Chamber closed and ordered the fascists to lie low. Turati, still trying desperately to instil fire into the socialists, proposed a common front against the regime but it was blocked by the Vatican. In due course, Amendola's liberal conservatives, with some socialists, communists and a few Catholic deputies – some hundred men in all – walked out of parliament and formed the 'Aventine Secession', taking their name from the moment in

The Lancia car in which Matteotti was kidnapped

494 BC when the Roman people withdrew to the Aventine Hill in protest against the patriciate.

But even the Aventine Secession was little more than a show of principles. Within their ranks there was no unity and none could envisage a solution other than within strict parliamentary legality, preferring to pursue a 'moral campaign' rather than set up an anti-parliament. As one critic phrased it: 'The Aventino lost the battle on which not only Italy's future, but possibly that of the world, depended.' When it refused to endorse the communists' proposal for a general strike, the communists withdrew and declared that the socialists and democrats 'had neither the strength nor the will to win'. As Gobetti put it, the Aventino 'spun a myth, the myth of caution'. The days passed and nothing happened. Turati wrote to Kuliscioff: 'Time is working for the enemy.' In Turin, lorries of fascists drove through the streets singing: 'Matteotti, Matteotti, *ne farem dei salsicciotti*' ('we'll make sausages of him'). A few days later Turati wrote again: 'The enemy has caught its breath'; Matteotti's death 'has perhaps yielded all that it has to give.'

With the death of Matteotti, Amendola was emerging as one of the strongest remaining moral voices. But he was a monarchist and a parliamentarian and could see no change other than with the king and the electorate, though he was deeply gloomy. 'Now', he declared, 'will come silence, inexorable, tenacious, invincible.' Italy was turning into a country he no longer liked. The working-class movement had not recovered from the defeat and destruction of its organisations and cooperatives and its leaders were beaten or in exile. The Catholics were constrained by fears of any opening to the left, and by the fact that many among them welcomed Mussolini's conciliatory tone towards the Vatican. Had others joined the secessionists, had Giolitti not declared that he intended to give Mussolini another chance, had the Aventine not been so craven, so lacking in imagination and so divided, had the king threatened to stand down, had the army and civil service come out in support – then Mussolini might have fallen. All during the summer and autumn of 1924, more and more embarrassing details emerged to haunt him. But he played them all with skill, courted the vacillating liberals and made promises to the restive and powerful *ras*. He then got the king to sign a second decree further curbing the powers of the press: when it went through, *squadristi* celebrated by burning newspapers in the public squares.

Was Mussolini directly responsible for Matteotti's murder? Some historians believe that he was, pointing to the fact that the existence of Dumini's squad was known to several leading fascists, as were the arrangements for Matteotti's abduction, and that the Lancia was traced to the editor of the *Corriere Italiano*, a known contact of Mussolini's brother Arnaldo. But not everyone is so sure. Both the nature of the murder and the choice of burial place, where the body was sure to be found, seem too amateurish. Mussolini clung on, denied all knowledge of events, blamed rogue fascists, and declared that not only was such an act 'anti-fascist' but 'anti-Mussolinian'. He told Sir Ronald Graham, the British ambassador, that he believed Matteotti's murder had been a case of personal vendetta, a 'bestial crime' that had started out as a warning and a lesson, or perhaps a practical joke, and had clearly gone wrong when a coat was wrapped over Matteotti's head and he suffocated. Matteotti, he said, 'was a delicate man'.

For Carlo, Nello and their friends, the murder of Matteotti, the man defined by Gobetti as the 'most staunch and intelligent of them all, the youngest in years and in spirit', was a defining moment. While the Aventine secessionists prevaricated, the young dissidents, most of them still in their early twenties, were shocked into political action. None would ever feel the same again. It was as if, across the whole of Italy, the political map had been abruptly altered. Gobetti immediately declared war on the *apolitici*, those who refused to sully their hands in the political arena. 'It is no good sitting in the middle,' he told his friends. 'You have to become fighters.' Carlo wrote to him: 'The time has come for us all to assume our battle positions.' It was their duty, wrote Rossi, 'arduous but sacred', to enter the battlefield. The time for compromise, for hesitation, was over.

One of the Rosselli brothers' first moves was to look for a political party to join: Nello was drawn to Amendola's newly formed Unione Nazionale, a movement calling for a return to the 'noblest traditions of the Risorgimento' and sufficiently wide, he hoped, to form the basis of a future government. Carlo, along with Salvemini, looked to Turati's United Socialist Party, of which

Matteotti had been the general secretary. All shared what Gobetti called 'revolutionary liberalism'; inspired by an 'inexorable passion for liberty', all hoped that it might now be possible to awaken such a wave of revulsion across Italy that it would bring Mussolini down. Fascism, said Gobetti, was a peculiarly Italian phenomenon embracing narrow-minded, dogmatic nationalism and had to be fought as such. He was more urgent than the two brothers, calling for a nationwide network of intellectuals, united by cultural affinities, but all three agreed that though they would not join the communists, fascism would only be defeated with the support of the working classes.

What they regretted was having wasted so much time on discussions. 'The old parties, the old cliques literally prevented us from fighting,' Carlo wrote later. 'They took shelter behind impotent moralising, boycotted bold action and were themselves swept away. And we with them.' The ideas that he had been turning over in his mind for the past few years were beginning to acquire shape and form. While Mussolini had been vigorous, the left had just wandered around feebly rather like bankrupts who keep living the luxurious life, instead of taking to the streets. Wanting 'normalisation', they had thought they would get it by granting Mussolini exceptional powers, and by the time he came to use them, they were without powers of their own. Post-war Italy had been betrayed by the 'blind and tortuous dogmatism' of its craven and 'sclerotic' socialist leaders, and had therefore been an easy prey for a 'tribe of fast-thinking predators', who, seeing no need for legality, had waged an energetic, youthful battle, leaving its opponents in possession only of the high ground. What was needed now was a new socialism, a bulwark against fascism, a transformation of the old liberal state into a new mass democracy built on trade unions and cooperatives, capable of confronting both fascists and Marxists.

One thing, however, was blindingly obvious to all of them: Mussolini could never be defeated by legal means. They now had just two choices: servitude or confrontation; a calm life or one of infinite danger.

The year before, in June 1923, a small group of young republicans calling themselves Italia Libera had heckled Mussolini in Piazza

Venezia, shouting '*Viva la libertà*!' and calling for free elections, an independent judiciary and the dissolution of the fascist militia. Mussolini quickly dismissed them as 'melancholy imbeciles'. But not long after Matteotti's death in 1924, a Florentine chapter of Italia Libera was formed, and Nello abandoned Amendola's party to play a leading part in it. One of its driving forces was Dino Vannucci, a twenty-nine-year-old Alpini veteran who had come home from the war with a limp and missing a finger, and who was now studying anatomy at the hospital of Santa Maria Nuova. Vannucci was tall, with a long, horse-like face, smiled constantly and appeared to take nothing seriously. Another founder was a railway-worker called Nello Traquandi who took the pseudonym Satiro (satyr), and began to interview possible recruits, among them the romantic, revolutionary Englishwoman, Marion Cave. A third was an exceptionally brave young doctoral student from Savona called Sandro Pertini.

Within weeks, fifty young Florentines were writing, printing and distributing flyers, and painting slogans on walls. They called themselves '*combattenti*', 'fighters'. 'We do not wish to be thought of as a race of slaves,' read one of their posters, 'worthy only of being dominated and humiliated by violence and intimidation.' Already it was clear that the fascists had them in their sights. One day a policeman arrived to search the Rosselli house in Via Giusti. Going through Nello's desk, he seized on some notes on Carlo Pisacane and his revolutionary activities. When Nello returned, the policeman threatened to arrest him for his seditious writings, and Nello took great pleasure in explaining that the Neapolitan patriot had been dead for over half a century.

When, not long afterwards, Italia Libera decided to hold a secret 'general assembly', they alerted supporters via passwords. Over a thousand people turned up, among them doctors, shop-keepers, postal-workers and students. Rossi and Traquandi were elected leaders. There were to be no names, no registers; a code was derived from the weekly lottery, and the city divided into four quarters, each under a different man. Police sensibly kept away when Salvemini led marchers through the streets one day shouting '*Eviva Matteotti*', but they were watching, biding their time. Nello spent a great deal of time distributing manifestos, driving his new car, which had been nicknamed Bianchina. He plastered photographs of Matteotti on the city walls, pasting them over the large yellow posters put up by the fascists. His thoughts too were taking shape; he was becoming bolder, less tentative, but unlike his brother, he was in search of a more contemplative life. For him, entering politics was 'like swallowing a toad'. As for Marion Cave, she had found her cause, and now took on the role of keeping the flyers and posters hidden in chosen spots around the city. The two brothers were in a fever of activity. A young supporter later wrote that, while he loved Nello like a dear friend, he felt for Carlo a 'kind of veneration'.

Early in September, Carlo returned to London to learn more about guild socialism, and to observe the first ever Labour government at work. He travelled to England via Belgium and Holland, where he and a friend hired bicycles. In Strasbourg he caught a cold and bought himself a woollen waistcoat.

London was in the throes of the British Empire Exhibition, with crowds flocking to the Palaces of Industry, Engineering and Art, and he had trouble finding lodgings. There were now separate *fasci* in many of the larger British cities, and two were opening in Scotland, in Leith and central Edinburgh. All were busy wooing the Italian community with summer outings, after-school activities, receptions and balls, attended by the men in their black shirts. A 'Gruppo Femminile' had been set up in London.

Matteotti's death had initially been greeted in England with dismay. There was a demonstration in Trafalgar Square and two minutes of silence were observed. A 'Friends of Italian Freedom' league was formed and its manifesto signed by Rebecca West, C. P. Trevelyan and Bertrand Russell. The tone of the financially ailing paper *Il Commento* had become despairing. In one of its last articles, published on 10 September, in Italian, English and French, it lamented the murder of Matteotti: 'Fascism', it said, 'is the triumph of mediocrity, violence and shamefulness.' The former editor of *The Times*, Henry Wickham Steed, who knew Italy well and had met Mussolini, observed that he was a deeply sinister man who reminded him of the famous burglar and murderer Charles Peace, hanged not long before.

But Mussolini had good English friends and allies, not least Sir Ronald Graham, who never ceased to file adulatory despatches from the embassy in Rome. Lord Rothermere, who was introduced to Mussolini for the first time in the summer of 1924, wrote that the Duce 'is the greatest figure of our times, dominating the history of the twentieth century as Napoleon dominated that of the nineteenth'. Order had first to be reintroduced into Italy; then liberty would follow. As *The Times* neatly put it, in Italy 'murder is more common than in most of the civilised nations'.

Though Amelia grumbled that Carlo did not write to her often enough, a steady stream of letters made their way back from England to Florence. He had met Professor Tawney, he told her, attended a reception for the International Peace Congress, bought the *Times Atlas* on special offer in Selfridges, was reading Bertrand Russell on China and had been made a visiting member of the 1917 Labour Party Club, where he was able to sit and read during the day. The weather was so terrible, so 'despairingly' rainy, that he had to keep having his damp clothes ironed. The portions of food in restaurants struck him as minuscule. One night he went to see Sybil Thorndike in *'la grande novità Shawiana'*, *St Joan*, the beginning of which he loved but then grew bored. He was trying to get an introduction to Keynes.

Closely following the news from Italy, he observed to Amelia that the Aventine Secession was continuing its path of 'collective suicide' and that the situation was 'grey'. On 15 September he wrote that whatever happened, those who opposed Mussolini had no alternative but to battle on, even if the battle lasted a lifetime. 'For me, at least, this is a moral imperative.'

In October, Carlo decided that he would stay on in England for the elections – Ramsay MacDonald was hoping to increase his parliamentary majority. Would his mother be *'molto* cross?' His plan was to travel across the Midlands and Wales, to talk to people at a moment when, preparing to vote, 'their souls are naked', and to write articles for the Italian papers. He was short of money, but 'since I am already at the ball, I might as well dance to the end'. He heard Asquith speak and thought that he was a 'worthy heir to the great Liberal tradition'; but declared that Lloyd George, though an able orator, was a buffoon and a demagogue. Carlo was excited by his encounters with factory-workers, miners and political campaigners, but had decided that the life of the roaming journalist was not for him: he hated having to come up with instant opinions and write '*sciocchezze*', inanities, on complex subjects. He wanted to be a player, not an observer. That he was already, at not quite twenty-five, being taken seriously was clear when the socialists invited him to contribute to their paper, *La Giustizia*.

Carlo was back in Florence in time to take part in one of Italia Libera's most audacious stunts. Early on the morning of 2 November, the Day of the Dead, just as the Cemetery delle Porte Sante opened, Rossi and Marion slipped in and placed a large picture of Matteotti inside the gates of the Vannucci family chapel, then secured them with a chain and padlock. Word went out for people to come with wreaths and flowers. Dozens arrived and knelt in prayer. The flowers were soon spilling out into the alleyways. A furious woman, supporter of the fascists, made a scene. Policemen and carabinieri arrived, followed by a local fascist chief, who broke the chain, ripped up the picture of Matteotti and ordered the carabinieri – it was telling that he had the power to do so – to prevent people from laying more flowers. But they kept coming. At the gates to the cemetery, police began to make arrests. One of those grabbed was Salvemini, who was taken off to a nearby police station, recognised as a *professore*, a man of standing, and released. He hastened back to the cemetery, where he was again arrested and returned to a now furious police inspector, who shouted at his subordinates: 'Don't you understand? He *wants* to be arrested!' Salvemini treated all fascists he encountered with open contempt and he advised his friends to do the same.

Carlo, Nello, Marion and Rossi all escaped arrest. That evening, Rossi and Dino Vannucci went to the police station to negotiate the release of those held for '*violazione di domicilio*', house breaking, having entered the Vannucci private chapel without permission. Dino explained that he had invited his friends in, but not the police or the local fascists, and would now like to bring a case against them for breaking the law. The inspector, seeing no way out, let his prisoners go. The newspapers that were still bold enough to speak out gave the event considerable coverage. With uncharacteristic and absurd optimism, Salvemini wrote to Lina Waterfield: 'Mussolini is in his death throes.'

It had indeed been an excellent, humorous stunt; but the fascists were not in a mood for stunts. Their leaders were calling for blood, specifically that of Amendola and Turati. There was talk of a '*seconda ondata*', a second wave of punitive expeditions.

Sometime that autumn Nello had been introduced to the nineteen-year-old daughter of a former colonel, Maria Todesco. Maria wore her fair hair down to her waist and was not allowed to leave the house without her governess. Her family were Sephardic Jews and she had been educated at home, in Florence's Via Jacopo Nardi, near the city centre. The Todescos were well off, owning property in Tuscany, but Maria's father suffered from manic depression, brought on, it was said, by having been forced to sit on a tribunal handing down death sentences to deserters in the First World War. The family had resolutely distanced itself from politics. Maria was quiet and affectionate, Nello loving and amiable. They fell in love.

The 4th Jewish Youth Convention was held in Livorno early in November and Nello decided to attend. Many young Jews from all over Italy were already looking towards Palestine for a Jewish homeland, and speaker after speaker insisted that there could be no true Jew who did not imbue his life with the values, language and culture of Zionism. On the second day, Nello rose to speak. His words might have come straight from the mouth of Amelia, for whom 'Jewish, yes, but Italian first' was an often-repeated saying. In a long, eloquent and sometimes emotional speech, coming across to his listeners as youthful, energetic and full of charm, Nello laid down the parameters of his own beliefs. He was, he said, Italian, and he felt himself to be profoundly Italian, heir to the great traditions of the Risorgimento. But 'I call myself Jewish, I hold to my Jewishness ... because I look with Jewish severity on the duties of our life on earth, and with Jewish serenity on the mystery of the after-life, because I love all men as in Israel we are commanded to love them ... because I have the clearest sense of personal responsibility ... because I have that religious commitment to family which all those who look at us from outside agree is a fundamental, adamantine characteristic of Jewish society. I am thus – I believe – a Jew.' That he did not go to synagogue, spoke no Hebrew and that Judaism was not the driving force of his life, did not make him any less a Jew. Nor did the fact that, 'in the citizenship of his thoughts', he was not a Zionist. His Jewishness might appear feeble, but it made him happy, alive and strong.

Nello's speech was much remarked on. He was attacked by the Zionists but warmly congratulated by those who told him that he had spoken out for the 'tormented' and the uncertain. 'But the Zionists are extremely impressive,' he wrote to Zia Gì. 'What awaits us? Where are we going?' The fervour with which he had spoken was all the more surprising in that religion had played such a small part in his upbringing. It was a mark of how the young Italian dissidents now regarded morality – truth, integrity, honesty, as opposed to fascist venality and bullying – as lying at the heart of their anti-fascism. For both Nello and Carlo, it was also about personal responsibility, inculcated in them from their earliest childhood (one has to look no further than Amelia's morality tales of the errant Topinino), which had become a faith in its own right, 'a spiritual torment', as Carlo would later put it, 'which forbids all indulgence'.

Later that month, Arnaldo Mussolini, one of the very few men whom Mussolini trusted and who was now editor of *Il Popolo d'Italia*, announced that he would visit Florence on 7 December. It would take the form of a ceremony conducted with great pomp in the Piazza Mentana. On the night of the 6th, Carlo, Ernesto and Paolo Rossi and Traquandi, with Nello driving Bianchina, met by one of the high walls that give on to the Arno River, immediately opposite the Piazza Mentana. Paolo was lowered over the side, and while the others kept watch, carefully painted in large white letters, using thick, indelible paint, '*Viva L'Italia Libera*' along the wall. The Florentines on their way to work next morning gathered to stare and laugh. Arnaldo was furious. The local fascist leaders, struggling and failing to erase the words, were deeply embarrassed. It was another pinprick to fascist pride.

By late 1924 it was beginning to look increasingly unlikely that Mussolini would be toppled. The Aventine Secession had proved impotent, its leaders divided and irresolute; the king was silent, fearing to make a 'leap in the dark', the public accepting. Many possible antagonists had deftly been co-opted into positions of minor power. Mussolini, to save himself from being swamped by a wave of moral indignation, had cleverly blocked all constitutional channels by which criticism could have been expressed legally and peacefully. For six months, Italy had oscillated between what Salvemini called 'a moralistic and puritan rebellion' and plotting in the corridors of power. But the plotters were proving the stronger force.

Meanwhile, Filippo Filippelli, the owner and driver of the Lancia in which Matteotti had been kidnapped, and Cesare Rossi, the head of information, had both written statements that directly implicated Mussolini in Matteotti's murder. 'We live', wrote Kuliscioff to Turati, 'on a knife edge.' Rossi's revelations were published in *Il Mondo* on 27 December. For a moment, it was thought that the king would act, but he did not. As Salvemini wrote, he 'slid from capitulation to capitulation, from complicity to complicity, from shame to shame, ever seeking a foothold from which to make a stand and never finding it. He is the *roi fainéant*.'

By now, in any case, Matteotti's assassination had lost the power to shock. And still the opposition havered. But the *squadristi* and the fascist militia, to whom the army had helpfully handed over 100,000 war-surplus rifles, did not. As Ernesto Rossi would write, to oppose what came next was 'to mount an assault on Monte Bianco armed only with a toothpick'. Until now, it had all been boyish antics; the real war was about to begin.

CHAPTER EIGHT

'Non Mollare'

On 30 December 1924, the *seconda ondata*, the second wave of fascist violence, was unleashed. It struck in many parts of Italy, but Florence was its epicentre – by 1924 a quarter of all the *fasci* in Italy were said to be in Tuscany. Just as the city and its surroundings gave birth to an exceptional number of anti-fascists – entire families who by upbringing and instinct were profoundly hostile to fascism, young men and women driven by a sense of deep disgust, Catholics who considered it at odds with Christian teaching – so it was also home to Italy's most corrupt and brutal *squadristi*.

In Florence, as elsewhere, the first *squadristi* had been war veterans and the *piccola borghesia*, shopkeepers and artisans, inspired by a hatred of the Bolsheviks and of the 'mutilated victory' of the war, and filled with a mishmash of pseudo-revolutionary ideas drawn from Garibaldi, Freemasonry and socialism. They were quickly supported by much of the aristocracy, who had never concealed their fury at having been ousted from local government by the socialists, along with military men, lawyers, notaries and rich industrialists. Many of the new *podestà*, the men who replaced mayors under the fascists, came from patrician families. Landowners in particular were eager to take revenge on the peasants who had rebelled against them, and happy to turn their estates into assembly points from where the *squadristi* could set out on their punitive raids. Further encouragement came from the Florentine Futurists and a handsome young man with glossy black hair and long black eyelashes called Kurt Erich Suckert, later known as the novelist Curzio Malaparte, who had greeted fascism as the rebirth of a virile Italy and who Gobetti called 'fascism's mightiest pen'.

Of the several different quarrelsome *squadre* in Florence, constantly struggling for supremacy, the most enduring and powerful in late 1924 was that run by Tullio Tamburini, head of the recently formed 92nd Legion of the city's Militia. Tamburini had an office in the Post and Telegraph building in Piazza Santa Maria Novella and could count on some 2,000 members. Aged thirty-three in 1924, Tamburini was a wily, profoundly corrupt man, who had extorted cars and money in return for protection, and had once spent five days in prison for swindling. With his scented pomades and various bits of jewellery, he regarded himself as a modern proconsul. He had a terrible temper and a facial tic, which caused him to purse his lips and screw up his eyes, giving him a cynical and malevolent expression. But he had a gift for making people if not exactly like him, then depend on him, and had built up an intricate web of spies and informers. His enemies referred to him as another Nero or Attila, but Mussolini trusted him. During the darkest hours of the Matteotti affair, Tamburini had sent him a telegram, saying: 'For you, for Fascism, for Italy'. When letters came to Rome accusing Tamburini of excessive corruption and brutality, Mussolini threw them away.

Renato Ricci, a member of the Fascist Party's executive junta, arrived in Florence on 30 December to help Tamburini orchestrate the second wave of violence. The choice of targets for their

The Disperata, one of Florence's most brutal *squadre*

'surgical strike' was to be left to them. Tamburini called for a 'general mobilisation' of fascists for 2 o'clock on the afternoon of the 31st. Hundreds, then thousands, of men began to converge on the city by bus, train, lorry and car, carrying rifles, sticks, agricultural implements and *manganelli*. They carried banners with the words 'Opponents, you have done enough!' and 'Duce, free our hands!', and sang 'For Benito Mussolini, dictator, *Eia! Eia! Eia!*' Tamburini and Ricci addressed the excited crowd in the Piazza della Signoria and then despatched the men to march through the deserted streets from which the Florentines had fled to hide behind bolted doors. When they reached the offices of the *Nuovo Giornale* periodical, which had published attacks on Mussolini, they set about breaking them up, threw the furniture and the archives out of the windows, destroyed the printing presses and then set fire to the building. Firemen called to the scene were prevented from approaching. Their next stop was the Association of Independent Veterans, which they looted, after which they turned their attention to offices belonging to left-wing lawyers and to a Masonic lodge in the city centre. Any unfortunate passer-by who was slow to doff his hat was beaten up. Carabinieri and policemen stood by and watched. A small plane circled above, dropping leaftets: 'Anti-fascists: Your last hour has come!'

Towards six in the evening, the mob reached the Borgo Santi Apostoli. It was New Year's Eve, and the Circolo di Cultura was empty. The reading room, which had seen so many heated debates on the meaning of democracy, was ransacked. Carlo's comfortable armchairs, the newspapers and books, the rugs, the lamps and the American stove were all thrown out into the square below, where a pyre was lit. Soon, there was nothing left. The mob moved on. As soon as the fire died down, a rubbish lorry arrived to sweep up the ashes.

News of the attack soon reached Carlo, Nello and the other club members; they decided to make the Rosselli house in Via Giusti their headquarters. Amelia was out, there were gates at the front, and the garden behind would make it possible, in case of need, to escape. Look-outs were posted. From time to time the younger members were despatched to find out what was happening.

A 'punitive expedition' against a socialist trade-union headquarters

Late that night, Amelia returned. She found armed guards by the door, Carlo and Rossi writing press releases and young people asleep in the hall. Not long before, she had admonished Rossi and the others for the dangers into which they were leading her sons. Now, she said nothing beyond complaining mildly to Carlo that her favourite walnut table had been lost. Smiling and calm, looking elegant among all the dishevelled young men, she slipped away to her room.

The Rosselli house survived the night unscathed, but next day news came that the prefect of Florence had ordered that the Circolo, a nest of 'anti-national agitators', be formally abolished as 'disruptive to public order'. The second wave spread to Arezzo, Livorno and Lucca. In Pisa the damage was such that the archbishop, Cardinal Maffi, sent a telegram to Mussolini expressing his 'disgust as a Christian, and humiliation, as an Italian'. By 3 January, the raids had reached Emilia-Romagna and Lombardy. In due course, a sculpture of a Madonna and child, brandishing a club, was erected in Monteleone. It was known as La Madonna del Manganello, Protectress of the Fascists.

It was now, while Italy was in turmoil, that Mussolini staged his most brilliant *coup de théâtre*. He recalled parliament, which had been closed for the Christmas holidays, telling the deputies that

he planned to deliver a major speech. Since the Aventine secessionists were continuing with their boycott, he knew that he could
count on a clear majority. On 3 January, rising theatrically before
a silent and partly empty Chamber, he announced 'a me la colpa',
I am to blame, and that he personally, he alone, took responsibility for everything that had happened. He was responsible for the
wave of violence, for the castor oil, the *manganelli* and the beatings – and for Matteotti's death. He told the assembled deputies
that he had admired Matteotti, whose courage and determination
'sometimes equalled my own', but Matteotti was, lamentably,
dead, and Italy needed a firm hand; and he, Mussolini, alone, was
the man capable of 'dominating the crisis'. If parliament was
willing to endorse his personal dictatorship, then he would speed-
ily put the country to rights. The attributes of a great political
leader were many, he said, but one of the most important was
that of 'having the power to halt, with a decisive show of will . . .
the collapse of a situation which appears in every way to be
crumbling and lost'. There were a few feeble protests, a few mur-
murs of dissent, but they fizzled away. The speech had been an
audacious gamble, but it had worked. It was now a question, he
said, of '*fascistizzare la nazione*', imposing the full weight of fascism. 'The opposition won't be curbed: well, I'll make them obey!
In forty-eight hours, all will be sorted out.'

Hearing from Turati what had been said, Anna Kuliscioff
observed: 'We live in a country of slaves. They don't lack certain
sentimental values, but they are incapable of standing up to
political brigandage.' When the Chamber formally reopened on
12 January, one fascist deputy noted with satisfaction: 'The blackshirts are now ready for everything that the opposition has to
send at us. They are in a state of complete efficiency.' It was
indeed brigandage, at its most naked. The king, meanwhile, had
approved a new cabinet, in which Mussolini, bit by bit, would
assume control of all the major ministries. Under him, he brought
in loyal fascists – Dino Grandi to foreign affairs, Italo Balbo to
aviation. Roberto Farinacci, the former *ras* of Cremona, became
party secretary. He was a crude, gross, vituperative man with a
jaunty manner, immense black eyebrows, and a peculiar, V-shaped
moustache. It was said that Mussolini kept hidden in his drawer
a copy of Farinacci's university thesis, with proof of plagiarism.

Across Italy, telegrams went out to local prefects to suppress all hostile reaction to Mussolini's speech. Ninety-five suspect clubs and associations were closed down, 150 'public establishments' suppressed, 25 'subversive' organisations disbanded, and 111 'dangerous' people arrested. And the cult of Mussolini himself took flight, that of a virile, decisive, paternalistic, above all sporting Duce, who swam, rode, fenced, flew, boxed and took cold baths. Thousands of photographs were taken of him, in hundreds of different poses, many with his manly torso on display, his piercing eyes glaring out at the camera, his mouth pouting and scowling, his large balding head thrown back. Even his colleagues grovelled. A journalist called Leo Longanesi coined the phrase: 'Mussolini is always right.'

On 31 December, even before Mussolini's triumphant speech, Carlo, Nello, Salvemini, Rossi, Traquandi and the others in Italia Libera had met in the Rossellis' house to discuss starting an

Nello in his early twenties

Carlo in his early twenties

underground paper to stir up those they called the 'feeble spirits' who had appeared to accept fascism as a *fait accompli*. Someone proposed calling it *Il Crepuscolo*, 'Twilight', but the word seemed ambiguous and defeatist. Then Nello suggested *Non Mollare* – 'Do Not Give Up' – and the others agreed that this was precisely the message they wished to get across: resist fascism, work for Mussolini's overthrow, despite the violence of the militia, the impunity of the *squadristi*, the decrees signed by the cowardly king. As Carlo wrote in the first issue early in January 1924, printed on two sides of a single sheet of paper, 'We particularly honour Mazzini because he did not weaken ... Since we have been denied the freedom to speak, we will take it upon ourselves to do so.' Only by fighting back would Italians be able to regain their stolen liberty. Matteotti would be their inspiration, the man who had shown the world that it was possible to '*non mollare*'; the Risorgimento would be their ideology. Rossi said that it did not matter what they wrote, because the point of *Non Mollare* was to inspire disobedience, incite others to exercise their rights, available to all citizens of civilised countries. The young men had taken to repeating a joke doing the rounds of Florence: 'There are three things that don't go together: honesty, intelligence and fascism. He who is honest and fascist is not intelligent; he who is intelligent and fascist is not honest; he who is honest and intelligent is not fascist.'

Salvemini and Carlo were to do much of the writing; Traquandi and Rossi agreed to find and deal with the printers. Marion typed and kept the files, and was soon to be seen with the pockets of her clothes bulging with bits of paper. Carlo and Nello would cover much of the cost from the income from their Siele shares, which had grown greatly in value since the end of the First World War. Traquandi's talent lay in his ability to recruit trustworthy people and soon dozens of former supporters of Italia Libera were distributing copies all over the city, with instructions that, when read, *Non Mollare* was to be passed on, from hand to hand. 'If we want to win,' wrote Salvemini, 'we will. Winning signifies for us a return to the laws of our fathers, a return to those liberties that guarantee a civilised life.' 'I sense', wrote Carlo to Salvemini, 'that it is our duty to provide evidence of character and moral strength to the generation that will come after us.'

No one had yet dared to make public the memorandum written by Filippelli, the owner and driver of the Lancia in which Matteotti had been kidnapped. In the fifth number of *Non Mollare*, in February, it was printed in full, with a run of 12,000 rather than the usual 3,000. Circulating from hand to hand, the paper was taken north by Rossi and given to Riccardo Bauer and Ferruccio Parri to distribute in Milan. Giovanni Amendola, fully realising the dangers he was running, published the second memorandum, by Cesare Rossi, in one of the very few newspapers still willing to print his contributions. What both statements made perfectly plain was that Mussolini was deeply implicated in Matteotti's murder, that he was, in Filippelli's words, the 'inspiration' behind it. Then Salvemini got hold of other incriminating documents and these were published in *Non Mollare* too. They caused a huge stir. The fascists were outraged. A hunt for these mysterious and subversive writers and editors was launched.

But the little group in Florence was both imaginative and canny.

The editors changed their printers with every issue. Vannucci, the student doctor, kept the clandestine material in the freezer of his hospital morgue. Rossi had a secret compartment built at the back of a cupboard in his house. A former socialist deputy, Gaetano Pilati, who had lost his right arm in the war and had since risen from being a bricklayer to owning his own successful building firm, used his workers to distribute copies and went out at night himself and glued copies on to the walls for people to read as they went to work. Why not give me more copies? Pilati kept asking. As they came off the presses, they were collected by the district leaders, and in turn handed over to train-drivers and postal-workers. Each had a note: pass this on. Sometimes an issue would be printed in Milan or the Veneto. Though Carlo, Nello and Salvemini had yet to be formally identified by the fascists, Ernesto Rossi had his house raided eleven times. The police came away with nothing, but he was a marked man.

At the end of March, police closed in on a communist type-setter called Renzo Pinzi in the San Frediano district of Florence. He got away before he could be caught, and Rossi advised him to leave Italy. He gave him 1,000 lire, while Salvemini provided him with introductions to friends in Nice and Cannes. A month later, the offices of three socialist lawyers were raided and packets of *Non Mollare* found on the premises. The militia decided that this was the paper's headquarters and charged the men with pub-lishing attacks on the king and his government.

Pinzi, meanwhile, had been growing restless in the South of France and began demanding more money. Angry at not being given as much as he asked, he secretly approached the Florentine militia and negotiated a reward and immunity from prosecution in exchange for giving evidence at the lawyers' trial. By now, the editors of *Non Mollare* had grown suspicious. After they inter-cepted a letter from Pinzi to his wife saying that he had made a deal with the fascists, Rossi, Salvemini and Carlo, fearing arrest, went to hide in a villa outside Cortona. *Non Mollare* continued to appear. When the king announced that he would be paying a visit to Florence, *Non Mollare* advised the Florentines to stay at home, saying that he could no longer be regarded as the King of Italy, but only that of the fascists. It bore unexpected fruit. On the appointed day of the royal visit, two rows of Blackshirts lined the route between Piazza della Signoria and Piazza Cavour; but of the Florentines there was little sight. A few bemused tourists looked on.

The trial of the three lawyers was set for 2 June. Two of them were released for lack of proof, and the last eventually sentenced to 19 months and 7 days in prison. But while giving evidence, Pinzi had also given names. He did not have those of Carlo and Nello, about whom he knew nothing, but he did give those of Salvemini and Rossi. Hearing that he had been denounced as a spy, Rossi was persuaded to escape to France. Salvemini, insisting that he had nothing to fear, decided to continue with his normal life. He went off to Rome, where he was sitting on a jury at the university. At 3 p.m. on 8 June, while he was at the Ministry of National Economy, police appeared, arrested him and took him in handcuffs to the prison of Regina Coeli. Salvemini had long been an irritant, and on more than one occasion fascists had tried to break down the door to his classes, and he had been saved by his students. 'It is time', announced *Battaglie Fasciste*, a party paper, 'that this corrupter of minds' be silenced.

Nello was away from Florence for much of the spring. Months earler, urged by Salvemini, who was constantly worried about the brothers' safety, he had gone to pursue his research on Pisacane, Bakunin and Mazzini in Berlin, in the archives of the German Social Democratic Party. Stopping briefly in Munich, Nello's first impressions were of architectural grandeur, disgusting food covered in sauces, and 'catastrophic' hotel beds. It was snowing. But he was working hard at his German, and he liked what he saw as far less class consciousness than in Italy, and the fact that the German girls seemed so free and independent.

In Berlin, Nello went to many operas and concerts, wrote long letters to Maria in Florence and kept a diary, covering the time between the death of Friedrich Ebert, the Social Democratic first president, and the election of Paul von Hindenburg, whose speeches he was taken to hear by the correspondent for *La Stampa*. Von Hindenburg, he wrote, had hair the colour of the froth on top of a glass of beer, a double chin, two pendulous cheeks, little damp eyes, and a 'modest paunch, soft hands, characterless'. Guided by

Salvemini, he enrolled himself in a course given by Friedrich Meinecke, the nationalist historian, observing that Meinecke's reflections on the conflict between power and ethics had a horrible echo in Italy. Away from the day-to-day agitations in Florence, his sense of anger and indignation against the fascists had turned, he said, into one of profound sadness.

One day, walking down the street, he observed a Jewish man trying to stand up to a hostile, jeering crowd. In his diary, he wrote: 'I heard, in that crowd, a wave of hatred.' To be a Jew in Germany now, he wrote to his mother, meant having to pretend not to be one: otherwise he would not be able to do all the things he planned to do. It made him feel 'more Jewish'. He had felt very uncomfortable on the night of the elections, when he kept hearing, in mocking tones, the word '*Jüden*'. Asking his landlady whether she would like to see the Jews expelled from Germany, he was appalled to hear her say that she felt 'a sense of physical repugnance whenever she happened to find herself near to one'.

Whenever he was alone, all Nello's sense of worthlessness returned to haunt him. 'I spend my time tormenting myself over everything I haven't done,' he wrote to Amelia, 'over who I am and who I hoped to be.' Another day he wrote: 'This morning life seems to me a beautiful thing, yes, but something that passes us by (or passes me by?) without our ever being able to seize it ... It seems to me always that everything escapes me ... that everything I have not done and don't do is beautiful, while all that I have done and do is mediocre.' Was this normal? he asked her. Was it his age? Was he really a mediocrity? He doubted now that he had the talent to become a university professor, or, indeed, a writer. 'A dilettante? the very thought humiliates me.' The endlessly troubled Nello never shared Carlo's mostly robust sense of himself, though others admired his candour and honesty and loved his affectionate and generous nature. As Calamandrei would later write: 'It was enough to look him in the face to have faith in the future.'

Nello was still in Berlin when news reached him of Salvemini's arrest. The abyss which now divided them, a small band of anti-fascists, from the mass of Italians, was, he wrote to his mother, growing rapidly deeper. For the first time, codes, which would soon become a standard part of all their letters, made their appearance. Salvemini had become 'the child'; prison, 'a clinic'.

Carlo, also mindful of the danger he was in, had been dividing his life between Turin, Milan, Genoa and Florence. For Amelia's birthday, he ordered carnations and violets to be sent to her from the Riviera. He told her that he was lecturing to 500 students, that he felt twenty years older when they called him *'Professore'* and wondered whether they would take him more seriously if he wore glasses. He had been to see Turati, who had made him 'come alive again', and Anna Kuliscioff, *'sempre deliziosa'*, always charming. For Anna's part, she noted that Carlo was 'tall and big and very dear to us', and that he would turn up at all hours, was never punctual, talked incessantly and was always laughing. A new note of restraint had crept into all their letters. 'Of this', he said repeatedly, 'it will be better if we speak face to face.' In the late spring, somewhat injudiciously, he wrote gloomily: 'Things are going very badly indeed. We are becoming flabby. Within the next three months, either we organise ourselves for a wide-based social revolt, or we will be slaves for eternity.' What he suspected, but did not know, was that his letters were already being intercepted by the fascist police.

Carlo was back in Florence when, on 9 June, a young member of Italia Libera called Carlo Campolini painted a portrait of Matteotti on to a sheet, while his mother kept guard at the window – their house had been repeatedly ransacked – and then handed it to a former telephone engineer, who rang the bell of a convent on the Lungarno, saying that he had to check the wires. This man climbed from the convent roof onto that of the Palazzo Frescobaldi next door and fixed the rolled-up sheet to a gutter, leaving a cord hanging discreetly down. That night, another young man rowed a boat across the Arno, pulled the cord and released the painting.

Next morning was the anniversary of Matteotti's murder. Crowds gathered, and it took firemen, carabinieri and militiamen several hours to remove the effigy. That same day – saying that these stunts were essential to make those who still resisted fascism feel less isolated – Marion, Carlo, and Alessandro and Sarina Levi led a party to lay a wreath of carnations in memory of Matteotti at the feet of the monument to Garibaldi on the Lungarno Vespucci. They were quickly arrested and taken to police headquarters, where the five men were despatched to spend a few days in Florence's Murate prison, while the three women were released, the police saying smugly: 'We fascists are gentlemen.' In *Battaglie Fasciste* appeared a chilling warning: 'To such provocations we always respond, and with persuasive arguments.'

For the first few weeks after his arrest, Salvemini was kept in Rome, in the Regina Coeli prison, and then moved to the Murate in Florence, formerly a convent. From his cell window he could see the hills of Fiesole and watch the swifts as they dipped and circled in the evening light. Among his fellow prisoners were a number of burglars, and they gave him lessons on how to break into a safe; they also taught him to play cards. Not long before, Salvemini had married Fernande Luchaire, mother of Carlo and Nello's friend Jean, the talented young journalist, and she was now in Paris with her children. Daily life in jail, Salvemini wrote to her, 'is not at all painful'. He joked that, as a student and a scholar, he was accustomed to long stretches of time shut up in small rooms. His one regret was that he could not finish correcting the proofs for a new edition of his book on the French Revolution. His trial had been set for 13 July. It would be one of the last moments of legality in Italy's slow descent into total dictatorship.

There was a great turnout of friends, students and supporters inside the courtroom, but also a number of fascist militia, strutting about clutching their cudgels. Alessandro Levi was there, along with Marion, several former Aventine members of parliament, and university colleagues. Salvemini was in a cage, big, hirsute, with his wild grey beard covering most of his face, pacing up and down, cheerful, chatting, reminding people of a bear on a chain. When he caught sight of Carlo, he was furious: 'Go away!' he called out. 'Your presence here is absurd. Do you really want to put your head into this trap? Go away. I beg of you. I order you.' Reluctantly, Carlo left.

The judge, on learning that the prosecution witness Pinzi had not yet even been tried himself for distributing prohibited material, and finding the evidence before him so feeble, took the surprising decision to adjourn proceedings and free Salvemini. As Salvemini's friends left the court, the enraged *squadristi* swarmed out of the side streets like angry bees. The friends scattered. Some took refuge in a pet shop nearby, others in a typists' office. Police and carabinieri were shamed into trying to protect them while waiting for a lorry which had been summoned to get them away. But more fascists had been alerted and came running. They surrounded the lorry, forcing it to a halt. Then they burst into the pet shop and the office, ransacked the premises, hauled out Salvemini's friends and set about them with their cudgels. The British writer Sylvia Sprigge, in Florence to cover the trial for the *Manchester Guardian*, received a blow to her head. Alessandro Levi spent eight days in hospital. Nino Levi, one of Salvemini's defence lawyers who had come down for the trial from Milan, was left with one hand permanently disabled. An old friend of Salvemini's, the distinguished archaeologist Umberto Zanotti Bianco, was chased to the *pensione* where he was thought to be staying. When it proved to be the wrong one, the fascists moved from *pensione* to *pensione* in search of him, severely beating any owner who refused to hand over their register. Zanotti Bianco got away, but worse was to come. Salvemini's other lawyer, Ferruccio Marchetti, was attacked a few days later in Siena and died not long after of head injuries.

Salvemini himself would certainly have been lynched had a carabinieri officer not hidden him in the basement of the Palace of Justice. At midnight, he was driven home. Instead of dropping him by his front door, however, the police pushed him out at the far end of his street. Rightly sensing a trap, he made his way instead to the Rosselli house in nearby Via Giusti. Amelia was with Zia Gì at Il Frassine, Carlo had gone back to stay with friends near Arezzo, and Nello was still in Germany. But Ada the cook and Mariapò the maid were there. The women greeted Salvemini affectionately and gave him a bed. He left next morning before dawn to take refuge with a friend in Rome.

The following night, towards 10 o'clock, there was a banging on the gates of the Rosselli house. Ada and Mariapò temporised, but in the end were persuaded to allow the two men standing outside to come in to see for themselves that Carlo and Nello, '*i due signorini*', were not at home. When the women opened the gates, they saw, hidden in the shadows, a dozen more men, who now forced their way in, and, brandishing revolvers and twirling their cudgels, rampaged their way through the house. As Ada and Mariapò begged and pleaded, they set about shattering a magnificent Sèvres vase, then a Venetian cupboard full of valuable objects. Having discovered Carlo's study, they tore the lid off the grand piano, then pulled an immense bookcase on top of it, smashing both. Before leaving the house, they made a vast pile of the furniture, with Carlo's desk upside down on the top, and crashed their way through the bedrooms.

Amelia's old friend Angiolo Orvieto appeared at Il Frassine the next morning. She was still in bed. Bit by bit, trying not to frighten her unduly, he described what had taken place. As they drove down towards Florence, Amelia thought that the countryside had never looked more beautiful, the air sweet and soft in the early morning summer warmth. The hall of the house in Via Giusti had a carpet of shattered glass and porcelain. The two sitting rooms and Carlo's study had 'ceased to exist'. In her own study, Amelia found a police inspector going through her papers. When she remonstrated, he told her that he would arrest her unless she showed him proper respect. She remained composed and dignified. As he left, taking with him letters from her brother Gabriele, now a member of the Senate in Rome, he told her, slowly and deliberately, that what he had found was 'very, very interesting'. Amelia felt a sense of profound menace closing in around them all.

Later, two *squadristi* were arrested for the destruction of the house, but when Amelia pressed charges she was given to understand that it was all a question of 'national security' and that no one was therefore to blame. The judge at the hearing was rude and hostile. Later, too, Amelia worked out that it was the gardener, Arturo – whose wife was a *'fascista furiosa'* – who had informed the militia that Salvemini had taken shelter in the house. Arturo was, she wrote later, 'a real spy, camouflaged as a rabbit'. Amelia stayed in the house, camping in the three rooms that had not been destroyed. Carlo, ever robust in the face of calamity and deeply relieved that his research notes had escaped unscathed, said jokingly that he had never much cared for his Steinway and would now be able to buy a Bechstein. 'If *i signori fascisti* don't have a better idea,' he wrote to a friend, 'then they might as well go to sleep. They will have to wait a very long time indeed before I give up the struggle.' To Amelia, he said that it was vital that the family appear 'almost hard, indifferent and not damaged' by what had taken place. From Berlin, Nello wrote a calming letter to Maria. For the moment, he told her, he would extend his 'forced holiday' in Germany. 'But I feel extremely serene, and will remain so, even if these troubles keep on coming. I am *"decisissimo"*, most decided *a non mollare.'*

Salvemini was very reluctant to leave Italy, but friends were trying hard to persuade him that it was now quite simply too dangerous for him to remain. The American art historian Bernard Berenson was living at I Tatti, a villa at Settignano in the hills above Florence, with his wife Mary. I Tatti had become a meeting place for art-lovers and intellectuals and Salvemini had been a frequent visitor. There was now a thought that Salvemini might use Berenson's passport to travel abroad – the two men looked vaguely alike – but Berenson demurred, not least perhaps because it soon became known that the fascists, thinking that Salvemini might take shelter in I Tatti, had laid siege to the villa. Salvemini realised he had to flee. But he did not plan to leave empty-handed. Through good contacts in Rome, he managed to buy, from a corrupt official and for a substantial sum, 350 pages of incriminating documents against Mussolini, tying him still further to the Matteotti murder. Then Salvemini slipped quietly down to a friend's house in Sorrento and, a few days later, across the border into France, taking with him only the documents and a change of clothes. Rossi was waiting for him in Paris. Exile, now, was becoming an option that increasing numbers of the dissidents were being forced to take. Foreseeing the likely seizure of all Salvemini's possessions, Mary Berenson spirited twelve cases of his books out of his apartment and up to I Tatti. From Paris, he wrote to tell her that he was planning to spend some time in England, which he considered 'the land of my heart, free among free people, a man among men'.

In the middle of the summer, Amelia, Carlo and Nello met up at Siusi, in the Alto Adige. There they were befriended by a group of sympathetic anti-fascists. Later, Amelia would write that these people had all taken to Carlo, saying that he was exceptionally eloquent, but all felt that he was behaving too rashly, and should learn to be less foolhardy. During the days they had together, Amelia and her two sons talked and talked. Reflecting on the lawlessness into which Florence had descended, she said that it felt like living at the time of Dante. Carlo had taken over the full editorship of *Non Mollare* and was continuing to put out damaging attacks on Mussolini, fed by the additional documents now sent by Salvemini from Paris. It was becoming insanely dangerous, not only to publish proscribed material, but even to read it. The fascists had got hold of the names of subscribers to all papers of a vaguely independent nature, and were now going after them. By the summer of 1925, *Il Caffè*, Bauer and Parri's irreverent and accusatory magazine – one issue was wittily composed solely of quotations from the fifteenth-century visionary Savonarola, Garibaldi, the writer Manzoni and the philosopher Cattaneo – had been raided so often that it was obliged to close down altogether. As the fascist paper *L'Impero* noted, the time had finally come to do away for ever with all these 'pestilential sewers'.

But *Non Mollare* kept appearing.

The violence did not stop. In *Critica Fascista* in May, an article had appeared saying that the most 'terrible and determined' enemies of fascism were not the communists, but the intellectuals, whose habit of 'verbosity, compromise and equivocation' contrasted so glaringly with that of the 'mature, virile, self-aware' fascists. Of these intellectuals, Gobetti was one of the most hated. In March 1924, Mussolini had sent a telegram to the prefect of Turin asking him to be 'vigilant in making life difficult for this stupid opponent of the Government and of Fascism'. The prefect did what he was told. Gobetti was followed, beaten up, his house repeatedly searched. Towards the end of the summer 1925 came a particularly brutal attack: as he was walking towards his parents' house one day he was set upon by a dozen young men with cudgels. He haemorrhaged blood, but told his mother that it was nothing. Ada was pregnant, and Gobetti was beginning to think that they had little choice but to join the anti-fascists already in exile. Friends who saw him at this time found him frail, his smile gentle, his skin like 'alabaster'.

Identified by the fascists as the leading and most outspoken 'man of the Aventino', and loathed by Mussolini for his

Giovanni Amendola, another thorn in Mussolini's side

publication of the Rossi memorandum, Amendola too was in considerable peril. The once staunch monarchist and parliamentarian had become Mussolini's loudest critic. He had already received four 'lessons' – beatings and arbitrary arrest – when, towards evening on 20 July, he left a spa at Montecatini to drive to Pistoia. Conscious of the probability of further attacks, he had requested protection from the local prefect. A lorry full of carabinieri turned up to escort him. But they did nothing when a crowd of fascist thugs, summoned from all round the countryside, blocked the road with a large rock, dragged him out of his car, set about him with their cudgels and broke his sternum. He was taken to hospital and underwent several operations. 'This time,' he told a friend, 'they mean to make an end of me.'

Non Mollare was still going. Working ever more frantically now that Salvemini and Rossi had gone, and conscious that the paper's days were numbered, Carlo continued to put out bulletins on fascist brutality. Tamburini and his men, unable to track down the authors, decided that the Freemasons were behind it, not least because 20 September, the day on which *Non Mollare* published yet more evidence tying Mussolini to the Matteotti murder, was also an important day in the Masonic calendar. And the Freemasons, who had initially supported Mussolini, had indeed recently withdrawn their approval. *Battaglie Fasciste* now published a manifesto, calling on fascists throughout Tuscany to 'strike at the Freemasons in their persons, their property and their interests'. Over the next few days, Freemasons in Florence were duly hunted down and beaten up. While this was going on, Mussolini was in Vercelli, addressing a group of Blackshirts: 'If necessary, we shall use the cudgel, and also steel. A rising faith has to be intolerant.' Lest the message had not been fully understood, on 3 October *Battaglie Fasciste* repeated the point. 'Freemasonry', it declared, 'must be destroyed and to this end all means are good: from the cudgel to the revolver, from the smashing of windows to cleansing fire.' And, as it turned out, to murder.

That afternoon, in Florence, a squad of fascists under the leadership of a small-time local boss, Giovanni Luporini, went to the house of a Freemason called Napoleone Bandinelli. They would not have found him at home, for he had taken his wife and child to the cinema, except that he had come back to collect a coat for his child. A neighbour, a train-driver and head of one of *Non Mollare*'s sections, Giovanni Becciolini, came to his help, drew out his own revolver, and in the confusion, with everyone firing, Luporini was shot dead. Who precisely fired the bullet that killed him was never established. But Bandinelli was chased across the rooftops and gunned down, after which his house was ransacked; the sound of his piano crashing from the window on to the cobbles below resounded down the street. Becciolini was battered, taken to fascist headquarters nearby, brought home half dead, stabbed again, then had his head held under the water in a nearby fountain. He died in hospital soon after.

Giovanni Becciolini, courageous supporter of *Non Mollare*

From his headquarters, Tamburini sent out a call for fascist volunteers. Handing them lists of names and addresses, he told them to 'take the initiative of serious reprisals for Luporini's death'. Luporini had been, he said, 'one of the most brilliant figures of Tuscan fascism', lured to his murder in an ambush. Vengeance must follow. In what became known throughout Italy as the Night of St Bartholomew – after the 1572 massacre of the Huguenots in France's wars of religion – thirteen lawyers' offices, a dress shop in Via Tornabuoni, and seven other shops were ransacked. Papers, dresses, typewriters, files, shoes, bags, tables and chairs were flung into the street and set on fire. These bonfires had become standard *squadrista* practice.

Nello had just returned from Germany, and he and Carlo learnt that their names were on the list of wanted men. Persuaded with great difficulty by Amelia to leave the city, they were driven by Zia Gí to collect Nello's car, then set off for a friend's house out-side Cortona. Amelia, wanting to remain close by, left Il Frassine and went to stay in a *pensione* in San Domenico. That night, a fellow guest called her to look at the strange rosy light in which Florence seemed to be bathed. The two women stood at the window looking out over the city below and asked each other whether some kind of fireworks celebration was taking place. It was at almost exactly this moment that *squadristi* reached the Rosselli house in Via Giusti. Failing to get an answer to their repeated banging, they fired a fusillade of bullets into the heavy doors. Ada and Mariapò kept the lights off and lay low.

Just after midnight, the *squadristi*, having commandeered two buses and moving from house to house, ransacking as they went, reached the home of Gustavo Consolo, one of the lawyers arrested previously for having copies of *Non Mollare* in his office. The family was woken by shots against the shutters. Consolo rang the police, who did nothing, and then hid under the maid's bed. The fascists broke down the door and herded Signora Consolo, her two children and her niece on to the terrace, while she pleaded on her knees for her husband's life. The *squadristi* then searched the house, discovered Consolo under the bed and shot him dead.

A second *squadra* had gone in search of Gaetano Pilati, the audacious, much-loved builder who had distributed so many cop-ies of *Non Mollare*. Two men put a ladder up the side of the house and climbed into the bedroom in which Pilati and his wife were sleeping. They fired two shots at him. Using his one good arm to try to protect the room in which his son was sleeping, he was shot again, after which the fascists left, one man saying: 'Let's go and get a drink. I have silenced him.' An ambulance was called. In the hospital of Santa Maria Nuova, Pilati was found to have been wounded in his face, his leg and one shoulder, and his intestine had been perforated in five separate places. Before dying three days later, he said to his wife: 'The Austrians disabled me, and the Italians have killed me.' Later, Rossi would describe Pilati as a man of 'luminous humanity'. Both Consolo and Pilati had made themselves much hated for refusing to be bribed or blackmailed.

The attacks went on. More fascists, summoned from the surrounding countryside, arrived in Florence and gave themselves up to an orgy of looting. By the time the violence was spent, eight people had been murdered, the villa belonging to Domizio Torrigiani, the Grand Master of the Freemasons, had been sacked and set on fire and forty businesses and houses belonging to Freemasons and lawyers who had been brave enough to act on behalf of some of the fascists' victims had been reduced to rubble. In the streets, anyone remonstrating against the violence was forced to kneel before a portrait of Luporini.

A campaign of whispers, lies and rumours was spreading around the city, terrifying people into telling on their friends. Old scores were paid off. As Nello's friend Leo Ferrero wrote: 'Every ring on the bell can signal the arrival of the police to arrest us, or that of friends come to warn us that the concierge, the cook, the concierge's daughter, the concierge's daughter's friend, the maid's friend . . .' had denounced them. He kept a diary, in which he described his father Guglielmo, a distinguished historian now in his fifties, as having no mental skills with which to deal with the '*pazzi*', the lunatics who patrolled the streets, or with the harassment and surveillance. 'All his wisdom', wrote Leo, 'is like an instrument that no longer works, a key when the lock has been changed.'

When Amelia returned to Via Giusti, she found the streets of central Florence littered with broken glass and crockery. Over the city hung a pall of acrid yellow smoke. Had they been there, she knew, Carlo and Nello would certainly have been murdered. People were speaking to each other in whispers and looking over their shoulders. Florence, she observed, lay 'under a monstrous incubus'. When she went to the local police station to ask for armed guards to protect the house, she was told that there were very few available, so many having already been called to protect others.

As the extent of the damage and the violence emerged, St Bartholomew's Night sparked widespread shock and indignation. Florence swarmed with foreign visitors who had been man-handled, seen their favourite restaurants and theatres closed and witnessed the looting and burning. There were protests, complaints, unfavourable articles in the newspapers. One of the lawyers whose premises had been destroyed was the legal adviser to the British colony. The Italian Financial Commission was due to leave for the United States to negotiate new terms for war debts. The anarchical rampages in Florence could not be seen to go unpunished, and the Fascist Grand Council decided that the time had come to curb the violence.

Roberto Farinacci was despatched from Rome to clear up the mess, but his lightning inquiry concluded that the troubles had all been caused by anti-fascists. Since this verdict satisfied no one, the buccaneering *ras* of Ferrara, Italo Balbo, arrived in Florence to conduct a more thorough investigation. He needed scapegoats. The city's prefect was forced to retire, the *questore* was transferred elsewhere, Tamburini was sent to the Italian colony in Tripolitania and it was not long before the hot-tempered and brutal Farinacci himself, whose whitewash report had done nothing to restore Italy's reputation, lost his position as secretary general of the Fascist Party. At the end of October, fifty-three prominent Florentine fascists were expelled from the party. Writing in the monthly *Gerarchia*, Mussolini announced: 'Violence is moral, provided it is timely and surgical and chivalrous ... private and individual ungoverned violence is anti-fascist.'

What few people seemed to grasp was that all this left fascist powers fundamentally undiminished. A series of trials of *squadristi* accused of the worst excesses followed, but each was more absurd and corrupt than the last; the few that ended in convictions saw them rapidly overturned. Signora Pilati was threatened, offered bribes, told that if she identified her husband's killers her son Bruno, too, would die. The family business was bankrupted. But she was a brave woman. Insisting on appearing in court, she pointed to the principal killer and declared, her voice barely audible for the jeers, that her husband had 'made of Italy something great. You have dragged it into the mud.' The five men accused of the murder were all absolved, and a banquet was held by local fascists in their honour. Signora Pilati and her son emigrated to South America.

Peace, of a kind, returned to Tuscany. Florence, noted Amelia, 'began to breathe again'. Marion Cave, writing to Salvemini in Paris in her perfect Italian, said that the city was indeed calm, but that legal oppression was beginning to take the place of *squadrista* violence. The killing of Pilati and Consolo had effectively dealt a death blow to the city's socialists. 'All but the arch intransigents like us', she wrote, were either withdrawing from public life or tacitly joining the fascists. Their letters, now, were full of oblique references to things going well or badly and friends were spoken about only by their code names. Rossi had become '*il burattino*', the puppet.

Marion's rheumatic illness had returned and she had begun to suffer from heart troubles; she had been put on valerian and digitalis and forbidden tea, coffee and cigarettes. In the preceding months, she and Carlo had become very close, and there were thoughts of an engagement. Amelia, however, was not in favour. There was something about this spirited, bold, emancipated young Englishwoman that made her uneasy and she begged Carlo not to meet Marion while he reflected on his future. Amelia, herself so determined and independent, remained curiously old-fashioned about women who chose to pursue careers, suspecting that it was self-indulgence; her instinct was that wives should keep house and support their husbands in their work. She could not quite see Marion Cave doing either.

In any case, it was no longer safe for Carlo or Nello to remain in Florence. Nello wrote to Maria that he felt 'humiliated, humiliated because we are Italian, and in spite of this, we are hunted down by Italians as if we were game'. Carlo was reluctantly persuaded to close down *Non Mollare*. His jobs in Genoa and

Milan required him to spend his weeks between the two cities and Amelia and Nello decided to join him for the next few months. By coincidence, Marion was on the train that took them north; she was much hurt when Nello pretended not to see her. She was sure, she wrote sadly to Salvemini, that he and Amelia, so apprehensive after the loss of one son, would keep a close watch on Carlo all winter. What she feared, in her revolutionary heart, was that they would entice him back into their comfortable world, and that then he would never achieve anything politically. Because, as she put it, 'that world is like a heavy eiderdown which suffocates every generous impulse, and in which a man of character or an act of daring cannot exist'.

The Rossellis were all in Genoa when Anna Kuliscioff died soon after Christmas 1925. The funeral took place on a very foggy New Year's Eve in Milan. Flowers and wreaths poured in from all over Europe, and Turati laid a cushion of violets on the coffin. Thousands of people came to pay their respects to this remarkable woman, calling out '*Viva Turati! Viva il maestro!*' as the coffin was carried past. But among the crowds were many fascists. Setting about the mourners with their cudgels, they ripped the ribbons from the wreaths and tried to break through the cordon of friends guarding the coffin, which was almost tipped over in the scrum. Turati had to be helped to escape by climbing over the cemetery wall. He and Kuliscioff had been together for almost forty years; he despaired of a life without her.

This was only the first of several painful deaths. Amendola, unable to recover from his last attack, died of his repeated injuries in Cannes. He was just forty-three. Lina Waterfield, who visited him shortly before, wrote that he was calm and not at all bitter. Amendola had been, Carlo wrote to Gina Lombroso, a 'second Matteotti . . . the best of men during the worst of times'.

Next to die was Piero Gobetti, alone in a hospital in Paris. He had stayed on in Turin for the birth of his son Paolo, then left for exile in Paris, telling a friend that it was a sad thing to be '*spaesato*', ejected from one's country. Ada and Paolo were due to follow shortly. But Gobetti had been much weakened by his many beatings. On 11 February 1926, he came down with bronchitis and was unable to shake it off. Four days later, he was dead. He was twenty-five. In his short life, he had edited three periodicals, founded a publishing house and written several books of history and politics. At a memorial gathering in his book-lined study in Turin, a friend spoke of him as a captain, who had led his troops to their first victory, then vanished like one of the mythical heroes of antiquity. Gobetti's mantle, he went on, should now pass to Carlo, who would inherit his 'bloodstained legacy'.

'When everything that crushes and humiliates us now is over,' Salvemini wrote to Ada in one of the thousands of letters she received praising her young husband, 'then he will be remembered as one of the noblest and most effective' of all the thinkers who had begun the anti-fascist movement.

'I weep for you, *Signora mia*,' wrote Carlo. 'I don't know what else to do or say.'

CHAPTER NINE

Breaking Free

Amelia and Nello stayed on in Genoa, in a little *pensione*, until the end of January 1926. An uneasy sense of servitude had settled over Italy. In November a former deputy, Tito Zaniboni, had been caught with a rifle and a telescopic sight in a hotel room facing Mussolini's offices in the Palazzo Chigi in Rome. Mussolini himself did not appear much concerned about the plot, but he cleverly used the occasion to convince Italians that it was right, since the opposition were now resorting to assassination, to curtail their freedoms a little more. The streets of the northern cities were calm, but there were few opposition papers still brave enough to publish attacks on fascism.

While Nello worked in the archives turning his thesis on Mazzini into a book, Carlo travelled back and forth between Genoa and Milan, occasionally pausing in Milan to see Turati, who was inconsolable without Anna Kuliscioff. Carlo continued to love his teaching and his students, but hated the limits on what he could now say to them. All civil servants and government employees were being asked to sign an oath of allegiance to the regime, and before his classes Carlo would pace up and down, saying that he was finding it unbearable to be a salaried member of a government to which he was so vehemently opposed. In the evenings, he would return pleased and buoyed up, for his students clearly liked his relaxed manner and the way he roamed around, perching on their desks; but by next morning the doubts would have returned.

Nello told Maria that he felt 'sick at the thought of violence' but that he was beginning to think that 'there is nothing for it but to bow one's head'. He and Carlo spent long hours discussing what they could do next to oppose the fascists. It was telling that when they heard of Zaniboni's plot, Nello was critical, Carlo admiring. The two brothers also disagreed over Salvemini's decision to remain in exile in Paris, from where he had sent his resignation to Florence university. Nello wrote to him to say that he should take great pride and consolation in what he had done for his small band of scholars, and the way in which he had taught them the value of sincerity and openness. Carlo, on the other hand, urged him to return, to come to Milan, put himself at the head of an 'elite' of the most combative young people, whom he would 'educate, incite and organise'. 'The only man is you. There is no one else in Italy.' To stay abroad would be a 'very grave error'. The fundamental work, 'whether material or spiritual', he kept saying, can only be done 'inside Italy'.

Salvemini himself was much saddened by exile, writing to the rector at Florence university that, since the fascists had done away with the 'existence of freedom, without which there is no dignity left in the teaching of history as I understand it', he would return only when Italy again had a 'civilised government'. Telling his friend Calamandrei that he would continue to do the 'fascists as much harm as I can' from abroad, he added: 'They would have done better to kill me when they could.' He soon learnt that he was no longer an Italian citizen and that everything he owned, except for his books in safe keeping at I Tatti, had been confiscated. 'My future', he wrote to Ernesto Rossi, also still in exile, 'is as dark as yours.'

Amelia was standing at her window in Genoa one day when she saw a parade of schoolboys in their little fascist uniforms march past. They were singing one of the new fascist songs, its refrain 'Bombs! Bombs!' 'I saw the abyss into which we were falling,' she wrote later. 'For the first time ... I realised that this was a bottomless pit, which could not be filled in. That night, in bed, I wept.'

In the wake of the October violence, the Tuscan fascists had been reorganised into 270 sections, with 30,000 members, and four legions – 6,398 men – of militia. Amelia went home to find Florence calm and the house in Via Giusti intact. The tourists had returned. She discovered that many of her former acquaintances had made their peace with the fascists; some, indeed, had taken official positions in their ranks. She stopped seeing them. Some of her Jewish friends had been reassured by an article in *Critica Fascista* stating that the fascists felt great 'respect' for the Jews and their 'profound and ardent fidelity' towards the *patria*. Amelia's circle in Florence had now shrunk to a very few, very close, friends: the Orvietos, Alessandro and Sarina Levi, Zio Giù and Zia Gì.

Carlo was convinced that the only way forward was to come up with a new kind of socialism, to reject all the old orthodoxies – especially the 'blind and tortuous dogmatism' of Italian Marxism – and to turn instead to the young and channel their youthful enthusiasm to better ends. Despite growing evidence to the contrary, he continued to insist that fascism still inspired moral revulsion in a great number of Italians. His new philosophy was, above all, to be pragmatic, plain-speaking and insurrection-ary. He found an ally in Pietro Nenni, a republican from Faenza, veteran of the post-war workers' revolts, and former editor of *Avanti!* He and Mussolini had once been friends, which meant that Nenni knew only too well the ruthlessness of which Mussolini was capable.

Unlike most of the other socialist luminaries, who were hanging desperately on to the notion that Italy might yet regain its sanity, Nenni was prepared to accept that the old guard had been defini-tively defeated. Though in many ways very different, both in temperament and age – Nenni was thirty-five, Carlo twenty-five – the two men were convinced of two essential things: that no compromise with Mussolini was possible, and that something had to be done, quickly, to galvanise a public rapidly becoming qui-escent and lethargic. But Nenni had fallen into a state of inertia and discouragement himself, and it was some weeks before Carlo was able to cajole and bully him into agreeing to start a new clandestine paper, to take over from where *Non Mollare* and Gobetti's *Rivoluzione Liberale* had left off. 'Above all,' Carlo wrote to him, chiding him for his apathy and apologising for his own urgency and outspokenness, 'I want to give proof of energy, char-acter and initiative.' It was his absolute 'duty' as a 'socialist and a rich capitalist', and he would feel it to be 'liberation' from the money which weighed on him.

With most of the clandestine papers closed, there was a fund of excellent writers to call on. Nello would contribute articles of historical analysis, examining the reasons for the defeat of the left and the rise of fascism. Carlo would put up the money, and between them all they would put behind them the paralysing obsession with class struggle that seemed to enfeeble left-wing Italian thinkers. Then they would navigate a new path through the 'enervating and unworthy' crisis into which the country had been plunged, stir their readers out of their 'intellectual paralysis' and prompt them to demand a society in which ideas were more important than self-interest.

Carlo was persuasive. Nenni capitulated. What mattered, Carlo told friends, was that Nenni was prepared to take risks in these horrible and perilous times. The first issue of *Il Quarto Stato*, a 'socialist magazine of political culture' appeared on 27 March 1926. Before long, it had well over a thousand subscribers and seven times that number of readers. Though Nenni and Carlo wrote as '*noi*' – 'we' – Carlo's tone of unquenchable energy and enthusiasm came through loudly. 'We don't see ourselves as beaten or resigned,' he wrote. 'On the contrary, our real future begins today.'

They were not left in peace for long. In April, a Milanese police inspector arrived to arrest Nenni. He was taken to spend twenty days in the prison of San Vittore; he would have been there far longer but for his international reputation. When he emerged, he too spoke of joining Salvemini and Rossi in exile.

Carlo was now sole editor. In the next edition, he published tributes to Gobetti, Amendola and Anna Kuliscioff. 'In just a few months,' he wrote, 'the highest peaks of the Italian opposition have fallen. Three mountains, three generations ... who shared a common longing for an absolute morality in life.' More and more he felt as if he were one of the embattled patriots of the Risorgimento, and in a review written at around this time quoted a letter of Mazzini's: 'When it comes to action, I am more determined than ever, more firmly resolute, to be of some use to a future Italy, and I will live and die, I hope, for her.' When Nenni told him that he would have liked to have given his life for an idea, Carlo wrote back: 'I too have often dreamt of being able to finish life so usefully for a great cause.' What he admired most about Mazzini, he said, was 'his boundless faith, his tenacity, his constancy, his courageous optimism, his utter determination'. Amelia had every reason to feel proud of Carlo.

To judge from two letters written by Nello to Amelia during the spring of 1926, Amelia was still far from reconciled to having Marion as a daughter-in-law. The first of them, written perhaps after some altercation, assures his mother that, whatever happened, Nello and Maria would try to give Amelia nothing but 'serenity'. The second is more revealing. He had been certain, Nello wrote, that once Carlo was away from Marion, 'he would turn off the tap called Marion and open another'. Since this had not happened, then Amelia had actively to seek 'tranquility'. 'You have done all that was humanly possible to do: now your, our, efforts at erosion will only become negative and corrosive.' If only for Carlo's sake, as well as his own, Amelia needed to play an 'intimate and daily' part in all their lives.

For himself, he added, though he was not yet sure that Maria loved him as much as he loved her, for his love was 'gigantic', he could not imagine ever again being so much in love. He spent his days, he said, feeling like a 'leaf wafting through space on a capricious wind'. It was not long before he and Maria were engaged, and Amelia felt nothing but delight at the prospect of their marriage. Maria was both loving and sensible, though not very robust in health. With great tact, she wrote to her forthcoming mother-in-law: 'Dearest Signora Amelia, I want to send you especially tender and affectionate greetings.'

How aware Carlo was of the depth of Amelia's reservations about Marion is not clear. He was also in love. Perhaps choosing to disregard his mother's feelings, he told her firmly that Marion was '*bellissima e deliziosa*'. Marion too was in love. From Capri, where she was staying in a *pensione* run by German nuns, she wrote, 'Dear little Carlo ... I would never have believed it possible to feel such happiness. *Buona sera,* my dearest and most handsome boy, *buona notte,* sleep well.' Salvemini had been to visit Marion's parents in England and wrote to tell her how much he had liked her intelligent and highly strung sister, but realised that her parents' life in Uxbridge was not Marion's world and that she had needed to get away.

Carlo had been living under the illusion that no one had noticed his presence in the north. But in March the fascist newspaper *Il Littorio* opened an offensive against the 'opponents of the regime' and Carlo's name was on the list of those they intended to pursue. What he continued not to realise was that his police file was growing fatter by the day. At 9 o'clock on the morning of 27 April, as he was walking down the street, he was stopped by three young men, ostensibly to ask some question about his class. They started to punch him. He fought back, shouted loudly and a crowd gathered. His attackers ran off before he was badly hurt. In the police report made of the incident, Carlo was described as being 'heavily built', with a wide forehead, fair hair with no parting, blue eyes, a snub nose, long ears, and hands and arms like those of a blacksmith. When he arrived in his classroom at 3 o'clock, there were cheers and claps. Then a small group of students began shouting '*Viva il fascismo!*' They were quickly bundled out. To Amelia, Carlo made light of the attack.

University teachers were now required to produce certificates of 'good character and citizenship', and soon orders arrived from Rome that Carlo must be dismissed for 'actions against the national government'. The rector demurred. But Carlo, for whom the attack by students had been a symbol of intolerable fascist interference, had had enough: he was sick of the restrictions that had come to exhaust and humiliate him. Greatly to Amelia's disappointment – which she made no effort to hide – he resigned from all his teaching positions but decided to stay on in Milan, taking a flat from where he intended to go on editing *Il Quarto Stato*. The uncertainty about whether or not to be an academic, which had plagued him for so long, was abruptly put to one side when he learnt that the university was under intense pressure to remove him altogether from their books. 'Kaput at last!' he said to Amelia. He would now give himself up fully to fighting the fascists. The moment had come, he told Salvemini, to do what others before him had done, and that was to sacrifice all 'for the triumph of ideas' and renounce 'the easier honours and successes of the official world'. The magazine was selling well and providing him with precisely the forum he needed in which to explore his thoughts. He appeared unbothered by Nenni's arrest and what it meant for his own future. When the premises of a typesetter whom he was using was raided by the fascists, with the loss of 5,000 copies of *Il Quarto Stato*, he cheerfully moved to another.

His professors were sad to see him go. Before he left, they told him that he had been an inspired and distinguished teacher, a brilliant conversationalist with an 'uncommon elegance of expression' and an entertaining lecturer, even if better as an analyst than as a theoretician. Both the staff and the students had loved him. His departure was a 'real loss'. To his mentor Luigi Einaudi, Carlo described himself mockingly as a 'semi-innocent and a heretic' when it came to real economics.

Carlo and Marion were married in the town hall of Genoa on 25 July 1926. He was twenty-seven, she was thirty and somewhat bitter about the long delay. Amelia, Nello and Santino Caramella, a philosopher recently sacked from his university for anti-fascism, were present. No one from Marion's side came out from England. The couple went for their honeymoon to a hotel in Santa Margherita, a small seaside resort on the coast north of Liguria. One day, Alberto Moravia turned up with pages from a novel he was writing about the alienation of young people in post-war Italy; he planned to call it *Gli indifferenti* and read parts of it aloud to them. A chilling tale, started when he was still nineteen, it laid the groundwork for his later books, with their sly, venal, narcissistic characters. Largely thanks to Amelia, he had been completely cured in his sanatorium in Cortina, and he professed to feel enormous gratitude towards her. Towards her sons he was cool and critical. 'I thought', he wrote later, 'that my cousins belonged to the eighteenth century and were deluding themselves, their heads filled with a mass of generous but impractical ideas.' In the house of Amelia's brother in Rome, fascists were regular visitors.

In September, Carlo and Marion went to Stresa, to a hotel on the lake, where the heat was sweltering and Carlo spent his mornings at his desk. After lunch, they sat on the terrace practising their German by translating the letters between Marx and Engels, before taking a boat out on the lake in the cool of the evening. After dinner, they returned to the terrace and talked or read books on the history of philosophy. '*Voilà tout*,' as Carlo described it in a letter to Amelia. Neither he nor Marion was exactly light-hearted; in any case both felt deeply involved in what was going on around them. Even before they married, Carlo had told Marion that for the moment he had no choice: politics, the fight against fascism, had to come first, before her, before any children they might have. He meant it. The charming, humorous, teasing boy was still there; but the urgency of the times had brought with it an impatient and steely determination. What concerned Marion was being strong enough to share Carlo's life. 'I want to be a lively companion to you, always ready to take an active part in your political life.'

Finding the heat excessive, they moved on to Portofino. They were still there when a letter came from Amelia. It said much about how difficult she was finding it to break the intimate tie that had bound her for so long to her sons. With a lack of restraint and self-knowledge perhaps surprising in one so attuned to the fleeting nuances of human relations, she wrote to Carlo: 'I beg you, write me a line ... Silence is the worst thing. To tell you the truth, the distance between us now and to which I must reconcile myself would be nothing if you wrote to me. You no longer tell me anything, and I can no longer follow what you are doing. This makes me very sad and fills me with a great sense of emptiness and loneliness.' What Carlo replied is not known. One can only imagine what Marion must have felt.

Back in Milan in late September, they found Carlo's flat too small for them both. Leaving the offices of *Il Quarto Stato* there, they moved into a large, quiet apartment at 5 Via Borghetto, near the Porta Venezia. It was, Carlo wrote to his mother, worrying as ever about spending money on himself, too big and too beautiful. But he loved its light airiness.

Mussolini called 1926 '*l'anno Napoleonico*', the Napoleonic year, of fascism. During its first ten months, he survived three more assassination attempts, and turned Italy into a dictatorship. Others would remember 1926 as a year of waiting.

The first attack on Mussolini was carried out by the rebellious and eccentric fifty-year-old daughter of an Anglo-Irish peer, Violet Gibson, who had fallen in love with Italy and wished to save it from his thuggery. On 7 April 1926, while Mussolini was raising his arm in the fascist salute during a visit to the Campidoglio in Rome, she fired a revolver at his head. Looking much like a pauper in the crowd, dressed in a shiny black dress and with her straggly long greying hair pulled up into an untidy bun, she had not struck anyone as menacing. The bullet grazed Mussolini's nose, which bled profusely. Reacting much as he had over the Zaniboni affair, he had his nose bandaged, then proceeded with his plans, declaring, whether consciously or not paraphrasing a leader of the French Vendée revolt in 1793, 'If I advance, follow me; if I retreat, kill me; if I die, avenge me.' As an act of clemency, Violet Gibson was sent back to Britain, where a society doctor declared her insane and sent her to spend the rest of her life in a lunatic asylum.

The second attempt on Mussolini's life took place on 11 September, as he was being driven to Palazzo Chigi. It was very hot and the car windows were down. A loud bang, as if a stone had been thrown against the car, was heard. The quick-witted chauffeur accelerated and the car was thirty metres away when the grenade exploded, wounding eight passers-by and shattering the windows of nearby buildings. Again, Mussolini made light of the attack, which was discovered to have been made by an anarchist marble-worker from Carrara called Gino Lucetti, who was seized by police before he had a chance to lob a second grenade.

The third event was more mysterious, and had immediate, drastic consequences. It took place just six weeks later, on 31 October, in Bologna, as Mussolini was being driven in an open Alfa Romeo by the local *ras*, Leandro Arpinati, having just been serenaded by the triumphal march from *Aida*. This time the bullet was apparently fired from the crowd by a fifteen-year-old apprentice printer, Anteo Zamboni, but since the boy was immediately set upon and lynched and his body paraded around the streets on a spike, nothing could be proved about him. The bullet narrowly missed Mussolini. Anteo's father, a well-to-do printer, was arrested, along with his mother and ten other members of his family. All over Italy, fascists went on the rampage.

This was just the beginning. It had been possible to dismiss Violet Gibson as insane. But the attacks by Lucetti and Zamboni showed how vulnerable Mussolini had become, even if all he had to show for four assassination attempts was a small wound to his nose. On 5 November, a series of 'exceptional', *fascistissime*, laws were enacted. All parties except for the Fascist Party were dissolved; anti-fascist organisations and publications were closed down; passports were withdrawn and the police ordered to shoot anyone trying to leave the country clandestinely; the death penalty, abolished in 1889, was reinstated for anyone attempting to murder the king or the head of government. The 120 Aventine secessionist deputies, who had prevaricated and stalled so uselessly and for so long, were dismissed from parliament. They had become so irrelevant that, as Turati observed, what they did or did not do was of no more than 'archaeological interest'.

Most crucially, a Special Tribunal for the Defence of the State was set up to try 'any activity whatsoever capable of damaging national interests'. Presided over by a senior officer from the army, navy, airforce or militia, with five assistant judges who had sworn an oath to 'obey the orders of the Duce', the Special Tribunal was given powers to hand down warnings – *ammonizioni* – prison sentences, and periods of forced residence – *confino* – in a village or penal settlement far from home. There was no anti-fascist activity of any kind which was not illegal, and no newspaper that was not incorporated into the totalitarian state: by the time it was definitively suppressed, *Avanti!* had been confiscated 132 times in two and a half years.

Fascism was now no longer a means but an end; as Mussolini told an audience gathered in Milan's Teatro alla Scala, the Italian citizen was nothing more than a cog in the great machine of state power. Realising that he had to bring Italian intellectuals into line, and get from them some kind of legitimacy, he turned to the right-wing philosopher Giovanni Gentile, who obediently came up with a *Manifesto of Fascist Intellectuals*, the fruit of a conference held in Bologna to prove that no gulf existed between fascism and culture. A large number of otherwise respectable academics were persuaded to sign it. In response, the *Manifesto of Antifascist Intellectuals* was drafted by the historian and editor Benedetto Croce, and this was signed by Salvemini, Piero Calamandrei, Guglielmo Ferrero and many of their friends. In it, they dismissed Gentile's paper as a 'schoolboy's exercise', and said that it was as incoherent as it was bizarre. Mussolini responded by calling Croce an 'impotent professor' whose work he would not deign to read.

After this, Gentile inaugurated a National Institute of Fascist

Culture, which began to churn out books and pamphlets designed to give fascism a gloss of respectability. To ensure that there would be no dispute, all independent-minded writers and particularly journalists were warned that they risked imprisonment on charges of 'pederasty or fraud'. Croce withdrew into what he called 'inner emigration', and lay low in his house outside Naples, trying to see the comic side of things; when asked whether he thought fascism would last, he would say only that he was not a prophet.

One of the first people to lose his freedom under the new laws was Antonio Gramsci, the leader of the Communist Party. Gramsci had long been warning that the communists should pre-pare themselves for many years of secrecy and exile, but had crucially delayed his own departure for Switzerland because he wanted to make a final, formal protest to parliament about the reintroduction of the death penalty. He left it too late. On 8 November he was arrested in Rome. Accused of plotting against the state, Gramsci, a small, graceful man with a large head, stood very still in his iron cage in the dock, exuding unshakable rectitude and contempt. 'We must prevent his mind working', the prosecu-tor declared at his trial, 'for at least twenty years.'

The task of implementing all this public security fell to Mussolini's newly appointed police chief, Arturo Bocchini, the forty-six-year-old former prefect of Brescia and Genoa. Bocchini was the son of a southern landowner, rich enough to send his six children to university, and enjoyed speaking in Neapolitan dialect with the cronies he brought in to serve him. He was a big, flashy, cynical, sharp-tongued man, with an eye for a pretty woman, a gargantuan appetite and a prodigious memory. It was said that he never forgot a name or a face, and that he regularly worked sixteen-hour days. Although Bocchini smiled and chuckled a great deal, and was full of witticisms and anecdotes, he also greatly enjoyed talking about pornography, and liked to say that God's greatest creation was *vendetta*. It was rumoured that he had almost come unstuck in Genoa when a young secretary, pregnant by him, died during an abortion carried out in the prefecture.

Already, Bocchini's anteroom swarmed, like the levée of a French king, with policemen and army officers, prefects, industri-alists and informers, and many pretty girls. Bocchini's house outside Rome recalled the villas of the late Roman period; visitors

Arturo Bocchini, Mussolini's faithful and portly chief of police

never forgot the fountain with statues of naked girls, squirting coloured jets of water from their nipples, or the entrance hall crowded with smiling wax dolls in different costumes, whose physical charms were exposed at the press of a button. In the mornings, dressed in a sumptuous brocade dressing gown, the police chief liked to wander round his estate while his minions came to kiss his hands.

What obsessed Bocchini, from the day of his appointment in the early autumn of 1926, was how to make absolutely certain that no one could assassinate Mussolini. The police apparatus that he inherited was antiquated: he set about reforming it. To run a successful dictatorship, he declared, you needed a highly efficient police force. This meant first of all putting a cordon sanitaire around Mussolini, chosen from a praetorian guard of hand-picked men, and ensuring that no one came within a fifty-metre radius of his house. When Mussolini travelled, roads along his route were closed. It also meant penetrating all anti-fascist groups, of whatever kind and size, both within and outside Italy. As Mussolini put it, what he wanted were 'octopus-like tentacles' – everywhere. Soon, Bocchini's system of repression, complete with spies and informers and agents provocateurs, was indeed many-tentacled. One of these spies was said to be his mistress Bice Pupeschi, whose code name was Diana, but just what she contributed in the way of secret information was not clear.

One of the casualties of the 'exceptional laws' was *Il Quarto Stato*, whose last number appeared on 30 October. The paper had survived a remarkable seven months and acquired 10,000 readers. At a clandestine socialist congress not long before, Carlo was one of a small group of younger men elected on to the executive; but all plans for reform, along with all political parties, had now been swept away. Another casualty was the distinguished liberal editor of the *Corriere della Sera*. Luigi Albertini, associated with the paper since 1898, was ousted and left saying, 'I conserve intact a spiritual patrimony ... and I save my dignity and my conscience.' Within days the paper had turned into a fascist rag. With him went another regular contributor, Carlo's mentor Luigi Einaudi, to whom Carlo now wrote: 'I know perfectly well ... that the storm is approaching.'

Threats were issued against Turati and Treves. Fearing that the net was tightening around them, Carlo sent Marion to stay with a friend's grandmother. Carlo, wrote another friend, 'was everywhere at once ... he formed little groups of friends who were in danger, he gave secret rendezvous, and all with such skill and grace that he made it seem as if he were playing a game.'

One evening, he called a meeting in the flat in Via Borghetto. To it came Riccardo Bauer and Ferruccio Parri, the two former editors of *Il Caffè*, and Sandro Pertini, who had helped with Italia Libera and had since had his arm broken by *squadristi* for writing a pamphlet on 'barbaric fascist domination'. All three had been repeatedly beaten up at different times. Parri had become very close to Carlo. He was thirty-seven, an economist by training, a calm, modest, unemotional man, with very precise and clear ideas, and much loved by his friends. The fact that Bauer and Parri were not exactly of the left – Bauer said endearingly that he was '*molto confuso*' when it came to liberty and justice – yet were prepared to risk their lives to oppose Mussolini, made the idea of the pure 'Mazzini hero for the first time no longer a rhetorical abstraction', but a reality to Carlo. He spoke eloquently about his long-term hopes for a closer link between all the anti-fascists of the left, whatever their political beliefs. Since all legal avenues for escape were now closed, they would have to resort to illegal ones. Most of the older leaders of the left were now in considerable personal danger, and those who had been deputies had lost their parliamentary immunity. Carlo intended to set up a network to smuggle them out of Italy to safety in France. Sandro Pertini wrote to his sister: 'I feel that my whole soul is coming alive ... This difficult task will transform us all.'

*

Marion soon returned, and Amelia arrived in Milan to help her finish doing up the apartment. Relations between mother and daughter-in-law were better, and Marion was now pregnant, worrying that a baby would get in the way of their political commitments, and telling Carlo that she feared something was ending between them 'before something else begins that we don't yet know ... The irreparable end of Marion Cave'. Amelia had expected to find a snug and peaceful home. Instead she found a 'real port in a storm': people coming and going at odd times, strangers appearing in the middle of the night, secret rendezvous, plans made to meet in churches, in the dark spaces behind the confessional.

One night Amelia, Carlo and Marion were asked by friends to join them in a box at La Scala. It was all very lively. Carlo and Marion were fêted as a new couple and many old friends, whom Amelia had not seen for years, came up to wish them luck. Gazing at her son, so apparently calm and content, Amelia thought he was looking around him at a world which in his heart he had already left.

One of the young men waiting to be helped to safety outside Italy was a slightly sinister journalist called Giovanni Ansaldo, a slippery, resentful young man, envious of Carlo's casual confidence. When Ansaldo asked him sourly whether he did not realise the danger he was running, and told him that he made it all seem like a travel agency, Carlo replied cheerfully that he did not believe the police had yet caught up with his new address. He went on using his flat as the headquarters of the escape operation, and at various times had both Nenni and Treves living with him and Marion. A postal system between Italy, Switzerland and France had been arranged with a friendly local councillor in Lugano, and letters went backwards and forwards in a series of codes: books, which were or were not in a library; exams, which were or were not taken; 'failures', which meant arrests. The borders were ferociously guarded, not least because Mussolini wanted to avoid his more articulate opponents escaping and spreading the word about conditions in Italy. Two routes were mapped out by Parri, who, like Carlo, thrived on plots and danger. One went across the bridge of Susak in Fiume into Yugoslavia; the other over the mountains into France or Switzerland. Smugglers found by Parri were paid to guide people across, leaving luggage to be taken by a bank clerk who travelled between Italy and Lugano every week-end. After each successful escape, Carlo rang Marion to say that he had received yet another telegram congratulating him on the forthcoming baby. In ones and twos, Treves, Nenni and others were spirited out of Italy across the Alps.

Then came the disastrous day when Bauer, accompanying Ansaldo and another journalist called Silvestro, was caught on the border with Switzerland and taken to the prison in Como. Parri went into hiding.

But Carlo would not stop. He wanted to pull off one spectacular escape to show Mussolini the dedication and strength of his adversaries, and to cause a furore in the world beyond Italy. He found the perfect person in Turati, in very poor health with heart problems, his spirit broken by the death of Kuliscioff. He was living in semi-darkened rooms, destroying his old papers in a 'dark, angry fury' and writing to a friend: 'My life is no longer worth the living.' Turati was now sixty-nine and had requested a passport to take a cure at a spa in Germany. It was refused and the fascists used the occasion to redouble the men at his door, who sung out, whenever he left the apartment, 'Con la barba di Turati – noi faremo gli spazzolini – per lustrare gli stivali – di Benito Mussolini.' ('We will make brushes of Turati's beard with which to shine Mussolini's boots.') He threatened to kill himself and had written a new will, blaming the government. Even so, he was very reluctant to leave the city where he had been so happy. It took much persuading on the part of Carlo to get him to agree, but the decision was made easier when the local questore rang at 4 o'clock one morning to say that he could no longer guarantee Turati's safety.

Carlo planned Turati's escape down to the smallest detail. On the evening of Sunday 21 November, Turati shaved off his long white beard, put on a capacious overcoat and a wide-brimmed hat, and was led by Carlo and Marion down to the ground floor, then up the back stairs to the attics and down a passage which joined his house to the one next door. From there they descended to the road behind, where his doctor, Pini, was waiting with a car. As he was bundled out, Turati had an asthma attack and the escape was almost aborted. He had left everything behind, knowing that he would never again set eyes on the things that he and Kuliscioff had bought together and loved, or the magnificent view across to the cathedral in which both had taken such pleasure.

The escape party stopped first at the house of his other doctor, Gillardoni, in Piazza Duse, but since a porter watched them arrive, it was thought safer to move Turati to a villa near Varese owned by Ettore Albini, former theatre critic for *Avanti!* and an old-school socialist who had already been in trouble with the fascists. Turati was to have stayed there for just one day, but plans to get him out of Italy had run into difficulties, and he was too frail to walk any distance. Meanwhile his escape had been discovered. Mussolini was furious and sent the inspector general of public security to Milan to track down the fugitives. Bocchini mobilised his local forces. Friends were pursued and hauled off to the prison of San Vittore. Warned that the police were closing in, Carlo hastily collected Turati. Two hours later, Albini's house was surrounded: Albini was arrested and spent the next eight months in prison.

A new plan was hastily put together to get Turati to Corsica and from there to mainland France. Pertini, still in pain from his broken arm, was sent ahead to charter a boat and recruit sailors. A thirty-nine-year-old experienced sailor, Italo Oxilia, who held strong anti-fascist views, volunteered to act as captain. Two other men came forward to help pilot the boat. Driving at night through the freezing countryside, avoiding roadblocks, aware that the fascists would be searching trains, Carlo and Turati travelled through Liguria, Umbria and Tuscany. Turati sat quietly in the back of the car, saying little, smoking his miniature Tuscan cigars. When they reached Savona, they registered in a hotel as father and son. An arrangement to leave from Vado had to be abandoned because officers from the Guardia della Finanza were patrolling that stretch of coast. At last, at 8 o'clock on the evening of 11 December, the boat with the six men pulled out of Savona harbour into the open sea. Pertini sang the 'Internationale'. A fisherman, seeing them pass, shouted out: 'Good fishing!' The big fish, wrote Carlo later, had broken free from its nets and was now running in the high seas.

A strong wind was getting up and water was soon washing

Lorenzo da Bove, Turati, Carlo, Sandro Pertini and Ferruccio Parri in Calvi, after Turati's successful escape

over the small boat. A thick fog had settled over the sea and for hours they battled on, not knowing where they were, bailing ceaselessly to prevent the boat from sinking. Oxilia remained calm. From time to time, Carlo went over to Turati to see how he was, to comfort him, to discuss what he would do when he reached France. To the others, it looked as if he were a son talking affectionately to his father. In the faint light of dawn they saw lights and a shoreline. It was indeed Corsica, but not where they had expected to land. The journey had taken twelve hours. A small crowd gathered to watch them come ashore, 'exhausted, drenched but happy', and a policeman appeared to conduct them to his superior officer. But Turati was well known and much loved. He was allowed to send a telegram to Briand, the French minister for foreign affairs, requesting asylum for himself and Pertini, who had realised that he too was now in grave danger of arrest. Both were welcomed to France.

Meanwhile a reception was hastily organised to honour Turati. He was extremely tired, but 'It was miraculous,' Carlo wrote later. In perfect French, Turati gave a speech describing Italy in chains and the struggle of the anti-fascists for liberty. 'Exhaustion, the crossing, seasickness, all was forgotten. The old war horse pawed the ground.'

The escape party slept the night in Calvi. Next day, leaving

Turati and Pertini to catch the ferry to Nice, Carlo, Parri and the sailors set off back for Italy. As he said goodbye, Carlo bent down and kissed his old friend. Turati, standing on the quayside, waved his handkerchief until they were lost from sight. His eyes were full of tears. He had hoped that Carlo would escape with him. Turning to Pertini he said: 'I am old, I will never see Italy again in my lifetime.'

There was a thought of the boat putting in at La Spezia but Carlo and Parri preferred to be dropped at the Marina di Carrara where they had friends. There, however, the police were waiting. Soaked, filthy and unshaven, their hair ruffled by the wind and salt water, they were at first suspected of being bandits. They were taken to a police station, where their details were transmitted to Milan. Word soon came back with their identities and orders for their arrest. Still protesting that they had merely been on a tourist outing, they were transferred to the prison at Forte di Massa.

Nello and Maria's wedding had been set for 22 December. The evening before, there was to be a party at which Nello was to be introduced to Maria's many relations. A telegram arrived from Marion: 'Carlo ill in hospital in Massa.' They knew exactly what it meant: 'ill' was arrested, 'hospital', prison.

Nello took off at once in his car to Massa, but was not allowed to see his brother. Amelia then tried, but was not let in either. It was only later that they read in the papers of Turati's escape, and of his triumphant arrival in Paris, and of Carlo's part in the adventure. The *Popolo d'Italia* carried a sneering article about this 'impotent and feeble-minded Mephistopheles ... a sad exponent of the old barbaric and vile Italy', now conveniently spirited abroad. But to the prefect in Milan, Mussolini, beside himself with anger, was said to have shouted, 'You are a donkey!'

CHAPTER TEN

Defying the Barbarians

On Christmas Eve, Carlo and Parri were moved to San Donnino prison in Como. Marion was able to be on the same train and the carabinieri let her sit and talk to Carlo; she was haunted by the chained prisoners and their sinister clanging that made her think of Tsarist Russia. In Milan, where the train stopped, Alessandro Levi was waiting at the station and saw Carlo in handcuffs between two carabinieri, his nose in the air, looking 'defiant and ironical'.

Bauer, Silvestro and Ansaldo were already in San Donnino, but the slippery, spiteful Ansaldo was already sliding his way towards the fascists. He would later say that the only reason Carlo had been so active in helping others to leave Italy was that 'he wanted to remove the competition'. The prison was a former convent, rather dark and poky. Carlo asked if he could have a bath and was reluctantly taken down into the cellars and offered an old wooden vat into which two buckets of hot water were poured. He remained determinedly cheerful and kept everyone's spirits up by his teasing, exuberant behaviour. The friends had been put into a cell together, and slept in hammocks. One night Carlo arranged a pillow fight. A police report noted that he had 'an eager, merry face and a ringing voice'. Ernesto Rossi, who had smuggled his way back across the border from France, managed to secure a pass to visit the prisoners. Carlo was 'noisy and extremely lively, just like a high-spirited Maremmano puppy'. To Amelia, Carlo joked that prison was the place to be, now that all his friends and all right-thinking people were either in jail or internal exile.

One of Amelia's first thoughts on hearing of his arrest was

relief. After the deaths of Matteotti, Gobetti and Amendola what she feared most was that her two remaining sons might be assassinated by the fascists. She requested and was given permission to visit Carlo. A note from the prefect of Florence testified that Amelia was of 'good moral conduct' and took no interest in politics, though she was 'opposed to the current regime'. When the train on which she was travelling north stopped in Milan she saw a group of expensively dressed people gathered just outside her carriage. They turned out to be seeing off Mussolini's mistress, Margherita Sarfatti, her childhood friend from Venice. Amelia observed the crowd's obsequious behaviour, and remembered all the times that Margherita had come to visit her in Florence before the war. Now Amelia was the mother of a disgraced political prisoner, and Margherita the mistress of the most powerful man in Italy. There came a moment when someone, clearly recognising Amelia, whispered into Margherita's ear. She looked up, their eyes met, but neither made any sign of recognition.

Amelia had feared that she would find Carlo in some way altered. Apart from being pale, he was resolute and full of plans. He asked her to contact his socialist friend Gonzales and see whether he would act as his defence lawyer; he was sure that he would be only too pleased to defend the cause for which they were all fighting. However, Gonzales, when Amelia went to his offices in Milan, was clearly embarrassed; soon after came elaborate excuses. Accommodations with the fascists had become contagious. Amelia expected Carlo to be angry, but when she told him, he merely said briskly, in his good-humoured way: 'He refused. That's all that matters.'

Carlo's next choice was Francesco Erizzo, a lawyer from Genoa. He was a small man with a little white pointed beard; everything about him was sharp, enquiring, beady. Treating Amelia with old-fashioned courtesy, he assured her that he would be delighted to do battle on Carlo's behalf. The trial, as he saw it, would essentially take the form of an attack on the fascist state. It was more than likely, he said to Amelia, that this would be the end of him personally as a lawyer. But then he was old, and he had always been a fighter. Marion, who had taken a house at Varazze in order to be close by, said that she felt optimistic about its outcome. 'Is it a given', she asked Carlo, 'that things always have to go badly?'

*

Nello in Venice with his new bride Maria

On 22 December 1926, Nello and Maria had gone ahead and married, according to Jewish rites, in the house of her grandparents in Florence. He was twenty-six; she twenty-one. From their honeymoon in Rapallo, Nello wrote to Amelia to say what he minded most was not being able to do anything for Carlo. For himself, 'our happiness is such that no blows or knocks can harm it. Every day that passes the sense of my own happiness grows inside me. I feel happy because every morning, when I wake up, I feel pleased at the thought of our long day ahead ... Every evening I smile when I think of our shared nights. This is happiness, no?'

For Nello, his marriage to Maria was quite different from that of Carlo to Marion. He was no less committed to the cause of anti-fascism, but the natures of the two brothers became more clearly defined with their choice of wives. If for Carlo marriage was a partnership, for Nello it meant escape into loving domesticity with a girl entirely untouched by politics and who expected to spend her future in family intimacy. 'This point is crucial,' Nello wrote. 'How far can a man, a husband, sacrifice his family for an ideal?' In Maria he had found a sense of security and purpose; he did not intend to throw it away. He told his friend Leo Ferrero that until then he had never known a 'true and complete friendship' as he had never dared to expose his hopes, the 'fragmentary' nature of his interests, to anyone, preferring only to present all that was 'best or at least most lively' in himself. With Maria it was different. He had found a new closeness, a new adventure in intimacy 'which fills me every day with serenity and delight'. It was a 'double event' in the Rosselli stable: matrimony and friendship.

Nello was still on his honeymoon when he learnt that his work on Mazzini had won a competition for the best thesis in modern history at the Scuola di Storia Moderna e Contemporanea in Rome, one of the few remaining relatively liberal institutions. He had not expected it, and appeared more surprised than pleased. He returned to Florence to learn that the award included a scholarship with the Scuola, which was run by Gioacchino Volpe, a distinguished modern historian who was managing to navigate the uneasy waters of fascist academia. The position brought with it a salary and considerable prestige. Volpe steered him towards research into the diplomatic relations between Piedmont and England in the early nineteenth century.

The solitary life had never suited the gregarious Nello and he looked forward to meeting fellow scholars and historians. As he said of himself, he was by nature a family man, a patriarch, a historian in need of colleagues. It was decided that the young couple would convert the second floor of the house in Via Giusti, with its views over the gardens and the mountains beyond, into a separate apartment. While waiting for it to be done, Nello spent his days in the National Library in Florence, making occasional forays into the archives in Rome and Naples. To their delight, Maria was pregnant. 'My duty is done,' Amelia wrote to Gina Lombroso. Her two sons were married and from now on she 'would live in their reflection, and their lives will illustrate mine'. She felt, she said, a great sense of peace: she had done her best, and all one could do was prepare one's children 'to know how to confront [life] with serenity and peace'. Like Carlo and Nello,

Amelia talked constantly about serenity; what made their use of the word so absurd was that serenity was not something any Rosselli actually felt.

Nello was indeed happy, but he was never without his doubts: the main shadow that lay over his contentment was that Carlo remained in prison, and he might soon go before the Special Tribunal. Asking himself why he was not taking risks, as his brother had, he resolved to set an example of how it was possible, in fascist Italy, to remain a dedicated anti-fascist: never weakening, refusing all invitations that came from the state, declining to join the Fascist Party, 'like a tower in the middle of the desert.' It was to be his form of rebellion. But there were times when he envied Carlo's bold clarity and purpose.

Meanwhile they waited. It was, for all of them, as if time had somehow stopped.

Carlo was still in prison in Como, just as robustly cheerful but less plump, having to his pleasure lost some weight, when he received a copy of Nello's newly published book on Mazzini and Bakunin. Carlo was spending his time thinking through his political ideas and enjoyed reflecting that Mazzini too had languished in an Italian jail shaping his own thoughts. What mattered to him now, he concluded, was exactly what had mattered to Mazzini: to bring about a 'popular revolution'. 'All I ask is this,' he wrote to Gina Lombroso. 'That one day I may find myself in the middle of a small group of friends who escaped, with dignity, from the furies, to work together to break the vicious circle of our errors.' He was now facing sentences of not less than three years in prison for each of two charges: helping first Ansaldo and Silvestro, and then Turati, to leave Italy.

But then, unexpectedly, Carlo was informed that he had been absolved of the two journalists' failed escape – but not of Turati's – and that he would be sent to one of Mussolini's new penal islands off the coast of Sicily to await his trial. In a letter to Nenni, Nello reported that his brother was behaving as if he had just won the lottery. 'The time may come,' Carlo told Amelia, when he would regret his decision to help Turati escape. But the die was cast, and there was no point looking back. What was important now was that he had shown proof of 'morality and absolute intransigence', true Mazzini attributes. Knowing how hard she found his absence, he wrote consolingly to Marion: 'For the hundredth time, I bless the hour that we met ... For us too hours of calm will come, hours of peace, hours of happiness.' When Carlo left San Donnino prison, the other inmates found it all very silent.

The train taking him south stopped in Florence. Amelia, Maria, Nello, Zio Giù and Zia Gì were at the station to meet him, but not Marion, whose heart condition had been aggravated by her pregnancy. Carlo suggested to the two carabinieri escorting him that they go back to the house in Via Giusti for dinner; surprisingly, they agreed. It was ten at night and when they got there Carlo bounded up the stairs to find Marion, calling over his shoulder to the startled carabinieri officers 'Don't worry, I won't escape.' As usual, noted Amelia, he looked like a 'king, surrounded by his subjects', with his customary ironical smile. She offered the men dinner, and when they grew restless, went up to get Carlo. She found him looking at the crib, made ready for the coming baby, with tears in his eyes.

In Rome, where Carlo's train paused, his uncle Gabriele came to see him. To Nello, Amelia wrote: 'Ever since the moment I saw him leave, I hate Florence, the house, the people, everything.'

It was late May and the wisteria that covered the house in Via Giusti was out; the garden, full of sweet-smelling plants and flowering shrubs, had never been more beautiful. Maria and Nello had moved into their apartment on the second floor and though Maria had just had a miscarriage, it had been early and she quickly recovered. Nello spent his mornings in the National Library, returning home every day for lunch. But on 1 June, he did not appear. Two o'clock, then three o'clock passed. Alessandro Levi, summoned by Amelia, went to find out what had happened. He returned to say that Nello had been arrested and was now in Murate prison.

For a while, it was thought that he had been picked up for an attack on fascism written by one of the handful of liberal senators who had dared to stand up to Mussolini, and who had inadvertently sent it to him in Florence, where it had been intercepted by the police. Another theory was that a spy in the bank, noting his regular withdrawals of money to pay the men working on the house, had assumed they were going to finance anti-fascists. A police report prepared for the prefect of Florence spelt out the real reason: Nello, it said, was of 'normal character', esteemed by his colleagues, and very hard-working. He was reported as tall, robust, with dark hair worn long, rather small, deep-set grey eyes, a somewhat big nose, a large round chin, large shoulders, long legs, big feet, medium-sized hands, and a good-tempered expression. He dressed with care. But his work was 'inspired by his very great aversion to the current regime ... He is exceptionally cunning at evading the vigilance of the authorities,' and with Matteotti's death he had become 'a violent and dedicated opponent'. He was, in short, a danger to the state, and needed to be removed to where he could do no further harm.

Like Carlo, Nello treated his incarceration with light-hearted disdain. 'For my part,' he wrote to Amelia, 'I feel full of energy and youthfulness. In fact, I am very pleased about this disagreeable experience. It will enable me to test my nerve and my character.' The days were 'flying by'. He felt, he told his mother, both totally innocent and 'extraordinarily serene' – again using the word so often repeated in the family. But one day, while Maria and Amelia were at the prison visiting him, Nello was handed a typed note. He went first red, then white. It said that he had been sentenced to five years' *confino*, internal exile on a penal island. No reason was given; there was to be no hearing; and he was not told where he would be going.

Three weeks later, Nello followed Carlo south. Amelia and Maria's father were allowed to see him off. Nello appeared on the platform, handcuffed, his head held high, smiling, supremely dignified. Amelia thought 'his expression amazingly pure, his eyes clear, limpid, transparent like those of a child'. As the train pulled out, the guards removed his handcuffs and he waved from the window until they were out of sight, his smile leaving behind it a 'luminous trail'. Gabriele was once again at Rome station to see this second nephew pass by.

Before crossing to the island of Ustica, one of the penal islands off Sicily, Nello spent several days in the Ucciardone prison in Palermo. Conditions – as described by Carlo during his own stay there – were appalling. Built for 1,000 inmates, it was housing 3,500 in 'filth and confusion'. He was put in a cell, empty of even a bed, and given two blankets, a spoon, a straw mattress; his belt, shoelaces, cufflinks, braces and tie were taken away. Bugs of every kind – fleas, lice – were rife. He would not have eaten had another prisoner not shared his food with him. In the jail were entire families of fathers, sons and brothers, picked up by the fascists in their trawl for subversive families in southern Italy. Some had been inside for several years, without trial or contact with their wives and children. In the ever-optimistic style with which the Rosselli brothers seemed determined to handle their misfortunes, a tone so cheerful that it became almost a parody, Nello now wrote to Amelia and Maria: 'I am extremely happy and very proud ... this will enrich my humanity.' He was making friends with the other prisoners and whistling Beethoven symphonies to himself.

Amelia herself was wretched, sleeping badly, worrying. Many of her Florentine acquaintances shunned her and she had resigned from all her positions. No less than her two sons, Amelia was now an outcast.

With Carlo and Nello apparently on their way to indefinite detention on the penal islands, Amelia, Marion and Maria settled down in Via Giusti to await the birth of Marion's baby. Giovanni (from Amendola's Christian name) Andrea (from that of Andrea Costa, hero of the revolutionary left) arrived on 8 June. Amelia was pleased that the child was a boy and said that he looked 'like a miniature Carlo'. His parents nicknamed him 'Mirtillino', 'little blueberry', from the day when, on holiday in the Alps and, having just learnt that Marion was pregnant, they were walking in a field of blueberry bushes and Carlo said: 'You'll see what a beautiful little blueberry we'll make.'

'I have <u>always</u> felt that Carlo's character was that of a hero,' Salvemini wrote to Marion after the birth. 'He is worthy of you, and you are worthy of him. But I cannot bear to think of what is happening to you both ... Kiss your baby for me.' From Colle Isarco in the Trentino, where they had taken Mirtillino to escape the summer heat, Amelia wrote to Nello: 'And I say that not all the sugar in the world would suffice to wipe out the bitterness I feel in my heart.'

By the summer of 1927, the myth that Italy had been on the brink of a Bolshevik takeover, saved by the bold and prescient fascists, had outlived its usefulness. But a new myth was needed, a positive one, and it took the shape of the 'corporative' state, the 'totalitarian' nation – the word originated in Italy – in which, as Mussolini put it, 'everything in the state, nothing outside the state, nothing against the state', a phrase that would be repeated often in the years to come. The time for history was over; it was now a 'time of myths. Everything is yet to be done.' It is against the background of this new Italy – dictatorial, repressive, intolerant – that Carlo and Nello, with their defiance, obstinacy and refusal to conform, stand out.

During the first half-century of free government that followed the Risorgimento, Italy had been a country of clubs of every kind, cooperatives, societies for mutual aid, associations of landowners, of teachers, of civil servants and of students, meeting freely and under a range of political and religious banners. These now had vanished. In their place came thirteen national confederations, six for employers, six for employees, and one for the professional classes, men of letters and artists that was broken down into seventeen separate associations. The right to strike was abolished. In theory, freedom of association was not actually forbidden; in practice, it became almost impossible to function outside the fascist body. *'Italianità'*, *'Romanità'*, *'fascistizzare'* became the words of the day, with Rome as the centre of the world, as it had been and would be again, once centuries of decadence were swept away and Italy returned to the age of Augustinian purity. *'Lei'*, the polite form of address, deemed incompatible with the new bold, unservile Italian, was replaced with *'voi'*. Foreign words acquired new variants: *pied à terre* became *piede a terra*, sandwich, *tra le due*. Fascism loved slogans, superlatives. 'Mussolini is always right' was stencilled on to walls, carved in stones, chalked on to blackboards, along with portraits and photographs of Il Duce, his black eyes staring, his jaw jutting into the air.

In order for this model state to run properly, its citizens had to be educated not only to work in the national interest but to use their leisure time productively, not fritter it away as 'loafers, dandies and drunkards'. Leisure, as the fascists saw it, was no longer an end in itself, but a means of improving mind and body, of acquiring self-discipline and self-control. On no account, said one keen fascist organiser, 'was the worker to be left to his own devices in his free hours'. Under the Dopolavoro, a national agency set up to regulate the hours after work, Italians of all ages were corralled into playing team games, cycling, doing calisthenics, going on group outings, and singing 'Giovinezza' on all possible occasions. (Toscanini, who had originally supported the fascists, refused to play it, saying La Scala was not a beer garden.) Boxing, said Mussolini, was an 'exquisitely fascist means of expression'. A new sport, *volata*, somewhere between football and handball, was introduced as a throwback to Roman times, and therefore truly indigenous and truly fascist. Magazine articles showed pictures of comely peasant women in national dress, and sturdy peasant men 'mirthful', yet 'sober and thrifty in their habits', enjoying 'healthy' and 'praiseworthy' pastimes. Private dance halls were closed 'for reasons of morality'. People were urged to become lean, willowy, sinewy. 'I have no pity', declared Mussolini, 'for the fat.' The new Italian was to be 'Herculean', potent, granite-like, made of steel.

In the wake of the Dopolavoro came the Opera Balilla – the name taken from a young Genoese boy killed in 1746 during the revolt against the Habsburgs. It catered for boys – very young children were made the sons and daughters of the *lupa*, the Roman she-wolf – aged between eight and fourteen, who wore uniforms modelled on the militia – black shirts, grey-green shorts, a fez – and presented arms with little wooden rifles. They took

Small boys marching in their Balilla uniforms

an oath to 'carry out the Duce's orders' and were organised into legions and cohorts. Discipline, said Mussolini, was 'the sun of armies' and Italy was to be served with 'work and with blood'. He was a man ever alert to the magic of words. He sent a mission to England to study Baden Powell's boy scouts and made the king's cousin, the martial Duke d'Aosta, the Opera Balilla's president.

The 'new man' was to be a synthesis of thought and action; the 'new woman', considered incapable of creativity or leadership, was instructed to stay at home and have children. Eager to increase Italy's population, the fascists banned abortion, sex education and all forms of contraception. 'He who is not a father', said Mussolini, introducing a punitive tax on male celibacy, 'is not a man.' In Florence, vice squads carried out a 'pogrom' of prostitutes, roaming the streets with 'the strategy of sportsmen lying in wait for larks in the shrubbery'. Fascist propaganda had two images: the *'donna crisi'* – cosmopolitan, urbane, skinny, hysterical, decadent and sterile – and the *'donna madre'* – rural, devout, tranquil and fertile. In healthy, hardy, fascist Italy, women would never be serious players. They were urged to swim, run, play tennis, hockey, handball and volleyball, but not on any account to throw a discus or lift weights.

To help put across this myriad of often confusing instructions, the fascist propaganda machine took to the airwaves. Radio came

Mussolini inspects a group of young fascist girls

relatively late to Italy, but by 1927 streams of *romanità*, bulletins and directives crackled out across the country, along with martial music, many renderings of 'Giovinezza' and bracing talks by the Duce. Newsletters, magazines, posters all reinforced the message, along with ceremonies, hymns, special dress, punchy slogans, aphorisms, lapidary phrases. If totalitarianism was anathema to Carlo and Nello, this spectacle of unthinking, subservient woman repelled Amelia.

For over a million Italians, fascism and its coercions had already proved too much. They had fled Italy and were living in exile in France, Switzerland, Belgium and South America. Though Mussolini would never be the equal to Hitler or Stalin in brutality and bloodiness, and Italy under fascist rule would never be like Russia or Germany, and though he liked to pretend that he was genial and forgiving, Mussolini was calculating, cruel and vindictive. Two of his mistresses, Margherita Sarfatti and Angelica Balabanoff, later said that he reminded them of a *teppista*, a brawler or hooligan. His own brother, Arnaldo, said that he was very nearly a criminal.

By 1927 – the year in which Churchill, who like much of Europe admired Mussolini's firm hand, announced that 'his only thought is the enduring welfare of his people' – Italy had become a one-party police state. Mussolini was not only prime minister and head of state, but minister of foreign affairs, of the interior, of war, of the navy and airforce and of corporations. Elections had been abolished, the rule of law subverted, teachers regimented, textbooks rewritten, journalists sacked 'for having manifested aversion to the regime' or forced to join a National Syndicate. There were to be no stories of epidemics, national disasters or even bad weather. Content, declared Mussolini, 'is as unstable as the sand formations on the edge of the sea'. Only mass organisation, a nation forced into a fascist political culture, would be able to drag the country out of its regional quarrels and economic divisions.*

---

* Matteotti's assassins, Dumini, Volpi and Poveromo, had finally been tried and sentenced to 5 years, 11 months and 20 days in prison in a trial notable for its bribery, intimidation of witnesses and obfuscation of every kind. Because of a special amnesty, they were already free. Dumini announced he wanted to raise chickens but soon returned to violence.

With the laws of so-called public security, no one was secure any longer: letters were intercepted, phones tapped, houses searched, suspects followed. Spies multiplied, because they were paid well, and because the profession of informer conferred status. Since there were spies everywhere, it had become safer to trust no one. In his drawer, Mussolini kept secret files on his enemies, on the quarrelsome *ras*, constantly jostling for power, on his colleagues and subordinates.

Bocchini, meanwhile, had reorganised the central office of the state police into seven separate divisions, two of which dealt explicitly with politics: Polpol (Divisione Polizia Politica) and DAGR (Divisione Affari Generali e Riservati). Polpol collected and processed information on anti-fascist movements; DAGR coordinated repression through the regional prefects and police commissioners. But in 1927, Bocchini began to put in place a secret political force, OVRA, an acronym deliberately kept mysterious for some years to make people feel anxious and constantly watched. Accountable only to Bocchini and Mussolini, OVRA inspectors had the power to intervene and investigate wherever they saw fit. The first office was set up in Milan, behind the facade of a wine dealer. Its head, Francesco Nudi, was a methodical, painstaking, portly, stubborn man with white whiskers. He was given twenty agents and a generous budget. Files on 'subversives' were opened and constantly updated, and before long there were 100,000 dossiers, arranged according to region, degree of threat, type of opposition, and as much material on character, habits, family, attitudes and sexual orientation as could be gathered. If Polpol was the brain, the central memory in the fight against the anti-fascists, OVRA was its operating branch, entrusted with infiltrating and ultimately crushing, if need be by assassination, Mussolini's enemies.

On 26 May 1927, the Duce told the Chamber of Deputies that public security in Italy was '*quasi perfetta*'. All opposition, he said, had been dealt with; dissidents were 'dispersed, finished, reduced to dust'. There is no place for opposition, he added, 'in a totalitarian regime such as Fascism'.

None of this boded well for Carlo and Parri, awaiting trial for the Turati escape, nor for Nello, facing five years of internal exile, his brief academic career in ruins. Of Mussolini's many enemies it was the intellectuals whom he most feared. With Matteotti, Amendola and Gobetti dead, and Salvemini, Turati, Nenni and many others in exile, only a few prominent ones now remained in Italy. The most admired, Benedetto Croce, had retired to his house in the south and no longer openly opposed the regime. The Rosselli brothers, however, refused to be silenced. Unlike the women, the farmers, the teachers, the factory- and farm-workers, the civil servants, all crushed and supervised, they remained not only alive and still inside Italy but also vocal and absolutely determined; and thus extremely dangerous.

What quickly became known as the 'Trial of the Professors' opened in Savona on 9 September 1927. For reasons of space it was moved from a small courtroom to a larger one. Eleven men were on trial: Parri, Carlo, Oxilia and the others who had helped with Turati's escape, along with Turati himself and Pertini, these last two being tried in absentia. The public prosecutor was asking

Carlo's wife Marion and their first child Giovanni, known as Mirtillino

for five-year prison sentences for their 'openly rebellious behaviour against the powers of the state'. We are, wrote Carlo, 'clutching at straws and at the mercy of a cyclone'.

For several days beforehand, the cafés, streets and squares of Savona were full of groups of people, talking excitedly. Friends and supporters of the accused had arrived from all over Italy. Marion and Amelia were there, as well as Parri's wife Esther and his father, and Alessandro Levi. As she walked into the public gallery, women gave Marion flowers and told her that if the verdict went against Carlo, they would storm the prison.

A few days earlier, Carlo had met his small son for the first time. He told Marion that Mirtillino looked very sweet, but that he probably liked babies when they were a little older. Mirtillino, as it happened, was teething and not at his sweetest, having been kept waiting for several hours to see his father. Marion wrote to Amelia that their meeting had been 'a bit sad'. Carlo was well, a little thinner, 'serene and tranquil and calm', but he had the look of a 'more serious man'. 'I ask myself if they are going to throw away the *whole* of our youth.' He was reading Dostoevsky and Victor Hugo and remarked to Marion that they had now spent almost more time apart than together since their marriage. Amelia told Nello that Marion herself was behaving with 'admirable dignity and courage', though her health was not good and she had had to find a wet nurse for Mirtillino. The two women had grown closer.

From Paris, Turati had sent a long letter to the president of the court. Touching only lightly on his escape, he wrote about the 'insupportable' conditions imposed by the fascists on any Italian who had a 'backbone'. His native land had, he wrote, been turned into one vast prison, in which it had become a crime both 'to remain in dignity or to leave in freedom'. His words on the immorality of the fascists quickly became the theme of the very public trial.

Carlo picked up these words when he spoke, early on, of Turati as a man of the highest moral clarity, 'one of the noblest and most unselfish spirits' Italy had ever produced, obliged to flee the 'desolation' into which the fascists had plunged Italy. It was only fitting, he said, that he, Carlo, the descendant of a Rosselli who had hidden Mazzini when he fled from his persecutors, should save another hero of similar moral stature from 'fascist fury'. Fascism, he declared, 'stands accused by the consciences of all free men'. Since all legal opposition had been suppressed by 'blind violence' and 'unjust laws', 'it has confronted them with the tragic alternatives of either supine acquiescence or starvation or exile.'

He then described, calmly and in great detail, the attacks on himself and his family and the murders of Pilati and Consolo.

Parri, too, spoke eloquently about morality. The months in prison had made him very pale, and his white skin stood out against his very black moustache. As a teacher and a much-decorated war veteran, he told the court, he had never been an exponent of subversion. But his moral aversion to what the fascists were doing to Italy had left him with no choice but to act. The fascists could 'persecute, disperse, strike down' people like him, but his moral disgust would never go away.

Carlo's lawyer, the wiry, white-haired Francesco Erizzo, made a brave, combative speech in which he argued that the laws under which the men were being tried were 'absurd, unconstitutional and persecutory'. Parri's lawyer, Vittorio Luzzatti, another small, modest, middle-aged man, who looked swamped by his huge robes, asked whether Rosselli and Parri might not be, as Mazzini had been, the true 'precursors of a new age of liberty and justice'.

But it fell to Carlo to make the most moving speech, long remembered in the annals of anti-fascism. 'I had a house,' he said, speaking quietly to a totally silent courtroom; 'they destroyed it. I had a magazine: they suppressed it. I had a university chair: I was forced to give it up. I had, as I have today, ideas, dignity, an ideal: for these I have been sent to prison. I had teachers, friends – Amendola, Matteotti, Gobetti – they killed them.' Among the spectators – the shopkeepers, the fishermen, the office-workers who had come to listen to the trial – there were audible sounds of weeping.

On the third day, the prefect of Savona summoned to his office the many journalists present, among them Carlo's English friend Barbara Carter, come to cover the trial for the *Manchester Guardian* and smuggled into court by Marion as her cousin. Under orders clearly issued from Rome, the prefect instructed them to keep their articles very brief, since the trial was 'no longer very interesting'. One young reporter scribbled: '*Hic jacet mortua justizia*', 'Here, dead, lies justice'.

At 6 o'clock on the evening of 13 September, the three judges withdrew. In the dock, the defendants sat smiling and Marion and Esther went over to talk to their husbands. The corridors outside the courtroom were overflowing with people; in the square outside some 2,000 others had gathered and were waiting for the verdict. Seven o'clock came and went; then eight, then nine. No one went home. Shortly before 10 o'clock a bell rang. The door of the judges' chamber opened and the three men filed solemnly back to their places. There was total silence. The president of the court, Pasquale Sarno, read out the verdict: ten months in prison.

There was a gasp, silence; then shouts and cheering, '*Viva! Viva la giustizia! Viva l'Italia di Parri e Rosselli!*' which spread out from the courtroom, along the corridors and into the square. People cried, kissed each other.

The defendants had already been in jail for over eight months; this meant that Carlo had forty days left in prison in Savona. But this was not really the point: in essence, they had been absolved. In the five days of the trial, as Carlo said, 'We really believed that something new had taken place.' The judges had proved that justice was still alive in Italy, and that, as independent magistrates, they had refused to be coerced or bullied. Sarno would later say, with an understandable touch of pride, 'We obeyed only the voice of our conscience.' As one of the fascist lawyers sourly observed, ten trials like this one, 'and the regime is done for'. It was, as Barbara Carter wrote for the *Manchester Guardian*, 'as if a hole had been opened in a sultry sky'.

The defence lawyers too, Erizzo and Luzzatti, had refused to be cowed or silenced. And the fight against fascism had been portrayed, unambiguously, as a matter of morality, honest men speaking out against a dishonest state. Though all too soon such trials would become nothing but rubber stamps for illegal fascist actions, though the Special Tribunal would soon be handing down, behind closed doors, one corrupt and unconstitutional sentence after another, the fact remained that on this one day justice had triumphed. 'These were the last rays', noted one of the men present, 'of a light that was slowly going out.'

The news spread rapidly throughout Italy and abroad, to the exiled Italians all over the world. To his young friends Parri and Carlo, Turati wrote that Italy had been shown not yet to be a 'country of the dead ... You spoke for all those who still dream and breathe and sigh for liberty ... In that moment, you proved that you were the true and real Italy, an oasis in the desert that the nation has become. You defied the barbarians occupying Italy.'

But Mussolini had no intention of letting the men go. Within hours a telegram from Rome reached Savona. Parri and Carlo would not be freed at the end of their sentence. They would be sent instead to spend five years each on one of the penal islands off Sicily. Carlo was surprisingly unfazed. He wrote to his mother that his path ahead was now absolutely clear. Wherever he was, in whatever circumstances he found himself, he would find satisfaction only in taking action, 'which is, and will be, my kingdom'. The year 1927, he told her, would forever be their black year, 'unremittingly dark, in which we all touched the very depths. Now we are rising.' Meanwhile he was 'living in books', discovering new fields of interest and planning a programme of work for his years on the penal islands, and in 'an almost idyllic frame of mind'. But to Turati, revealingly, he wrote something else: 'I am making no plans for the future. However, I don't believe I will stay longer than a year ... Read, twice over, between the lines.'

Carlo was about to follow Nello to the islands. The trial, for him, had been more than just an extraordinary victory over the fascists. It had made him, at the age of twenty-eight, a very public figure, a name to be admired by every anti-fascist of every political persuasion; and one to be still more hated and feared by Mussolini. The accused had become the accusers.

CHAPTER ELEVEN

Il Confino

To the Italians, there was nothing new or very surprising about *il confino*, sending troublesome and unwanted citizens to house-arrest in remote villages or on barren islands off Sicily. The Romans had used these islands as places of exile, as had the Bourbons, who confined their most threatening opponents to a deep, wet, black hole under a barracks on Ustica. The history of banishment in Italy runs up to and through the struggles for independence and beyond, with laws on internal exile for 'enemies of the state' passed, rescinded, reintroduced. Even the relatively liberal prime minister Crispi despatched unruly socialists and anarchists to the island of Lipari at the end of the nineteenth century, until they smuggled out descriptions of appalling conditions and the scandal was such that they were brought back to the mainland.

In 1926, when Mussolini introduced his 'exceptional laws', *il confino*, law number 1848, was thus the perfect solution to his growing number of enemies. It would neutralise, silence, physically remove people without the nuisance of a proper trial. It mattered little whether they kept or changed their views: it was enough that they could do no further harm. 'We will remove these individuals from circulation,' Mussolini told the Chamber of Deputies, 'in the same way that doctors isolate their contagious patients.'

Better still, no actual crime needed to have been committed. Simply 'intending' to commit a 'conspiracy against the state' was deemed subversive, of '*estrema pericolosità*', 'extreme peril', to the safety of Italy. It was enough, after 1926, to mutter or sing offensive words about the Duce, or to whistle at a *squadrista*, to be hauled before the Special Tribunal, after which a sentence of up to five years in some distant outpost was an almost foregone conclusion. One of the first men to leave for the islands was a Roman workman, overheard in his factory saying that he was surprised that no one had yet murdered Mussolini. He was followed, not long afterwards, by thirty-eight Florentine carpenters, cobblers, barbers, typesetters and train-drivers, all men, except for one woman dressmaker, suspected of 'favouring armed insurrection against the state'. All had been members of the Communist Party. After them went a knife-maker from Frosinone, who had inscribed 'W Lenin' on to the handles of four knives.

To read accounts of the perfunctory hearings is to understand how tenacious, brave and innocent were Mussolini's early opponents. Many of them were conducted in absentia, and all were closed to the public. There were few absolutions and the Special Tribunal had retroactive powers. By the spring of 1927 lines of manacled prisoners had become a familiar sight on trains going south, unshaven, dirty, often in striped prison clothes, a number printed on the left side. Among them were Freemasons, socialists, anarchists and above all communists, from the '*più rosse*', the reddest Italian regions in the north: boys of fifteen, grandfathers of seventy-five and the wives of trade-union officials, along with artisans, journalists, writers and many prominent political figures.

Soon, there were well over a thousand men and women in *confino*, scattered between Ustica, Favignana, Lipari, Pantelleria, Lampedusa and Le Tremiti, the harsh, scorched, waterless volcanic islands lying far off the coast of southern Italy and Sicily, from which many of the destitute original inhabitants had long since emigrated. Greeted with a mixture of dismay and curiosity by the few who remained, the visitors brought with them a director for their penal colony, most often a senior policeman, and a number of guards, both policemen and militia. On arriving, the *confinati* were told that if they shed their 'aberrant' ideas and became totally submissive, then they might just be pardoned, through the 'infinite goodness and generosity of Il Duce'.

For many, the initial relief at reaching the islands – after interminable journeys manacled on trains, with halts along the way in verminous, overcrowded jails, medieval in their horror – was overwhelming. No sooner had they stepped on shore, than they were given a rule book which spelt out how they were to behave: find work (where?), conduct themselves obediently, not fight, not wear scruffy clothes, not be rude to the guards and on no account to play cards, frequent bars or discuss politics. The *confinati* were also forbidden to speak a foreign language, to gather in groups of more than three or to wander beyond a small, carefully denoted area. There was no need for a prison: being islands far off the coast, no escape was thought possible. Articles 5, 6, 7 and 8 specified that a *confinato* was not allowed to have a weapon, a means of transport, a radio or a camera. (The 11th commandment, the men joked, was 'Thou shalt not hope.') Failure to obey would result in a one- to three-year prison sentence, to be served after the period of *confino* expired. Once a year, every prisoner was issued with a suit, a pair of shoes, a shirt and a 'military style' pair of underpants.

Carlo had been on Ustica between prison in Como and his trial in Savona. Nello, sent to Ustica early in July 1927, had hoped to find Carlo still there, but by then his older brother had been returned to the north. By the end of the year, however, both young men were on the islands, Nello on Ustica, Carlo on Lipari, each facing five years of discomfort, extremes of cold and heat, scant and unhealthy food, incessant curfews and roll-calls, little water, restrictions of every kind, complete political and intellectual isolation and crushing boredom. All mail was censored, and Bocchini made certain that he had spies planted among the prisoners.

Nello reached Ustica, in chains, on 4 July, to be greeted by Carlo's friends as he stepped off the boat on to the rocky beach. His first but misleading impression of the island was, as he wrote to Amelia, of 'splendid colours and reflections in the water, a picturesque little village, the uninterrupted song of the cicadas, an occasional light passing at night on the horizon, beautiful sunsets'. The single-storey houses had an Arab look to them. While the common criminals and the poorer *confinati* lived in various small dormitories behind heavy wooden doors with padlocks and barred windows, Nello had enough money to pay for his share of what had been Carlo's house, a pretty red building belonging to a priest, in which, as Carlo had written to him, 'I have left a little of my heart.' Sleeping in what had been until a fortnight earlier Carlo's bed, writing at his table, looking around at the 'elegant' objects with which his brother had furnished the room, Nello felt both charmed and saddened. 'They consider me to be his representative,' he told Amelia, 'and his friends enjoy comparing me to him and saying: he is worthy of Carlo.'

One of the first sights that struck the new arrivals was a plaque to a nineteenth-century local hero, reading: 'What could you possibly lack here, which you would find in the big metropolises?' The answer was simple. Ustica, which lay seventy kilometres off the coast of Sicily, a speck in the vast surrounding ocean, lacked almost everything. Its single village, in which lived most of its population of 900, was partly derelict, many of its original inhabitants having emigrated to become the early pioneers in Louisiana. It had no electricity, no wheeled vehicles, no school, no chemist or hospital – though one of the prisoners had once been a nurse and, when not drunk on the execrable local wine, dispensed a few drugs from a chest. There was no tarmac road and no jetty, the original one having long since been washed away in a freak storm, and when cows were occasionally brought over to the island to provide fresh meat, they were made to swim the last few metres before being led up to the single square and tied to one of the very few trees on the island.

Ustica was very dirty: after the prisoners were locked in at nights – the political ones were allowed two hours more freedom than the criminals – pigs were released to clear up the rubbish. If heavy seas prevented the arrival of the thrice-weekly boats, the island ran out of food and water and the inmates were obliged to drink from the heavily polluted wells. When doctors in Palermo saw a patient clearly dying of hunger and disease, so ran the joke, they would ask him if he came from Ustica. There had already been many deaths among a large contingent of Arab prisoners – rebels from the days of the Libyan campaigns – from tuberculosis, dysentery, bronchitis, gastric flu and pneumonia, brought on by being kept fifty to a room. The few survivors crouched on the rocks in their white robes, staring mournfully out to sea.

But the island was not without its charms. Prickly pears grew along the shoreline and over the dry stone walls, and though there were never enough to go round, the rich volcanic soil produced peas, beans, lentils, courgettes, capers and cucumbers, which could grow to almost a metre in length. Melons did well, as did small, sweet grapes, harvested, wrote Nello, 'as in Virgil's time'. In the autumn, the rocky ground was covered in the delicate white flowers of the asphodels. And if most of the houses had floors of beaten earth and dung, some of them had coats of brightly coloured paint, and in summer delightful geckos prowled across their walls. Along the dusty streets, a special crossbreed of grey donkeys wandered at will. Spring brought nightingales and on clear days you could see Etna. The sea was the centre of life, its contours, its moods, its horizons; the *confinati* gathered sea snails and urchins along the seashore and gazed out across the water, dreaming of freedom. But when the winds got up, and howled over the little houses, it seemed as if island and sky were as one and their homes might be blown away in the gale.

Having settled himself in Carlo's room, Nello took stock. 'We read, we discuss, we grumble and sleep,' he wrote to the Ferreros in one of his dozen or so weekly letters. 'This is our life.' It was, he said, 'neither exhilarating nor boring; rather, it is a peaceful flow of equal days, their monotony broken by the vivacity and variety of thoughts about good friends, about new work, about the past.' He was not idle. Among the first *confinati* to reach Ustica in 1926 had been the communist leader Antonio Gramsci who, sentenced to 20 years, 4 months and 5 days for calling for a general strike, had arrived manacled and chained with his few belongings stuffed in a pillowcase. One of Gramsci's first acts had been to start a library in a whitewashed room and arrange classes for his fellow *confinati*. Ustica, he wrote later, was a 'kind of paradise of personal freedom' compared to what came later.

The men who arrived with him had since been teaching the local inhabitants to read and write, while giving talks on all possible subjects. Nello immediately volunteered to teach a course on the Risorgimento, thinking it might become part of a new book that he was planning, and offered to work in the library, which was already well-furnished with books sent by friends. The police and militia, baffled by all these scholars, asked the prefect in Palermo to send them some 'intelligent guards', able to follow what was going on.

The well-organised communists, some of whom had taken to wearing high-collared Russian-style tunics with embroidered borders, had started communal kitchens in order to make the most of the little food and money by buying collectively, directly from producers. The political prisoners tended to eat according to their party affiliations, the criminals by the region of Italy they came from. When the 'maximalists' were found to be eating with the 'unitarians', Nello joked, there was talk of socialist unification. He started a mess himself, and invited a Masonic friend of his uncle Ernesto to join it. Antonio Bordello, a communist engineer from Naples, was fascinated by astrophysics and held Socratic sessions on the stars; he was also an excellent cook and his mess was much in demand, though the one run by the men from Emilia was considered the finest. 'With an engineer for cook, a lawyer for scullery maid, a jurist for waiter . . .' sang the *confinati*. Another communist had turned a field into a football pitch and his matches aroused much passion. A third had asked his family to send vaccines against typhus; others had got their families to send olive oil and smoked hams.

Giuseppe Scalarini, the former political cartoonist on *Avanti!*, arrested for his irreverent depictions of fascism, asked his wife to bring games and toys for the local children. Later, he hid his drawings of Ustica inside the stuffing of his daughter's dolls, in packets of medicine and even inside a chicken, announcing that it was a special hen 'stuffed with the islands'. One boat brought a dentist, who, having no instruments, was forced to dig out rotten teeth with a nail. The clock in the square, long silent, had been started again by a *confinato* watchmaker and plans were afoot to bring over a radio from the mainland, the only receiver or transmitter on the island being limited to morse and off-limits to all but the police. And this cooperative prisoner life, first started on Ustica among this band of exceptional men, was beginning to spread to the other penal islands.

Nello was captivated by his companions, particularly Carlo's friend Bauer, whom he was beginning to regard as another older brother. 'Everyone is extremely kind,' he wrote to Amelia. 'There is a sense of instinctive solidarity between the *confinati*; all formality has been abolished, and we are friends at once, even before we learn each other's names.' When a photograph of Mirtillino, the nephew he had never seen, arrived in a letter, he carried it round on a series of visits. 'Luckily', he wrote to Gina Lombroso, 'we are adaptable people and not at all ill-tempered.'

Nello's house on Ustica with a crowd of *confinati*

Best of all, he had received permission for Maria to join him. One of the anomalies of this odd form of punishment was that, providing you had sufficient funds, you were allowed to bring your family to live with you. When not seeking out and making friends with the few women prisoners or the wives of other *confinati*, so that Maria would have female company, Nello started searching for a suitable home. There were few to choose from, though he was offered plenty of pigsties and chicken coops, hastily cleared out by islanders eager to make money from their new visitors. He settled on the ground floor of a square whitewashed house in the lower part of the village, with a terrace overlooking the sea, a barracks on one side and a woman who raised chickens on the other. To his mother-in-law Luisa, he wrote: 'I am waiting for my little wife with fantastic impatience.'

'On a fine autumn morning', as Nello later described it, Maria arrived on Ustica. It was 12 September 1927. The only way you could tell the seasons apart, he noted, was by a certain freshness in the air, because the trees in the square were evergreen and mild temperatures lasted well into the winter. Maria, now twenty-two, had not been well and had been ordered to rest and take the sun.

Having successfully cleared their new house of cockroaches, and come to terms with the fact that the lavatory was in the kitchen next to the stove, she took up a position on the terrace under an awning, or went to sit on the rocks to watch Nello bathe between the permitted hours of ten and eleven, on alternate days, under the watchful eyes of a patrolling boat of militiamen. 'You might say', Nello wrote to his mother, 'that we are still enjoying our honeymoon.' What Maria made of the women on Ustica is not known, but the community was not without social niceties. As a *confinato* wrote to his wife and daughter, due to join him shortly, 'Bring what you have in the way of good and elegant dresses . . . the colony of *confinati*'s wives does not scorn a certain richness and ostentation in their dress.' An elderly local woman was heard to say: 'Ustica has become a little Paris.'

Though herself a suspect, as the mother of convicted anti-fascists, Amelia remained at liberty. Eager to see Nello and Maria, she requested, and was granted, leave to visit them. No more than her sons, however, did she think of complaining. Accustomed to the care of cooks and maids, she took to the simple life with a kind of humorous pleasure. 'If anyone had ever told me that I would see *mammà* with an apron going into ecstasies over four meatballs,' wrote Nello to their friend Gina Lombroso, 'I would have thought it a joke.' Foraging for food in the surrounding countryside was an essential part of the *confinato*'s life, and Amelia was soon roaming the hillsides in search of edible grasses, keeping an eye out for a fishing boat, which might mean fresh fish. Unlike the *confinati*, Amelia could go where she liked, but each time she crossed the invisible barriers beyond which Nello could not stray, it reminded her of just what it meant to be so circumscribed. Being sent to the *confino*, she would later write, was like 'slipping without noise into a marsh, which slowly absorbs, swallows, suffocates, kills with no other weapon than silence'. Though the three of them, Amelia, Nello and Maria, lived together in amiable, uncomplaining harmony, Amelia did not always share her son's boundless optimism.

Maria was once again pregnant. She seemed to take well to this harsh exile, though she was always hungry. There being no gynaecologist on the island, one was summoned from Palermo. He arrived so sick from four hours of rough seas that he took to his bed. As Fernande Salvemini, who had taught Maria as a girl, wrote to their mutual friends the Ferreros, 'It's surprising how much strength there is in Maria, who seems so fragile – strength, rectitude and goodness.' Like Marion, Maria was full of resolve. Nello, Amelia wrote to Zia Gì, 'remains as good-tempered as ever. What wonderful company, this son of mine.' The weather stayed warm and they had made the house 'pretty and comfortable'. On the days that the boat was due, she watched its arrival from the terrace thinking about 'the very thin thread that links us to the world'. On Nello's twenty-seventh birthday, they celebrated with chocolates sent by Zia Gì, and a 'disgusting bottle of pseudo horrendous champagne' and wished each other 'many hopes and many dreams'. This was, wrote Nello later, a 'truly happy period of our lives'.

In Paris, Turati was celebrating his own birthday. He was seventy. At the party given for him, he raised his glass to Carlo and Nello, 'the most worthy, the few still truly alive: they are *nostri maestri* – our masters'.

However, Ustica was never free of tensions. When the mood was peaceful, sounds of the mandolin and the guitar could be heard coming from the rooms occupied by the Roman and the southern prisoners. But as the island filled up with ever more feisty communist, anarchist and socialist men and women arriving to serve their sentences – to be packed into small, stifling dormitories into which the rain dripped ceaselessly, locked in from dusk to dawn and plagued by lice – tempers frayed. When the dates for transfers or amnesties approached, the *confinati* gathered in agitated groups in the village square. Because there were so few women, there was a growing number of homosexual relationships, men taking the names of women – 'Carmen' and 'Tosca' were two of the most common – and being referred to as 'the criminals' tarts'. On an allowance of 10 lire a day, always hungry, prisoners used the money to drink instead of eat. Even one of the administrators admitted that the rations 'would have made Gandhi lose weight'. There were political rows, fights, jealous tantrums, after which the culprits were punished. With work available for barely 30 out of the 500 or so men, idleness made the others envious and angry. Militiamen were ordered to stay close, listen to conversations, pick up incriminating talk. Nello and Maria, safe in their house with sufficient money, were fortunate.

One of the first directors of the penal colony was a level-headed man called Sortino, who recognised the importance of the school and the classes in keeping people busy. But one day a Roman anarchist, Spartaco Stagnetto, reported witnessing one of the common criminals rob another, and he was knifed in his own mess. Had there been a proper doctor, Stagnetto would probably have survived. As it was, he died, and his funeral became the occasion for open hostility between prisoners and guards, stirred up by the militia, who brought hand grenades with them to the graveside. Sortino, judged too lenient, was removed. In his place came a far more ruthless figure, Michele Buemi, who had little liking for the *confinati* and took great pleasure in enforcing petty rules. A brutal, thuggish centurion, Alberto Memmi, was appointed to run the militia. One of their first acts was to put in a request for more weapons, including machine guns. The *confinati*, Buemi complained to the *questore* in Palermo, were doing 'exactly as they pleased ... and boasting openly about being in a holiday resort rather than under house-arrest'. The prefect warned Rome that there were signs of a 'dangerous common front' of anti-fascists on Ustica.

What particularly annoyed Buemi and Memmi was that men were now wandering around with books by Hegel and Nietzsche, and that between them the '*confinati eccellenti*', the educated ones, were running a very efficient settlement. Memmi sent his men to sit in on the classes and listen for seditious talk. Tensions rose further when a chemistry professor was overheard describing how certain substances, when put together, caused explosions. His students had also been heard speaking English and German 'openly and freely'.

The night of 10 October was particularly stormy. The wind howled. There was a rumour that a 'foreign' ship had been seen and the dormitories were full of excited chatter. Buemi and Memmi decided that the moment had come to act. Police and militiamen were despatched to search the rooms. Men, protesting, were led out and made to stand in the storm. Women were threatened with guns. Children cried. Next morning, thirty-nine of the supposed ringleaders were manacled, chained and rowed out to where the water boat, full of carabinieri, was waiting to take them back to Palermo. Because of the heavy seas, the little boats pitched and banged into each other until the captain called out that he would not transport anyone unless the chains were removed.

Cleverly, Buemi had selected the intellectual 'elite', and now accused them of plotting to overcome the guards and escape to the mainland on the 'foreign boat'; for good measure he added that he knew of a plot to poison his coffee and that of his men. One of those singled out was Amadeo Bordiga, one of the founders of the Italian Communist Party. There were fears that Nello might be included after he was accused of making a 'very violent speech' and inciting a group of communists, anarchists and Freemasons to rise up and kill Mussolini, but in the event he was spared. Next day, 272 other people, named as accomplices, were transferred to the island of Ponza; 17 more were sent to join their friends in the Ucciardone prison in Palermo.

The upshot of this turbulent night was surprisingly fair. Though it took some months, an honest and impartial magistrate declared that the whole incident had been 'absurd', dreamt up in the fevered minds of 'ill-intentioned informers'. The 'foreign' boat was found to have been a French vessel, the *Orléans*, which had been in too great a difficulty in the rough seas to answer the semaphore requesting information. The unfortunate and wrongly accused men were allowed to complete their sentences without further punishment. But Ustica itself had changed. All classes were now closely supervised, and every restriction was enforced; it had become a wary, tightly controlled place.

On 8 January 1928 Amelia left the island; she was worried about Marion, alone with Mirtillino in Rome. 'But what is to be done?' she asked. 'It's impossible to divide myself in two.' Maria and Nello stood on the new dock, recently completed by the prisoners, and watched the boat draw away. 'The intimacy of these last two months', Nello wrote to Zio Giù, 'has been so close and so warm that it doesn't seem possible that it has come to an end.' His grief at her going was made worse, as he wrote to her, by the fact that 'I feel a huge sense of pity for your sad life of sacrifice.' Maria's mother Luisa had arrived to take Amelia's place and Maria was now safely well beyond the third month of her pregnancy. 'We are beginning to breathe a little,' Nello wrote. 'We NEED at least this to go well.'

As it happened, luck from an unexpected source was about to befall them. Before coming to Ustica, Amelia had been to Rome to see Gioacchino Volpe, the director of the Scuola di Storia Moderna e Contemporanea. She knew that Volpe admired his young protégé, and that Nello was attached to him. But Volpe, once a man of pronounced liberal views, had opted to serve the fascist state and was acutely conscious that his every move was closely watched; one mistake would cost him dear. He received Amelia at home. Volpe's manner, she wrote later, perfectly reflected the uncomfortable position in which he found himself: it was clear that he wanted to help, but equally that he feared that any word of sympathy might be used and distorted. His facial expression was 'that of the liberal' and at one point she even saw a glimmer of tears in his eyes; but his words, 'composed and measured, belonged to the fascist'. Tentatively, Volpe proposed that Nello should write a letter explaining that he was just a historian, with no political interests . . . Amelia stopped him. Nello, she told Volpe, would never apologise or beg. It was not in his nature. However, she added somewhat sternly, it was in Volpe's power to see that justice was done. Leaving his house, she concluded that no more would be heard.

To his uncle Gabriele, who had intervened on his behalf, Nello wrote that he considered his university career over. 'It's a miracle that it lasted so long!' A long letter of comfort arrived from Carlo. 'I want you to feel me close by, by your side, solidly with you . . . on this perilous, the most perilous, road that you have chosen.' He told his younger brother that he fully agreed with his decision not to ask for clemency: 'To be at peace with oneself is the premise for happiness.'

But Volpe's more generous instincts prevailed. He asked the university president, the distinguished and very elderly Senator Boselli, to petition Mussolini to free Nello to pursue his research; and he got in touch with Gabriele Pincherle to suggest that he, as a senator and Nello's uncle, petition Mussolini for Nello to be sent somewhere he could continue his important studies. Boselli duly wrote to Mussolini, pointing out that Nello's family were

prominent people, that his eldest brother Aldo had been a decorated war hero and that his wife was pregnant. Mussolini, who
underlined these last words, sent back word to say that Nello
could indeed be freed – providing he wrote in person to ask for
a pardon. Boselli informed Nello that he now needed to write a
letter in which he promised henceforth to concentrate only on his
research. It was to be a letter of submission, even if only implicit.
At the same time, Volpe wrote to Nello that he needed to be
tactical. Why not put aside his scruples, undertake to engage in
'no practical activity' of a 'political nature', or show any 'open
hostility' to the regime?

But Nello was not to be swayed.

Much as Carlo's speech at Savona would go down in anti-
fascist history, so would Nello's reply to Boselli. His words were
brusque and clear. He would never, he told the president, 'renounce
the fundamental rights and duties of a citizen', for to do so would
be to 'voluntarily paralyse my brain and my heart'. Furthermore,
he was convinced that no real research was possible 'if it is not
conducted by a free spirit in a free atmoshphere'. A self-censoring
historian was an absurdity. Boselli felt that he had no alternative
but to forward this letter to Mussolini. All would now depend
on the Duce's mood.

The reply came in the form of a letter from the under-secretary
in the Ministry of the Interior, Giacomo Suardo. Its tone was
sharp. Nello's letter was full of 'unacceptable views' and falsehoods. Furthermore, it bore no trace of submission. However, he
went on, Mussolini had made the 'generous and high-minded'
decision to award him conditional liberty, in the hope that his
spell in *confino* had taught him the 'most elementary duties of a
good citizen'. On 29 January 1928, Nello learnt that he was to
be set free.

'The autumn passed, the winter passed,' Nello wrote later;
'when the swallows returned I was freed.' The day came when
he and Maria, accompanied to the jetty by their friends, climbed
on to the boat to take them back to the mainland. Both of them
had tears in their eyes. Nello felt that in Ustica he had learnt a
great deal, been 'formed' and made many 'unforgettable' friends.
As the boat pulled away, they looked back at their companions,
at the little white church, the low houses, the rocky coastline;

then the whole island came into view, 'like a black whale'. Against all the odds, they had been very happy there.

A young militiaman, going on leave, sat down next to them and began to play his guitar and to sing. Maria, who suffered from seasickness went below. But Nello continued to sit on deck, in the cold wind, watching two seagulls dipping and flapping above him. Later, he wrote to a friend: 'Balance: two months in prison, seven in *confino*, a child on the way, a vast and incomparable experience lived through, the relationship with my wife become intimate and profound. Future? Uncertain.'

CHAPTER TWELVE

The Island of Winds

On a windy morning towards the end of December 1927, a young *confinato* lawyer called Francesco Fausto Nitti, nephew of the former prime minister, saw a man in the usual manacles and handcuffs step ashore in Lipari's Marina Corta. He had 'an open and pleasant face, he was *gigantesco*, and his blue eyes smiled from behind his glasses'.

This was Carlo. 'I arrived into a glory of light and sun,' he wrote to Amelia the next day, 'and was greeted extremely warmly.' In a postcard to his uncle Gabriele, he wrote that 'Lipari is very civilised and leaves nothing to be desired from a material point of view ... The climate is spring-like ... After a year of greyness, this return to life is delicious.' The port of Lipari was both 'affluent and clean', there were four chemists', several well-stocked groceries and butches, and a clockmaker, 'all in all a veritable Eden' compared to Ustica. He felt drunk, he said, on the sea, the sky, the light, the overwhelming joy in being able to move around freely again. Like Nello, he was determined to see only the best of things.

Within days, Carlo had found one floor of a house to rent on the edge of town, a whitewashed villa with views over the mountains and the sea, surrounded by cypresses, palm trees, eucalyptus, medlars and lemons, and bushes of capers with purple leaves. It reminded him of Tuscany. It had a terrace with a flowering vine over the pergola, and a garden large enough to grow vegetables and flowers and to keep chickens – though it lacked a lavatory, and his landlord had not provided sheets, blankets or plates. From the terrace you could smell the orange blossom, and there was a tortoise creeping through the undergrowth. Writing to Parri, still in prison in the north, he said that he was revelling in this new form of detention with an 'unprecedented intensity . . . everything pleases me.' He had applied to have Marion and Mirtillino join him and was busy equipping the house for their arrival.

Lipari was generally considered the best of the *confino* islands. Home in classical antiquity to Aeolus, King of the Winds, it is the largest of the Aeolian Islands, fifteen kilometres long and nine kilometres wide, ten times the size of Ustica, with two volcanic peaks and thermal baths said to be the oldest in Italy. In 1927, half of its population of 7,500 lived in the port of Lipari, which had two main streets and a castle, built on a rock above the water on Greek and Roman remains, a Norman cathedral, a bishop's palace and four other churches. The rest were scattered in hamlets on the hillsides, or around a second port, Canneto, a few kilometres to the east, where they worked in the obsidian and pumice industries. Though in autumn and winter Aeolus's winds could blast and howl, whirling up blinding clouds of dust, the climate was mild and the mountains very green. There were no cars and very little electricity. The Café Eolo showed silent movies.

But Lipari, like Ustica, was a place of tensions. When, in the spring of 1926, medieval houses round the castle were demolished to make way for two vast dormitories for convicts, a cortege of angry women had marched up the steep flight of steps, occupied the new buildings and rung the cathedral bells. They wanted no more convicts on the island, and brought with them peasants armed with hoes and rakes.

All through 1927, the locals watched Mussolini's political enemies land at the Marina Corta twice a week from the *Adele* or the *Etna*, the richer among them, such as Carlo, to rent houses, the poorer sent to occupy the dormitories by the castle. Among them was a growing number of dissident fascists, punished for various misdeeds and soon ostracised by the anti-fascists as the *'gruppo merda'*, the shit group. When there was trouble, these men were locked behind bars in a prison block with four large cells, suffocatingly hot in summer, arctic in winter. But the islanders loved their distinguished and educated inmates, greeting the anarchists, socialists, communists and Freemasons with enthusiasm as they shuffled and rattled off the boats in their chains. Nervously expecting taunts of 'traitor' and 'renegade', the political prisoners were instead given fruit and glasses of the excellent local wine, made from Malvasia grapes which thrived on the volcanic soil.

Just a few weeks before Carlo's arrival, there had been an uproar when two *confinati*, hoping thereby to secure pardons, had informed the director of the penal colony of a plot. The authorities used the occasion to strip the very well-furnished library, run by a *confinato* tax inspector, of many of its books. Anything with the word 'revolution'– including Carlyle's *History of the French Revolution* – was taken away, along with everything Russian, and all works written by *malpensante* authors such as Voltaire, Mazzini, Upton Sinclair and Anatole France. Bernard Shaw was allowed to stay. Many of these books had originally been smuggled in by the families of the *confinati*, hidden in the bottom of their suitcases.

Whether in their rented houses or in the castle dormitories, the *confinati* were allowed out at seven in the morning, attended a roll-call at eight, when their daily allowance of 10 lire a day would be handed out, and then allowed to roam 'free' – within a tightly circumscribed area, watched over by patrols, militia and policemen from forty-three watchtowers positioned at regular intervals. At dusk, two blasts of a trumpet sounded the curfew. Those living in rented houses were allowed to choose between having peepholes in their windows and doors, open at all times, or being subjected to two-hourly roll-calls all through the night, when militiamen would pound on their doors.

When the boat from Milazzo arrived with new *confinati* and the mail, the port was briefly closed. Otherwise the prisoners strolled up and down the Corso Vittorio, went down to the port to look at the boats, attended classes started by *confinati* teachers and professors, and ate in each other's canteens. On Lipari the most popular kitchen was that run by Matteotti's former cook. In summer, swimming was allowed, the *confinati* from one beach, the convicts from another. Occasionally, the director gave permission for men to walk with their families up the donkey tracks into the hills. When the boat brought newspapers, their lucky recipients would be followed around by a line of hopeful readers, though there was little in the press that did not follow the Fascist Party line. The former mayor of Orvieto, a socialist, wrote a hymn about the *confinati*, describing them as the '*cavalieri dell'umanità*', 'knights of humanity', deported for their ideals. Though forbidden, it was sung, loudly, on all possible occasions.

But Carlo was not like Nello. While Nello's sunnier nature meant that he searched hard for ways to make the best of all misfortunes, Carlo railed. Within days of reaching Lipari, the delights of semi-freedom had given way to anger and grief. '*Confino* is a cell without walls,' he wrote to Marion, 'all sky and sea. The patrols of soldiers act as walls, walls of flesh and bone, not cement and stone. The desire to break out becomes an obsession ... No, no, I was not born to be shut up in a chicken coop.'

Carlo had few illusions about his own character. In one of his most candid and self-reflective letters, he wrote to a friend that he was 'thirsty for action, concrete, realistic; my whole being is orientated towards it. My happiest days are those of frenetic activity ... rooted in the overpowering certainty of facts.' He would never be a historian like Nello, he added, but he hoped that some small act of his might one day make history. Had things turned out differently, he would have lived quietly and happily, teaching, writing, enjoying family life. 'But at times like these, when the most fundamental principles of life are at stake, I am drawn towards all the beauty and importance of a life of battle.' Three days later, exploring another aspect of himself, he wrote to Parri: 'My inner life and my outward acts are very tightly linked to the surroundings in which I find myself ... That's to say that I am, I think, I act, I react in terms of the people around me ... I am, to the very tips of my fingers, a political animal, for whom a life without politics would have neither sense nor light.' Did this side of his character, he asked, show a 'dangerous weakness'? All Lipari's little freedoms served only to make his captivity more bitter.

Carlo was, however, as gregarious as he was political, and he immediately set about making friends among the 500 or so men, and the few women, sent to Lipari as enemies of Mussolini, a task made easier by his genial manner and his obvious sympathy for those in difficulty. One of the first was Nitti, the young lawyer who had watched him arrive. Like Carlo, he was twenty-eight, a thin-faced, dark-haired man with round spectacles in heavy, dark frames. Having studied law in Rome, he had been involved with a group of anti-fascist students, and made a pilgrimage to the ditch in which Matteotti's body was found; he had subsequently befriended Matteotti's widow, Velia, under whose windows fascist patrols sang ribald ditties. He had been working in a bank when he was arrested and charged with 'subversive acts' and had arrived on Lipari nine months earlier, after a long journey on trains shunted around Italy, locked up in the little steel boxes with no light or air in which prisoners were transported. In the state archives in Rome there is a copy of the prefect's report on him. Nitti, it claimed, was 'an individual as dangerous for his propaganda as for his actions'. He and Carlo soon became close.

Another new friend was the former parliamentary deputy for Sardinia, lawyer and co-founder of the *Partito Sardo d'Azione*, which was calling for regional antonomy. Emilio Lussu was in his late thirties; with his receding brown hair, small moustache, pointed beard and stern stare, he had the look of a Russian revolutionary. He seldom smiled. Returning after the war to his home in Sardinia with four medals for valour, he had tried to tackle the high illiteracy, malaria and backwardness into which the war years had further plunged his already impoverished island, but in so doing had come up against the hostility of the fascists. There were mutterings that he should be lynched.

On 31 October 1926, a mob of *squadristi*, carrying staves, ropes and chains, had followed him home. Lussu had managed to get inside and take refuge in his study on the first floor. But the fascists broke down the door and one climbed on to the balcony. Seeing the man's shadow, Lussu fired his old hunting gun. The young assailant fell back and later died. Lussu was arrested and spent several months in prison in Cagliari, where he developed pleurisy, and then began to spit blood. Mussolini had pressed for a charge of manslaughter. But as with Carlo and Parri, Lussu had come before a rare, honest judge. He was found to have acted in self-defence and pronounced innocent. But not so innocent as to avoid a five-year sentence on the penal islands as an 'incorrigible opponent of the regime'.

Lussu, still coughing blood, had taken a room in a house in Lipari largely destroyed in a recent earthquake, its floors perilously sloping; but it had a large terrace surrounding the whole building. He had been invited to join the republican canteen – his political allegiances lay with the republicans – but in the winter of 1927 his health remained precarious and he was seldom well enough to leave the house.

Three days after his arrival, Carlo was taken to meet Lussu. He found the Sardinian creeping around his semi-derelict room, coughing. They had barely exchanged a few polite sentences about the Risorgimento when Lussu told him that he dreamed of saving himself from the 'poisonous, lethargic influence of this isolated, unfree existence'. He longed only to escape and spoke with what Carlo would later describe as 'frenzy . . . [escape] at all times and in all tenses, past, present, future and conditional. Escape by boat, motorcraft, steamer, airplane, air balloon. Escape, escape, escape.'

But no one had ever escaped from Lipari. Or, indeed, from any of the penal islands. They were too remote, too well guarded, and censorship was absolute.

Just the same, the two new friends agreed to become what they laughingly referred to as a Club della Fuga. Lussu and Carlo were founder members, along with Nitti. A fourth was Gioacchino Dolci, a thin, short, very dark young Roman of twenty-three, with a laughing, guileless manner. Dolci had spent much of his childhood in an orphanage in Trastevere, before becoming the secretary of the youth wing of the Republican Party. Forced to flee to Paris, where he had survived by washing dishes, he had foolishly returned to Italy in pursuit of a girl, been arrested, sent first to Ustica, where Gramsci befriended him, and then to Lipari. Dolci was hungry for learning, interested in everything that came his way. In the Club della Fuga he found not just friends but mentors. 'Dolci does gymnastics with ideas,' noted Carlo.

Mussolini's Special Tribunal was hard at work, sentencing dissidents and despatching them to the penal islands. Lipari was filling up. By the spring of 1928, the number of *confinati* had reached 900 – both political and criminal – guarded by 400 militia Blackshirts and a contingent of policemen. While the islanders were prepare to tolerate the police, many of whom were local men, they were wary of the militia, arrogant young men from other parts of Italy who strutted about, refused to pay their bills, and preyed on the young girls. The Liparesi continued to look on the political *confinati* with a certain respect and admiration, called them '*galantuomini*' and gazed at the soberly dressed '*onorevoli*'– the honourables – as they took their afternoon stroll up and down the port or sat in the Eolo drinking coffee, deep in conversation.

Not long before Carlo's arrival, the boats from Milazzo in Sicily had brought some fifty of the Aventine secessionists – arrested and sent before the Special Tribunal the moment they lost their parliamentary immunity. With them came Luigi Basso, secretary of Turati's party, a small, chubby man with curling whiskers who sauntered along impeccably turned out in a dark suit, a bow tie and starched collar, accompanied by his formidable wife in a lace stomacher. Domizio Torrigiani, Grand Master of the Freemasons, had also arrived, a man considered so dangerous that he was always accompanied on his walks by two guards carrying guns. Since he had been described by the local priest as 'the brother of the devil', a little girl, watching him alight from the boat, marvelled that he was only a man. Torrigiani was famously mean, but cultured and shrewd. His health was poor and every evening, as he walked the 500 metres one way and 500 metres the other, conversing with all around him, he coughed and coughed. The *confinati* called him the 'king of the road'; the locals thought he was a magician.

Among the newcomers were many communists and anarchists – who between them made up the great majority of the *confinati* – but also men and women arrested for 'equivocal behaviour', or for smuggling, or for supplying birth-control devices. They came from every corner of Italy, from the Veneto down to the toe of Sicily, lawyers and journalists, teachers and farmers, metalworkers and fishermen, woodworkers, carpenters and bricklayers, drivers, barbers, coachmen. For many of them, *confino* would become their education, their university, the place where they learnt subjects they had never before heard of, and where their political understanding was sharpened. It was in the *scuola dei confinati*, they would later say, that they learnt to think.

And among the political prisoners there were women too, but never very many of them. The archives in Rome hold files on every individual sent to the *confino*. Some are fat, with dozens of documents containing details of arrests, sentences, supposed crimes, changes of address. Others contain just a single page. The women's files are very thin. On Lipari, when Carlo arrived, there was Florinda Salvatelli, a thirty-seven-year-old peasant woman from Monterotondo, arrested for singing a rude song about Mussolini and described as an 'ignorant, foul-mouthed . . . disgusting subversive'. Vera Santoni, twenty-six, was a Florentine dressmaker brought up by anarchist parents. She was arrested when she went to lay flowers – together with seventeen other people – on the grave of a communist killed by *squadristi*. She was described as pretty, intelligent and 'eloquent', but active in the 'Bolshevist campaign.' At forty-two, Agata Bertollini was one of the older women, of 'staunchly republican' views, accused of receiving packets of anti-fascist literature from her brother in New York. Agata was the mother of five young children, and her husband was struggling to keep their farm going without her. In a letter to Mussolini, she begged him to pardon her, 'with my hands joined in prayer and on my knees'. There is nothing in the archives to indicate that he did.

And, as the months passed, the boats brought a growing number of wives and children of the *confinati*, many deeply relieved, despite their small, cramped, dark lodgings, that here at least they were safe after months of constant fear of physical attack by the Blackshirts. 'This new life', wrote a woman called Giaele Angeloni, who arrived on Lipari with her new husband Mario, 'felt like liberation.' A school was set up for the children, though Bocchini sent word that it be taught by 'persons of certain fascist faith'.

Because many of these political prisoners were intelligent, energetic and very bored, they set about devising ways to pass the time. A man called Paolo Fabbri opened a laundry, using the water in the cistern on his terrace and sending his fifteen-year-old son Pietro round the houses to collect the *confinati*'s dirty clothes. His wife worked in one of the communal kitchens and she and some of their friends also did the ironing. (When Pietro took Carlo's laundry back to him on Wednesday mornings, he always found a biscuit waiting for him.) Ernesto Sagno from Salerno made doughnuts, which he sold from a basket along the Corso. Filippich, from Trieste, mended bicycles; Ceruti, from Como, opened a carpenter's shop; Guatelli from Parma arranged for deliveries of Parmesan; Tagli, who had been a famous maître d'hôtel, took charge of the republican canteen. Professor Lazzarini, an expert on Dante, gave talks on *The Divine Comedy*. Mario Magri, D'Annunzio's adjutant, organised swimming races, ball games in the water, and boxing matches, which were invariably won by one of the two anarchists from Civitavecchia. The director of the penal colony, Cannata, was a civilised and fairly liberal man and he looked approvingly on all these activities, but some of the militia were already beginning to complain that it was all too lax, and that drunken *confinati* could be found wandering around at night.

Every Thursday afternoon, at 4 o'clock, a small group met at Carlo's house for French conversation under the orange trees. One of the circle was Ettore Albini, theatre critic of *Avanti!*, arrested for his role in Turati's escape. They drank glasses of Malvasia, bought by Carlo from the local priest. He had already acquired a reputation for tactful generosity, and the penurious among his students would be given food and a little money to take away. Another couple known for their generosity were Pasquale Binazzi and his wife Zelmira, joint former editors of an anarchist magazine. Binazzi was a small, ruddy-faced man, with his hair *en brosse* and a piercing stare; Zelmira was tall, slim and elegant and kept everyone's spirits up by singing old ballads in the sweet, pure voice of a young girl. The Binazzis were known as the 'true apostles of anarchy'.

It was an odd existence, free but not free; and no one would ever forget these strange yearning years on Italy's most southern islands.

On 18 January 1928, Marion arrived on Lipari with Mirtillino. He was seven months old, a happy baby who seldom cried. Carlo had never yet spent a night in the same house as his son. He was much taken by his small boy, 'so sweet, so lively, so calm, so amusing – enough to gladden the heart of a father theoretically immune to the charm of babies'. The boy's smiles, he said, made him realise how much Mirtillino would mean to them all. 'I believe that he has a special feeling for me: he must have understood, at last, that I am, and will be, set in stone, someone in his life.' But he was not without apprehension: could anyone as involved as he was in 'humanity' really be a good father? Carlo had asked Dolci, who was always short of money, to whitewash the house and paint a coloured frieze along the walls of Mirtillino's bedroom. He was to share it with a Tuscan nanny,

Maria Porcellotti, whose fiancé was a *confinato* anarchist from Pistoia and who had herself been declared 'exuberant and troublesome' by the fascists.

Life quickly settled into a routine. They rose early, in time for Carlo to attend the 8 o'clock roll-call. He had managed to find a piano and both he and Marion were taking lessons, and he had also recruited a newly arrived political prisoner to teach him German. Marion agreed to give three English classes a week to Nitti and two other men; they found her very strict. Though the soil was sandy and somewhat poor, and when it rained the earth turned to mud, they planted a vegetable garden. Carlo was taking his turn in the kitchen, in the 'cakes department.' Spring came early, and in February Marion wrote to Zia Gì: 'I have to tell you that Mirtillino is even more beautiful than he was!' The snowdrops were out, a 'demon' wind had been blowing for fifteen days and the garden was full of weeds, but there were the first signs of beetroot, radishes, lettuce and celery. They had also put in pansies, sweet peas and lilies. Carlo, she said, was against bulbs, but she herself had ordered some from catalogues. She asked Amelia to send coffee and Quaker Oats from the Old England shop in Florence and a bucket and spade for Mirtillino. As the weather got warmer, she was given permission to walk up into the mountains, from where she watched Stromboli's small volcanic eruptions. Amelia arrived on a short visit and met Nitti, Dolci and Lussu, who said that she was just like Cornelia Africana, the upright, virtuous widow of Tiberius Gracchus the Elder, whose two reforming sons had challenged the Roman senate in the second century BC. She and Marion paid a visit to the neighbouring island of Vulcano.

Carlo was restless; whenever the boats bringing post failed to arrive, sometimes for days on end, he fretted. Letters were crucial to his life, as they were for all the family. They had long used affectionate nicknames for each other – Amelia was 'Mietta', 'Mimmola', 'Lilla', 'Bobolink', 'Pippola', 'Tiullina'; Salvemini remained 'Father Bear', and 'Marion 'Biancofiore'. But now, to circumvent the censors, they used Tuscan expressions, words in English and French, private jokes, slang, rhymes, jumbles of words, terms of endearment, blending both intimacy and the need for secrecy. Sarina Nathan became 'Don't say', for her fondness for English. 'Negro' was used to describe something dark, something to be avoided. What the censors and the police in Rome, who received, copied and filed many of their letters, made of them, no one knows.

'For myself,' Carlo wrote after Amelia left, 'I can't say that I am going through a very brilliant period ... the tedium of this humiliating life oppresses me.' The days passed, one just like another, broken only by 'little crises of inner rebellion'. After a few days of 'cerebral life', he told Nello, 'I feel a sense of nausea and revolt, a desire for action.' He had been on Lipari just three months; four years and nine months remained of his sentence. He could never, he said, accept this life of 'resignation and oblivion', which others seemed to tolerate. His existence, he wrote to Gina Lombroso, had become 'all form and no substance, like bread without yeast, a day without light'. It was telling that both Carlo and Nello kept in touch with some of Amelia's friends, remarkable people with whom they had grown up and to whom they continued to feel close.

In the evenings, as it grew warmer, the family sat out in their garden, Marion knitting, reading aloud to each other from Molière or the Greeks. She was trying to work out what Carlo would wear come the summer heat: linen trousers, an open-necked sports shirt, a light flannel blazer, possibly striped or blue, and she asked Amelia to find them in Florence. They should be, she wrote, 'outsize!' Though Carlo had lost some weight, he was still somewhat plump. Even as he rebelled against what he called the daily 'contemplation of domestic harmony', Carlo knew that he was lucky to have found Marion. She was a woman, he told his mother, who was prepared to follow him anywhere, stop doing what she was doing to attend to him, and yet someone who remained essentially independent. And this, he said, was exactly what he needed. 'But who knows how long this wave under which we are submerged will last?' How long would he have to live in this 'strangely deformed' existence? Without Marion and Mirtillino, he kept saying, his life on Lipari would be truly unbearable.

Help arrived, in the shape of Ferruccio Parri, his wife Esther and their two-year-old son Giorgio, known as Dodo. Having been refused permission to serve his sentence somewhere in the north, where he would be close to his family, Parri had found himself on Ustica, before persuading the authorities to let him move to Lipari, where the climate was said to be better for small children. During their long months in prison together, in Como and Savona, Carlo and Parri had grown very close. It was from Parri that Carlo had learned 'the value of spiritual discipline, of rigorous moral habits, of stoical indifference (perhaps exaggerated) towards the practical and ordinary aspects of life'. Parri was a man who 'gave, gave, always gave but never took'.

Rooms had been found for the Parri family in the Villa Diana, a fine two-storey yellow-stucco house not far from the Rossellis, with electric light, 'almost' running water, 'views and fresh air' and the use of the garden and terrace. They were to share the house with the Grand Master of the Freemasons, Torrigiani, and other *onorevoli*. There was talk of Parri joining the Club della Fuga, but he said that he feared repercussions against his wife and elderly parents. Like many of the men arriving from long months of confinement, his health was poor: he had bad rheumatism and found walking hard.

Politics was the daily bread of the *confinati*, for there was little else for them to do. The amorphous nature of fascism meant that everyone searched constantly for meaning. Even those who had arrived feeling tepid about politics were soon drawn in. Despite the ban on political conversations, the *confinati* were constantly talking, analysing, interpreting, rewriting the past, as they walked up and down the Corso in their neat dark suits or sat in the Café Eolo, their conversations fanned by rumours and information gleaned from new arrivals. Like the Rossellis, all had been quick to learn the art of metaphor and disguise. Some of their phrases were both obscure and absurd: an 'oyster farm' had come to mean the monarchy. The consensus among them was that fascism had been the inevitable result of the war, and of the fact that working-class Italians had been mobilised and manipulated by the privileged classes. Where they disagreed was on how to beat the regime.

The communists were the most disciplined, and were already forming themselves into cells: four or five comrades under an '*amico*', five *amici* under a *parente*, four *parenti* under a *famiglia*. They were also at work keeping up the morale of their members. Their view was that any future bourgeois democracy was to be rejected; they would endorse only a government of the working class. The anarchists scorned all forms of organised government. The socialists havered, some saying that what was needed was a return to a pre-fascist, but greatly improved, democracy.

Carlo, who had for some time been plunged into what he described as a 'regime of utter laziness', now felt ready to turn his mind to politics. The arrival of Parri had galvanised them all, and the two men, together with Lussu and Nitti, sat around the garden of the Rosselli house pondering the possible shape of a future Italy. 'What we were looking for', Parri would write, 'was a new rallying cry, persuasive and powerful enough to bring about a new revolution, an anti-fascist revolution'. As Carlo saw it, if *The Communist Manifesto* of 1848 had been the 'revolutionary Gospel' for almost a century, what was needed after the bitter experience of fascism was a 'new promise, more humane and more liberating than Marxist ideology'.

Though these four left-leaning men differed in the details of their political beliefs, they shared a total refusal to accept the state into which Italy had sunk, an instinct to fight, and a negation of all that fascism stood for. Most importantly, they kept telling each other, they did not want to create a new party, but to transform socialism so that it reflected a fairer society. Drawing their thoughts from Gobetti, from the Aventine parliamentarians, from Matteotti, Turati and Salvemini, they kept coming back to the two same words: liberty and justice.

Very quickly, Carlo emerged as the strongest voice. 'I have never seen a man so eager to explore, to conquer, to grow,' wrote Parri later. 'He was like a volcano in continuous eruption, both physically and intellectually,' And when the four men were not deep in discussion, Carlo sat down to formulate these new thoughts, to produce a programme, a modern manifesto. As he wrote, Marion hid the pages inside the piano.

Nello, ostensibly free but in fact kept under constant surveillance on the mainland, was also at work on the shape of Italy's future, only in his case it was a question of getting at it through the lessons of history. Volpe, keen to prove that his young protégé was dedicated only to his studies, had assigned him research in the archives in Rome, Naples and Palermo. Maria loved Rome, and they rented a house in the city centre. Nello had come round to thinking that the seeds of fascism dated from long before the recent right-wing governments. They lay in the nature of Italy itself, its backwardness, its unhealthy, uneducated, illiterate population, its weak infrastructure, its few resources, and its south largely under the yoke of bandits. It was, he maintained, a country independent only in name and rightly regarded with extreme wariness by the rest of Europe.

Working alone in the archives, however, Nello was feeling increasingly cut off. 'Every flag I see flying in the sun, every little fascist boy in uniform I pass in the street, every poster I read, says to me: you are not one of us,' he wrote to Amelia. 'There's no place for you here. Go.' To counter this sense of isolation, he told his mother how close to her he needed to feel, how often he wanted to see her. He said that he was thinking of looking for a house in the country, where he and Maria and all their future children could live 'peaceful, rich, inner lives'. In May he went with his childhood friend Leo Ferrero to Naples and they called on Benedetto Croce, living his secluded, watched existence. Surreptitiously, Nello had also contacted some of the few young anti-fascists still at liberty and there was talk of him contributing to *Pietre*, one of the last independent magazines not yet suppressed by the fascist government. Given his promises to Volpe, and the fact that he was closely observed, these acts were perilous.

On 11 July, at 2.25 a.m., Maria gave birth to a daughter. The baby was to have been born at home in their flat in Rome, but at the last minute complications arose and Maria was taken, 'uttering great cries of pain', to a hospital and the little girl delivered by forceps. They named her Silvia, which seemed to them 'both intimate and robust and also very Roman'. She weighed three kilos and was 'pale pink' in colouring, with small, perfect ears. Nello wrote to give the news to Zia Gì: 'Pretty? No. Ugly? No. A dear sweet little Silvia, yes.' Nello's happiness, Amelia added, was 'really touching', and though the baby was indeed charming, her nose 'occupies rather a large surface on her minuscule face'.

Silvia was thirteen months younger than Mirtillino and she too soon acquired a nickname: Pisellino, little pea. From Lipari, Carlo wrote that for a Jew and a non-believer like himself, only pro-creation gave any guarantee of 'relative immortality'. But, he added, thinking over the intensity of his and Nello's feelings about their mother, and about their wives, 'perhaps this is why Jews have such a potent and profound feeling about family'. Duty and responsibility, in some shape or form, were never far from their thoughts.

In September, Nello travelled to Udine to oversee the reburial of Aldo's remains at Timau in a vast cemetery for those who had died in the First World War. Aldo had been dead for twelve years. It was raining hard but Nello walked up towards the pass where his brother had died, past waterfalls and meadows and deep forests. Other families, he wrote to Amelia, had hereditary lands; they would have this grave, which they would all visit together every year. Aldo, he said, was warm and alive in his heart and he would make certain that Silvia would always hear his name mentioned with love. Before leaving, he gave 100 lire to the young soldiers who had dug the grave with such tact, asking them to drink to Aldo.

Not long after Silvia's birth, Nello and Maria moved to Turin. Nello spent his mornings in the archives, his afternoons in the library; Maria was learning to type so as to be able to help with his research. Nello's mood was cheerful: 'Tell my brother that he is a little pig,' he wrote to Parri, complaining that he had not had a proper letter in many weeks. When Carlo did write, it was in the serious tones of an older brother, telling Nello that he should settle on one subject and make it the focus of his life. They exchanged letters, guarded, cryptic, about the nature of Carlo's new work, which had received a boost when a pile of notes, left behind on Ustica and confiscated by the police, were mysteriously returned to him.

But Nello had not resigned himself to political inactivity. Despite the very real risks, he met up surreptitiously with Carlo Levi and Riccardo Bauer, recently released from *confino*, both of them precariously at liberty. They managed to put out one issue of a clandestine paper, and then were forced to accept defeat. But they were not traced or caught.

*

Nello and his second daughter, Paola

Maria with Paola and Silvia

Though Marion had dreaded the moment when she would have to abandon Carlo, they had always known that, given her heart problems, she and Mirtillino would leave the great heat of the Lipari summer and visit her parents in England. A letter requesting a passport on the grounds of ill-health went off to the Ministry of the Interior in Rome. The note in her file is revealing. 'A very brave and hysterical woman,' it says, 'to be considered as dangerous as her husband or perhaps even more so. Capable of committing desperate acts. Vigilance.'

The passport was granted. But now it was Mirtillino who needed to get away. Though he had thrived during his months on Lipari, and was walking and chattering like a little bird, he had come down with suspected amoebic dysentery. Marion set out immediately for London and Mirtillino went into Great Ormond Street Hospital, where doctors feared typhus. Without news for days on end, Carlo fretted miserably. But Mirtillino recovered and Marion took him for a couple of weeks to a nursing home and then to stay with her sister in West Kirby. Marion missed Carlo so much that she had a constant knot in her stomach. Before returning to Italy, she bought Mirtillino a red coat with a velvet collar and a little suit with leggings, and herself gloves and a leather jacket.

Back in Italy, their train stopped in Turin, where Nello was waiting with a bottle of fresh milk and some cooked apples. The crossing from Milazzo to Lipari was extremely rough and getting on shore from the pitching boat was terrifying. Marion was pleased to be back in this 'dear intimate life'. Carlo found Mirtillino much changed, 'interesting, amusing'. He and Marion got used to eating pigeons, but decided that goat, one of the few reliable sources of meat on the island, was too strong. One day they found a large wild turkey strutting around their sitting room; they ate it for supper with the Parris.

The autumn of 1928 was hot and sunny. Carlo worked in the mornings, swam in the midday warmth, collected the post at 4 o'clock, and went early to bed. He was rereading *The Brothers Karamazov* and *War and Peace*, noting with pleasure that 'great minds' write fundamental things. He had got into the habit of continually taking the temperature of his own moods and thoughts and transcribing them in long letters to his mother. The need to pin down, to describe, to analyse and understand, begun in their early childhood, had grown stronger with the years: there was no event, no person, no encounter, no idea that Carlo did not feel the need to communicate. 'In truth, I regret nothing,' he wrote one day. Though he would be 'asphyxiated' by a life of academia, his earlier university work had been a useful experiment, and he had chosen every subsequent step in full consciousness, never hesitating and never doubting. He was grateful for his present state of safety, but his need to get something done, now, 'on earth', was becoming increasingly intense and violent: it 'fills my time, my space, my world, my reason for being alive'.

For the first time, at the age of twenty-eight, he felt that he really knew himself, knew what mattered and this, he said, gave him great strength. He urged Amelia not to worry about him. 'I have travelled a long way. But I am not tired. I'll travel further. I won't lose myself. I can see the path ahead. I'll get there.' And, he added, teasing her, she could at least take pleasure in the sons she had created: 'We may of course burn up ... but only because we tried to get too close to the sun.' For all his happy marriage, there was always a sense that, with Aldo dead, it was the three of them, Amelia and her two sons, against the world.

Amelia returned to Lipari for another visit. As Nello wrote to a friend: 'My mother trots from one end of Italy to the other.' Amelia was now fifty-eight, as upright and beautiful as ever, her posture and manners those of an earlier age, her long hair still piled up elegantly on her head. Carlo told Zia Gì that he was delighted to see that she had put on weight and seemed more cheerful. Late one night, he wrote to Nello: 'There is no one on earth equal to our adorable mother, persecuted for the last twelve years and confronting it with such nobility ... Oh Nello, don't we see ourselves in her? That it is to her that we owe the best, yes the best, in our characters?' Spending these weeks so happily with her had almost made up for the horrors of 1927.

But then came the sad news that Gabriele had died. Amelia, for whom her brother had provided unfailing comfort and strength her entire life, was crushed. Carlo urged her not to shut herself up in Florence but to go to Turin to stay with Nello. His uncle had taught him, he told her, the importance of holding on to the truth, and never betraying 'that religion of duty', of which

Gabriele – modest to the point of absurdity, genuinely good, honest almost to excess – had been such a shining example. On his twenty-ninth birthday on 16 November, Carlo spoke of the 'sad and beautiful destiny of our family'.

Carlo was greatly liked among Lipari's *confinati*. People found him friendly, approachable, as interested in the lives of the ordinary families as in those of his intellectual friends. He and Marion continued to gather people for tea in their garden, and sometimes played the piano for them. Carlo handed out little boxes of candied oranges which he made himself. There was something almost childlike in his ready, sunny smile.

On the afternoon of Epiphany, 6 January 1929, he and Marion invited all the children of the *confinati* to a party. They expected forty; sixty-four turned up, along with their mothers and grandmothers. Carlo had cut coloured paper patterns and hung them around the walls. Games were played, followed by a tombola with prizes of socks, sent by Amelia from Florence; there were sparklers, false noses and balloons and a small present for every child. Nitti made an appearance as a menacing witch. A few fireworks were let off. Then came sandwiches, hot chocolate, biscuits – unimaginable luxuries on Lipari and also sent by Amelia – and Malvasia wine for the adults.

Behind it all, behind the ever amiable and unflappable facade, however, Carlo suffered. He felt trapped and impotent and angry. 'Monotony, monotony, nothing new ...' he wrote. 'The winter is slow in passing ... Obsession returns. Escape. Escape. Escape.'

CHAPTER THIRTEEN

Not Even the Flies Escape

There was only one way to leave *confino* early: complete submission. From time to time, to mark dates on the fascist calendar, Mussolini released people who were prepared to renounce their dissident ways and extol fascism. The *confinati* themselves, or their families, could also send a subservient letter to the Duce, pleading to be pardoned; but once this became known, they were often ostracised and called traitors. Giovanni Ansaldo, Carlo's journalist friend caught escaping to Switzerland with Bauer but now eager to profess a new-found fascist allegiance, sought and obtained a pardon after a suitably begging request. On Lipari the others lined the road as he walked to the boat taking him to liberty, staring in disapproving silence. When Parri's family, unknown to him, petitioned Mussolini for his early release he was furious and cut short further negotiations. 'You must find the strength never to give in to false illusions,' he wrote sternly to his mother. 'To wait; to be patient; to remain sane and serene just as we are.' True anti-fascists did not capitulate.

This left only escape. But, as the Club della Fuga understood all too clearly, escape was impossible. Lipari had 36 kilometres of coastline, patrolled by three fast naval motorboats with machine guns, and one with a cannon, and they kept watch from a hidden inlet. The guards had radios; and on nearby Vulcano was a searchlight with a powerful beam that lit up Lipari port and its surroundings. On the island itself, between militia, police, carabinieri and Guardia della Finanza, there were now some 500 guards. There were also spies, for the most part *squadristi* who had committed small acts of disobedience and were trying to win their way back into favour.

Even as the Club della Fuga plotted – a hydroplane sent by friends to pluck them out of the water while they swam? Stealing one of the motorboats? – other *confinati* seized the initiative. A young Tuscan student, educated in England, joined up with a Venetian workman, a Genoan shopkeeper and Mario Magri and hatched a plan to break out. All four lived in the dormitories inside the castle precinct. One night, having plaited their sheets into a rope and stood on each other's shoulders to reach the high windows, they let themselves down the walls. Magri was disguised as a priest; one of the other men wore women's clothes. Their idea was to find a rowing boat. Next morning the alarm went up and locals were given shotguns and drafted in to help track down the fugitives. For five days the men wandered around the mountains, growing increasingly hungry and thirsty. When they could stand it no longer, they approached a farm and asked for help. The farmer was willing but his wife, terrified about possible reprisals, denounced them to the police. They were caught, beaten up, then sentenced to four years in jail in Messina. The farmer, who had failed in his duty to report them, was sent to Ustica for five years' *confino*.

In spite of this exemplary lesson, three months later a young Venetian called Spangano stole a canoe used by summer visitors, intending to row himself to the mainland. Almost immediately, the sea got up and he was forced to put back to shore. He left the boat drifting, thinking that it would be washed up and every-one would assume that he had drowned. For a month, he avoided the patrols and was fed by other *confinati*. Then one day he made his way to Lipari's second port, Canneto, and managed to climb up an anchor chain on to a German boat loading a consignment of pumice. The captain agreed to stow him away; but his second-in-command handed him over to the carabinieri. Spangano was given a three-year prison sentence.

These failed attempts were studied closely by Carlo and his friends. If anything went wrong, they knew there would be no second chance. All four men – Carlo, Lussu, Nitti and Dolci – were, each in their own way, desperate and impatient. Nitti spoke of being consumed by 'murderous boredom'. Lussu feared that unless he reached somewhere with proper medical facilities he would not live to see the end of his sentence. He wished to die, he said, not a chained, but a free man. Carlo, who ached constantly for action, and wanted to take his ideas for a future political Italy to a wider audience, fumed and fretted. Lipari, he grumbled, was all right for 'political old-aged pensioners' but not for men who wished to fight and to work. To Amelia, in veiled terms, he said that he did not envisage his destiny as a captive, but added, always quick to make fun of himself, that he was not the stuff of martyrs. 'Have you ever heard of a tall, fat, bespectacled, optimistic, extremely healthy, teacher of economics martyr?'

When they met, which they did every day and often several times a day, the four friends returned ceaselessly to the subject of escape. 'We dreamed of every kind of ending,' Carlo wrote later. 'Drowned. Recaptured. Jeered at, executed. Rarely did our imagination bring us through safe and sound.' To his surprise, for he had feared her opposition, Marion entered enthusiastically into their plotting.

For a plan to work, they agreed, a number of things had to happen. They had, first of all, to persuade the authorities that they were all four of them model prisoners, totally resigned to their sentences, with no thought of rebellion. Both Lussu and Carlo were watched with especial care, Lussu because of his violent brush with the fascists in Sardinia, Carlo because of Turati's escape. Then they needed to have a group of friends outside Italy to orchestrate the rescue and buy a fast boat, a task made considerably easier by the fact that Carlo had money. Importantly, they needed to find a way of communicating secretly with these friends, to coordinate timing and place. This was solved by Marion who, on one of her return visits to Lipari, brought with her invisible ink, smuggled in a scent bottle, and chemical reagents in the form of bright green crystals, which she sewed into the hem of a coat of the same colour.

As for the friends outside Italy, there was no lack of candidates: Italo Oxilia, the sailor who had helped spirit Turati to France, agreed to take charge of the boat; Raffaele Rossetti, a member of the former Republican Party and a decorated war veteran, took on the day-to-day logistics; and Alberto Tarchiani, a tall, calm, broad-shouldered man with glasses and wavy hair, editor of the *Corriere della Sera* until it was taken over by the fascists in 1925, was given the task of putting together the escape plan. All three of these men were in exile in Paris. Letters were now written to Marion's father in London, who then sent them on to Paris, where the rescue team deciphered the invisible words as they appeared in vivid red.

What none of them realised, however, was the extent to which they were all watched. Even Marion's father, Ernest, who never left London, was the subject of an Italian Ministry of Foreign Affairs memorandum. He was a man, it said, 'professing revolutionary ideas and frequenting meetings of anarchists'. Marion, meanwhile, had been persuaded, with great difficulty, to take no part in the escape, because of Mirtillino.

On Lipari, the four men set about making themselves trusted. Lussu decided that he would construct an image of absolute predictability and orderliness. He mixed little with the other *confinati*, but took two short daily walks – adopting a frail and somewhat jerky stride – every day at precisely the same time, followed by his two bored guards. In order to feed the idea that he was sickly and tubercular, obsessed by routine, he never left the house without a large coat and a scarf pulled up to his ears.

The Club della Fuga on Lipari

It was soon being said that one could set one's watch by Lussu's routine; he himself liked to think of himself as Kant, by whose precise walks Königsberg's inhabitants had kept time. To prepare himself for what he foresaw might be a long period in the sea, he forced himself to take icy showers; and since he had never learnt to swim, he now taught himself and added daily plunges from the beach to his routine.

Dour and severe with those who did not know him, Lussu was warm with his friends, a brilliant talker, entertained by everything. Since he had had four years' experience as an officer with the *Arditi*, and the *Arditi*, as he told the others, could do anything, he volunteered to take charge of the logistics of their escape. From his terrace, he studied the moon's cycle and where and at what hour it cast its light. He had become friends with the fourteen-year-old daughter of an anti-fascist trade unionist, who had arrived with his family on Lipari in 1926. Bruna Pagani often joined him on his walks and was soon known to the *confinati* as *'la signorina di Lussu'*. She would soon play her part in the plan, but for now Lussu, a natural teacher, described life on Sardinia to her, talked about French history and nature. One day he taught her to sing Sardinian songs. 'You must become an educated Signorina,' he told her.

Dolci took the part of an eager young draughtsman, intent on spending his sentence on improving himself. He got permission to sketch the island, and soon completed a series of detailed drawings. Together they identified an excellent spot where a boat might approach the shore, a rocky cove at the far end of the port, little guarded and just outside the beam of Vulcano's searchlight. Nitti studied the daily routines of the naval patrols, the rocks, the reefs, the coast, 'as though we were deep-sea mariners'.

Carlo and Marion decided to build up an image of a contented, settled family. This was not altogether a fantasy: Carlo spoke of 'this unexpected gift of happiness'. He played the piano a great deal, tended the vegetable garden, and was always deferential and genial with the guards. In his letters to Amelia, knowing that they would be read, he described a long-term plan to install a pump to bring more water to the house. There was a momentary alarm when he was suddenly arrested, taken off to Palermo and questioned, but Marion hurried over to Sicily, and was able to persuade the authorities that they had confused his identity with that of someone else, though it was never clear what it was about. Carlo returned to Lipari. One day they were given permission to take a picnic up into the hills. While Marion and Mirtillino played, Carlo and Dolci drew maps. Carlo had taken on the job of navigator and was busy studying the tides.

Their tactics were paying off. On 6 October, the director, Cannata, informed his superiors 'The colony is secure ... from Lipari not even the flies think of escaping.'

Music brought Edoardo Bongiorno into their lives. He was an islander in his late forties, a passionate musicologist, a socialist, a man of great sympathy and discretion, much liked by his fellow islanders, who referred to him as 'Don Eduardu'. He had been the leader of the local band until, obliged to play 'Giovinezza' on all public occasions, he had resigned and now devoted himself entirely to his shipping agency, giving Carlo music lessons on the side. A Liparese by birth, Bongiorno knew every inch of the coastline and after their lessons Carlo would go home with nautical maps hidden in the score of *L'elisir d'amore*.

The Club della Fuga had grown to six people, of very different political and religious ideas: there was the Jewish Carlo, Nitti, who was Protestant, and Lussu and Dolci, both Catholics; their helpers were Bongiorno, another Catholic, and Paolo Fabbri, a Marxist. When not doing the *confinati*'s laundry, Fabbri studied French. He was a farmer from Molinella, a resourceful, dry, humorous man with rather large ears and small deep-set pale eyes, who had been extremely brave in the agrarian battles against the fascists. The others were very fond of him.

In Paris, the plans for the rescue were moving ahead. Tarchiani went to London to discuss them with Salvemini, who was now living in England. A boat, the *Sigma N*, was bought and Marion's friend Mrs Peacock agreed to reconnoitre the canals and waterways for its journey down to the Mediterranean. The *Sigma N* set forth from northern France, ultimately bound for Tunis, and then on to Lipari. Progress was slow; hours were wasted negotiating locks. Raffaele Rossetti, never an easy man, became arrogant and bossy. There were repeated minor disasters. Having only now realised that there were 300 locks between Marne and the river Saône alone, Tarchiani decided that they would do better to put the boat on a trailer and drive. Since time was passing, they agreed to travel through the night, but while Tarchiani was napping, the hired driver fell asleep and the car and trailer plunged into a field. When the boat finally reached the coast, its engine, specially ordered by Rossetti, was found to be ailing. No spare parts could be found. A new engine was ordered. Rossetti was irritable and silent; Tarchiani fretted. Nothing augured well for a 600-mile round trip between Tunis and Lipari.

Everything that could go wrong continued to do so. When the group reached Marseilles, they discovered that a general strike had been called and the port was closed. The mechanic they had hired lost his nerve and disappeared, saying that he was terrified of drowning. Eventually, two months after leaving Paris, the *Sigma N* and its crew crossed the Mediterranean and reached Tunis, where Tarchiani and his wife were to wait for the boat to return from the rescue operation. The boat had been registered as a pleasure craft in the name of Mrs Vandervelde, the wife of a Belgian ex-minister. There was trouble with customs. The new engine went wrong.

All these delays were relayed to Lipari in secret ink or coded messages in newspapers, letters, cards and books, but they sometimes took weeks to be delivered. Fourteen-year-old Bruna had become their courier. One day she was approached by a sailor in the port asking her whether she was '*la signorina di Lussu?*' He then gave her a folded newspaper to give to Lussu. On another, she was called into the grocery shop, run by a Sardinian woman, who gave her a packet and told her to tell the '*onorevole*' that a parcel had arrived for him. Lussu sent her back to collect a special Sardinian cake, covered in bright decorations. It contained a pair of binoculars, which Lussu hid in a cupboard, telling Bruna that if the carabinieri should ever come to search his house, she should take them, climb over the terrace and hide them somewhere. One day he asked her to help him dye some clothes dark green, which would not show up in the dark – they all refused to wear the fascist black – and there was much laughter as the vat boiled over and green dye splattered the room.

A plan was now in place. On a given day, Carlo, Nitti, Lussu and Dolci were to gather on the beach by the rocky cove behind a sea wall. They would go into the water around dusk when the sun had dipped to the point that a swimmer would barely be visible. They would swim out about 150 metres from the shore and tread water, sending a message by torch to the *Sigma N*. In case of disaster and no boat showing up, they would still have time to make it back to their houses before the curfew.

The date was set for the night of 17 November 1928, Carlo having calculated that it was a week after a full moon, so that it rose late in the evening. The weather was grey, the sea cold and choppy. That morning Carlo had received a coded telegram from Marion, who was back in Paris, which told them that the *Sigma N* had left Tunis. Towards dusk the four men, in their dark-green clothes, met on the rocks and swam out. Dolci had drunk most of a bottle of cognac against the cold. There was no boat. For thirty minutes, their teeth chattering, they swam round and round. Finally, knowing that there were just minutes left before the curfew, they turned back to shore, clambered out of the water and ran for home.

Carlo had scratched his glasses, and in the dark tripped over a barbed-wire fence and fell into a spiny bush. He raced past a terrified little girl and when he got home, found that his face was covered in blood. Next morning, he told the neighbours that he had fallen over in the garden; knowing Marion to be away, they looked at him suspiciously. The *Sigma N*, he later learnt, had indeed put out to sea from Tunis, but huge waves had soon driven the boat back. Then the rope attached to the tender carrying the spare fuel had snapped and they had lost it. The mission had been aborted. On Lipari, the four men felt crushed. For half an hour, said Lussu, he had felt like a free man, his 'whole soul bent on the open sea'. Winter was setting in and there would be no further chance of escape for many months.

What was crucial, however, was that the entire event had passed unnoticed.

Recovering from their acute disappointment, Carlo and the others resumed their orderly lives; Lussu and Bruna took their walks; Nitti and Dolci returned to their calculations. Then there was a announcement that a number of *confinati* were to be pardoned early: Dolci was one of them. They realised that this would be a great help. Dolci planned to return to Rome, then sneak over the border and make his way to Paris, where he would be able to give the others a complete picture of Lipari, and then help pilot a new boat. A new date was set: July 1929. There had been nothing wrong with their plan, and there was no reason not to try it again. It was the *Sigma N* which had been a doomed boat, and it continued to be jinxed. Transported back to Marseilles to be sold, it slipped out of the net swinging it to shore from a trawler and crashed heavily into the sea. The French authorities decided that Tarchiani's licence had not matched the true weight of the boat and issued a fine. By now Tarchiani was out of funds. He took the few francs he had left and went to the casino in Monte Carlo. And here his luck changed. He placed all he had on a single number: it won. He did the same again, and won again. He emerged with enough money to pay off all their debts.

On Lipari, the winter of 1928 was bitterly cold. It rained incessantly and one day it even snowed. Waves pounded the islands. Winds rattled the ill-fitting windows and blew so hard under the doors that the rugs on the floor flapped. When Dolci left, Nitti moved in to live with Lussu, but at the same time he rented a room from Bongiorno giving directly on to the cove they intended to use again, with stairs leading down to the rocks. The dull, monotonous days crept by. The militia, bored and frustrated themselves, endlessly provoked and humiliated the *confinati*. Many new petty rules were imposed. Carlo sat in his little house and played Beethoven and Chopin, read Marx, worked on his new political theory. There were days when he found it almost a relief not to have to think constantly about escape.

Finally it was spring again. The Club della Fuga resumed its plotting. The almanac showed that the lunar phase would be at its best on 5, 6 and 7 July, and again on the 26th, 27th and 28th. A new and better boat had been found, the *Dream V*, belonging to an Egyptian prince, Djelal Edine. Grey above the line and red below, it had two powerful motors of 90 horsepower each and could do 26–30 knots – which made it faster than the Italian naval launches. Through Salvemini and Ernest Cave, it was bought for 115,000 francs and registered to Cave. Oxilia, with Dolci's help, was to be the captain and more useful charts had arrived in Paris from Bongiorno. Tarchiani was continuing to plot and plan but was laid up in bed with sciatica. The usual coded messages went backwards and forwards between France and Lipari, where Lussu, Carlo and Nitti continued to meet, to talk, to pick feverishly over arrangements.

What none of them knew was that rumours of an escape from Lipari had reached the authorities in Rome. Spies had reported that Marion was smuggling letters in and out on her regular visits. There was talk of the French ex-consul to Ljubljana being in some way involved. A telegram sent by the Ministry of the Interior to the prefect of Messina on 3 March was uncannily accurate: a rescue was being planned by motorboat, to take place at night. Carlo's name was mentioned and surveillance was increased. At the end of April came a flurry of telegrams urging constant vigilance. A spy in Paris intercepted a letter which spoke of a boat being bought in Spain. Another mentioned Tunisia. A watch was put on Tarchiani. But then the director, Cannata, returned from his holidays and reassured the ministry in Rome that Carlo's behaviour was not that of a man planning to escape. On the contrary, he was leading a settled domestic life. 'Rosselli model *confinato*', he cabled his superiors. 'Wish they were all like him.'

News that the boat would take the men off from Lipari in the first fortnight of July arrived written in invisible ink in the pages of Arthur Schnitzler's *Fräulein Else*, sent from Paris to Marion, who was on one of her periodic visits to the island. She was again pregnant, and Mirtillino was not well. Making much of both facts, mother and child left Lipari. Carlo fretted about them. 'I feel oppressed and extremely worried,' he wrote to Marion on 30 June. Meanwhile he continued with his calm and regular life, played the piano, and went swimming. A mandolin player and a tuneless choir, which struck up nearby in the evenings, were, he said, driving him mad. In London, Marion met the women running the Italian Refugees' Relief Committee, who helped her transfer the money for the boat and carried letters to Salvemini in Paris.

Now that a date had been set Carlo tried again to persuade Parri to go with them, but Parri still anticipated repercussions against his family. Parri, said Carlo, was 'my second conscience, my elder brother'. His melancholy friendship had taught Carlo how pure, high-minded men felt alone and sad, and not, as he had always believed, 'abstract and rhetorical'. Parri was also devoted to Carlo, saying later that he considered him to be the most energetic, determined and impressive of leaders, and he feared only that he would wear himself out young. Injudiciously, Carlo now invited the Grand Master of the Freemasons to accompany them, but Torrigiani refused, saying that his eyesight was too poor and his health too frail. This could have cost them all dear, for informers got wind of his words and hastened to report them to Cannata, but the director, constantly bombarded by the gossip of the malicious, venal and untrustworthy spies, decided to ignore them. In his letters to Amelia, Carlo, knowing that every word was scrutinised by Cannata, described his calm life, his visits to his friends, his schemes to improve his house.

At the beginning of July, the *Dream V* reached Tunisia. In the end, Raffaele Rossetti had backed out and Tarchiani had been too ill to accompany them. Oxilia, Dolci and a new mechanic, Paul Vonin, ate a lobster to celebrate their progress. They prepared to leave for Lipari.

On the evening of the 5th, Carlo, Lussu and Nitti made their way stealthily to the rocky cove, swam out 150 metres and trod water. The sea was calm, the sky clear. No boat came. They waited 30 minutes, then swam back to shore 'like whipped curs'. Nitti was the most despondent. 'It's our destiny to die either in prison or on this island,' he told the others. 'This obsession with dying free men is absurd.' Carlo paced his terrace trying to work out what might have happened. A coded telegram the next day explained that there had been a sudden storm and trouble with the motor. The 6th and 7th were impossible. The next date was 26 July.

Carlo resumed work on his manuscript and wrote contented letters; and he smiled at everyone all the time. He told Marion that he had lost ten kilos and that he was happy about the coming baby, even if it meant that he would have to spend 'a pretty solitary winter' all alone on Lipari. The 23rd was their third wedding anniversary and he wrote her a loving letter. Would they ever have, he wondered, a life 'definitively together'? Early on the 25th, he wrote again to say that the sea was flat, and there was a slight breeze. He had dreamt about a lion chasing him down an escalator. Lussu said it was a good omen: a lion meant Africa. Carlo felt tense, 'melancholic, not bitter ... questions, doubts, vast new horizons, dreams and hopes, even ambitions, but not of an ordinary kind'.

On 26 July, the three men swam out, waited, grew frantic, returned to shore, tried to work out what could have happened. There were just two possible days left.

On 27 July, Carlo lunched with the Parris and asked them to keep and hide a copy of his manuscript. He played with the Parris' young son Dodo, gave him rides on his back, and said to him: 'When we meet again, you and Mirtillino will be friends.' He seemed particularly cheerful and laughed like a young boy. As he shut the garden gate, he looked back and waved. Later, Esther Parri would remember the expression on his face: 'Anxious and happy, sure of himself.' Nitti spent the day giving his usual Italian lesson to two young anarchists and took pleasure in setting them an essay with the title 'He who sleeps does not catch fish.' Then he went to a café and sat talking to friends.

Dusk fell and Fabbri, who had volunteered to help, met Nitti in the cove. There was no sign of Carlo or Lussu. At 9.15 p.m. the faint purr of a motor was heard and a black shadow slipped out of the dark. Fabbri swam out to make contact with the boat while Nitti set off to look for the others. In his haste, he tripped over a hen coop. The chickens squawked, a woman rushed out and shouted 'thieves' and two militiamen appeared. Nitti ran back to the rocks and swam out to the boat. Minutes passed. The boat began to drift in the direction of the well-lit port, where a group of militia and policemen were sitting drinking in a café. The curfew sounded and there were now just ten minutes left before the patrols began their rounds.

Fabbri swam back to shore to see what was happening. There was still no sign of Lussu or Carlo.

To calm the militia who came to investigate the squawking chickens, Fabbri went up to them and apologised, saying that he had been rather drunk and had foolishly tripped. This diverted the two men and allowed Lussu and Carlo, who had been hovering behind a wall, to slip past and swim out to the dangerously drifting boat. Arms reached out to help them on board. The boat was now so close to shore that they felt themselves brilliantly lit up. They could hear every syllable uttered by the police in the bar.

Oxilia fired up the engines, the sound of the motors explosively loud in the silent air. Putting it on full throttle, he turned its prow out to a 'glassy sea, leaving behind a white sparkling wake on water as smooth as oil'. From their house near the port, the Parris listened as angry shouts rose up.

The *Dream V* sped past Vulcano. The moon got up, huge and yellow, casting its light on Lipari as it faded gradually from sight. Carlo, Lussu and Nitti changed into dry clothes their friends had thoughtfully provided. They drank brandy and could not stop talking; laughing, they pictured the scene they had left behind. Carlo's job was to keep the petrol tank full, Lussu's to puncture the empty canisters and throw them overboard so that they filled with water and sank, leaving no trace. As the petrol was consumed, the boat became lighter and faster. They passed an Italian merchant ship, whose captain would later say: 'They were going like the devil!'

By dawn they had left Sicily's western tip far behind them. Fearing pursuit, they took turns at scanning the horizon with binoculars. When they saw boats they picked up the weapons that Lussu had requested be put on board. At 3 o'clock that afternoon, the *Dream V* reached the coast of Tunisia. 'Our hearts were bursting,' wrote Carlo later. 'We could not stop smiling. It was as if we had changed our skins ... New interests, new hopes, urgency. In a flash, *confino* became a memory. We could think

Francesco Fausto Nitti, Carlo and Emilio Lussu, on their way to freedom

233

only of the future.' They sent a telegram to Tarchiani, who had made it as far as Tunis and was in an agony of anxiety: 'Baby born. Mother in excellent health.' Tarchiani had been waiting for this moment for two years. He had never met Carlo, Lussu or Nitti, but as they walked towards him under the plane trees of L'Avenue de France in Tunis he felt that he had known them all his life. 'All well', he cabled his wife. 'Very glad.'

The men left behind them pandemonium. It was a Saturday night and many of the guards were not at their posts. Those who were ran around shouting orders. The officer on radio duty refused to send out the alarm without the signature of his superiors, who could not be found. Cannata dithered, and when at last he sent word to the naval base in Naples, it was hours before anyone acted; it was only late next morning that a flying boat was despatched to search for the fugitives. By the time the prefect of Messina contacted Rome, the *Dream V* had reached the shores of Tunisia. Mussolini, outraged, ordered that he should be constantly updated on progress. Everyone was extremely reluctant to tell him that there was none.

Forty-eight hours later, a team of men from the Ministry of the Interior descended on Lipari. From their interrogations they learnt that the carabinieri had indeed heard the sound of a boat around 8.30 p.m., but concluded that it was the one belonging to Cannata; and that the head of the police, Tommaso da Ponte, grown bored and lazy, had never bothered to check that the lightbulbs around the cove were working, and had not even known of the existence of the flight of steps down to the rocks. A furious Bocchini accused Cannata of 'indolence and an absolute lack of intuition and initiative'. Described as 'opportunistic, corrupt, inefficient', he was dismissed. (He had long wanted to leave Lipari: as a fervent Mason, he had hated being jailor to Torrigiani.)

Fabbri and Parri were both arrested for complicity; Bongiorno was repeatedly questioned. Surveillance was tightened up and the whole area around the cove was sealed off. New prohibitions were introduced. The number of roll-calls, patrols and police boats were increased and the militia, who were busy taking out their rage and humiliation on the prisoners, were given more powers. A barbed-wire fence was put up to enclose the whole *confino* area and sentinels posted day and night. The daily sum given to the inmates for their food and lodging was reduced from 10 lire to 5. When, one evening, a goat sneezed on the mountainside the militia, jumpy and watchful, thought it was some kind of signal: in the ensuing chaos, 35 *confinati* and 16 islanders were injured.

But nothing dented the immense excitement, admiration and pleasure felt by most of the prisoners, for whom the escape had been not just a triumph of ingenuity but an act of overwhelming public rebellion against the fascists. The Lipari 'raid', as Lussu later said, was like a stone thrown into a calm lake on a sunny day: 'Around the spot on which it falls ripples form, multiply, fan out and ruffle the flat water, bringing sudden life to apparent death.'

For Mussolini, it was a small calamity. Not only had three dangerous and articulate critics of the regime escaped an apparently impregnable penal settlement, but they were now free and outside Italy, where they would obviously lose no time in describing in detail a side of fascism that most of the world knew nothing about, or had chosen to ignore. He did not plan to let it go either quietly or unpunished.

CHAPTER FOURTEEN

To Be an Exile

On 29 July, Carlo, Lussu and Nitti woke to freedom. They bought suits, shirts and Basque berets, so as to pass unnoticed, though Carlo had some trouble finding anything in Tunis large enough to fit him. Back on the boat, they informed the authorities that they were bound for Sfax, along the coast towards Libya, then set out in the opposite direction towards Algeria, but were soon driven ashore by heavy seas. While the three fugitives hid, Oxilia reported, as instructed under Tunisian law, to the port authorities. At 4.30 the next morning, hugging the shore, they set out again. A party of mounted spahis kept them company for a stretch of the way, cantering along, their arms raised in salute. Forced into Bizerta by the continuing bad weather and too impatient to delay their arrival in France any longer, they boarded the night ferry for Marseilles. Before they left, Oxilia, who had volunteered to stay with the boat, took photographs. The four men stare out, smiling exultantly.

During the night, when no one could sleep, Tarchiani filled them in on the world of the anti-fascists in exile, their feuds and penury and endless gossip. At Marseilles, a customs officer asked whether they had anything to declare. No, they replied, 'we are the smuggled goods'. Carlo, normally the most exuberant member of the party, was quiet, worrying about possible reprisals against his family.

Their train reached Paris at 11 o'clock on the evening of 1 August. Tarchiani had sent a telegram to Turati and Salvemini, asking them to meet him at a bistro by the Gare de Lyon, but not explaining why. When Carlo, Lussu and Nitti walked in, there was first silence, then cries of excitement. 'It seemed', noted Lussu later, 'as if fascism itself had fallen.'

'They have arrived!' wrote Turati in *La Libertà*, the newspaper of the exiled Italians. 'Fugitives? No, men who have returned to fight under the Italian flag. In a civil war, as in every war, it is the first duty of every prisoner to escape . . . humiliation, shackles, slow death.' These 'victors and vindicated' were the first, but they would not be the last of those who escaped Mussolini's clutches. The story was picked up by the French newspapers, then sped around the world. Paeans of lyrical praise descended on these courageous and 'brilliant sons' of Tuscany, Sardinia and southern Italy, finally at liberty to draw the world's attention to the 'agonies of an enslaved people'. Since Carlo spoke English and French, they made him their spokesman.

What no one could have anticipated was the speed of Mussolini's response. Even as Carlo's train was making its way up through France to Paris, he ordered the prefect of Aosta to arrest Marion at the hotel in Courmayeur where she and Mirtillino were staying. The police took them off to Aosta prison and put them into a cell with prostitutes. It was dirty and full of fleas. Discovering, to their discomfiture, that Marion was six months pregnant and suffering from heart problems, the authorities moved her next day into a hotel in Aosta, under police guard. She was forbidden to speak to anyone or to write or receive letters. A young friend, hearing of her arrest, hurried to Aosta, but was only able to watch her pacing around the square, in between her guards. It was thought that the next step would be to send her as a *confinata* to the penal islands.

Nello and Maria were on holiday in Fiuggi when they received news of the successful escape from Lipari. They sent Amelia a telegram: '*Tutto bene*', all well. It was intercepted by the police, who assumed that Nello was in on the plot. There was no proof, but the prefect of Messina, in search of scapegoats, gave his name as one of the organisers. Nello was arrested and taken to the prison of Frosinone, where he was put into a small cell with twelve other men.

But Mussolini had not reckoned with Carlo's energy and determination, nor with the British spirt of fair play. Within hours, Carlo and Salvemini, who had excellent contacts in England, had launched a clamorous and indignant campaign to get Marion released. Favours were called in and letters from prominent British academics and politicians began to arrive on Mussolini's desk. Marion's English family issued protests. Much was made of her frail state of health and her pregnancy. *The Times* reported that Mussolini had taken Marion and Nello as 'hostages' and the *Manchester Guardian* warned that any country pretending to great-power status would suffer 'fatal discredit' by such behaviour. The New York *Daily News* sent Mussolini a telegram asking for clarification. A headline in the *Evening Standard* spoke of a 'pure vendetta'. The *Daily Express* mentioned 'barbarians'. Newspapers throughout France, Germany and the United States devoted long, highly critical articles to fascist brutality.

While in London organising Carlo's escape, Marion had made friends among the circle of clever, strong, well-educated women who had worked in the suffrage movement and now found themselves marginalised from power but still influential. One of these was Sylvia Pankhurst, who had visited Italy in her art-school days, and met Gramsci and the Italian radicals. She sent a telegram expressing solidarity and congratulations to the Rosellis. But there were also Bertha Pritchard, secretary of the Italian Refugees' Relief Committee, and Barbara Carter, who had covered the Savona trial for the *Manchester Guardian* and was putting together a series of pamphlets highly critical of the fascists. They and their friends, highly competent and articulate feminists, began feeding stories to the British papers about Marion, 'cast into a cell', and used her story to throw more light on fascist Italy.

Amelia, meanwhile, had arrived in Aosta and been allowed to visit her daughter-in-law and grandson. In public, she was able to remain 'brave and cool', but inside she was crushed. 'This blow', she told Nello, 'is really too much for me.' She felt old, used up, pointless, '*arcistufa*', totally fed up with 'this old carcass of mine'. Her sons had already had all that was 'best and truest' in her and she had little left in reserve. 'I send you much love, my dearest, with all my despairing tenderness.' Amelia was also worrying about Marion, who had fallen ill and seemed fretful and depressed, and she was cross with Carlo for embarking on such a dramatic step with no thought of what it might do to his wife.

For his part, Carlo was mortified. 'Here I am,' he wrote abjectly in a joint letter to his mother and wife from Paris, 'having obtained my own personal freedom, even if only temporarily, at the expense of yours.' Were he not absolutely certain that he would become a 'great force in the struggle for the freedom' of his country, then he would find what was happening truly unbearable. He battled on with his newspaper crusade, seeming never to sleep, reassuring his family that he would not be deported, since he had committed no crime. 'Courage, my dear Marionellina,' he wrote. 'Have faith, don't lose your nerve.' There was no proof against her, 'none, none, none. They will be forced to give in.'

Two weeks passed; the campaign in the newspapers continued. Finally the Italian ambassador to London was instructed to put out a statement: 'Signora Rosselli has not been arrested or molested in any way ... She is entirely free and nothing whatsoever has been done to curtail her full liberty.' An official told the *Daily News* that his 'countrymen were as tender in their dealings with women and children as anyone else' and that the Italian people would be deeply wounded to be thought capable of imprisoning 'a young, expectant, mother'. By now, Carlo had given long interviews to dozens of newspapers, most of which included the word 'hostage'. Marion and Mirtillino were released.

To Carlo's great chagrin, Nello did not fare so well. By 8 August he was back on Ustica, treating the whole thing with his customary good temper. The island, he wrote to Maria, was much as he had left it eighteen months before, and when he landed, not having shaved for a week and wearing a shirt rather like Robespierre's, his friends told him that he looked like a Risorgimento martyr. Adapting himself to disagreeable surroundings very quickly, he added, had become so much a part of him that he wondered whether he was not suffering from an 'advanced form of Arab indifference and fatalism'. But, he went on, it was probably only that he had grown a protective carapace against the calamitous times. 'Not to take the world as it comes, now that would really be an act of folly.'

Amelia felt none of her younger son's cheerful resignation. 'The persecution levelled so remorselessly against me by destiny', she railed to Nello, 'has become almost grotesque ... I am sick to the very death of this life; and I am full of envy for people who are happy.' She had put in an application to be allowed to visit Nello; it was refused.

Mussolini had at first forbidden any mention of the escape in the Italian papers. Only on 9 August, twelve days after the three men left Lipari, did a terse three-line item appear in *Il Popolo d'Italia*. By now, however, what little remained of the underground press in Italy had circulated the story which, like Chinese whispers, had picked up many fantastical embellishments along the way. As an informer reported to Bocchini on 13 August, the 'anti-fascist murmurations' overheard in cafés would not have sounded out of place in the novels of Jules Verne.

In Paris, even as Nitti was putting together a quick book on their escape with details about conditions on the penal islands, and Lussu was writing an article for the *Atlantic Monthly*, a counter-offensive was launched from Rome. Harold Goad, Marion's former employer at the British Institute in Florence and a passionate fascist supporter, wrote an article for the *Spectator* describing Lipari as a charming island of grapes, figs, olives, wine and warm springs. Carlo replied instantly, pointing out that Siberia, too, had hot summers, cloudless skies, melons and corn, but that did not prevent either of them from being penal settlements. Goad responded with a patronising rejoinder that every 'thoughtful' Englishman regarded the 'great moral and spiritual' values of the 'Fascist creed' with justifiable admiration. Soon after, an adulatory article, written a year earlier, was reprinted in the *North American Review*. It took the shape of an interview with Mussolini, carried out by an American visitor, Katharine Dayton. The Duce, whom she compared approvingly to Napoleon, possessed 'tremendous native dignity – a dignity with nothing of the strut about it'. His eyes flashed lightning and rolled and sparkled with humour as he chuckled, 'shyly tapping the side of his nose', before he kissed her hand.

Mussolini was plotting his revenge. He ordered that more punitive conditions should immediately be put into place across all the penal islands. Then, to prove that Carlo and his friends' words were nothing but fabrications, Mussolini sent Thomas B. Morgan, Rome manager of the United Press news agency to visit the islands. Morgan was evidently a good friend to the fascists, for the articles he sent back described a 'charming picture . . . a spectacle of scenic beauty', the men tipsy on the delicious local wine, reading, walking or 'just loafing'. Next, Mussolini despatched the

Mussolini's love of Roman antiquity

president of the Italian Red Cross, Filippo Cremonesi, to write a report on Lipari and Ponza, another colony just off Naples. Cremonesi was a mild and courteous man, but he was prudent and had no desire to fall out with the fascists, nor to alarm the International Committee of the Red Cross in Geneva. He returned praising the beauty of the islands, the generous amount of space in which the *confinati* were allowed to roam, the 'fairness, justice and equanimity' of the regime. Cremonesi said that the men slept in a 'sunny dormitory' and that the illnesses they suffered were no different from those of the general population. What he failed to mention were the clubbings, the damp and dirt of the dormitories, the infections and loss of weight from lack of vitamins and proper food among those desperately trying to send money home to their penniless families. Nor did he touch on the punishment of forty months in prison meted out against Fabbri for his part in the escape, or the fact that Filippich, the mender of bicycles from Trieste, had been so badly beaten up by the militia and his head held underwater in a cistern, that he later died. The ICRC expressed itself 'satisfied and reassured'.

On 27 August Nello, apparently on Mussolini's direct orders, was transferred to the island of Ponza. The journey took twenty-eight hours, in pitching seas. Ponza was generally regarded as the prettiest of the penal islands, but also the hottest, and the place where the most 'dangerous' anti-fascists were sent. The police and carabinieri had long since given up trying to keep order, and the *confinati* were ruled over by a particularly brutal militia centurion, whose wife egged him on to ever harsher measures, saying that the prisoners did not show her sufficient respect. His men, wearing a medley of uniform and civilian dress, swaggered around, half drunk, brandishing whips and cudgels. The walls of the little port were covered in obscene graffiti. Those the political *confinati* considered the 'dregs', the drunks, informers, spies and bullies, were all kept together in one dormitory, known as Manchuria, for its bleak, freezing conditions in winter.

Nello admitted that he had been obliged to spend some days in a 'stinking' dormitory, but, as ever, praised the room he was finally allocated, looking out over the port and the surrounding hills. He said the houses were clean and well built and the road that ran along the seafront was the pride of the islanders. This 'derelict' place, he wrote, had a 'pleasing crust of primitiveness'. He was particularly delighted by the close and loving relationship that had developed in Florence between Maria and Amelia. 'In the midst of so many blows,' he wrote to his mother, 'what we have left is our incomparable intimacy and the solidity of our dispersed family.' He was confident that Amelia would give Maria something of her own extraordinary richness and strength in the face of adversity, and that Maria herself, who shared his mother's 'moral stamp', had much to contribute. His young wife, he said, was a woman who never had a bad thought, was trusting and lacked all artifice. With her, 'one could imagine founding the kind of family you find in the Old Testament'. Seemingly so frail, and not yet twenty-four, Maria was turning out resilient and resourceful. Nello missed his family, and told Amelia that he found himself pulling faces like Silvia's, 'to remind myself even a bit of her dear little face'.

Though he was without many of the books he needed, he went back to work on his three current projects – the political right in Italy, Piedmont between 1849 and 1860, and Italy's foreign policy towards Britain. As he wrote ruefully to Gina Lombroso: 'It is my destiny that just as my labours are coming into port, a sudden squall throws them back on to the high seas.' However, Ponza was the very island to which the nineteenth-century patriot

Pisacane had been sent, and he began to think that he might write his biography; since he had no documents, he would use his imagination 'to make him come alive inside me'. Carlo Levi had sent him paints and part of his days were spent outside with his drawing pad. 'It is certain that if I loved and admired you very much before,' Levi wrote, 'I love and admire you and your family even more today. You endure all these reversals not only without complaining, but you find in them ways to stay alive and even to be happy ... You are, in short, an extraordinary family.' It made him, he said, almost embarrassed to be so weak and so idle.

On learning of Nello's arrest, Volpe wrote him a tetchy and reproachful letter. 'I would like to believe that the charges levelled against you are once again only suspicions ... I would feel most pained if you had broken your promises to me.' Somewhat re-assured by Nello's protests that he was innocent, Volpe again intervened on his behalf with the Ministry of the Interior, saying that he had seen no sign of any kind of political activity in Nello. Maria was now in the eighth month of her pregnancy. To every-one's surprise, Nello was allowed to leave Ponza and travel to Florence to be with her, though he took two guards with him. On 5 November came the even more unexpected news that the case against him had been dropped. The next day, at eight in the morning, Maria gave birth to their second daughter. She weighed over 3½ kilos and had a loud voice and chubby hands. Compared to the delicate and doll-like Silvia, Amelia wrote to Carlo and Marion, she looked distinctly '*borghese*'. Having expected a boy, her parents had no name for her. Eventually they settled on Paola.

The family's fortunes had taken a turn for the better. Neither of Amelia's sons was any longer a prisoner. And though Carlo was in exile, Nello was free, in a cautious way, to move around. He and Maria bought a former convent in the hills above Flor-ence at Bagno a Ripoli. A large sixteenth-century villa reached by a long dirt road, there were olive trees, an orchard, a vegetable garden and a magnificent view of the city laid out below them. It had a terrace of cypresses and an old chapel, which Nello turned into his study. Here, taking Amelia with them, they planned to spend the summer months.

Amelia was now fifty-nine, and still beautiful; her hair, of which

L'Apparita, the Rosselli house at Bagno a Ripoli above Florence

she was very proud, was completely white; she rinsed it with a blue wash to stop it looking yellow. Conscious of her looks, she dressed in lilac and grey, and wore a wide ribbon around her neck, in white rather than the usual black. She carried a lorgnette in a little bag which closed with a button, and told Silvia and Paola that she could make it open by blowing on it. When the little girls went to bed at night, she kissed them all over their heads, as if flowers were falling down on them.

Long before Carlo, Lussu and Nitti arrived in France in the high summer of 1929, Paris had become the capital of Mussolini's enemies. It was an excitable, affectionate and disputatious world, riven by feuds, prey to rumours, full of hope and despair. Turati, in his iron-grey coat, large bow tie and scuffed wide-brimmed hat, chain-smoking, his expression one of permanent gentle irony, was its undisputed patriarch and elder statesman. Alongside him were Claudio Treves, his fellow socialist leader, small, with thick red hair cut *en brosse* and red whiskers, much respected but too austere and trenchant to be universally liked, holding his loneliness and passions behind a cool, courteous manner; Carlo Sforza, one-time Italian ambassador to France; and Francesco Saverio Nitti, uncle to Francesco Fausto, and briefly prime minister of Italy in 1919. These were the '*pezzi grossi*', the big fish.

Around these men were representatives of every faction of Italian politics – maximalist and reformist socialists, communists, liberals, republicans and anarchists – and, as in the penal islands, every variety of man and woman who had fallen foul of the fascists. There was also Salvemini, who came and went between London and Paris, and refused to follow any political line, referring to himself as the wandering Jew of anti-fascism.

The Italian exiles had reached France in three waves during the 1920s, joining not just the earlier generations of Italian patriots, driven abroad by the revolutions of the Risorgimento, but the Russians, Armenians, Latin-Americans, Poles, Algerians and Jews, drawn to France by its liberal views. A country that welcomed political exiles, France was where the League of Human Rights was born among a disparate group of syndicalists, pacifists, Freemasons and republicans. The first wave of Italians, arriving in the wake of the March on Rome in 1922, had brought anarchists and socialists, active in the labour confrontations and hounded from home by the *squadristi*. Many of these had settled in Argenteuil, fifteen kilometres to the north of Paris and soon known as '*la petite Italie anti-fasciste*'. Next came men such as Salvemini and Turati, targeted by the fascists after Mussolini's triumphant speech in January 1925. Finally came those who, after the fascist decrees of November 1926, understood that there was no longer any place for them in the new Italy and who, after Mussolini closed the borders in 1927, had survived often hair-raising journeys over high mountain passes. By 1929, all Italian political parties in exile had their headquarters in Paris, reproducing what they had been forced to leave behind, including their differences and their schisms. Nevertheless, at a meeting held in the south-western town of Nérac in March 1927, the exiles had formed themselves into a coalition, the Concentrazione Anti-fascista, dedicated to keeping alive a sense of opposition, and to bringing some kind of unity to their deliberations. Only the communists had refused to join; they looked after their own.

Many of these refugees – most of them men – were now impoverished. As one man put it, exile represented 'the very outer limits of unhappiness'. Accustomed to respect and affluence, as lawyers, professors, engineers and parliamentarians, they were grateful when they could find jobs as waiters, garage mechanics, clerks.

Filippo Turati (centre) and the Italian exiles in Paris

Carlo's friend Sandro Pertini washed cars at night, then became a bricklayer. The exiles lived frugally, like students, in small dark rooms in modest hotels around Rue de La Tour-d'Auvergne, in the 9ième, and met in smoke-filled halls above cafés run by other Italians. At the Unione delle Cooperative, they ate at one long table covered in a white cloth with a small bottle of red wine before every place. With their beards, some wispy, some lush, their pince-nez and dark clothes, they looked neat and serious.

The more fortunate were sometimes invited to Nitti's uncle's house on Boulevard de La Tour-Maubourg, where the former president and his wife Antonia, who had managed to bring money out, provided an 'oasis of faith and hope in this desert of resignation, inconclusion and dissatisfaction'. To every new arrival, the former prime minister said cheerfully: 'In three months we will be home.' Turati, who shared none of his optimism, was to be found in a fifth-floor studio, where he rose before dawn, washed in cold water and made coffee on a primus stove from special beans bought from La Maison du Café – his only luxury – before sitting down to work very close to the window as his sight was increasingly poor. He kept a large framed photograph of Anna Kuliscioff on his table.

As the months of exile had passed and turned into years, and their funds had kept shrinking, so the Italians had moved to ever smaller and dingier hotels. They often went hungry. Their neat suits frayed. All they had left was words. When not talking – loudly, indiscreetly, heedless of eavesdroppers – the exiles wrote articles and memoranda, position papers and speeches and pamphlets. With the Concentrazione Antifascista had come *La Libertà* newspaper, written almost single-handed by Treves in two grimy rooms in the Faubourg-Saint-Denis. There was also the satirical *Il Becco Giallo* – 'The Yellow Beak' – co-founded by Alberto Cianca, former minister in the Bonomi government and editor of *Il Mondo*.

As for the French, they had been very generous to these refugees – there were said to be some 150,000 Italians living in and around Paris at the end of the 1920s, and over a million across the whole of France – but they were growing wary, particularly since a prominent fascist called Nicola Bonservizi had been shot dead in a restaurant not long before. His killer, an anarchist, would have gone to the guillotine had it not been for the outrage of the French public over the Matteotti murder. Aristide Briand had just replaced Raymond Poincaré to create his eleventh cabinet in a long and uneasy run of shifting political allegiances. Six months before Carlo's arrival, the government had announced that no political fracas from the exiles would be tolerated, and anyone caught breaking the law would be deported. Since politics were all the exiles had left, this decree had been greeted with great apprehension. In the French newspapers, Carlo, Lussu and Nitti's arrival was noted in a mixture of ways, the left celebrating 'a contagion of courage – crowned by success – which might yet change into an epidemic', the right anxious lest the three men transform a hitherto peaceful Italian community, albeit one sometimes disparagingly described as '*i macaroni*', into one of troublesome agitators.

It was into this quietly seething, impoverished, rivalrous grey world of exile that Carlo erupted, youthful, bursting with vigour and resolve. Greeted, as he told Amelia, 'like a brother and a hero', he moved into a small hotel in Rue de Chabrol, not far from the Gare du Nord. The moment he knew that Marion and Mirtillino were free and safe, he got down to work with Salvemini, Lussu and Nitti. It was immediately clear to the newcomers that the parties and political leaders already in exile had grown inward-looking, inert, bogged down by doctrinal differences. As Treves summed it up: 'Don't look to us, we are the defeated, the failures.' The Concentrazione Antifascista was interested only in propaganda, talk, rhetoric, but not in action or in supporting those anti-fascists still clinging on in Italy. But action was precisely what Carlo had in mind. As he wrote to Amelia, 'My thoughts and my heart are in Italy. It is there that lie our hopes, our field of action.' What was needed was not more talk, and certainly 'no old parties, no old names'.

Within two weeks, a movement – strictly not a party – was formed. This 'veritable laboratory of ideas' was to be called Giustizia e Libertà, the name they had chosen on Lipari, and was to draw inspiration from Salvemini's teachings in Florence, from *Non Mollare*, from Gobetti and from *Il Quarto Stato*. It had nine founder members: Cianca, a stocky, whiskery man with a prominent nose who, as a serious, well-regarded editor, kept up a moral crusade against Matteotti's murder; Vincenzo Nitti, son of the former prime minister, a cool, sarcastic young man, excellent at deflating absurd ideas; the high-handed Raffaele Rossetti, original plotter in the first Lipari escape; Cipriano Facchinetti, with whom Rossetti had founded an important anti-fascist magazine in Turin; Tarchiani, architect of their freedom, silent, impassive, but extremely tenacious; and Salvemini. Carlo, Lussu and Francesco Fausto, one socialist, one republican, one liberal, three faces of an *'inscindibile trinomio'*, became the joint directors.

Giustizia e Libertà, attached to no political party and anxious to distance itself from the timorous legality of the Concentrazione, had more than a touch of anarchy in its tone. It would fight for 'Liberty, the Republic, Social Justice' in a single 'unity of action', which, though respectful of the 'great dignity and rights' of the exiled community, would be committed to revolt, to actions, 'noisy, vast and violent', inside Italy itself. 'We Italians,' they announced, 'and no one else, will defeat fascism.' After much debate, they took Lussu's suggestion for their slogan – *'Insorgere! Risorgere!'* – and a flaming sword as their symbol. Carlo was indefatigable, working fourteen-hour days, 'modest and disciplined, heedless of all obstacles, seeing only the flowery, sunlit valley of his hopes'.

Having successfully launched Giustizia e Libertà in a fanfare of publicity, Carlo set about finding somewhere for his family to live. Marion would have liked a house in the countryside, mostly because she wanted her children to grow up surrounded by trees and grass, but also because she thought Carlo would be safer. Carlo himself, mindful of the grey, wet Parisian winters, would have preferred the bustle of the Left Bank, close to the shabby hotels and offices of the Italian exiles. They compromised on a light, sunny flat on the sixth floor of a new block of flats in Passy, close to Salvemini's *pension* and to the Bois de Boulogne, an area largely unchanged from the eighteenth century, with tree-lined avenues and imposing houses.

By the end of September, Marion and Mirtillino were installed and their furniture had arrived from Italy. To his mother, Carlo wrote that he had at last 'found a still point after so much agitation and so many problems'. Here, in the peace of Passy, surrounded by his family, he planned to complete his book on what he called *Socialismo Liberale*. Marion's baby was due in the spring. She longed to play a more active role in Carlo's life, but was constantly checked by her ill-health, saying sadly that she was nothing but a useless 'barrel' of a wife. On his thirtieth birthday that November, Carlo wrote a long letter to his mother. 'Do you remember me as a boy,' he asked. 'Wily, impetuous, generous, bad-tempered, lazy?' And as a young man, 'voluble, prey to every passing fancy?' Today, he told her, he could at last see the path ahead. 'I will get there.'

He paid a quick visit to London, where he gave a talk at the National Liberal Club on 'Fascism: Its Latest Phases'. He spoke at the LSE, to the Fabian Society, the 1917 Club and in Conway Hall, and he was invited to meet Dora Russell, Gilbert Murray and Lady Astor. He was not yet a very polished speaker, but he was fast on his feet and the English were charmed by his sense of humour, his modesty and his passion. Everywhere, to everyone, he described conditions on the penal islands. His country, he told his listeners, was now 'silenced and cowed, regimented, spied on . . . controlled by an army of police agents'. The new Italy was 'rapidly acquiring the soul of a slave'. 'The day we overthrow the fascist regime,' he told the *Manchester Guardian*, 'it will be in Matteotti's name. This is Mussolini's dread.'

In Rome, *Il Popolo d'Italia* angrily depicted Carlo as a 'renegade', a repugnant traitor trotting out 'bitter and scurrilous' lies, and accused him of making money, like Judas, out of his treachery. It was all good publicity. Fêted everywhere, Carlo had time for little more than a dinner with Bertha Pritchard, to whom he wrote: 'After three years of impotency, I feel full of energy . . . We will work and we will win, even if the fight lasts another twenty years and exacts from us extreme sacrifices.'

None of this activity was lost on Mussolini or Bocchini in Rome – not Carlo's plans, nor his movements, nor his life with Marion and Mirtillino. For by the summer of 1929 Bocchini had made great progress with his many-tentacled secret services.

Two years earlier, Bocchini had decided to despatch a number of men to infiltrate the communities of exiles in various different countries, recruiting his agents from within the Fascist Party and for the most part attaching them to embassies and consulates. He gave each of them a code name, chosen from among the Homeric heroes – Ulisse, Achille – and the gods – Apollo, Diana, Castore. When he ran out of these, he moved into classical culture: Aristotle, Socrates. Now Mussolini announced that he would form his own 'exquisitely fascist' consular corps. In theory, these men were to be 'authentic fascists and veterans of *squadrismo*', aged between thirty and forty-five, have a university degree, and speak perfect French and at least one other language. In practice, some of those sent to France were ill-educated and thuggish, priding themselves on being graduates of the 'school of the *manganello*'. The Italian embassy in Paris acted as logistical support for these diplomats-come-spies and their satellites of informers, while the consulates provided valuable information about the movements of the anti-fascists around France. In Marseilles, a particularly zealous consul had a dozen men helping him draw up lists of 'subversives', subdividing them according to their physical appearance: 'lame', 'wears glasses', 'bearded', 'with scars'.

For the moment, the sinister OVRA was still operating mainly inside Italy, while Polpol handled the foreign spies, paying them through secret funds and shady deals with money from the Ministry of the Interior. Not that all the informers needed paying: subtle threats against family members or promises of work were often enough to persuade the impoverished and frightened exiles to turn spy against their friends and colleagues. It was a murky world, and the various spy rings struggled for supremacy.

Bocchini's '*fiduciari*', his trusted agents, were given precise instructions: to report 'facts, situations, opinions, criticisms'; to keep an eye out for any weakness which might be usefully exploited; to listen for rumours of plots. They were told to tap phones, read mail and carry out house searches. The idea of a 'terrorist' attack, particularly against Mussolini, continued to haunt Bocchini. Every report sent back to Rome was filed in the central police archive. The agents were given red dossiers, and known only by their pseudonyms and numbers.

The escape of Carlo, Lussu and Nitti, and particularly the enormous amount of bad publicity about fascist Italy it gave rise to, had been a severe blow to Mussolini. Bocchini circulated a letter to all his outposts saying that these men were 'persone pericolose', 'dangerous people', capable of committing 'injurious acts' and warning that Lussu, as a much-decorated war veteran, might well instigate his 'partisans' to carry them out. A report from the Italian ambassador to Paris at the end of October advised that Carlo was already 'blowing life' into the anti-fascist movement. His 'principles', reported one spy, 'are absolutely different from those of the former leaders'. Another, clearly present at a meeting in Turati's house, noted that he had seen Carlo 'gesticulating, talking enthusiastically, telling everyone of the sufferings of the Italian people, enslaved to an armed and tyrannical minority'. On Carlo's personal file in Rome, opened around this time, is stamped in large letters, 'PERICOLOSO'. Bocchini ordered that surveillance on him should be increased.

At the same time, the French Sûreté was doing a little spying of its own, some of it fanciful. Marion, a policeman noted, was thinking of opening a salon for the exiles and for the women who ran the Friends of Italian Liberty. The Rossellis were reported to have 'large sums of money, acquaintances, sympathisers, and they propose to create a vast movement of anti-fascism'. A report written on Oxilia, still in the South of France, is revealing. A rumour had been picked up in the Italian community that the fascists were planning to kidnap him, and he had told friends that he was terrified of being attacked in the street, bundled into a car and driven across the border. Since the French were anxious not to arouse anti-Italian sentiment, they decided to tell border police to look out for anyone looking suspiciously cowed in the back of a car trying to cross into Italy.

Not surprisingly, perhaps, the Italian anti-fascists in France were growing increasingly aware that they were being watched, though most remained curiously innocent of the perils. At about the time of Carlo's arrival, an anarchist called Camillo Berneri, another former disciple of Salvemini's, had started a file of his own on suspected spies. Though he concluded gloomily that 'there is nothing but confusion in Paris, and it's no longer possible to distinguish one's friends from one's enemies', he continued to compile names and potted biographies and put out a paper on 'Fascist Spies Abroad'. But neither he nor the uneasy anti-fascists were any match for Bocchini and his men.

The spies were much helped by the presence in Paris of a small, but vocal and growing, band of fascists. The first Paris *fascio* had been set up by a personal friend of Mussolini, Nicola Bonservizi – the man assassinated by an anarchist in 1924 – with a duke, a count, a professor and two doctors on its board. 'Centurions' of the 'Bonservizi cohort' were busy instilling '*l'anima italiana*', the Italian soul, into otherwise sadly 'denationalised' Italian children. As in the London *fascio*, there was much singing of 'Giovinezza' at banquets and gatherings attended by the grandees in their fascist uniforms, and children were sent home to Italy at the expense of the state to be bathed in *italianità* during the summer holidays. Expectant mothers were also offered a free passage home so that their offspring would be born in the *patria*. Their meeting place, the Casa d'Italia, just off the Champs-Élysées, had been done up with sumptuous elegance, intended to reflect an image of 'the Italy of today, ardent, young, active, dedicated to discipline ... respectful of hierarchy'.

Mussolini was right to fear the power of Carlo and his friends, for they were indeed committed to making trouble. As Lussu wrote long afterwards, 'In those first years of exile we thought of nothing but plots, attacks, insurrection and revolution.'

The first plot, however, was not of their making. A twenty-one-year-old student called Fernando de Rosa, active in the Turin anti-fascist movement until forced to flee Italy in 1928, had made friends among the more conspiratorial members of the exiled Italian community. They called him the '*beniamino*', the youngest son. Since he firmly believed that the old Italy he loved had been crushed, he told his friends, he did not mind dying for the cause of its freedom. Telling no one of his plans, he caught a train to Brussels on 22 October 1929 and went to the Colonne du Congrès, where the Italian heir to the throne, Crown Prince Umberto, in Brussels for his wedding to the Belgian king's daughter, was due to lay a wreath to the Unknown Soldier. De Rosa managed to slip through the police cordon, pulled out a gun and fired. But he had aimed far too high and his bullet missed the prince. De Rosa was thrown to the ground and almost lynched by the crowds. Later, he would explain that his gesture had been intended to draw the world's attention to the complicity of the Italian monarchy in fascism.

His trial drew many friends and supporters, including Turati, who spoke affectionately of a young man 'overcome by the folly of self-sacrifice, like the first martyr in the catacombs', and described Italy as a country in which 'violence and crime' now held sway. De Rosa's lawyer argued that it was the effect of fascism on young and impressionable minds, when they saw their homeland battered and dishonoured, that should be judged. De Rosa was given a five-year prison sentence. Carlo, not surprisingly, was full of praise for his act. Tyrannicide, he had taken to saying, was not something that should be rejected out of hand. His words were not lost on the spies.

The next plot, in which Carlo was an unwitting player, was somewhat more complicated. It involved one of Bocchini's early recruits, Ermanno Menapace (No. 98 in the police dossiers) who, passing himself off as a salesman of used cars, had been courting the journalist Cianca and anarchist Berneri for some time with a view to provoking an incident that would reflect badly on the anti-fascists. With Carlo's arrival and the setting up of Giustizia e Libertà, the prospect seemed even more appealing. Tarchiani, observing Menapace's machinations, had grown suspicious and tried to warn his friends, but Berneri was a complicated character, full of candour and a longing for martyrdom. And he, like Carlo, yearned for action. Menapace fed him the idea of assassinating Alfredo Rocco, architect of Mussolini's new corporativism, while on a visit to the League of Nations in Geneva.

Berneri, deftly played by Menapace, took possession of some gelignite and fuses, and was then caught in his flat in Paris, in a cleverly orchestrated sting, which soon implicated not only Cianca, but Tarchiani, Lussu and Carlo. The French authorities were surprisingly lenient. Cianca spent 100 days in the Santé prison. Berneri served a longer sentence, and then paid a high price for his gullibility. Ostracised by the other exiles, he wandered from country to country in search of asylum. As for Tarchiani, Carlo and Lussu, they were formally expelled from France, but friends in high places managed to convert immediate expulsion into renewable temporary visas. Menapace, exposed as having planted the incriminating gelignite, fled to Italy.

None of this dented Carlo's longing for a truly sensational stunt. The furore that had surrounded his escape from Lipari had died down, and it was time to stir it up again. He had just finished writing his book, his thesis that Italian socialism had to be rescued from both communism and fascism in a 'third way', harking back to the democratic dreams of Mazzini, Pisacane and the Risorgimento. And in March, Marion had given birth to a daughter, with, as Carlo wrote to his mother, a large mouth, a great deal of fair hair and 'a little nose belonging to the potato family'. They decided to call their new child Amelia, after her grandmother, but she was soon known as Melina. Mirtillino had started to talk, and his sentences came out in a mixture of Italian, English and French. 'The family grows in a most harmonious way,' Carlo wrote to Amelia, adding that the one bitter note in his life, '*mammolina cara*', was that she was so far away: otherwise, he was content, and 'following my chosen path'. Amelia now had four grandchildren, but two were in exile and likely to remain there.

The new plot was the kind of adventure that Carlo most relished. Giovanni Bassanesi was a twenty-five-year-old teacher from Aosta, formal in manner, Catholic as well as liberal, who was supporting himself by photography while studying at the Sorbonne. With his very pale skin and straight dark hair slicked back, he looked a little like Rudolph Valentino, unsmiling and intense. He had been nineteen when Matteotti was murdered, and the event had marked his life. Soon after Cianca was released from prison, Bassanesi came to him with a plan. He had tried the communists but they had turned him away. He told Cianca that he had once scattered anti-fascist leaflets from the upper box of a theatre over the audience below, and this had given him a better idea. He would learn to fly, pilot a plane over an Italian city, and drop leaflets. Like many of these schemes, Bassanesi's plan had a sort of absurd innocence about it. But when he heard about it Carlo was delighted. He said that he would buy the plane, pay for the leaflets and organise the whole venture.

Bassanesi duly learnt to fly. Because small planes have limited fuel capacity, an airfield was identified by friendly local socialists in the Swiss canton of Ticino, close to the Italian border, at Lodano. In a remarkably short space of time, minutely orchestrated by Tarchiani and Carlo – by now experts in this kind of planning – a Farman biplane had been bought, an experienced

French pilot found to fly the plane with Bassanesi on the first leg of the journey, the leaflets were printed, and Dolci had volunteered to fly as passenger in order to throw them out over Milan. Bassanesi, though by nature highly volatile and nervous – and also prone to airsickness – remained resolute.

Early in July 1930, Bassanesi and the French pilot flew to Bellinzona, the capital of Ticino, where the pilot was dropped off. Bassanesi then flew on to Lodano, where Carlo, Tarchiani, Dolci and the leaflets were waiting. Everyone was jumpy. At the last moment the parachutes had to be jettisoned because there was no room for them. At 11.30 a.m. on Friday 11 July, the plane took off, with the anxious Bassanesi at the controls. They crossed the frontier, flying at 150 kilometres an hour, and by midday were above Milan. For the next fifteen minutes they flew low over the city, Dolci throwing out the leaflets, which fell, like multicoloured snowflakes, on to the workers emerging from offices and factories for their lunch hour. One pack, which failed to come apart, broke a factory window, but no one was hurt.

Having dropped Dolci back at another airfield just over the border, Bassanesi flew towards the St Gotthard Pass. There was

Giovanni Bassanesi, before his flight over Milan

heavy cloud and he had no instruments. Unable to see where he was going, he made a crash-landing in a rocky field. The Farman fell apart and he was briefly unconscious before being pulled from the wreckage with a broken leg. He was arrested by the Swiss police and taken to a prison hospital in Andermatt.

The effect of the stunt was extremely satisfactory. The first news of the flight appeared in a Ticino paper, which gave it a special edition. The story was picked up, repeated, reprinted throughout Europe. In Italy, there was at first total silence. Then a short article appeared about a 'rogue' plane with a 'renegade' pilot, spewing 'words of hatred' in the form of leaflets, all of which had been quickly recovered and destroyed. The aeroplane, said the *Corriere della Sera*, symbol of all that was glorious and progressive, had been turned into a 'hateful device' and a reminder of treachery.

The truth was somewhat different. The snowstorm of leaflets had caused a sensation in Milan, and far from being recovered, all but 15,000 of the 150,000 thrown out were spirited away, to be passed on from hand to hand and city to city. The daring of the enterprise was much admired, and the name of Giustizia e Libertà was on everyone's lips. Mussolini called for the maximum punishment for these 'violators of the inviolable sky' and for a trial for endangering the security of Switzerland. The Swiss refused, saying they would bring charges only for violation of the rules on flights.

Carlo, Tarchiani and Dolci all volunteered to appear before the court, believing it would afford them much welcome publicity. The trial did not go Mussolini's way. Held in the city of Lugano under a judge, Agostino Soldati, known for his independence of spirit, it became a replica of the famous Savona trial. Lawyers from all over Switzerland volunteered to defend the men. Once again it was not those in the dock but fascism itself that was on trial. Speaker after speaker described the brutality of the fascists. There was a huge turnout of lawyers, politicians and journalists, many of them from foreign newspapers. Carlo Sforza and Turati testified on Bassanesi's behalf, Turati saying that the stunt had been a beacon of light amid the terror and unhappiness of an 'oppressed and depressed Italy'. Do not hope, he said, that in fining Carlo Rosselli you will make him mend his ways. 'He is incorrigible. And he will commit many other such acts ... until the *Patria* has been redeemed and restored to liberty.' Sforza spoke at length about 'sacred ideals' until stopped by the judge.

Bassanesi had broken Swiss law and received a four-month prison sentence, but since he had already spent several months awaiting trial, he was immediately released. His 'idealism' was praised, and he received no fine. Carlo, Tarchiani, Dolci and the French pilot were all acquitted. As in Savona, the cheering flowed out into the streets. That night, there was a celebratory banquet before the plotters boarded their train for Paris. At stations along the way were waiting enthusiastic crowds. Bassanesi returned to Brussels, where he was much congratulated; and soon set about dreaming up new stunts. Once again, Carlo, Tarchiani and Dolci were heroes. But Amelia was full of angst. 'I beg of you,' she wrote to Carlo, 'be sensible, do not push your luck. I am terrified that your constant little pinpricks will result in some disaster (though I fervently hope that moment never comes).'

The flight over Milan had put Giustizia e Libertà firmly on the map. But its leaders were now squarely in Bocchini's sights.

CHAPTER FIFTEEN

Just One Heart

As Piero Calamandrei later described them, Carlo and Nello were 'two spirits, two attitudes of mind, two kinds of life, but just one heart'. While Carlo chose to fight the fascists from abroad, 'the land of freedom', Nello considered it his duty to challenge them within Italy, 'the land of slavery'. Pressed by friends to join Carlo in France, he would say that someone had to stay behind to give an example of how not to give in to the fascists, to '*salvar l'anima*', save his soul, in the very midst of them: it had fallen to his lot to do so. The two brothers' natures were not so much alike as complementary: Carlo excitable, impatient, optimistic; Nello calm, even-tempered, full of self-doubt. Where they met, somewhere in the middle, was over the beliefs inculcated in them since early childhood by Amelia and carried into their adult years: a certainty that they had to take responsibility for their own actions, a shared honesty, loyalty and deep sense of family, and their profound love for each other. There were no voices of criticism or disapproval between them. They were now thirty and twenty-nine. That they looked so similar, both tall, fair-skinned, somewhat overweight, with open faces and warm manners, only added to their closeness.

Both possessed, as Amelia did, curiosity, a need to understand, a moral centre, a belief in human dignity, and implicit in everything they said and wrote was their attachment to liberty. For both of them, the evils of fascism lay not in questions of class and privilege but in the mistakes of the past, and neither one believed that, once fascism was defeated, it would ever be possible to go back to what had come before. Something new had to happen. Carlo was seeking it in action, Nello in history, as seen through the men and women who had shaped it. The fact that Nello's part was by necessity more oblique, more guarded, made him seem the less involved of the two. But he was not. He, like Carlo, was a fighter, always conscious, as he told a friend of 'all the beauty and value of a life of battle'. As Carlo put it, they both knew that the battle might last many years, and that it was likely to entail many sacrifices; but there was no avoiding it. 'We are working for eternity! This is our strength.' Amelia, reluctantly, with fear and misgivings but also with pride, accepted this. Both her sons knew how much she minded not being near them. This, Carlo wrote to a friend, also in exile in France, was the sad fate 'of our mothers who are growing old'.

At the Scuola Moderna, Volpe had not ceased to manoeuvre on Nello's behalf. He was clearly attached to his young colleague and prepared to put up with criticism that he was supporting 'an open enemy of the regime, a socialist, a Salveminiano'. Nello's *Mazzini e Bakunin* had been praised by critics for its meticulous accumulation of material and for its style, free of flourish and vested interest, unusual in the world of Italian academia. He had already done what research he could for the Scuola di Storia Moderna e Contemporanea's project on British and Italian diplomatic relations in the archives in Palermo, Naples, Turin and Rome. Volpe wanted him to pursue them in the Public Record Office in London, and he now persuaded a reluctant Mussolini to grant Nello a passport. Though the material was too dry to be congenial to Nello, for he was increasingly drawn to a wider, more discursive and biographical view of history, seen through men's ambitions and drives, he was a willing and diligent worker and accepted the possibility of a stint abroad with pleasure. It was made clear to everyone that he was not considering flight.

All the Rossellis, in their own way, loved London. Englishness, like the Risorgimento, was part of their rational image of themselves, as people not easily buffeted by oratory or obfuscation. Carlo had briefly considered making London his base, but quickly realised that, for the anti-fascists, its staid social circles were no match for the volatile cross-currents of Parisian life.

In June 1930, leaving Maria, Silvia and Paola with Amelia in Via Giusti, Nello set out for England. 'I am wonderfully happy,' he wrote from the Thackeray Hotel in Bloomsbury. He loved the cordiality of the people he encountered and their 'passionate respect' for individual liberty, and he even liked the weather. It was, he told them, as if he had come home 'after a long mental illness'. His 'old English blood' thrived. In the mornings, he went to the archives, despairing about the sheer amount of material he was finding; in the afternoons he joined his painter friend Carlo Levi, also on a visit to England, and they took their easels to Hampton Court, catching a boat up the Thames. One day, they hired bicycles and set off to explore the English countryside.

Through Carlo and Marion, he had introductions to Bertha Pritchard and her circle of clever women friends, who in turn were being fed material on Italy by Salvemini, whose appetite for work was prodigious and who never tired of fresh onslaughts on the fascists. His book, *The Fascist Dictatorship in Italy*, had been published to considerable publicity, both in the US and in England, and a thousand copies smuggled into Italy. Salvemini, noted Mussolini, was full of madness and hatred; an Italian police report described him as 'touchy, vindictive, proud, presumptuous, cultured and intelligent'.

There were also invitations to dine with Don Luigi Sturzo, one of the most remarkable of Mussolini's opponents, a tall, thin, beaky Catholic priest from Sicily. In 1919 Don Sturzo had bitterly attacked Mussolini, and become one of the founders of the Partito Popolare Italiano – a precursor to the post-war Christian Democrats – and for a brief moment the leader of 100 members of parliament. However, any coalition between socialists and his party had been unacceptable to the Vatican, and in 1924 Don Sturzo had been dismissed by the Cardinal Secretary of State Gasparri, on the wishes of Mussolini, and sent to London on prolonged study-leave for his refusal to endorse the fascists. Don Sturzo was still campaigning for a party based on Christian teachings, but not subservient to the Catholic Church. He was much loved by Bertha Pritchard, who helped translate his writings, and by Salvemini, who called him 'one of the best things in my life'. He had reviewed Nello's book, praising it highly. Together, they talked endlessly about liberty, 'for all, and always'. Mindful of their seditious talk, *Il Popolo d'Italia* referred to them as 'authentic international carrion'. Carlo and Don Sturzo had kept up an affectionate correspondence, which occasionally turned frosty when Carlo seemed too critical of the Church's support for the fascists.

In London, Nello saw Salvemini for the first time in five years. It was an emotional reunion. Soon after, Nello wrote his mentor and friend a loving, appreciative letter, in his usual open, almost jaunty style. Salvemini, he said, had taught him about political thought, about the great pleasure of serious work, about relating the present to the past. 'My dearest Professor, only you know how much I owe you. You made me a man. Alongside you, under your influence, I became a man.' But, once again, he needed guidance. He was about to be thirty, and felt himself both old, and yet still a child. What should he do? Could Salvemini suggest a subject that would both satisfy his need for historical research and at the same time have a bearing on contemporary politics? How could he steer his way between these conflicting sirens?

Carlo and Marion had applied for passports to visit Nello in England, but as aliens and political refugees in France, these were refused, neither the French nor the British willing to make difficulties with the fascists. Word went out for the port officials in Dover, Folkestone, Newhaven, Southampton and Harwich to keep an eye out in case they tried to enter the country illegally. Ramsay MacDonald was back in power, once again with a minority Labour government, and there had been hopes among the anti-fascists that he would stiffen up British attitudes against Mussolini. But MacDonald was not prepared to provoke his displeasure. The 'blood-thirsty organ grinder', as the *Illustrated London News* described Mussolini, remained more a figure of fun than a despot for the English, who continued somewhat condescendingly to say that, while there would be no question of a dictatorship in England, a firm hand was probably necessary for the unruly and theatrical Italians and their suspicious weakness for the Bolsheviks. Mussolini, observed Harold Nicolson smugly, would never have been a fascist if he had been 'an Englishman in England'. It would take the rise of Hitler for the British to see the dangers of totalitarianism.

In the six years since Carlo's visit to the Fabians, the London *fascio* had opened schools in Southwark, King's Cross, Marylebone, Hackney and Stratford, moved into new offices in Greek Street, and were busy corralling the sprawling Italian community, inveighing against all who transgressed against *italianità*, referring to them as 'fossils' and 'feeble crusts' on the manliness of the new virile Italy. An Italian countess going by the name of Maria Vanden Heuvel had written an ode to Mussolini, '*O tu, raggio di sole nascente*' – 'Oh you ray of the rising sun' – and sang it on all possible occasions, accompanying herself on the piano. But the Italian fascists in London also had their violent side: when Nitti's book, *Escape*, was published by George Putnam, there were threats to blow up its offices.

Amelia had also applied for a visa and when it came through she joined Nello in London. Bertha Pritchard and her friends were precisely the kind of women whose company Amelia most enjoyed. Then, at Nello's invitation, Alberto Moravia came to visit them in London. The success of his latest novel *Gli indifferenti*, with its disparaging portrayal of young people under fascism, materially greedy and empty of all ideals, had made him the *enfant terrible* of the Italian literary world. But his notoriety also gave him some protection from the wrath of the fascists, and particularly that of Mussolini. Ever slippery in his attitude towards politics, Moravia enjoyed moving in fascist circles, though he was greeted one day by Mussolini's mistress, Margherita Sarfatti, with the words: 'You're the cousin of that pig Carlo Rosselli.' Carlo, who had finished reading the book on Lipari, considered it 'amoral and morbid'. Amelia disliked its cool cynicism; she had become critical of her once much-loved, talented nephew and complained that he always seemed bored and disgruntled.

On his way home to Italy, Moravia paused in Paris to see Carlo, who asked him to post a letter in Rome, written to an anarchist friend, because he feared it might otherwise be intercepted by the secret police. Moravia demurred. What if he were spotted? Carlo laughed. It would be wonderful propaganda for the anti-fascists if a writer of his renown were arrested. Moravia took the letter.

Marion was again pregnant, despite taking precautions. 'We are in despair,' Carlo wrote to his brother; they were thinking about an abortion. Nello wrote a jocular letter to Amelia: 'Madonna, what a couple of cats those two are.' What worried them all was whether Marion's heart would withstand another pregnancy.

At the end of the year Nello met Maria in Switzerland. Mussolini had granted her a passport 'to avoid the nuisance ... of pressure by the Rosselli family'. The worry and uncertainties of the past two years had taken their toll and she was very thin; there were fears that she might have inherited something of her father's depressions. But a cure in the mountains, away from the two demanding little girls, left in Florence with Amelia, lifted her spirits. At the turn of 1930, they settled into a hotel in Montreux, and Nello painted a portrait of his young wife in bed. He was enjoying, he told Zia Gì, a 'second edition of my honeymoon', and he did not know which of the two he found sweeter, his own intense happiness or the spectacle of Maria returned to such 'joy and liveliness. She laughs at everything, is enthusiastic about everything, and has such a full and sane attitude to life.' He persuaded her to unpin her chignon and leave her dark curly hair loose. She looked, he said, 'adorable'. In late January Maria went back with Nello to spend a few weeks in London. When she was obliged to have a minor ear operation, Nello wrote an eight-page, closely spaced letter to Amelia, describing every detail.

After further consultations with Salvemini, Nello had settled on the subject for his new book, a biography of Pisacane, the Neapolitan patriot and officer who fought at Mazzini's side in 1848, was exiled in Lausanne and London and eventually committed suicide at the age of thirty-nine. One of his first readers was Amelia, who considered it a 'vast and profound bit of work', made all the more so because Nello had put so much of himself into it. Alessandro Levi agreed, but said that it made him feel nervous. He suggested that Nello tone down his words, since they seemed to allude so openly to the fate of the anti-fascists driven into exile. Salvemini's teachings on the importance of relating the past to the present had borne fruit, but these were dangerous times. Even when softened and made more ambiguous, Nello's book still read as a commentary on fascist persecution, with barely veiled references to Mussolini, and much praise for the 'very few' honest and decisive patriots, who *non mollerano*, would not weaken. Even the normally fiery Salvemini urged tact and caution. What they did not know was that a spy was on their trail even in London, and that he had reported that 'Rosselli, Mary, known in feminist circles', speaking good Italian, was raising money for anti-fascist causes.

Carlo and Nello had not met for three years. Though they wrote to each other constantly about their work, praising each other's efforts – Nello said that Carlo's short book on his escape from Lipari, *Fuga in Quattro Tempi*, showed the marks of a 'great' writer – what they longed to do was talk face to face. Since he was unable to come to England, Carlo kept pressing Nello to visit France. With his trusting and innocent nature, so heedless of possible dangers that it worried his friends, he reassured Nello that he was never watched, that his post was never intercepted, and that, providing they met somewhere other than Paris, it was 'mathematically impossible' that Nello would be compromised. 'There are so very many things that I want to say and ask you, dear Nellino, and I feel such happiness and tenderness at the very thought of embracing you again.' But Nello was wary. He had promised Maria that he would do nothing to provoke another sentence on the penal islands. And he was right to be anxious. His police file in Rome included notes on his every movement, on the names and addresses of the people he was meeting, along with Maria's comings and goings. Amelia too was now closely watched. A note circulated by Bocchini's men urged 'the most diligent vigilance in order to keep track of her movements and observe everything she does'.

And now Volpe, hounded by Mussolini over Nello's suspiciously long absence, wrote sternly to his young protégé to delay no longer. Reassuring Volpe that he had no intention of breaking his promise, Nello nonetheless asked Carlo to warn him if things were happening that might make his return to Italy dangerous. They devised a code: the words 'affectionate regards' meant that it was perilous; 'excellent, have a good journey' that it was safe. The brothers worried ceaselessly about each other's safety, telling each other again and again: take care, don't make a joke about the dangers, do not go out on the lake, do not take public transport, try always to have a friend with you. Still Nello hesitated about going home, while at the same time fearing that the longer he stayed away, the harder he would find it to go back. 'I cannot tell you', he wrote to Carlo, 'with what reluctance I return to my cage.' But with Maria and the children in Florence, he really had no choice.

The two brothers met only briefly as the train taking Nello back to Italy paused in Paris.

The cage to which Nello chose voluntarily to return was very nearly fully enclosed, a vast prison in which all aspects of life were regulated and all attempts to escape foiled. Since the liberal state had been unruly and disorderly, the fascist state would be all about order, unremittingly enforced. As Mussolini put it, 'In a certain sense, you could say that the policeman preceded the professor in history.'

The early 1930s were a golden age for fascism: the regime seemed secure, the anti-fascists, widely regarded as traitors, were exiled or silenced. From the top of Italy to the heel, men, women and children paraded in their uniforms – some senior fascist officials had twenty different outfits – to the sounds of 'Giovinezza'. They venerated the Duce and tried their best to obey the rules. Newsreels beamed around the world pictured natty child fascists mimicking grown men, saluting, singing, marching. In the Pontine Marshes south of Rome, malaria was retreating as a programme of public works drained the swampy soil. In Sicily, fascist policemen sent from Rome were busy purging the corrupt officials and curbing Mafia killings and extortion. A plebiscite reported 8½ million people as endorsing the fascists, and 135,000 refusing to do so. And where everything was not quite as it should have been, no one was allowed to say so. As Mussolini declared in 1928, 'Italian journalism is free because it serves just one cause and one regime; it's free because ... it can and does act to control, to criticise and to make progress.' There was very little, now, to distinguish one newspaper from another.

The acrimonious, mistrustful relationship between Church and state had been at the heart of Italian politics since the Risorgimento. Having suppressed Freemasonry, the Church's implacable enemy, Mussolini had spent the late 1920s inching fitfully towards accommodation with the Vatican. Early in 1929, at a ceremony of considerable pomp held in the Vatican Palace, he signed the Lateran Accords, making the Vatican a fully independent enclave and its citizens exempt from fascist laws. The Church was given authority over marriage, religious teaching was made obligatory and crucifixes were returned to the classroom. In return, the

Vatican recognised the fascist state, and Pope Pius XI graciously described Mussolini as the 'man whom Providence sent us' – though he cannot have been altogether reassured when Mussolini announced that fascism was itself a religion, 'a passion, a faith, an apostolate'. In Britain, the Catholic *Tablet* called the Duce an 'intellectual giant'. Journalists hinted that fascism had somehow even inoculated Italy against the economic depression sweeping the west. Don Sturzo was offered an appointment as a canon of St Peter's Basilica – on condition that he renounce all political life. He turned it down.

While the fascist propaganda machine was busy spewing out self-congratulatory statistics – litres of milk distributed, numbers of summer colonies for children set up – a 'corporate' state was coming into being, made up of a great many phrases, but also a great deal of what Salvemini described as 'humbug'. 'Don Quixote', said Mussolini, 'attacked windmills as if they were real monsters.' He would deal with them 'as if they were windmills'. Before the 'advent of the saviour', Italy had apparently been a country of loafers, dandies and drunkards. Now it was one of sportsmen and fecund mothers. This, at least, was the theory. In practice, Italians had been riding bicycles and producing large families long before the March on Rome. What was more, by the early 1930s, there were a million Italians out of work, and those in work had seen their personal rights, political liberties and bargaining powers vanish. In Bari, the southern showcase town for the fascists, a quarter of all inhabitants lived four to a room. In Sicily, the policemen sent to round up suspected *mafiosi* had used the occasion to mop up political opponents and had merely driven the Mafia underground.

The Italians were fed inconsistencies, falsehoods, contradictions, differing interpretations, all designed to mystify and confuse, many of it transmitted in stentorian, martial style over the radio. It was forbidden to mention failures. When, in the early 1930s, the young journalist Luigi Barzini was sent by the *Corriere della Sera* to report on Sardinia, he was instructed not to mention poverty, malaria or banditry for, officially, these no longer existed. In reality, much of the south remained as it had always been, mired in backwardness and lawlessness.

By 1931, when Nello returned to live permanently in Italy with

Maria and his two young daughters, a new generation of Italian children who had never known anything but fascism was growing up. The Opera Nazionale Balilla, with its two million children, controlled every aspect of sport and physical training. The First World War had revealed Italian men to be in poor condition, many with heart problems, rickets and congenital illnesses. The new physical instructors were to be 'biological engineers' and builders of a more perfect 'human machine'. Throughout the 1920s, federations of cyclists, footballers, motorcyclists, tennis and rugby players, roller-skaters, weightlifters, skiers and sailors had been set up. They were paying off. The Olympic Games held in Amsterdam in 1928 had yielded a mass of gold medals for Italy. Pot-bellied Fascist Party leaders were to be found crammed into tight gym clothes, bouncing on trampolines. In the new Foro Mussolini in Rome, huge naked male statues were stationed around a running track.

As for girls, who had to be protected from the 'unnatural desires of English suffragettes' and the frivolity and worldliness of 'French coquettes', they were made to dance, garden, iron and knit, and given 'doll drills', in which they were taught how to hold babies the correct way. When, in the early summer of 1928, thousands of girls between the ages of sixteen and eighteen were brought to Rome for the first gymnastic-athletic competition, they were told to discipline their muscles and take part in rifle practice, while at the same time to study 'good mothering', in order to become 'neither feeble ... nor gloomy'. (Pope Pius XI protested about the rifles: if girls raised their arms, it should 'be always and only in prayer and charitable actions'.)

And yet fascism sent out conflicting messages to girls. Young women who tried to join an air club in Bologna were turned away on the grounds that 'in fascist Italy, the most fascist thing women can do is to pilot the making of children'. The fascists wanted their women at home, producing babies. They liked wide hips, florid complexions, good bones and passive dispositions, but they also wanted girls to exercise, which made them thinner, more athletic and less passive. The press was instructed never to portray women with dogs (child substitutes), wasp waists (unsuited to motherhood and probably syphilitic), or as excessively thin (probably sterile).

Long before the end of the first decade of fascist rule, schools were resounding to Eia! Eia! Alalà!, the cry of the Roman legions. Both boys and girls wore white gloves, and marched along their school corridors in perfect order and silence like well-drilled soldiers. When visitors came, the children rose to their feet, and, at a given command, simultaneously stretched out their right arms in a Roman salute. On the walls of their classrooms hung framed fascist maxims and photographs of Mussolini, along with little lamps, surrounded by flowers, to honour fascist martyrs.

Under a new Ministry of National Education, real *'fascistizzazione'* began. Schools were no longer places to foster curiosity and learning, but rather agencies of indoctrination. Spontaneity and initiative had given way to stifling uniformity. Five separate commissions sifted through existing school books, rejecting all that seemed to weaken *'italianità'*, and replacing them with eulogies to heroic aviators and explorers. The story of Pinocchio was jettisoned as being mawkish and sentimental. Essays and drawing competitions were set on edifying themes: 'The glories of Ancient Rome', 'The mother of the hero' or, best of all, on the Duce as hero. Patriotic songs punctuated every class, every gymnastic exercise. Life, declared Mussolini's brother Arnaldo, 'should be attacked like a mountain range which can only be crossed with difficulty'. Action, not thought: thinking was harmful to health.

Of all activities, *l'arma azzurra*, aeronautics, was the one dearest to Mussolini's heart. With the appointment of Ferrara's brutal *ras*, Italo Balbo, as minister of aviation in 1926 had come a craze for flying, Mussolini himself taking to the skies above Milan in a bowler hat and grey spats. Flight, Mussolini declared, was 'the greatest poem of modern times ... the contemporary equivalent of Dante's *Divine Comedy*'. When in December 1930 Balbo took off from the lagoon of Orbetello in Tuscany with ten seaplanes to cross the Atlantic, the honour and prestige of Italy had never seemed to ride so high.

Filippo Tommaso Marinetti had spent the 1920s extolling Futurist versions of art, sculpture, poetry, theatre, aeronautics and even food, in ways that perfectly matched fascist aspirations. For Marinetti, as for Mussolini, the skies were the place to impose domination over the earth. The 1929 Manifesto dell'Aeropittura futurista, of which he was a signatory, glorified man's ability to conquer space and time through flight and he, like Balbo, had led seaplanes over the Mediterranean and to West Africa and Brazil. The pilot, said Marinetti, was the newest of the new men, one who soared over the pedantic realities of mere mortals.

It was not enough, however, to be bold. Marinetti wanted to 'fascistise' all culture, do away with classical architecture and fill Italy's Renaissance squares with electric trams and overhead wires. He wanted to industrialise Venice and ban everything foreign – films, food, orchestras and even languages – within 'our virile, proud, dynamic peninsula'. And since the new man had to be futuristic inside as well as out, he launched a crusade against pasta, saying that it made Italians gross, lazy, complacent and stupid, and led to pessimism and prostitution. 'Until now men have fed themselves like ants, rats, cats and oxen,' he declared in an article on Futurist cooking. The new man would do better to eat black olives, fennel hearts and kumquats, and as he ate, stroke sandpaper and velvet, enjoying the contrast in taste and texture, while a waiter sprayed carnation-scented water on to the back of his neck and from the kitchen were relayed the roars of aeroplane motors. At the Holy Palate, his proposed Futurist restaurant in Turin, diners would be given a boiled chicken accompanied by ball bearings in whipped cream, served by a 'woman of the future', bald and wearing spectacles. Compared to the remorseless severity and humourlessness of most fascist dictates, Marinetti's crazy fantasies had a certain innocent charm.

And over it all presided the towering figure of Mussolini, boastful, canny, vain, cruel and erratic. In 1929, he had moved from his old office in the Palazzo Chigi to the Sala del Mappamondo in the fifteenth-century papal Palazzo Venezia. It was 18 metres long, gilded and frescoed, with a ceiling 12 metres high and a polished mosaic floor, and had a balcony looking out over the piazza below, perfect for speaking to the people, hands on hips, jaw thrust out, unsmiling. Mussolini positioned his desk at the far end of the largely empty hall, so that visitors faced a long intimidating walk to approach him. He liked encounters to be kept brief, no more than fifteen minutes – a loud, ticking clock was placed strategically nearby – and he came across as brisk, speaking quickly, seldom listening. He liked dramatic pronouncements and vast choreographed occasions, reviewing troops or inspecting the peasants draining the Pontine Marshes. On his desk was a picture of his much-loved Angora cat.

Though his desk, like his hall, was kept free of clutter, Mussolini worked extremely hard. He made lists; the great speeches, designed to come across as spontaneous, were minutely prepared; as the head of several government ministries, he liked to be closely briefed about them all, even if he made little effort to work out how to turn words into actions. He would later say that in 7 years he had transacted 1,887,112 items of business. Boasting that he was never tired, he was a careful and calculating executive, controlling his entourage through a mixture of blandishments and bullying, playing one off against another, weaving a chaotic but cunning path between rational governance and fantastical myths.

Famously promiscuous and unfaithful, enjoying rapid seductions in the Sala del Mappamondo during which he seldom removed his trousers, Mussolini had eventually married his staid and squarely built Rachele in a church ceremony and moved into the Palazzo Torlonia near the Porta Pia. After the birth of their daughter Edda had come four more children, three boys and another girl, but the family had only recently moved to Rome to live with him. Meals were quick, not least because a severe duodenal ulcer kept him on a diet of fruit and milk. In April 1930, Edda, now twenty, married Galeazzo Ciano, the son of an admiral, in a vast and sumptuous ceremony to which 4,000 guests were invited. Ciano was a greedy, vain, elegant man of considerable charm and laziness, a good mimic and raconteur, most often to be found on the golf course, and already perceived as his father-in-law's possible successor. He possessed, said his enemies, 'the character and moral outlook of a popular gigolo'. Given to sexual dalliances, he enjoyed eating pheasants and oysters and kept an exercise bicycle in his office in the Palazzo Chigi.

As important to Mussolini as his image of a loving family man was his ambition to be the architect of a sparkling, cleaned-up Rome, restored to the splendour of the Emperor Augustus, with Roman roads and stadiums full of statues of naked men. The 'filthy and picturesque' was to be replaced by towering imperial buildings in shining white stone, on straight lines. A Via dei Fori

Mussolini as a family man, with his wife Rachele and their five children

Imperiali was planned to run between the Colosseum and the Palazzo Venezia, and an entire town, EUR, to rise on the road leading to the sea. There was to be a 263-foot statue, with the head of Mussolini and the body of Hercules, his hand raised in the fascist salute, and his foot larger than that of an elephant. Meanwhile the Duce's severe features, his triumphalist poses, were splashed on to posters, walls, coins. Now nearing fifty, he sometimes chose to jog rather than walk, in full uniform, the image of the steely soldier bearing the weight of Italy on his sturdy shoulders. As proof of his superior courage, he had himself photographed with a lioness.

By comparison, pictures of the royal family, the complacent King Victor Emmanuel and his statuesque wife Queen Elena, were somehow paler and more insubstantial. Their son Umberto – who had survived de Rosa's assassination attempt – was now married to Marie José of Belgium. Though her short-haired, stylish looks did not wholly conform to those of a comfortable fascist matron, Marie José obligingly agreed to be photographed breastfeeding her new baby. Mussolini considered monarchy, particularly one as supportive and accepting as that of Victor Emmanuel, useful to his notion of history.

It was only towards the end of 1930 that Italians learnt what the sinister letters OVRA stood for. As Mussolini had said: 'The more Italians are afraid, the quieter they will be.' Keeping OVRA's meaning secret had added to its sense of menace, in no way reduced by spelling it out in several different ways: sometimes the Opera Vigilanza e Rastrellamento Antifascista (Vigilance and Search), sometimes Opera Volontaria di Repressione Antifascista (Repression). It hardly mattered. Its function was perfectly plain. By the end of the 1920s, Bocchini's vast apparatus of surveillance had been put in place, consisting of a relatively small, tight-knit bureaucracy answerable directly to him, and several thousand 'trombellieri', stringers, some permanent, some casual, all jostling for supremacy and preferment. There were spies and informers in restaurants, hotels and cafés; in brothels, factories and military barracks; in schools and universities, where teachers denounced their colleagues and students their teachers, and, sometimes, their parents and their parents' friends. There was even a paid spy in the Vatican, Monsignor Enrico Pucci, a priest on the Pope's immediate staff. Pucci was given the number 96 and received 3,000 lire each month.

'We want', Mussolini told Bocchini, 'to create ... a kind of magical eye which keeps Italians under control and can at any moment provide me with a complete, up-to-date picture of everything being said and done in the whole of Italy. Men ... with the craftiness of a fox and the speed of a serpent, they need to learn the difficult art of provocation, how to insinuate themselves into a crowd, how to fit into every situation and every social circle.' Bocchini had done his bidding. Inspector Nudi's first inspectorate, Zona 1, in Milan had been followed by Zona 2, in Bologna and its surroundings; more were planned for Bari, Avezzano, Palermo, Cagliari, Naples, Florence and Rome. And against the communists, until the early 1930s the main target for the fascists, OVRA had already proved extremely efficient: some 2,000 people had been arrested, most of the communist leaders sent to jail or the confino, and thousands more now lived 'under surveillance'. Most of this was due to Bocchini and Nudi's men.

But the secret services had not been altogether successful. They had spectacularly failed to prevent a bomb going off at the entrance to a trade fair in Milan, minutes before the king was due to arrive. Eighteen people were killed and more than fifty injured. Though the police combed the city, 560 people were arrested, rewards were offered for information and a young man, mistaken for his anarchist cousin, had three ribs broken during interrogation, no culprit could be identified. Bocchini's failure to anticipate Carlo's escape from Lipari – despite warnings – was another black mark, as was Bassanesi's flight over Milan. The methodical, painstaking Nudi asked for, and was given, more men. Manhunts intensified.

Mussolini remained deeply ambivalent about the Italian intellectuals; he wanted their imprimatur, but he also feared their dissidence. He preferred them to be inside Italy, where they could be watched and threatened, rather than abroad where, like Salvemini and Carlo, they could mount campaigns against him. That Nello was able to live and work, and even travel abroad, relatively unmolested was revealing of the strange nature of fascism itself, a mixture of scrutiny and looking the other way, of menaces and promises of immunity, of violence towards those considered total enemies and accommodation with those who might be redeemed. It was a slippery world, and Nello would have to navigate his way.

Benedetto Croce, Italy's best known anti-fascist, was allowed not only to speak and write fairly freely, but also to continue producing his magazine, *La Critica*. Several times a year, he travelled north to Milan and Turin. Wherever he went, he was a magnet for those trying to keep some kind of independent thought, and this too the fascists tolerated, even if they usually kept a policeman outside his door. In the summers the anti-fascists still at liberty went south to visit him in his house near Naples, or they met somewhere in the mountains, in the guise of tourists. 'We felt that we were living on an iceberg,' one of them was to write. Even meeting just a few times a year broke their sense of profound isolation. When Nello managed to join them, tall, rosy-cheeked, he reminded them of a 'putto, grown enormous, with great candour'.

By the same token, Luigi Einaudi, Carlo's former mentor, was allowed to go on teaching at Turin university, making no secret of his liberal views, or the fact that he contributed articles to the London *Economist*. Nello was under no illusions that, not having the fame of Croce or Einaudi, he would be allowed any such latitude. It was just how far he could operate as an honest historian that he needed to discover. As he wrote at the end of his book on Pisacane, 'The traveller, anxious to cross the torrent, throws one stone after another into the depths.' Watching the stones disappear, he can only hope that they are there, out of sight, ready to bear his weight. 'Pisacane, too, seems to have disappeared into the void. But by his life and by his death, he laid one of the granite blocks on which the Italian edifice is built.' It was clear that he saw himself and Carlo as such blocks.

With *Pisacane* published to respectful reviews, Nello was thinking of starting a magazine to 'detoxify' the telling of nineteenth-century European history from the 'nationalist bacillus'. It would include articles by historians from across Europe and would deal with nothing later than the First World War in order to avoid the thorny topic of contemporary politics. By placing Italy firmly in a wider European context, he told friends, he intended to make Italian readers feel 'less alone'. His cousin Alessandro Levi, the Ferreros and the Orvietos were all encouraging, as was Croce; even Volpe expressed interest. Nello found the choice of the nineteenth century, with its articulate and heroic Europeans, comforting. 'When I am with these men,' he said, 'I am where I belong. I am at home. The men of today are foreign to me.'

It was as well that Nello had money, for Italian academia was now closed to him. Unruly and independent-minded schoolmasters had already been purged. In November 1931, after years of increasing restrictions, university professors, who were also employees of the state, were ordered to sign an oath of fealty to the king and to the fascist regime. It caused consternation in academic circles. Some professors were only too happy to obey; others procrastinated, and were threatened. (One joked that the letters of the Fascist Party, PNF, could also stand for '*Per necessità familiare*', for family reasons). But by 18 December, all but 12 of the 1,200 or so had signed and the recalcitrant dozen were dismissed or had resigned in disgust. The Pope had obligingly made things easier by issuing a communiqué allowing Catholics to take the oath. The academic world throughout Europe protested loudly and in London Mrs Crawford published a letter comparing the fascists to the Ku Klux Klan.

Florence, once the recognised cultural capital of Italy, had become the home of 'exquisitely fascist' artistic activities. A 'moral cleansing', was launched, with campaigns against swearing, pornography, immoral plays and indecent fashions. 'Eroticism' was to be done away with, wherever it occurred. Girls were enjoined not to dance the Charleston, and to wear thick stockings and blouses with long sleeves. Dance halls were closed down. There were calls to 'ostracise Northern habits', such as Christmas trees. The following spring, a meeting was called to discuss immorality on Tuscan beaches, and a Decalogue of Moral Hygiene urged readers not to take bribes, to rise early and not to believe that 'it is chic to appear discontented'. Number 1 of the Decalogue was 'Read Mussolini'; number 10, 'Reread Mussolini'. Some of this spirit of joylessness and fervour had entered the Lyceum, the club in which Amelia had spent so many interesting hours, and from which she now resigned. Those who took her place were committed fascists: in Mussolini's Italy, there were now very few arenas where intelligent, liberal women could have a voice. It was another indication of the ambiguities of fascism that the Lyceum invited Maria to become a member, despite the fact that she was known to be the wife of a declared anti-fascist. She refused.

With many of their former acquaintances reluctant to be seen in their company, Amelia, Nello and Maria lived quietly, meeting few people apart from the Orvietos and the Zabbans. Nello's 'moral conduct', noted his police report, was 'orderly'. Amelia had acquired a smooth-haired terrier called Bubi. Their friends the Ferreros had left for Switzerland. Amelia had resigned from all her publishing ventures and had ceased to write plays, but she continued to turn her hand to children's stories and to read aloud to Paola and Silvia. On Sundays, Nello went on long walks in the countryside around Florence with Piero Calamandrei, Alessandro Levi and the few other independent spirits still hanging on in fascist Florence. 'We deluded ourselves', as Calamandrei put it later, 'that we could find in the hills our lost freedoms.'

Nello was the youngest of the group and the most vigorous, a 'simple and sane' figure, striding out, sweet-natured, laughing. In his diary he wrote. 'We are fighting to acquire the pleasure of a normal life.' But it was scarcely normal. He and Maria had decided to protect their daughters from all contact with fascism: the girls neither went to school nor attended the semi-compulsory after-school activities, but had a Swiss or German governess instead. Whether they realised how closely they were watched is not clear. In their many letters to each other, to Carlo and Marion, to friends in exile, they were very guarded, using only nicknames – Lussu had become *carciofo* (artichoke), Tarchiani 'Matilde', Nitti '*il presidente*'; but their letters ended up copied, typed up, and filed in Bocchini's ever fatter dossiers. And for all his apparent cheerfulness Nello was often low. 'How sad, my dear professor, is our life in Italy,' he wrote to Salvemini. 'I mean the life of the '*non-ralliés*' (whether party members or not), condemned to perpetual discontent, isolation and social uselessness.'

CHAPTER SIXTEEN

Dancing for Liberty

'I am not living, I am burning,' Carlo wrote to Amelia in late 1930, six months after reaching Paris. Describing his life as 'cyclonic', he said that the days were devouring him. After the years of enforced inactivity on Lipari, he seemed possessed by the need to move, to meet people, to plan. He was everywhere, talking, organising, travelling. Marion, pregnant, with palpitations and constantly tired, was sometimes bitter and reproachful. She told him one day that Mirtillino, was asking 'Where has Daddy gone?' On another: 'I am not at all happy, dear Carlo ... I am also sick of so many paper kisses!!! ... Very angry. Addio.' Carlo was apologetic, but also stern. 'You have always understood the importance of what I do,' he wrote from one of his many journeys away from Paris. 'It is an *opera santa*, a great and sacred cause, and even you must see that everything, except for the health of the children, has to be sacrificed to it.' What Marion really minded was not being able to be part of it all; and when alone boredom quickly turned to depression.

By 1930, most of the Italian anti-fascists in exile who were not communists were envisaging a constitutional democracy once fascism fell but, believing that socialism would ultimately prevail, they preferred to analyse, rail and dream rather than to act. The communists, for their part, remained faithful to Marxism and a totalitarian ideology. Carlo, Lussu and Nitti still did not agree with what they saw as the Concentrazione Antifascista's culpable passivity. Since Mussolini's 'ruthless fanaticism' used violent methods, the only way to oppose it, they maintained, was through violence; since all legal means were closed, only illegal ones were left; since the old left-wing parties were mired in a failed past, and in any case political parties were too ponderous to respond dynamically, then what was needed was a wide-based, united fighting force.

Socialismo Liberale, Carlo's one major theoretical work, its themes endlessly refined on Lipari and further hashed out in Paris with Tarchiani and Salvemini, was published in French in December 1930. It advocated the two Mazzinian ideals of republican liberty and social justice; a separation between Marxism and socialism on account of the deterministic nature of Marxism, and an overhaul of socialism to make it less sclerotic. Italy should pursue a mixed economy, agrarian reform, and an end to the complacent monarchy and the complicit paternalism of the Vatican. Local committees could lay down the basis of a new state, to be completed once the fascists fell by a constituent assembly, elected by universal suffrage. But first, a militant vanguard, 'small nuclei' of active fighters, would prepare the path towards the liberation of Italy, after which freedom for all citizens would follow.

There was more. It was not merely a question, said Carlo, of overthrowing a bad regime, but of putting in its place a 'civilisation'. Like Gobetti, he believed that ethics, politics and culture should go hand in hand; like Amelia, that people should be responsible for their own actions. The difference between the fascists and the anti-fascists, he argued, lay not in matters of class but in moral sensibility: his 'creative revolution' envisaged spiritual redemption as a precursor to the renewal of the nation and its culture. In this, intellectuals had an important role to play in re-educating a people 'suborned by an ignorant and brutal dictatorship'. Italians had been made 'morally lazy' by fascism.

It would be a mistake to try to pin down too neatly Carlo's proposed new state. His ideas were not without flaws and even Salvemini found some of them a bit of an enigma. But what inspired him chiefly was the desire to destroy Mussolini as soon as possible. In any case, he regarded this concept of freedom not as static but as something fluid, constantly renewed in debate and argument, a set of rules for civil society rather than a collection of principles cast in stone. Carlo had sent his first draft to Nello, who commented: 'You really are a star.'

He had expected criticism from others. But he was not prepared for the tidal wave of indignation and opprobrium which followed the publication of his book. The anarchists declared that he was far too respectful of government and state. The communists said that he was too privileged. His much-loved friend Turati called him a 'presumptuous little bourgeois', a 'reactionary dilettante', and said that by contrast Gobetti had been a serious scholar. Other communists called him a *socialfascista*. Claudio Treves announced that Carlo was in truth neither a liberal nor a socialist. Croce, who joined in the attacks from Italy, said that his ideas were like the mythical hircocervus, half-stag, half-goat, 'an absurd and aesthetically unpleasant combination that purported to attach the rough, rude and shaggy body of socialist to the long and agile legs of liberalism'. The pages of the opposition papers in exile were filled with similar attacks, many of them vituperative and extremely hurtful, particularly when written by people he considered close friends. While the backbiting rumbled on, Carlo turned resolutely to what he really believed in: action.

The few young anti-fascists still at liberty in Italy had meanwhile formed themselves precariously into the very kind of networks Carlo was looking for. There was a small, mainly republican group in Rome; some followers of Gobetti in Turin; the railway-worker and *Non Mollare* distributor Traquandi in Florence; Lussu's friends in Sardinia; more republicans in Trieste. In Milan, there were Carlo's three close friends: Riccardo Bauer, austere, well-educated editor, recently released from Lipari; Ferruccio Parri, who had just benefited from an amnesty; and the lively, bold, brilliant, mocking Ernesto Rossi, Salvemini's third spiritual son, considered by some to be a complete 'madman'. A chemist, Umberto Ceva, who had helped with the escape from Lipari, provided invisible ink for their communications.

For a while there had also been Sandro Pertini, the young man who had escaped to France with Turati. He had proposed getting hold of bombs and clock parts and setting them off under the Palazzo Venezia, a plan that had to be abandoned when it was discovered that Bocchini, ever haunted about Mussolini's safety, had not only had steel bars welded over all the basement entrances, but formed a *'squadra di sottosuolo'* to patrol the sewers. In any case Pertini, who had slipped back into Italy, had been recognised by a childhood friend since turned fascist, subsequently picked up by the police, and was now serving a 10 year, 9 month sentence in solitary confinement in prison in the port of Santo Stefano, where 'exemplary punishments' with the *manganello* were often meted out by the guards. Pertini's friends, following his fate, knew precisely what they risked.

Bauer and Parri had immediately joined forces with various friends in Milan who had been working under the name of Italia Libera to help prisoners' families, arrange clandestine crossings to France and Switzerland, and send information on the fascists to those in exile in Paris. After his abrupt departure with Salvemini from Florence in 1925, Rossi, like Pertini, had infiltrated himself back into Italy – Rossi was a common Italian name – and managed to get a job teaching law and economics in a technical institute in Bergamo, avoiding Florence, where his mother Elide and sister Serenella lived. Elide was a woman in Amelia's mould: brave, dignified, uncomplaining, as close to Ernesto as Amelia was to her two sons.

Travelling around Italy with two large suitcases full of clandestine material, his black eyes shining with honesty and passion, Rossi had managed to cross the border into France undetected on six separate occasions. He told Salvemini that he was not so much a man of politics as a sceptic, and that what really mattered to him was sympathy and instinct. He had recently become involved with Ada, a teacher of mathematics from the University of Pavia whose surname also happened to be Rossi. A fervent Garibaldian, she, like him, was leading a double life. The police were not fooled. A report by the head of the carabinieri in Bergamo described her as a 'profound hater of fascism' and said that she needed close watching. Few of the leading anti-fascists were women, but occasionally one would carry material in false-bottomed suitcases over the border, and these women were known as *fenicotteri*, flamingoes.

Bauer and Rossi, using invisible ink and writing between the lines of a French textbook, had sent Carlo, Nitti and Lussu warm congratulations on their escape and an outline of plans for actions to be carried out inside Italy. Rossi's risky crossings had been replaced with a more secure route via socialist friends in Ticino and Lugano, where a young Greek scholar called Pietro Zani collected messages and propaganda material, hid them behind the panels in his car, and delivered them to couriers in Milan. Bauer's diminutive and combative housekeeper, Rina dei Cas, kept their most precious notes on her at all times.

What the Milanese group proposed, in a manifesto called *Consigli sulla Tattica*, 'Advice on Tactics', was a two-tier approach: the education of the masses and the setting up of small cadres of active fighters to carry out very noisy, very public, very embarrassing attacks 'with courage and sacrifice'. 'We gathered around us', wrote Bauer later, 'the best, the dispersed, the believers, the young. We danced for liberty, for the republic, for social justice.'

This was precisely what Carlo had in mind: insurrection, through *'squadre d'azione'*, taking the greatest care to avoid harming innocent bystanders. Indiscriminate killing, Carlo and Salvemini agreed, was a 'terrorist act', and therefore illegitimate; 'assassination' and 'tyrannicide' were legitimate responses to state violence. Lussu, the self-styled Jacobin, regarded by the others as a brilliant logician, was put in charge of devising spectacular actions. Leaflets and pamphlets, written by members of Giustizia e Libertà – now known as *giellisti* – began to arrive over the border.

In Rome, Bocchini and Nudi were chafing over their continuing failure to produce culprits for the Milan bombing; the documents on the case filled fifty-five fat volumes. It was a clever young colleague of Bocchini's, Guido Leto, who now proposed putting the blame on the *giellisti*, about whom they kept hearing rumours. Word had reached Rome that the printing of their material was being done in Milan and not in Paris, and that the conspirators met in the Café Tantal in Via Silvio Pellico. Two suspects were immediately arrested. Although Polpol and OVRA were never vicious in the way of the Gestapo, they were not altogether averse to using torture to get people to confess. One night, the two suspects were taken to the mortuary, shown the bloody remains of the victims of the bombing, and had their feet burned and their testicles squashed before being held for many hours in agonising positions.

Milan was clearly crucial. But Bocchini realised that it was Paris where the true heart of the conspiracy lay. He recruited more spies and ordered them to France to gather information, contacts, addresses, means of communication. Then were posted to ports and put on merchant ships; others were placed on the railways to act as couriers. A Captain Rey, controller of the wagons-lits between Rome and Boulogne-sur-Mer, was noted as having a '*zèle débordant*' for fascism; in the Paris secret-service notes, he was described with 'very piercing eyes', a small face and a little moustache *en brosse*. Another useful man was a sly and resourceful policeman called Guido Valiani, attached to the Italian embassy in Paris, who smoked little Tuscan cigars, spoke French with an execrable accent, but knew everyone. Yet another was Livio Bini, who passed himself off as a Florentine socialist in exile and was a very canny exploiter of weak or deluded refugees. Then there was a journalist called Aldo Borella, who wrote meticulous reports, excelled at combing hotel registers for hidden information, and was paired up with one of OVRA's most formidable emissaries to Paris, Vincenzo Bellavia, known as 'Acquarone'. Discreet and manipulative, Bellavia was said to have several French policemen in his pay. He was given the specific task of watching Carlo. There was also the former director of a cooperative in Ravenna, Antonio Bondi, who longed to recant and go home, but was persuaded first to worm his way into the Giustizia e Libertà offices. All these men were in a delicate position. They had to be plausible, able to explain away the fact that they had money to live on, and they had to produce and stick to believable stories about their pasts. If rumbled by the anti-fascist community, the spies ran the risk of summary justice or vengeance against their families still in Italy.

Soon, reports from these men were arriving in Rome, either by special letter-drops in hotels or private houses, or poste restante to the main post office in the Piazza San Silvestro. They would be collected, typed up in three copies for the various archives, and a summary sent every afternoon to Bocchini, who extracted the most important information and passed it on to Mussolini. In the Ministry of Information, 400 shorthand typists were kept busy transcribing intercepted letters and conversations picked up in phone taps or prison cells. One report spoke of Rosselli proposing a 'series of attacks', and of the absolute necessity of getting rid of the '*capo*'. Another named Lussu as the 'supreme commander of all the armed forces of the anti-fascist revolution'. Several others mentioned that quantities of explosive material were being shipped around.

The fact that many of these reports were full of exaggeration, invention and mystification only played to Bocchini's fears about Mussolini's safety. There was one wild assertion that terror attacks were about to be launched from Corsica, another that squads of militiamen were being trained in Paris. One of the more fanciful had Marion falling in love with Bassanesi, being forbidden by a jealous Carlo to visit him in Brussels, and having a row with Signora Nitti because, 'being a hysteric, she had apparently made suggestive proposals' to her husband. Though often absurd, the result of these daily bulletins was a climate of growing determination in Rome to break this 'odious and criminal anti-fascism'.

It would prove surprisingly easy to pull off a first victory. For the anti-fascists were turning out to be extraordinarily gullible and none more so than the easy-going and credulous Carlo, whose instinct was to trust everyone.

Bocchini made one further recruitment before setting his trap.

Carlo del Re was a twenty-nine-year old lawyer, a Freemason, a polyglot, an extrovert, always willing and very presentable. He came from Friuli and had a pale face, floppy black hair, and a scar along his right cheek from an accident in which he had also lost two fingers on his left hand. For a while, acting as a lawyer for receiverships, del Re had made a lot of money. But he was a gambler. The day came when he owed 124,000 lire in poker debts: he was ordered either to pay them or go to jail. But there was a third option, that of selling his friends in Milan to the fascists, and he took it. Through a distant friendship with Italo Balbo, the Minister of Aviation, he was introduced to Bocchini.

With friends among the former left-wing journalists in Milan, del Re was just the man Bocchini was looking for. They made a deal. Del Re would infiltrate the group of anti-fascists suspected to be working in Milan, and if possible trace the network back to Carlo in Paris. Then he was to pin the Milan bombing on to Giustizia e Libertà, and to rake as many people as he could into the conspiracy. In return, his debt would be paid off, he would be guaranteed total secrecy and, once the group was 'liquidated', a job. Bocchini forwarded the proposal to Mussolini, who simply wrote '*Sì*' on it.

Del Re set about his task with a degree of pleasure because among his many accomplishments he liked to think of himself as an actor. He went to Paris, met Carlo and Salvemini, and urged them to think up some really big action, preferably with explosives. Because he was able to travel in and out of Italy with no trouble, he was soon their preferred courier to liaise with Bauer, Rossi and Parri in Milan. Professing to have Masonic connections, he made friends among Paris's Italian Masons, also high on the list of Bocchini's suspects. Soon, he had become indispensable to Carlo.

Since the possession of explosives was useful in establishing guilt, del Re persuaded the chemist Ceva in Milan to experiment in making phosphorous bombs in one of their bathrooms. As luck would have it, exposure to air caused the phosphorous to explode, del Re's jacket caught fire and Rossi put out the flames with his hands, burning himself in the process. Del Re urged them to make more bombs, but Ceva, a mild, retiring man, never keen on violence, refused. They were surprised when del Re got angry and argumentative, and even more surprised when he followed and watched when they insisted on taking the ruined explosives and throwing them into the river Brembo.

Del Re made a second attempt to plant bombs when he tried to persuade Carlo, in his Paris flat, to fill the seasonal *panettoni* with dynamite and send them to fascist officials. Carlo, appalled, refused. He would not dream, he said, of killing children on Christmas Day. Next, del Re engineered a meeting in a cemetery in Milan, attended by Ceva and Rossi, so that plainclothed policemen could photograph them. By now, he had amassed an impressive list of names and addresses of *giellisti* suspects.

Despite Ceva's misgivings, plans were progressing to let off explosives in front of seven tax offices in different parts of Italy simultaneously. Because there had been so many botched attempts at capturing the group red-handed, Bocchini decided he could wait no longer. In any case, Mussolini was expressing considerable irritation at the delay and calling for 'arrests on a vast scale'. On 27 October, 1930, the day before the eighth anniversary of the March on Rome, he struck.

Bauer, Ceva and Parri were picked up in Milan; Rossi was

Ernesto Rossi and his mother Elide

arrested from his institute in Bergamo; Traquandi was caught in Florence; several others in Rome. Bauer's sister Adele, finding him gone from home, suggested to Ada Rossi that they ask del Re what was going on; the spy's manner was so 'urbane and strange' that she hastened away to warn others. Del Re reported to Bocchini that Ada had told him that she had been able to destroy a lot of evidence. She was, he said, a 'nihilist' with 'terrorist tendencies' and extremely dangerous.

That day, twenty-four people were caught. Most of them were professors, lawyers and journalists, described as 'whisperers, sowers of alarm and discontent'. They were transferred to Rome, to be held in solitary confinement in the prison of Regina Coeli. Mussolini was reported to be calling for the death penalty for the ringleaders, accused of being terrorists, bomb-makers, insurrectionists and assassins, in league with plotters abroad. They were put into death cells.

Del Re still had hopes of luring Carlo and Tarchiani into a trap. He phoned them from Lugano, asking them to come south urgently to give him orders. They told him to come to Paris instead. Rumours had reached them of a man with two missing fingers being a spy, and del Re's name had been mentioned. Del

Re caught a train north and turned up in Carlo's flat, where, clearly uneasy, he proceeded to tell a confused and tangled story. Carlo ordered him to produce his wallet: it was found to contain a small fortune in cash. Characteristically, Carlo let him go back to his hotel, having made him promise to return next day. After all, as he said later, he was not a killer. Del Re vanished.

Ernesto Rossi, meanwhile, had very nearly managed to escape. On the train taking him south to Rome late at night, he had made friends with his four guards, who had obligingly handcuffed him in front rather than behind. The carriage was extremely hot and stuffy. The guards dozed off. Rossi, helped by the sweat on his wrists, wriggled his way out of the cuffs. Because he had often made the journey, he knew that a moment would come when the train was forced to slow down. He eased the window up, and, before they could stop him, squeezed out. He fell hard, next to the rails, and briefly fainted. As he came to, he heard shouts and began to run; the guards had pulled the communication cord, but it was not working and the train carried on. It was now one in the morning. He came to a house, pushed his way in, and found a husband and wife in bed, 'naked, enormous, fat, terrified'. He explained who he was. The man leapt out of bed, shouted at him, and drove him from the house. He ran on towards the pinewoods near Viareggio, and lay on the sand until a storm drove him to take shelter in a beach hut. He moved on again, met a man with a horse and cart who refused to help him, and finally reached a naval barracks.

Dawn was just breaking. Rossi, who had lost his jacket and his coat, was freezing. He approached the barracks where the sailors, who were just getting up, seemed friendly. They gave him some food and lit a fire for him to warm himself; they listened to his story, but then handed him over to the carabinieri.

It took Ada several weeks to discover that he too was now in the Regina Coeli. She was told that all the 'Milanese dynamiters' were in solitary confinement and had been turned over entirely to OVRA. Rossi coped by keeping himself fanatically neat in jail and insisted on polishing his shoes, something he later said stopped him from contemplating suicide.

Bocchini's men had been quick to realise that the unassuming Ceva, alone in his cell, was defenceless and trusting. They played on his sense of guilt and loyalty and soon managed to persuade him that he had told them enough to incriminate the others, and that they intended to portray him in court as a traitor. The lonely days passed obsessively; to distract himself, Ceva solved mathematical problems in his head. Late on Christmas night, he decided that he could bear it no longer. He broke his spectacles, ground up the glass, mixed it with some mints and citric acid, and swallowed it; he died the next morning, in agony, soon after 7 o'clock. From his nearby cell, Rossi listened to his groans.

Ceva was a devoted husband and father. Before dying, he wrote two letters. The one to his wife Elena was long, full of memories and regrets and advice about how to bring up their two children. 'My angel ... forgive me. Not for what I am about to do, but because I was blind, lacking in judgement, unthinking over things that one should not take lightly. I didn't realise ... No one should mourn me.' To Police Inspector Nudi, Ceva wrote that he had committed no crime, that his conscience was clear, and that he

Umberto Cevo with his youngest child

had been inspired only by 'an overwhelming love of liberty'. 'I never had, living my happy peaceful life, a sense of the reality of things ... or of the perils towards which I was walking.' But, he added, he feared being manipulated by the prosecution into incriminating del Re, a man he considered his friend.

Ceva died still believing in del Re's honesty but the others were quickly disabused. In Milan and Paris rumours of del Re's treachery spread. On the walls of the prison yard in the Regina Coeli, Rossi used a bit of chalk to write: 'Del Re is a spy for the regime.' Elena Ceva was besieged by sympathetic visitors, among them Benedetto Croce and Toscanini. Bauer and Rossi, perceived as the ringleaders, were now in great danger of being executed by firing squad, and Carlo and Salvemini launched an international campaign to save their lives. In their letters and articles for the newspapers, Carlo referred to his two friends as 'my brothers', and Salvemini spoke of del Re as an 'agent provocateur'. The *Manchester Guardian* published an appeal signed by thirty European intellectuals, from Arnold Toynbee to Thomas Mann, asking that the trial be held, not before the Special Tribunal, but in an open court. Only Bernard Shaw refused to sign, saying that though he did not agree with everything the fascists did, he still admired their work. Carlo tried to persuade some of his highly placed Conservative friends to bring pressure on the British government to advise Mussolini to behave with moderation. As Salvemini pointed out, criticism from abroad 'was hitting him precisely at his weakest point'.

What became known as the 'Trial of the Intellectuals' opened in the Palace of Justice in Rome on 29 May 1931. The accused were in an iron cage. Women were banned from attending, which meant that neither Elena Ceva nor Rossi's mother Elide was present. Not long before, Rossi's much-loved sister Serenella had committed suicide, pushed over the brink by the horrors of his arrest. At three that same morning, Michele Schirru, an anarchist who had confessed to planning to murder Mussolini, and who, when caught, shot and wounded several policemen, had been executed. It was the first time that an intention rather than an act had been punished by death, and sent a clear message that this was the fate intended for those in the dock.

It quickly became apparent that Bauer and Rossi took full

responsibility for every aspect of Giustizia e Libertà in Italy – though not, of course, for the Milan bombing. The remains of the explosives, retrieved from the Brembo with del Re's help, were produced in court. Rossi gave an account of del Re's perfidy, describing himself again as 'distinctly and decisively anti-fascist'. Bauer, as he had in the Savona trial, turned the proceedings into an attack on the fascist regime. He had felt it his duty, he said, to try to break the cycle of violence and subjugation into which Italy had been plunged. Liberty, he declared, had been reduced to a 'putrefying cadaver', but he was convinced that the days of freedom would one day return. The thought of freedom alone would comfort and accompany him in the loneliness of his cell. His words were long remembered and quoted. There were brave cheers in the court, and even the president admitted that his speech had been 'noble'.

Bauer and Rossi's obvious moral honesty and courage paid off, and the campaign waged by Carlo and Salvemini clearly helped. The two men received prison sentences of twenty years each. Traquandi was given seven years. Parri, for whom no evidence of involvement could be proved, was absolved, but since he was deemed 'capable of committing further acts', he was ordered back to Lipari, where conditions had deteriorated further and TB was now rife. He begged to be allowed to go somewhere near a library and where the pains from the frostbite he still suffered after his first stay on Lipari might be treated. His request was refused. 'The island', a prisoner had written not long before, 'is turning into a cemetery.' The other fifteen people in the dock received short sentences or were freed for lack of evidence.

The Trial of the Intellectuals was considered a great coup for Bocchini. Mussolini used the occasion to announce that the Special Tribunal would be renewed for another five years. For the anti-fascists, 1931 had been a lethal year: 519 people had, between them, received sentences totalling 2016 years. Del Re was given 44,000 lire and a new name; in terror of retribution, he caught a boat for South America.

Ada was sacked from her teaching job in Bergamo and gave herself up to planning Rossi's escape. Rossi's mother Elide told Salvemini that she had never felt the need to appear strong so keenly, for Serenella and Ernesto had been very close and she feared what the solitary confinement in which he was being kept might do to her son. To a friend, she wrote: 'I am so unspeakably sad that every moment is an effort'; when praised for her powers of resistance it seemed to her 'almost like irony'. On one of her few permitted visits, she found her son in tears, but he asked her to say to Salvemini and Carlo that he thought about them all the time and that their friendship gave him courage. 'Only my resignation and my serenity', Elide said to Salvemini, 'can save him.' Forbidden to write anything, he had taken to scrawling on his window with a bar of soap until that too was taken away from him. It was Rossi who famously said, referring to the soup served in prison: 'After the third worm, stop.'

On one of her own visits to Rossi, Ada suggested that they get married. The ceremony was performed by the local *podestà* on the anniversary of her own parents' wedding, and they hoped to be as happy. She managed to get him moved to a prison in the north, which made visits easier. With the help of Carlo, who sent her money and a false passport, she explored the possibility of getting him out through the prison sewers. When that proved unworkable, she used the money to bribe a compliant guard and a helpful garage mechanic, but that too failed. When Rossi was abruptly transferred back to the Regina Coeli, she resigned herself to preparing courses in algebra, trigonometry, psychoanalysis, the classics and American literature, which she took to him in prison, and which he then shared with the others. Study kept them sane.

In January 1931, even as del Re's machinations were continuing to unfold around him, Carlo found a new flat at 5 Place du Panthéon on the Left Bank; he was delighted by the move, saying that Passy was too philistine and he wanted to be near the Sorbonne and the constant bustle of young people in the streets. On 12 March, Marion gave birth to a boy; they called him Andrea, but he was soon known as 'Aghi' or 'Eghi'. Marion had had two children in less than a year; she was thirty-four, but looked older. When Amelia arrived in Paris soon after the birth, she found the household in disarray. As Carlo wrote to Nello, it was all '*assai pasticciato*', a bit of a mess; whenever either of her sons were in difficulties, they sent for Amelia. An informer reported to Rome that Marion was 'very depressed, with bad heart troubles. She will soon die of a heart attack.'

On 14 April, elections in Spain brought a republic to power; King Alfonso XIII abdicated and left for France, where there was much rejoicing among the exiles. 'The Spanish revolution moves and elates me!' Carlo wrote to Nello. 'Maybe in Italy too dawn will break.' As the head of Giustizia e Libertà in Paris, he told his brother, he believed that he had 'magnificent duties' to go at once to lend solidarity to the new leaders, but these clashed, he admitted, with the 'sacred duties' he owed his family. 'Nellino,' he wrote, 'help me and above all understand me . . . I am so happy to see a chink in the grey horizon.'

The magnificent duties prevailed; it was too exciting a moment to miss. Leaving Marion recuperating in a hotel in Cap d'Antibes with Mirtillino, and his mother in charge of the two younger children in Paris, Carlo took off for Barcelona. Tarchiani and Bassanesi went with him; Carlo, who loved speed and had no respect for highway laws, did the driving. At Perpignan he lost the car keys, but when new ones had been cut and they had hastened on to Barcelona, he found it all 'majestic'. After the grey and lowering worries of Paris, he loved the light and the countryside and the fervour of the new republic. In Madrid, he had meetings with Manuel Azaña, architect of the new socialist-republican alliance, and a celebrated pilot called Ramón Franco. Carlo was hoping to win support and backing for new flights over Italy, but at dinner one night he quarrelled with Bassanesi, who suggested that they drop not leaflets but bombs over Piazza Venezia. What, he asked sharply, about the innocent civilians below? His letters to Marion were excited. Madrid, he told her, was 'frantic and feverish' and he longed for the day when he would see the same in Italy. A bullfight had first disgusted then entertained him. The Prado was magnificent. 'Rest,' he told her, 'grow strong and above all be calm . . . Addio, dear little thing.'

Marion's answers, perhaps not surprisingly, were curt. 'I envy you your lack of preoccupation with those far away . . . I wish that I loved you a little less so as not to suffer quite so much when you are materially and spiritually absent . . . A kiss from your Marionellina, who has become old old and is the mother of three children.' She was having constant palpitations, and

Amelia told Zia Gì that the doctor had said they were due at least in part to her nervous state; he ordered her to stop taking her temperature. Contrite, Carlo begged her to be patient. With their friends in jail, having made so many sacrifices, how could she not see that it was his 'tragic and imperative duty' to battle on? Marion too was now contrite. Her health was better and she and Mirillino were going back to Paris. It was just that she felt cut out of everything and she wanted so badly to be part of it all. And if 'for two days I don't hear from you, then the world goes black'. They made it up. Admitting that his visit to Spain had yielded little, he wrote: 'We love each other too much. I love you.' Spain, he told her, was 'delicious' but 'extremely Latin'.

At 8 o'clock on the evening of 3 October 1931, a snowdrift of 400,000 white leaflets floated down from the sky above the Palazzo Venezia, where Mussolini was sitting in council. For almost half an hour the little plane circled 300 metres above central Rome, down the Corso, past Palazzo Chigi and then over the Spanish Steps and the gardens of the Quirinale. It was still just light and the streets were crowded with people going home from work: they picked up the leaflets and read appeals for them to abandon 'the most tyrannical and corrupt of governments'. And then the plane flew off, never to be seen again. The only mention in the Italian papers was that it was the work of *'una carogna'*, a skunk.

The Pegasus, as the plane was called, was flown not by a member of Giustizia e Libertà, but by a twenty-nine-year-old poet and dramatist, Lauro de Bosis, best known for *Icarus*, his verse play about the man who dreamt of a new world in which all would be free and equal. As a boy, de Bosis had been inspired by D'Annunzio and had later worked for the Italian American Society in New York, peopled increasingly by fascist supporters. But, as with Carlo and Nello, Matteotti's murder had changed the course of his life. Having got to know Salvemini and Don Sturzo, and become the lover of the American actress Ruth Draper, he had founded the Alleanza Nazionale with friends, writing pamphlets calling on 'men of order' to bring back a more honest Italian government. He was in America when his friends were arrested, tortured and given long prison sentences. When a photocopier was discovered under her bed in Rome, the fascists also arrested his sixty-six-year-old American mother for helping with the pamphlets. Asked why she had done so, she reminded them that Mussolini had declared Italy to be a country of 40 million good sheep 'ready to give their wool to the regime: and I am not a sheep'. De Bosis decided to 'bear a message of liberty across the sea to people in chains'. The three plagues of Italy, fascism, monarchy and the Vatican, he told Salvemini, 'must all be eliminated, one by one'.

Though friends begged him not to, de Bosis moved to Paris and cycled every day to an airfield near Versailles, where he learnt to fly. He made friends with Dolci, who described to him Bassanesi's flight over Milan. De Bosis was a solitary figure, with something childlike and innocent about him. He bought the Pegasus in Germany, and took off for Rome from Corsica. The weather was good, the temperature 25 degrees, and the meteorological office reported clear skies all the way. A last photograph taken of him leaning against his plane shows a good-looking man in a suit, bow tie and white shirt. He probably never believed that he would survive; there was fuel enough for only part of the way back. Before leaving Corsica, he wrote a six-page testament and left it with a friend. The problem, he wrote in 'The Story of My Death', was that no one took fascism seriously. 'This is a mistake. It is necessary to die. I hope that after me others will follow and rouse public opinion ... they will reap what I have sown.' To Ruth Draper he wrote: 'Be happy for my sake! not only proud but happy ... I could not have wished for a happier solution to my wish to serve my country and my ideals.' It was later thought that the Pegasus had gone down 40–100 kilometres from the coast of Corsica. De Bosis' testament was published in *Le Soir* in Brussels, the *Sunday Times* in London and the *New York Times*. Mussolini was reported to be enraged; several airforce officers lost their jobs.

Carlo followed de Bosis' adventures with interest. Though the republicans in Spain had not followed up their goodwill with any practical help, he was still pushing ahead with plans for a new flight of his own, spurred on by the increasingly over-excited Bassanesi. This time, the idea was to fly from Konstanz in Germany over both Turin and Milan, where *giellisti* would organise demonstrations of support. A highly dubious German former army officer, Viktor Haefner, who had been jailed on various occasions for selling military secrets and for fraud, volunteered to produce a plane. Carlo paid 9,000 marks for a second-hand Junker Junior and at the end of October he and Tarchiani set out for Konstanz with 350,000 anti-fascist leaflets in the boot of their car.

There was almost nothing about the plan that was sensible. Bassanesi, who had taken to adopting the most improbable pseudonyms, was by now well known to informers and police forces all over Europe, as were Carlo and Tarchiani; de Bosis' flight had put security at airports on alert; and news had already been sent out by Bocchini's men about a possible flight by Italian exiles. On 11 November the conspirators met at the airstrip and loaded the leaflets on board. It had been raining hard, and the ground was not just covered in thick grass but very muddy. With the still inexperienced Bassanesi at the controls, the Junker lumbered its way down the airstrip, narrowly missed the terminal, and crashed into a ditch. Undaunted, they unloaded the leaflets, put them back in the car, and decided to try again the following day. But in the morning the police were waiting. Bassanesi was arrested as he approached the plane; Carlo and Tarchiani, observing what was happening, took off in their car unseen, but the French secret services put out an alert for a 'yellow-brown, 4 door Ford Cabriolet, with 2 spare wheels'. At Freiburg, near the border, it was spotted by a sharp-eyed youth, who reported the foreign number plate to the police, who quickly linked it to the botched Konstanz flight.

'*Bin in haft aber gesund Brief folgt.*' 'I am well but in jail. Letter follows,' Carlo cabled Marion.

In Konstanz prison, Carlo's cell was warm and clean. Meals were sent in by a local restaurant. As ever, he was cheerful, uncomplaining and optimistic. 'No candidate for martyrdom this time,' he wrote to Marion, asking her to send pyjamas, socks, toothpaste and German books so that he could 'take up the broken threads of my intellectual work'. Marion noted dryly that she was enjoying being useful and pleased to discover that 'the stupid life I lead has neither rusted nor put me to sleep'. On 16 November, Carlo celebrated his thirty-second birthday with a loving telegram from Amelia. Requests arrived in Paris for more books and deliveries of the *Corriere della*

Sera, the *Manchester Guardian* and *Le Temps*. To Mirtillino, Carlo wrote that prison was not at all bad and that he was going to bed every evening at the same time as the children. With so many of his friends in jail in Italy, he said that he was enjoying a rare sense of communion. 'When I am free,' he wrote lovingly to Marion, 'we'll have a second and a third honeymoon.' But Marion, after her initial burst of revolutionary energy, had fallen into loneliness and anxiety. 'No one writes to me any more,' she commented sadly when letters failed to come from Nello and Amelia. Carlo begged her not to let herself be led astray by 'distorting fantasies'. She said that she was dreading the coming winter, but taking comfort from five-year-old Mirtillino, to whom she was extremely close, and whose intelligence, she said, 'resembles an explosion'.

Carlo was intending to repeat his success at the Savona trial and turn the occasion into a further public attack on the fascists; eminent European democrats were offering to act as witnesses in his defence. But having initially bombarded Germany with ever wilder accusations against the plotters, then realised that he would be giving Carlo another platform, Mussolini dropped all charges, though not before hundreds of the leaflets had been spirited out of police hands by German social democrats and posted into Italy. A possible ten-year prison sentence was turned into a fine and expulsion from Germany. The three men were freed. Cheated of his day in court, Carlo was comforted by a letter from Nello: 'I am proud of you and your activities. Bit by bit, your name is being mentioned everywhere as a future leader in Italy ... If you sometimes feel alone and unheeded, forget it ... You will end up – we will end up – the victors as long as we never give up [*non mollare*], not for a moment, not by a hair on our body.'

Bold flights over Italian cities were now abandoned. They were too expensive, too unpredictable, too dangerous. Bassanesi continued to roam erratically around Europe, dreaming up ever madder schemes, alienating his friends by his truculence and closely watched by Bocchini's spies. He finally took up with a pretty law student at the Sorbonne called Camilla Restellini, described by Turati as the 'flower of exile', and had four children with her. But the *giellisti* never quite trusted him again.

CHAPTER SEVENTEEN

A World of Moral Richness

Amelia, Nello and Maria, with Silvia and Paola, now three and two, spent the last night of 1931 in Via Giusti. There was a strong wind blowing and the fireplace smoked, but at midnight they opened a bottle of champagne and raised their glasses to Carlo and Marion in Paris. To say that she thought especially hard about him at that very moment, Amelia wrote to Carlo next morning, would be a mistake, because she thought about him ceaselessly, in an almost continuous single thought of love and good wishes. They had put Beethoven's *Seventh Symphony* on the gramophone while they drank their champagne, and when Amelia remarked that it was really a funeral march, they agreed that it should be a funeral for 1931, which had turned out to be such a cursed year.

Though Carlo had not been prevented from re-entering France after prison in Konstanz, there were moves by the French government, and especially by the new prime minister Pierre Laval, to have him expelled, in order not to provoke Mussolini. But Carlo had met and become friends with Léon Blum, leader of the socialists, who intervened to get the order lifted; in exchange, he had to promise to refrain from all further 'disorder'. Carlo told friends that he had no intention of stopping his campaigns: he would simply try to make himself less visible. Lying low was not something that came naturally to him. The Italian embassy reported to Rome that there were satisfactory indications that Carlo was not much liked in some French government circles, but added: 'all the more powerful Jews, the 18-carat Jews,' had come forward to support him. A tone of anti-semitism was beginning to creep into the language of Mussolini's men, as it was, indeed, beginning to colour the tone of the French far-right papers. Nothing about the refugees, wrote one columnist, was more horrible to contemplate than 'this mixture of people with their peculiar features, their hooked noses, their too-black hair, their leathery, bronzed, earthy hues'.

Carlo loved the new flat, where the windows looked immediately on to the Pantheon; in the evenings, if he had spent most of the day at his desk, he would stroll along the Boulevard Saint-Michel and pause by the book stalls. A newcomer to Paris at around this time, the Russian writer Victor Serge, described Carlo as watchful, a good listener and extremely courteous, but someone who – with a sudden direct observation or 'merciless criticism' – would reveal 'the militant inside his soul'. Though some of the exiles were irritated by Carlo's refusal to be constrained by anything, and others objected to the way he attacked the '*anziani*', the ancients, he was on the whole much liked: his discreet generosity had become legendary. A new young friend, the musician Massimo Mila, heard him play Beethoven one day and remarked that though Carlo was not technically perfect, 'behind every note you could hear a world of unrivalled moral richness'.

Salvemini with Mirtillino

Carlo and Marion had begun to have trouble with three-year-old Melina, who was turning out to be very wilful. Marion found her almost impossible to deal with, complaining that she upset the sunny and contented Andrea and saw something to complain about in even the nicest things. Marion was making efforts to get out more. Attending a meeting of the Italian socialists in the Pantheon one night, wearing what a police report described as a 'pretty fur coat', she was heckled and called a *'sale bourgeoise'*, until she seized a red scarf and waved it above her head to demonstrate her true colours. There was nothing she or Carlo now did which was not recorded by someone, whether the French police or the Italian spies. Even Carlo's occasional colds were reported to Rome.

Carlo and Lussu continued to meet and to talk every day – Lussu would later say that their conversation had continued uninterrupted for seven years. Sometimes they quarrelled violently, but next day they were talking again. Lussu himself was penniless, unable to find work, walking everywhere to save money on Métro fares, eating scraps and visiting exhibitions only when they were free. No one, he joked, not even the Parisians, had ever visited the Louvre as often as he had. 'I am not complaining about my situation,' he wrote to his mother. 'I like it a thousand times more than I would one of dishonourable tranquility.' He was, however, in terrible shape, the damp and cold of his meagre lodgings aggravating his low-lying TB, and he often stayed in bed, passing the time writing caustic articles for the anti-fascist papers. He was keeping secret from his friends the fact that he had become involved with the pretty blonde blue-eyed twenty-year-old daughter of a friend, Joyce Salvadori, whom he had met when she had visited her father in *confino*. Lussu kept trying to put her off, pointing out that he was old and ill; but she was persistent and though she kept well away from the other exiles, she eventually moved into his hotel, where she cooked and filled his room with flowers.

Mutterings of criticism had been heard among the various members of the Concentrazione Antifascista that Carlo and Giustizia e Libertà were too stand-offish and superior. But Turati, to whom Carlo remained devoted and who continued to be regarded as the *'ombrellone'*, the 'big umbrella' of all the exiles, was anxious to broker some kind of accord. He feared that their incessant quarrels, along with their excessive prudence, made them appear both weak and unserious. 'We have to get out of this poisonous miasma ... We have to resist in every way possible: propaganda, airplanes, bombs? Everything rather than nothing. We have to remember always that they are the enemy and, as with a snake, we have to crush its head, wherever it hides.'

In February 1932 Carlo agreed to come up with plans for a unified movement in exile, making the Concentrazione responsible for all activities outside Italy, and Giustizia e Libertà for all those inside, becoming in effect their 'armed wing'. Salvemini, never one to mince his words, continued to complain bitterly about the 'cadaverous' socialists. 'I understand that it was inevitable,' he wrote sourly to Carlo. 'But what a pity you have had to swallow this filth ... How much more heroic it would have been to remain independent ... Instead, we have yoked together the living and the dead, shrouding the living with all the passivity of the corpses.' The communists, who Salvemini hated even more than the socialists, refused to have any part in the new movement, saying that they considered Giustizia e Libertà 'a masterpiece of hypocrisy, lies and stupidity'.

Hoping to rise above the endless sniping, Carlo opened the columns of a new paper, *I Quaderni di Giustizia e Libertà*, to all political views as a way of airing grievances and widening the

Turati, not long before his death in Paris

discourse. Privately, he fumed against the scepticism and Machiavellianism of his supposed colleagues, saying that they were always quick to 'deride anything of any value, and to turn the most devastating tragedies into farces'. Observing events, the spies reported to Rome that Carlo was rapidly emerging as the dominant figure, 'the real victor of the situation'.

Turati, the charming *ombrellone*, was failing. He continued to rise early in the morning, to make his sugary coffee on his spirit stove, and to walk slowly to the park, the pockets of his ancient loden coat stuffed with newspaper cuttings. There he would sit on a bench and watch the children playing. But his asthma was getting worse, and the friends with whom he lived listened anxiously to his slow, heavy tread up and down the stairs. One night in March 1932 he arrived home late from a political meeting almost unable to breathe. He refused all help and when he had shut his bedroom door they hovered silently outside wondering what to do. Next morning Turati was back at his desk again. Visitors flocked to the house. When Carlo came, he was horrified to see how yellow Turati's skin had become, how thin his face, and how his eyes seemed not to focus. He hugged his old friend and kissed him.

On the 29th, with Marion and Carlo and a few other friends by his bedside, Turati died. He was seventy-five. A hearse pulled by black horses and shrouded in a vast bower of flowers was followed to Père Lachaise Cemetery by every exiled Italian in Paris. Carlo helped carry the coffin of the man he had so loved and admired to the grave. In a forty-two-page obituary of his friend, Carlo described Turati as the 'moral leader' of Italy.

Claudio Treves, Turati's natural heir as leader of the community, did not long outlive him. Treves, too, had spent his six years of exile begging his companions to fight 'the cruellest, the toughest, but the most sacred fight' against the fascists, even unto death. Treves was just sixty-four, but ground down by poverty. He died alone, of a ruptured artery, in a dingy hotel room. Marion wrote to Amelia that when she saw the bleakness and barrenness of that little room, the full injustice of it all was suddenly brought home to her. It was another vast funeral; and once again the French police and the Italian spies took careful note of who was there. 'How sad to see them die in exile, so soon one after the other,' wrote Carlo to Bertha Pritchard, 'the best and the purest.' An era was over. He had often found Treves weak and irresolute, but had never ceased to admire his ferocious sense of justice.

Slowly, inexorably, the mantle of leader seemed to be passing to him; and he did nothing to deflect it. 'I feel in myself', he wrote to Marion one day when she had escaped briefly to convalesce in the peace of a country hotel, 'the strength, the impulse, the ideas, the possibility of making the others pulsate, come alive.'

In January 1933, Hitler came to power. Fascism was no longer an isolated phenomenon in Europe: on the contrary, it was democracy that was becoming isolated. In Italy, early in the new year, Mussolini decided to consolidate his dictatorship by inviting people to join the Fascist Party; those who refused would see almost every avenue blocked to them. He greeted Hitler's rise with pleasure, envisaging a fruitful collaboration, in which France and Britain would be obliged to revise the central European borders. Plans were under way for Hitler to visit Italy.

At the time, few people detected a pattern. But Carlo was one who did. He took stock of what he called a 'catastrophe of nature', the speed and ease with which a civilised continent had accepted a 'new form of barbarity'. Were it not for the concentration camps, the tyrannical decrees, the political repression, it would, he said, be perfectly possible to regard what was happening as a Wagnerian fantasy, full of operatic characters fighting it out with wooden swords. But, as he wrote to Don Sturzo in London, 'the European situation is a tragedy', a crisis in which morality had failed, and power and tyranny were being blindly accepted, and it had taken an 'authentic barbarian', Hitler, to awaken the continent. German Nazism was a harsher animal than Italian fascism, but these two animals were not, in the end, all that dissimilar.

'*La guerra che torna*', the war which is returning, arguably Carlo's most famous article, was published in I *Quaderni* in June 1933. The time was over, he wrote, for defensive politics; the position of the anti-fascists as 'defenders of peace', paralysed by intrigues, had to be jettisoned. Dictatorships were expanding in the face of the 'confusion and exhaustion' of old democratic traditions; the democracies had no option but to go on the offensive and launch a preventative revolutionary uprising, by raising a force as strong as that of the fascists. Without immediate intervention, 'intransigent, fierce, hard, with no compromises', there would be no avoiding a 'new massacre', a second world war. 'War is coming,' he wrote. 'War will come.' Not at once perhaps, but in a few years, when Germany felt sufficiently strong to challenge its enemies. Not all Carlo's forebodings would come to pass, but many of them, such as the British and French attempts to cling on to neutrality, were prescient.

Lussu and Carlo, who disagreed over many things, were at one on this. But Lussu was almost Carlo's only ally. Across the socialist world in exile, there were again outpourings of criticism and anger. Nenni, custodian of the Socialist Party in Paris, dismissed Carlo's words as rubbish and insisted that all war was imperialistic, and that only social revolution was worth dying for. The outburst of hostility only drove Carlo to rail more loudly against the pacifist orthodoxy of the socialist Second International, to warn against schisms, and to become increasingly impatient with the 'cadavers' and the taboos of the exiles. A war of words broke out in the *Quaderni*. Carlo remained calm. Hitler, Mussolini, fascism were problems now for the whole of Europe, not just Italy, and they had to be addressed together; and it was Italy, the first country to be hit by fascism, that should be the first to free itself, and then help others to do the same. It all fitted in with his convictions, first explored as a student in Milan, that the future lay with a united Europe, liberal and socialist, 'united morally and politically even before economically'. In this too, in his dreams 'to make Europe', Carlo was moving ahead of his friends.

On Christmas Eve 1932, 93 of Italy's most fecund women, mothers between them of 1,300 children, were brought to Rome to visit the Exhibition of the Fascist Revolution to mark the tenth anniversary of the March on Rome. They were led to the glass case containing, on a velvet cushion, the bloodstained handkerchief with which Mussolini had staunched the bullet wound to his nose from Violet Gibson's gunshot, and they kissed it. They were not the only visitors. Some four million Italians were more or less forced to make the pilgrimage to see the life-sized photographs of the young martyred fascists in their coffins, showing gaping wounds, the illuminated cases with Mussolini's pen and

letters, and the special shrine, behind heavy crimson velvet cur-
tains, with its large cross rising out of a pool of blood in the
middle of the room, while fascist hymns played softly in the
background. Foreign dignitaries came too, among them Anthony
Eden, Goering and the King of Siam. Oswald Mosley, who had
recently received money from the London *fascio*, brought his wife
Cynthia. Dedicating one room to the *squadristi* slain for the revolution, Mussolini spoke with reverence of the 'bold, proud, strong,
fearless young men' who, with their hearts, wills, faith, love and
purity, had broken the opposition and created the new Italy.

Fascism had never been more exultant. Mussolini himself had
become a tourist attraction. To impress those Italians who had
earlier gone abroad, he offered special train fares and hotel rooms
so that they could see for themselves all that had been achieved.
The cracks in the 'Corporate State', described as a happy balance
between capitalism and socialism and sometimes likened to
Roosevelt's New Deal, were not yet too apparent. Mussolini's
stranglehold over the media was absolute: the Ministry of Popular
Culture in Rome oversaw, with fanatical rigour, the publication
of 81 daily papers, 123 political weeklies, 3,860 magazines, 7,000
parochial news sheets and 32 foreign news agencies. A popular
magazine, *La Voce della Donna*, extolled the chic fascist woman,
showing her doing gymnastics. In cinemas and schoolrooms all
over Italy documentary films were screened about contented
labourers clearing the Pontine Marshes and happy families returning from horrible emigration to the prosperity of new Fascist Italy.

To many Italians, these were miracle years. Fascism, with its
Futurist aspirations, was going further and faster: the fastest
seaplane, the fastest transatlantic liner, the most successful football player, the most skilled athletes. What no one mentioned was
that behind the triumphalist talk, all over Italy petty tyrants ruled
through blackmail and beatings. Italy had become a country of
subservience, equivocation and graft.

Towards those who wished to leave, Mussolini was merciless.
In 1929, soon after reaching Paris, Carlo, Lussu and Tarchiani
had sent a message to Velia, Matteotti's thirty-five-year-old widow,
kept under strict surveillance by the fascists. Written in invisible
ink in the pages of a book, it asked her to consider leaving Italy
with her three children, and to give evidence of Mussolini's

atrocities. The invitation evidently reached Mussolini's ears. Bocchini issued orders for 'relentless, efficient, uninterrupted surveillance' of the entire family, leaving no moment when they were not watched.

Two years later, after the death of Matteotti's mother Isabella, Carlo tried again. By now it was known that Velia was living in miserable conditions, forbidden to wear black as no mourning for Matteotti was tolerated, followed whenever she left the house, and kept almost totally isolated, since very few visitors were brave enough to call. The eldest boy was allowed to attend school, but only in the company of a policeman; the two younger children were forced to stay at home. But Velia had a doctor friend, Giuseppe Germani, who was determined to spirit the family out of Italy, and while passing through Paris he met Carlo and agreed to take back to Rome some invisible ink so that they could be in touch and make a plan. A spy overheard the conversation. On his return to Italy, Germani was arrested and sent to the penal islands.

Carlo, with Salvemini's help, turned to Sylvia Pankhurst, who mobilised her international circle of feminists, among them Dora Russell and Ethel Mannin. They formed a committee, launched an appeal and began gathering signatures for a petition asking the British government to protest. One of the people approached was Bernard Shaw, noticeably unreliable on the subject of fascism. Shaw refused, saying that Pankhurst was an 'incorrigibly pugnacious woman' and that she suffered from the vice of lecturing other nations on their moral inferiority. 'No,' he wrote, 'you can't bully me, and you can't bully Mussolini. If you want to help Mrs Matteotti, and not merely sandbag him with her, you must be scrupulously polite.' Their correspondence quickly degenerated into a squabble over the fascist corporate state.

The British government, appalled by these proceedings, refused to accept a delegation to Downing Street, a member of the Foreign Office noting: 'Better leave, well or ill, alone.' Briefly, Pankhurst considered leading a delegation herself to Rome, but that too had to be abandoned. The Matteotti family remained under virtual house-arrest. When news reached Carlo and Salvemini that Velia had agreed to be taken under the wing of the Catholic Church, Salvemini observed sourly: 'We must be indulgent towards that unhappy and lonely woman. But it is so disgusting.'

Very little of the fanfare, ritual, regulations and strictures of fascist daily life touched the Rosselli family in Florence; they had enveloped themselves in a cocoon apart. Between April and October they lived at their villa, L'Apparita, a place remembered later by the children with great happiness, with its barn for grain, its chickens and rabbits, its storerooms full of jam and apples, and its farm, tended by a peasant family who also made oil and wine. They had a goat. When the weather was bad they played in the loggia on the top floor; when it was good they roamed about the gardens or on the terrace looking out over Florence. Visitors who came to L'Apparita were collected from the tram terminus at Bagno a Ripoli by donkey and cart. Silvia had been given the donkey, a small Sardinian animal with its distinctive dark stripe across its back, for her sixth birthday. Nello, who loved surprises, had presented it to her very early one morning, still in his dressing gown. There were excursions to Zia Gì and Zio Giù nearby at Il Frassine, and to visit Maria's family, not far away at Borgo San Lorenzo, where the children watched the maids do the laundry with ashes, played under an enormous old chestnut tree and ate the thick yellow honey for which the farm was famous. On hot days, they followed the dirt track down to the river, dragging their toes through the dust, to the acacia trees from which the bees fed. Their grandmother Luisa was a warm, homely woman, small and cosy, physically as unlike the tall, elegant Amelia as it was possible to be. She suffered from terrible migraines, and would lie on her bed with a cloth soaked in vinegar over her eyes. Silvia and Paola watched her at her devotions, reading softly to herself from a book of Hebrew prayers.

Winters were spent in Via Giusti, where an inside staircase had been built so that Amelia, in her rooms on the ground floor, should not feel isolated from Nello and his family above. Here, too, the family lived as apart from fascist Florence as they could, and here, too, it felt like countryside, with its large garden behind the house, and hills in all directions beyond. Whether at L'Apparita or Via Giusti, the girls were taught at home. A plan to let them do gymnastics at the Istituto Pastorini was abandoned when Silvia

Zio 'Giù' Zabban at Il Frassine near Florence

Marion, Zia Gì and Mirtillino

won a gala and was told to stand to attention on a dais and raise her arm in the fascist salute. In the afternoons, she and Paola would clamber up onto the step by the high windows giving on to the street and watch the children coming out of the school opposite, and envy the little girls in their Giovani Italiane uniforms. They saw no newspapers, listened to no radio, and no adult who visited the house ever mentioned upsetting facts in their presence. The son of a family friend recounted to them one day the grisly details of a body found drowned in the Arno. It was some time before he was invited to play again.

What Nello's daughters would always remember was the warmth of their family life, the closeness of the three adults, and Amelia's serene and loving presence. This intensity of emotion is borne out by the many letters that continued to flow between them all, affectionate, solicitous. In those written to and from Carlo and his family in Paris, or between Amelia, Maria and Nello when one or other was away – at the seaside, up in the mountains, visiting relations – they wrote about what they ate and how they slept, about schools and nannies and cooks, about visits to concerts and the opera, and about the children, their moods and state of health; and when they ran out of space on the page, they flowed over into the margins and up and down the sides. But what they did not write about was politics. The Rosselli dossiers in the police archives for these years are very thin. There was, or so it seemed, nothing to report.

Which was not, of course, entirely accurate. Nello, to whom domestic life had brought great personal happiness, continued to fret about doing so little publicly for the anti-fascist cause. His hopes to start a European historical magazine, with an implied stand against dictatorships, had been slowly dashed as possible contributors and collaborators fell away, fearful of too close an association with a known opponent of the fascists. Nello complained bitterly about defeat at the hands of 'these parrots, these eternal buffoons of the life of the mind'. Writing to Benedetto Croce, he remarked sadly that he and his close friends felt old and extremely out of fashion, detached from the present, without even the pride of the past. He had become a stranger in his own country, afraid, exhausted, bereft of ideas, 'as if we were just so many larvae from which no chrysalis had ever freed itself'.

He told his friend Leone Ginzburg that he found the collapse of his magazine all the more painful because it had represented a real effort to overcome his own sense of unsociability, inertia and isolation.

Nello's sense of public futility was made stronger when he heard that his childhood friend, the talented and remarkable Leo Ferrero, only son of Guglielmo and Gina, had been killed in a car crash in Santa Fe. Leo had managed to reach Paris and then become a scholar at Yale, where he continued to pour out a stream of plays, poetry and fiction, saying apologetically that he was one of the 'privileged', who had never physically suffered at Mussolini's hands. The Ferreros had become the hub for scattered anti-fascists in exile. On hearing of Leo's death, Amelia wrote a bleak letter to Gina; both these women now knew what it was to lose a son. When Leo's uncle asked Nello to write an obituary, Nello hesitated, saying that he felt too sad. But then he sat down to write, and described Leo as a boy, forced to trot along by the side of his friends because he was so small, and the way that in class he sat swinging his legs because his feet did not reach the floor, and the fact that they all despaired of him ever being anything but a dilettante, because his talents were so many, and his interests so scattered between art, music, literature and endless talk. He finished the piece while on holiday in Forte dei Marmi, where he was staying with friends of Leo's, and wrote, 'His shadow is with us.'

And there were more deaths. At the end of October 1933, after a short illness, and in the middle of a great storm of unusual ferocity which roared round the house, Zio Giù died. He had been Amelia's prop for nearly thirty years. Zia Gì was desperate, but, as Amelia wrote to Carlo, evidently thinking of Aldo, 'one does not die of grief'. Zio Giù, whose terror had always been to be buried alive, had asked that his body be kept at home for thirty-six hours and a further fifty in the mortuary. For all those hours, Nello and other members of the family watched over him.

Not long after, Amelia's much-loved sister Anna died, and Carlo, fearing his mother's descent into depression, urged her to distract herself, to get out more. Cut off from them all, unable to share their sadness, he wrote to Amelia that he felt so uprooted that he doubted, even once the horror of fascism was over, that he would ever be able to find his roots again. Keeping going, he said, had become a blind and dogged determination.

In the autumn of 1934, Maria gave birth to a longed-for boy: they called him Aldo, after Carlo and Nello's brother. It was, as Nello remarked, a much-needed bit of happiness.

With Zio Giù and Anna gone, with Gobetti and Amendola dead of their injuries, Matteotti murdered, Bauer and Rossi in prison, Parri and countless others on the penal islands, and almost every other friend in exile, the Rossellis' world had become very small. Even the news that Giulio Einaudi, son of Carlo's mentor Luigi, and one of the few people still at liberty, was starting a new publishing house in Turin and wanted him to write a biography of Mazzini did not dispel Nello's growing sense of isolation. It was made more acute by an unexpected but delightful event. He and Maria – as they wrote to a friend in code – were just back from a week on the Riviera, where they had spent 'very very happy hours' with 'relatives'. What he was referring to was meeting Carlo, Marion and Mirtillino at Juan-les-Pins. Nello and Maria had taken Silvia with them. It was the first time the two small cousins had met and they eyed each other with curiosity. A photograph shows the two children sitting on the shoulders of their tall, stout fathers. Going back into Italy seemed to Nello like returning, yet again, to prison.

It was fortunate that Nello's life revolved around Florence. For though he remained closely in touch with his friends in the north, particularly with Leone Ginzburg, and knew precisely what they were doing, his part in their activities was small. With the Milan branch of Giustizia e Libertà destroyed, the baton had passed to Turin, where Ginzburg and two other close friends, Mario Levi and Sion Segre Amar, had taken over the job of receiving anti-fascist material from Paris and sending it around the country. They also contributed to Einaudi's new magazine, *La Cultura*, in what Benedetto Croce called an 'open conspiracy of culture', using historical articles as barely veiled references to fascist immorality. Another friend, Barbara Allason, gave parties that provided a cover for anti-fascist meetings.

Bocchini had recently scored notable successes in his war on the anti-fascists with the arrest of two apparently lone would-be assassins of Mussolini. One was an industrialist from Rivarola called Domenico Buvone, who had taken up with an Austrian ballerina of expensive tastes in Paris and who had agreed, at a price, to plan an attempt on the Duce's life. A bomb he was carrying in a suitcase in Rome suddenly exploded, killing his mother and badly injuring his sister, and he was eventually caught after shooting dead a carabiniere. He was sentenced to death, not for the murder of the policeman, which was accepted as accidental, but for his planned assassination of Mussolini, and not before he had provided Bocchini with many interesting details of the world of the anti-fascists in Paris. Buvone was executed on the same day as another conspirator, Angelo Sbardelotto, a twenty-eight-year-old anarchist from Belluno, who had volunteered to kill Mussolini. Sbardelotto, a disorganised and vague man singularly unsuited to assassination, had been picked up wandering aimlessly round the Piazza Venezia, and had later confessed. Both these plots, particularly when ties binding the two men to Paris became known, fed Bocchini's terrors for Mussolini's safety.

But he had just acquired a most useful spy. Dino Segre was a cousin of Sion Segre in Turin, and because of this the Jewish-Torinese anti-fascists took him to their heart. He was a successful journalist, the author of bestselling soft pornographic novels – cynical, amoral satires with titles such as *The Chastity Belt* and *The Scent of the Female* – and though he was not short of money, he loved intrigue and adventure. Bocchini offered him a generous salary, gave him the code name 'Pitigrilli' and the number 373, and sent him to Paris to spy on Carlo and his friends. Pitigrilli had a particular loathing for intellectuals, suspecting that they despised him, and he revelled in the pain he was able to cause. As Lussu would later say, 'Pitigrilli did not become a spy, he was born one.'

In Paris, he had no trouble worming his way into Carlo's trust. He was a tall, elegant, well-dressed man in his late thirties, and with his easy, agreeable manner, he invited confidences. In his reports back to Bocchini, he spun webs of the relationships between the Rosselli brothers, Leone Ginzburg, Carlo Levi and many others, mixing the real with the invented, rumours with personal observations, using his novelistic skills to paint lively reports of them all, and describing them as perched in various 'caravanserai' around the capital. Carlo, he reported, took his breakfast in bed, served on a silver tray, while reading *L'Humanité*. 'Rosselli', he told Bocchini proudly, 'admires me greatly. I have definitely become close to his heart.' Soon, he was able to inform Rome that Sion Segre and Mario Levi would be driving back from France into Italy, their car boot full of anti-fascist literature. A police trap was set at Ponte Tresa on the western shore of Lake Lugano. In the confusion, Segre and Levi managed to escape by jumping into the water; Segre was caught and fished out, but Levi swam to the Swiss shore and made his way to Paris.

Pitigrilli was not the only informer to whom the trusting Carlo had become close. There was also an engineer called René Odin, 'Togo', number 570. He too moved between Turin and Paris, inviting confidences. He reported to Rome that Carlo Levi and Ginzburg seemed to feel an 'almost religious admiration' for Carlo. In his role as agent provocateur, Togo did his best to persuade Carlo to organise an attack on the Chamber of Deputies in Rome, and though that came to nothing, he continued to weave his fantasies, and Carlo continued to trust him.

Then came the day when, in Turin, Bocchini's men made sixty arrests, among them Nello's friends Leone Ginzburg and Barbara Allason. Moravia, fearing that he might be picked up too, hastened to burn all his letters from the Rossellis. Virtually every one of those arrested was either an intellectual or a university professor. The women among them were held in solitary confinement, their belts, suspender belts, hair pins, cigarettes and books taken from them, and repeatedly interrogated until they were stunned and confused. Then, unexpectedly, they were released. Leone Ginzburg and Sion Segre were sentenced to long prison terms; others went off to the *confino*. In Segre's car the police had found leaflets about a small Jewish study group in Turin, and now declared that they had stumbled on a Jewish conspiracy, and that from 'Treves ... to [Carlo] Rosselli, the organisers of subversive anti-fascism are members of the "chosen people"'.

Nello's good fortune was that his name was never mentioned, but having once again escaped the fate of his friends, he felt more than ever a 'grey and mortifying isolation'. In fact, Bocchini's men were well aware that when Nello travelled for his studies, he used the opportunity to make contact with other anti-fascists, but had decided that now was not the moment to arrest him. A spy reported, with the usual mixture of fantasy and exaggeration, that the Rosellis were rich Jews, that Amelia had a lover whom her sons condoned, and that the family lived in great luxury in an 'unhealthy moral environment'. In the evenings, he said, the men dined in black tie and the women in décolleté, waited on by manservants. Nello was described as owning many properties, among them a 'sumptuous country villa'.

The sly Pitigrilli somehow managed to escape all suspicion. He had a two-hour meeting with Carlo, who was mourning the capture of his friends, and told him that from now on no women must be used in the anti-fascist fight. Saying that he still did not understand what had happened, Carlo went on to tell Pitigrilli of future plans, talking of the need to get their material into factories, and saying sadly: 'We have become like ants which immediately begin to rebuild their granaries when they have been destroyed by someone's footstep.' The credulous Carlo described where and how he communicated with Italy, and soon entrusted Pitigrilli with more missions back to Turin, where he was able to assemble a list of more names.

On 8 August 1934, Pitigrilli sent Bocchini the recipe for the invisible ink Carlo used, with the formula for making it visible. He added that Carlo had told him that he had spent half a million lire on Turati's and his own escape and that much of his inheritance had gone to the anti-fascist cause. In December, Pitigrilli complained that they all seemed to prefer domestic lives, and seldom went to cafés, which made it harder to spy on them. As often as he could, he found pretexts for visiting Carlo at home. Carlo remained astonishingly trusting. As Pitigrilli smugly observed, though 'he sees spies everywhere' he had still not rumbled him.

Pitigrilli's sleuthing paid off. By the spring of 1935, Bocchini had enough information to order the arrest of the remaining Turin network. Over the next year, dozens of people were sent for trial, among them Carlo Levi, who used his months in *confino* in a village in the south to write his famous book, *Christ Stopped at Eboli*. The harsh sentences were such as to send warnings to other anti-fascists, both in Italy and abroad. But Bocchino was not altogether reassured. He had been unable to touch Carlo, Lussu,

Tarchiani, Cianca and the others in France. 'Among all the movements conspiring against the regime,' he wrote to the *questore* in
Turin, 'that of Giustizia e Libertà is without doubt the most dangerous,' not only because they were convinced that fascism would
end only when Mussolini was 'suppressed', but because they
intended to do all they could to stir up the quiescent Italian
people. Another spy had told him that one of the Turin group
had said: 'What counts for us is action, coups: words are pointless.' As for Pitigrilli, he persuaded Bocchini to arrest him too, to
deflect suspicion; but by the time he emerged from prison a short
time later, even Carlo had finally begun to have serious doubts
about him. Pitigrilli slipped into the shadows.

On 14 June 1934, Hitler and Mussolini met for the first time, in
Venice. Mussolini was in full fascist uniform, complete with boots,
spurs and a dagger; Hitler was in a yellow raincoat and looked,
said Mussolini, like 'a plumber in a mackintosh'. The meeting
was not a success. Hitler irritated Mussolini by talking on and
on in German and dismissing the modernist art at the Biennale as
degenerate. Mussolini annoyed Hitler by making a speech saying
that they had agreed to preserve an independent Austria as a
buffer between their two countries, and that if necessary Italy
would defend Austria by force. When, two days later, Hitler

Mussolini, Hitler and the King and Queen of Italy inspecting the troops

returned to Germany, Mussolini complained that it had been like having a conversation with a record player.

Mussolini's pledges over Austria had no effect on Hitler's plans. On 25 July, the Austrian Chancellor Dollfuss was murdered by Nazis disguised as Austrian soldiers, as it happened just as his wife and children were arriving to spend a holiday with the Mussolini family. Mussolini moved troops to the Austrian frontier. In the event, no intervention was needed: the revolt was put down and, for the moment, Hitler abandoned his intentions to interfere in Austria. At home and abroad, Mussolini was congratulated for his firm hand. However, he had plans for territorial gains of his own.

Mussolini's language had always been bellicose. Well over a million young Balilla boys marched with their toy guns to the beat of war. In the *Italian Encyclopedia* of 1932, Mussolini had written that 'war alone brings to its highest peak of tension all human energy and puts the stamp of nobility upon the people who have the courage to meet it. All other trials are subservient.' Italians, he told the Grand Council, had to be habituated to 'the sight of blood and the idea of death'. The slogan '*Credere, obbedire, combattere*' – Believe, obey, fight – was everywhere.

Over the years there had been considerable resistance on the part of the local population to the Italian colonisation of Tripolitania and Cyrenaica, and it had been dealt with harshly. It was time for further conquest, this time of Abyssinia, on which Mussolini had long had his eye as a country ideal for economic exploitation and one which would link the existing colonies of Italian Eritrea and Italian Somaliland. Neither Britain nor France, Mussolini believed on the basis of past conversations, would oppose him if he attacked Abyssinia, providing he did not infringe on their own colonial interests. And there was another good reason for going to war. For all the large-scale public works, and all his insistence that 'corporatism' had brought efficient and profitable state control, Italy's finances were shaky. An invasion of Abyssinia would distract attention from schemes that were doing little to alleviate Italy's enduring poverty, and mobilisation would reduce the numbers of unemployed.

In December 1934, there was a skirmish for the possession of wells at Wal Wal, on the ill-defined border between Italian

Somaliland and Abyssinia. The Italians demanded compensation, and the Abyssinians turned to the League of Nations to arbitrate. Diplomatic discussions, disagreements, proposals and acrimonious exchanges went on all through the spring and summer of 1935. Winston Churchill and Austen Chamberlain called for sanctions against Italy if she violated the covenant of the League, causing Marinetti to decry British '*snobismo*', alcoholism, degeneracy, lack of genius and above all 'their sexual abnormalities'. The crisis deepened. On 3 October 1935, Mussolini ordered the bombing of Addis Ababa and despatched troops into Abyssinia from Eritrea and Somaliland. 'Workers and fascists,' he told the crowds assembled in the Piazza Venezia, 'on your feet! Fill the skies with your shouts! ... shouts of justice, shouts of victory!' On 10 October the League threatened to apply economic sanctions, while continuing to negotiate.

Carlo had long been observing the approaching invasion with anger and disbelief. Now that it had come he was everywhere, talking, writing articles, making speeches, trying to mobilise opposition, exhorting people to rise up and protest. 'For fascism,' he kept repeating, 'war is the sole form of politics'; the fascists were 'reducing the Italians to massacre and ruin'; it was nothing but an attempt to deflect attention from the sorry state of the economy. Any war in Africa had to be opposed 'today, tomorrow, always'.

A new spy in Paris, Nicola Casavolta, reported to Rome that Carlo was saying 'We must at all costs rise up, we can't remain passive.' Whenever he left his house now, there was a spy behind him. Fifty photographs of him had been handed out among the informers. Spy number 512, Egidio Traina, told Bocchini that Carlo was saying to his friends that 'all methods to crush the enemy are good', and that what he feared was that others would defeat the fascists before the Italians rose up to do the job themselves. 'To us must fall the honour of bringing down [fascism] like a rabid dog. The hour of revolution has sounded.' When, on 6 October, Carlo made a speech against the war at the Palais de la Mutualité in Paris, there were four spies in the audience, each one of whom sent their own report to Rome. The Italian newspapers, describing him as a 'rubicund Jewish millionaire', claimed that he was the 'most violent enemy of Italy'.

An unnerving incident took place at around this time; Carlo

chose to make little of it. One day he received a visit from a young émigré, Giuseppe Zanata, who told him that he had deserted the army rather than go to fight in Abyssinia. A little later he returned with a different story. He told Carlo that the wife of one of the communist exiles in Paris had given him a revolver and some cartridges and instructed him to kill Carlo, telling him that he would receive 15,000 lire if he did so. Under cross-questioning, the young man contradicted himself, and said that he had thrown the revolver into the Seine. But when Carlo insisted on searching him, the revolver was still in his belt. Zanata confessed that OVRA had sent him from Rome, and that instructions for the assassination had in fact come from the Italian vice consul in Paris. Carlo ordered the terrified Zanata to write down his confession and sign it. He then filed it away, but characteristically said nothing.

The Abyssinian campaign was brutal. The Italians used poison gas on civilians, to horrific effect. Abyssinian casualties kept growing, to an estimated 70,000, while the Italians suffered few losses, not least because Abyssinia possessed neither artillery nor an airforce. The delegate of the International Committee of the Red Cross described the battle scene as a 'veritable hell', in which screaming and moaning women and children were 'dying like flies', their faces made unrecognisable by the burning poison gas. On 18 December 1935, Mussolini called for a 'Day of Faith' and invited Italians to donate their gold to the war effort. Many thousands of women gave their wedding rings; Pirandello sent his Nobel Prize medal to be melted down. Thirty-five thousand kilos of gold were collected. In England, the Italian *fascio* raised £18,480 for the war coffers, and declared that there would probably now be shortages – 'no more gorgonzola'. As one English journalist shrewdly observed, the Italians had become 'a nation of prisoners, condemned to enthusiasm'.

Carlo's opposition to the war took on a desperate note. He railed at the League for its pusillanimity and at Britain and France for their secret dealings, warning that 'this could become one of the determining causes of a new European conflagration'. He had thousands of flyers printed on rice paper urging the Italian soldiers to desert; he planned to distribute them to the troops on their transit ships, but they were seized by French customs. For a while, he almost believed that he could see signs of exhaustion in the Italians and a desire to climb out of the 'moral humiliation' in which they now lived. 'The war in Africa', he declared, with more hope than belief, 'will be the tomb of his Excellency.'

He was wrong. The speed of the Italian victory surprised everyone, as did the low number of Italian deaths. Though Mussolini had entered the war with little planning, and no thought of what to do with Abyssinia once the country was conquered, it was over by May 1936. On the 3rd of the month the Italians entered Addis Ababa and the Emperor Haile Selassie fled into exile. Ecstatic crowds in Rome learnt that Italy at last had its empire, 'a fascist empire, an empire of peace, an empire of civilisation and humanity'. Victor Emmanuel III took the title of Emperor of Abyssinia. Mussolini's prestige had never been higher, even if the cost of the war had been prohibitive, as would that of pacifying and ruling the new colony, and Italy's range of options had been narrowed, so that it would be driven ever closer into an alliance with Germany. The fascist papers spoke of Mussolini as 'infallible', and 'divine'. Nello, lying low in triumphalist Florence, wondered whether the moment might have come to join Carlo in exile.

For Carlo, the victory was crushing. To Giacomo Antonini, another spy whom he believed to be his friend, he wrote sadly: 'You know that it is in my nature to see the positive side in every situation. But how not to believe the evidence in this case?' Sylvia Pankhurst had started a new paper which published reports on the massacres in Ethiopia and the continuing brutality of the fascists in Italy, to which Carlo and Salvemini contributed articles. But for both the League and the anti-fascists, Abyssinia had been a terrible defeat, and when Carlo heard that the League of Nations had officially ended its sanctions against Italy, he felt 'nausea'.

These were not easy times. The Concentrazione Antifascista, riven by doctrinal differences, was coming apart. The stabilising element provided by Treves and Turati, with their passionate belief in the cause and their moral stature, had disappeared with their deaths. Far from becoming a united movement, the various parties within it had kept up their constant sniping against each other. A new pact of unity in Paris between the exiled socialists and communists was greeted warily by Carlo, who had just had a first encounter with Trotsky which he described as a 'cordially hostile verbal duel'. Bocchini's many arrests in Italy had driven more rebels to seek safety in France and these also fed into the sense of scratchy unease that had settled over the Parisian anti-fascists.

Among Carlo's friends too, schisms had opened up. Lussu, his constant companion for seven years, left to pursue a cure for his lingering TB in the Haute-Savoie, where he had seven ribs removed, largely financed by Carlo. Complaining that Carlo was not sufficiently 'revolutionary', he declared that his own real interest in the struggle lay in military actions, of which there were now none. Tarchiani, whose views had always lain some way to the right of Carlo's, and who was in any case in desperate need of money, drifted off. Carlo was also having disagreements with Don Sturzo over the Church's collaboration with the fascist regime, and even with Salvemini, who accused him of losing his way, flirting with Marxism and a proletarian revolution, and beginning to sound like a typical Mazzini exile, living on dreams and abstract ideas. And that, said Salvemini, 'would be a real disaster ... You are losing your once certain touch. One day a drift to the left, another to the right.'

Meanwhile the Concentrazione, after more ill-tempered meetings, disbanded itself. One of the many spies sent to Paris to report on the exiled community described it as confused, leaderless, bigoted, reduced to seditious talk; the exiles, he said, were a sorry bunch, 'totally ignored and isolated'. This news was greeted with delight by Mussolini. 'Not so much *concentrazione* as dead,' he noted. 'Very dead. Putrefied.' There was also more criticism from Bernard Shaw who, having heard that the International Committee of Writers was opposed to fascism, wrote to tell Sylvia Pankhurst that he wanted nothing to do with it: 'As against Salvemini, Rosselli and the Liberal parliamentarians, generally I am on the side of Mussolini.'

Carlo and Giustizia e Libertà were now alone, with Carlo in sole command. More than ever propelled into the limelight, he remained buoyant, telling the friends who came together for the anniversary of Matteotti's death that it was inevitable that he had been assassinated, as Amendola and Gobetti's deaths had also been inevitable. 'And, unless we save them, Rossi, Gramsci, Bauer and many other Matteottis' would die too, 'all of them by their very natures the opposite of Mussolini's character and sensibility'. The dictator, he went on, was 'singularly impotent with men who escape his mental horizons. He therefore suppresses them.'

What Carlo did not know was that the spies were warning Rome that he was now regarded as the 'main peril', a man 'ambitious to excess, cold, calculating, ready to risk when it appeared to him there was even a slender possibility of success'. As one anonymous informer put it: 'To my mind, it is absolutely necessary to eliminate him.' In the report in the archives, the last three words have been circled in red.

Characteristically, Carlo did what he always did when under assault. He counter-attacked, sounding optimistic. With the bickering Concentrazione gone, he said, 'great dreams' lay ahead. 'Many people who were slumbering are waking up.' Writing the editorials himself, he started a new weekly *Giustizia e Libertà* paper, small enough to be folded in two and put into an envelope, looking much like a page pulled out of a lesson book. He opened its columns to all comers, politicians, historians, economists alike. 'To you', he wrote in an article directed at the fascists, 'the Empire. To us, the nation. To you, decadent Rome; to us a republican, united Risorgimento . . . To you, a totalitarian dictatorship; to us, hope and rebirth. One period has ended. Another is opening.'

At the same time, he pushed the two ideas about which he felt most strongly: European unity in the face of fascism and the Nazis, and the need to entice the young to set up small mobile groups of youthful anti-fascists who had 'never betrayed'. It was time for fresh action, and to these newcomers, who had been turned into an enormous grey zone, ignorant, indifferent, sceptical, bored, servile, regimented and dulled by all-embracing fascism, he could offer guidance, help and experience. Revolution, he declared, had become not only an economic necessity, but a 'patriotic duty', and whoever captured the minds of the young 'will control tomorrow'. He wanted, he said, to 'detoxify' the atmosphere in which they were living, build a bridge between what came before fascism and what would follow, and give them 'almost a new faith'.

Depressed by seeing a photograph of Italian nuns giving the fascist salute, he had come to believe more strongly than ever that Catholicism was a 'fatal enemy' of all liberty, and that only lay people were capable of true progress, a stand that earned him a cold letter from Don Sturzo, who accused him of wanting to create a 'pagan religion of the state ... a Bolshevik cult of the anti-God'.

In his new paper he decided to include a literary page, drawing attention to everything in Italy that smacked of revolt. As his model, he chose his cousin Moravia and wrote an article saying that his new book, *Le ambizioni sbagliate*, had been banned because Mussolini rejected its depiction of young people in Italy disaffected by fascism. Carlo praised Moravia as an authentic and realistic writer. As it happened, the book had not been banned, but Carlo's article was shown to Ciano and then Mussolini, who decided that it should be, and also got the *Gazzetta del Popolo*, for which Moravia wrote, to sack him. If Carlo had hoped to win Moravia over to the cause of the anti-fascists, he was disappointed. Moravia wrote a grovelling letter to Mussolini, and, as censorship and soon racial persecution became stronger, resorted to ever more compromises.

In the summer of 1934, the Rossellis moved house again. Though Carlo had speculated successfully on the stock exchange, the anti-fascist cause was eating into his inheritance and the large sunny flat overlooking the Pantheon had become too expensive. They found a smaller one not far from Nenni's house in Rue Vavin, on the third floor of 79 Rue Notre-Dame-des-Champs, a long, winding street full of tall buildings, with little shops below and old-fashioned lamps which cast a pleasing yellow glow. Though Carlo was forced to leave his grand piano behind, and mourned the loss of the evening light on the cupola and the vast skies all around, the new flat was bright and Marion papered the children's bedrooms with flowered patterns and painted the dining room a light biscuit colour. Carlo's studio was once again entirely lined with books. He told Amelia that the move had done him good, taught him not to become too attached to familiar places. During the move, Marion took refuge in a hotel near Saint-Sulpice, where she lay in her bed looking out over the gardens of a convent school feeling guilty that she was not helping. But her heart problems were getting worse and she tired quickly. 'In our life,' she told Carlo sadly, 'there is no room for a sick woman.'

For his birthday that autumn, she gave Carlo a weekend suitcase in pigskin. Very early that morning, the three children climbed into his bed, bringing him their presents of marrons glacés, marshmallows and chocolates. Mirtillino had started writing poetry and was taking gym lessons from a Swedish lady who told them that he was as uncoordinated as a puppy. Carlo called the two younger children '*le bestioline*', the little animals. Aghi now had a mass of curls. Melina's outbursts of temper exhausted Marion, but the three children played happily in the nearby Jardin du Luxembourg. They spoke Italian at home, French everywhere else, and read *Winnie the Pooh* and *Dr Dolittle* in English. And yet, however hard Carlo and Marion tried to shield the children from the surrounding tensions, the household was permanently on edge. Many years later, Mirtillino would write: 'Ours was a political childhood. Treason, hedging, fellow-travelling, fanatical loyalty to one's own and hatred to the rest.'

Their surveillance continued. Bellavia, spy no. 353, reported to Rome that he was trying to rent a room in the house opposite the Rossellis, where he would station someone with a camera; he wanted to find a woman, with a cover story of having a lover, 'nothing unusual in a country where morality is of little interest'. Another spy noted that many of their visitors were Russian, and that Carlo was beginning to think of himself as a 'second Lenin'. When they did not know the names of his callers, the spies described them: fat, short, small, well-dressed, black hair. In Carlo's French dossier, kept by the Parisian police, someone wrote: 'They say that he is very lucky.'

Though Marion often found it hard to prise Carlo from his desk, she forced him out to hear Toscanini – to whom she sent flowers on behalf of the appreciative Italian exiles – conduct *I vespri siciliani*. When Amelia came to stay, they went to the theatre to see Cocteau and Giraudoux, and to a little cinema on the Left Bank to watch Eisenstein's films. The Rossellis often dined with the Nittis; Dolci, who had remained one of Carlo's closest friends, had become engaged to Nitti's daughter Luigia. In their hospitable house Carlo met many of the leaders of the French left; the historian Élie Halévy became a friend, as did André Malraux and Julien Benda and the Noufflards, who invited them to their house at Fresnay in Normandy. Though he did not always share their views, Carlo's warm nature endeared him to everyone. He worried constantly about not having enough time for the children, but when he was home he would gather all three of them on to his big leather armchair, with Aghi on his knee, and make up stories for them. The two little ones had new nicknames, Mea and Meo. He told Amelia that he was always running, always short of time, that he could never stop, not even for a minute. Giustizia e Libertà had opened a new office not far away in Rue Val-de-Grâce, but many meetings took place in the Rosselli flat, or spilled over into the Café Saint-Sulpice, lasting long into the night in a haze of cigarette smoke. Some of the more impoverished contributors slept in the office.

For Carlo, as Marion pointed out to Amelia, holidays were always a problem. The seaside bored him, for Marion could neither swim nor play tennis, though he made an exception for Cap Ferrat, which he described to Amelia as an 'idyl to end idyls', telling her that he had been to visit Amendola's grave and that his sense of anguish had been lessened by that 'triumph of light and colour'. A visit to Antibes ended with his early return to Paris. Another, to Royan, went better for it was close enough for him to go backwards and forwards. But the best of all was when their friend Paul Desjardins had summer gatherings of European intellectuals in a twelfth-century abbey and Salvemini came to join them. Very occasionally, and then always arranged in code, there were brief holidays, usually somewhere close to the border, with Nello and his family, and Amelia came as often as she could to Paris.

Early in 1935, Marion's health seemed to worsen. Leaving to go into a clinic for an operation, she wrote to Carlo that her life had become a nightmare, and that there seemed no limit to her despair and exhaustion. They decided reluctantly to send the two younger children to spend some months with Nello and his family in Florence, so that she could get more rest, and Carlo, constantly worried about her, turned down an invitation to give a series of lectures in the US, telling the man who had issued the invitation that his duty lay with his 'companion of many years, who has shared my efforts, setbacks, adventures'. Mirtillino, who was always conscious of being his mother's favourite, stayed in Paris.

In Evian, where she went to convalesce, Marion reflected on

Marion, Mirtillino and Carlo on a rare holiday

Nello and Carlo with two of their children on a beach in
France in the early 1930s

her 'physical decline'. It was no longer possible, she concluded, to fool herself that she would ever completely recover; that hope had gone. 'And if, in order to exist, I need so much comfort and so much looking after, would it not be better to give up? But then I think of the intolerable pain of leaving Carlo and Mirtillino.' When the weather was fine, she sat on her terrace at the Hôtel des Ambassadeurs reading *War and Peace*; Pierre reminded her of Carlo. Writing to Zia Gì about the children, she said that only Melina, of the three, had been born 'ugly'; Andrea was 'very presentable', but Mirtillino, with his golden hair and eyes of blue porcelain, 'was a beauty'.

Left in Paris with Mirtillino, Carlo took him on expeditions, sometimes joined by Salvemini, who was charmed by the little boy's liveliness and intelligence. Mirtillino had been given a canary, which he called Taguine, and together he and Carlo invented a bird club, keeping a list of all the birds they saw. When Mirtillino thought about his father in later life, he would remember this large man, always active, always enthusiastic, always loving, who brought energy and excitement to everything; and who, in the evenings, played Bach and Beethoven on the piano – the opening bars of Beethoven's *Fifth* had become the hymn of Giustizia e Libertà – and took him on imaginary journeys with an atlas, or read him passages from Plutarch. On Mirtillino's ninth birthday, 9 June 1936, Carlo and Marion took him to a Chinese restaurant, where he used chopsticks for the first time. As a present, according to a report written by a spy and filed in Marion's dossier in Rome, they gave him a bicycle.

Though Melina and Aghi arrived in Florence speaking little Italian, they quickly took to their cousins and to Italian food. Melina, they all thought, looked exactly like Carlo. She was shy, and clung to Amelia. Her temper remained unpredictable. Amelia told Zia Gì that there was something 'violent and primitive' in the little girl's nature, attributing it to the constant change in governesses and to the fact that no one had taken a firm hand with her. Slowly, Melina's moods grew calmer. There were walks in the countryside on Sundays, occasional outings to the cinema and holidays in the mountains. In the evenings, after the children had done their homework, they all played games: not Monopoly (about money) or cards (remembering their grandfather Joe's gambling) and never anything to do with weapons. Writing to Marion from Vienna, where she had escaped on a brief holiday with Nello and Maria, Amelia wrote that her happiness with them was like 'sunshine'. 'Otherwise, tell me, how would we go on, with all this blackness around us, and in our hearts.' She had decided to write her memoirs.

In July 1936, Carlo and Marion went to Morzine in the Haute-Savoie to celebrate their tenth wedding anniversary. A loving telegram came from Amelia, Nello and Maria in Florence. Marion was happy because Carlo had promised to spend an entire month with her. They had barely arrived when news came that civil war had broken out in Spain. After a week of frantic telephone calls, Carlo hastened back to Paris. 'The vile Hebrew Rosselli', reported a spy to Rome, 'refuses to accept that he is beaten.'

CHAPTER EIGHTEEN

A Free Man Again

On 17 July 1936, generals in the Spanish army launched a coup against the democratically elected Popular Front, which had been fatally weakened by the global economic crisis and the strikes and anarchist violence that had broken out between workers and employers. It was backed by the Guardia Civil and the Catholic Church. Two days later, General Franco, head of the Army of Africa in Morocco, asked Mussolini to lend him aeroplanes to ferry his soldiers across the Straits of Gibraltar to the Spanish mainland. Ciano, newly elected foreign minister, agreed and, having sent the planes, he went on to send weapons and men. Though the Spaniards came to dislike their Italian allies, calling them quarrelsome, bullying and despotic, Italy would soon become Franco's major contributing foreign power. Some areas of Spain supported the rebels, others the Republican forces; the civil war spread, as did atrocities on both sides. Nationalist commanders spoke of carrying out *limpienza*, 'cleansing'. Bodies of executed Republicans were left on the streets to inspire terror. The Republicans burned down churches and murdered priests.

It would later be said that in the Spanish Civil War, people saw what they chose to believe: a fight between good and evil, between bosses and workers, between Church and state, between enlightenment and the forces of darkness. For Carlo it was perfectly simple. Abyssinia had been a disastrous defeat for the anti-fascist movement and it had greatly strengthened Mussolini. Spain would be the place where the anti-fascists redeemed their past failures and returned democracy to its rightful place. A victory in Spain would decide the fate of Europe. What was more, Carlo was feeling bruised by a fresh attack on him by former colleagues, who dismissed Giustizia e Libertà as a band of useless agitators, bombastic and impotent. Carlo had never felt more isolated. Spies reported that he was dejected, confused, out of sorts.

But not defeated; Carlo did not countenance defeat. He called a meeting in the Giustizia e Libertà offices in Paris and set about raising men and material to support the Republicans, despatching the anarchist Camillo Berneri ahead to Barcelona to get a feel for what was happening. His mood quickly turned to one of elation. With the Spanish war, he was discovering a talent for stirring prose, his words moving and exultant. It was, he told the men who came to Rue Val-de-Grâce, like the Risorgimento all over again, a great light burning over the horizon. 'We declare,' he wrote, 'not in the febrile excitement of an hour, but calmly ... that the Spanish revolution is our revolution, that the working-class Spanish Civil War is the war of all anti-fascists, that the place of all revolutionaries is in Spain.' He was looking for volunteers to go with him to Barcelona, in the name of the 2,000 people killed in recent years by the fascists in Italy, and the 3,000 more who had been jailed or sent to the *confino*. Only his *giellisti*, the republicans and the anarchists were ready to listen; for the moment, the socialists and the communists hung back. To his great relief, Amelia had agreed to come to Paris to be with Marion and the children while he was away. To Gina Lombroso, Carlo wrote: 'The peace of Europe is hanging by a thread.'

Most of the pilots in Spain had gone over to Franco; what the Republicans needed most were technicians, planes and men who could fly them. Carlo provided money from his dwindling resources for the squadron of volunteers planned by André Malraux. Since Malraux himself was not a pilot, a French reserve officer was put in charge; the first forty-seven men were soon on their way to Spain. They intended to carry out their two daily sorties without parachutes, to leave more room for bombs. In the evenings, there were vast gatherings of supporters for the Spanish republic in the Vélodrome d'Hiver.

In Paris, the spies were following Carlo's frenetic activities closely. Bellavia reported that he was acting like a 'real Jew', 'a little Lenin, a daddy's boy', and that the weapons he was getting hold of would surely later be used against Italy. He had been spotted talking to the Soviet writer and journalist Ilya Ehrenburg;

his telephone was tapped and his intercepted letters were examined under a special quartz lamp which could pick out invisible messages. Antonini wrote that Carlo was bored with domesticity, and that Spain was providing him with a purpose to his life. He was right.

Carlo was now a portly, bespectacled man in his mid-thirties; as Salvemini said, he looked like a bookish intellectual, not a fighter. Nothing, however, was going to prevent him going to war, not even the fact that the Spanish Republicans were saying that they needed not men but weapons. Borrowing a white beret from Marion and wearing workmen's clothes, he left by train for Spain. By 19 August he was in Barcelona, in the infantry barracks of Pedralbes with some 130 Italian comrades, training to join the anarchist syndicalist Colonna Francisco Ascaso, under the auspices of the Catalan government. Though the barracks were in a grim and forbidding rococo castle, with vast halls and a tower, they were full of cheerful men and women of every age and political hue, wearing suits and overalls and berets, red and black scarves wound around their necks, clutching rifles and revolvers and pistols. More were arriving all the time, by car and bicycle and on foot, from Belgium and Switzerland, Algeria and Argentina. The leader of the militias was an anarchist intellectual called Santillan, who looked distinctly unmilitary. It all reminded Carlo of a university during a break between classes. 'I felt', he wrote later, 'a free man again, with a true sense of dignity.'

As a veteran of the Italian Alpini, Carlo was made joint commander of the Ascaso, in charge of 40 riflemen. The 90 machine-gunners were led by his friend from Ustica, Mario Angeloni, the Tuscan republican notary; Berneri was appointed their political commissar. Most of the men were distinctly middle-aged and had served in the First World War. They were told that they would find weapons waiting for them at the front line in Aragon. A few days later, they marched to the station to catch a train – not in line or in step, since none of the men cared to be seen as regular soldiers and the anarchists were instinctively opposed to discipline; but they sang and raised their fists in salute. Some wore suits, but had taken off their ties; others were in overalls, as if they had just come off the factory floor. As they straggled along, passers-by cheered them on. Carlo's myopic friend

Aldo Garosci was there, having come straight from his studies on Cézanne in Paris, as well as the writer and critic Umberto Calosso, a stout, pipe-smoking forty-two-year-old with spiky hair and a long nose, who had happened to find himself in Spain when the war broke out. Calosso's old Ford was loaded on to a wagon at the back.

At 1 o'clock in the morning the train paused at the station of Terrassa, and a crowd of cheering people climbed on board, bringing melons, ham, wine, bread and cheese. Next morning the Italians woke to the dry, burning plain of Aragon, its earth ridged, parched and stony. In the baking afternoon they were dropped off at Grañén, where the temperature had just touched 52 degrees. Carlo had always hated the heat. Of the three lorries sent to fetch them for the last lap of their journey to the front, two immediately broke down. The men walked the 18 kilometres in silence. The militia headquarters in Vicién had no beds for them, but gave them soup and bread and some straw to lie on. Carlo and Calosso slept in the Ford. They found themselves laughing: here they were, a respectable writer and a retired university professor, released from the monotony of their everyday lives, young once again, 'authors and actors in our own destinies'.

Next morning, cannon fire could be heard coming from the town of Huesca, six kilometres away. The Ascaso column had been given the task of cutting the road linking Huesca to Zaragoza. Rebel forces were dug in both to the right and to the left. '*Posizione* sandwich,' noted Carlo. He followed a patrol of half-naked militiamen up to the crest of a hill, passing abandoned hovels cut into the rock, panting as he scrambled over the hard, furrowed ground; then he went to swim in a nearby lake. 'The sun and the earth', he thought, 'command in this war.' In the distance could be seen two great pillars of rose-coloured rock 'like the entrance to hell'. Carlo had started a diary. 'Not a tree', he wrote, 'not a blade of grass . . . not only my feet but my shoes are on fire. Nausea is making things worse.' Since they had no cover, the men had to dig deep trenches in the packed earth. 'Extraordinary experiences,' he wrote to Marion, 'unforgettable . . . I am so happy to be here.' He had already fallen in love with this 'primitive, young, burning' land. At night, looking out at the stars which seemed to shine exceptionally bright against the dark sky, listening to the whispers of his companions, he felt a sense of great fondness for the men around him. The wind got up, blowing flurries of grit and sand and he did a round of the men standing guard. An owl hooted not far away. 'It's hard', he wrote in his diary, 'to take this war seriously.'

Since it was mid-summer, engagements took place at dawn. Before it grew light on 28 August Carlo was wakened by one of the sentries, who thought he could see signs of enemy tanks leaving Huesca. Carlo posted his men and named their position Monte Pelato, after a mountain on Lipari. The tanks advanced. The Italians, despite being outnumbered six to one and having no artillery and grenades that failed to explode, held their ground. Carlo remained, Calosso said later, totally calm. Four hours passed; seven Italians were killed, among them Angeloni, who died singing the 'Internationale' and talking about his family. Finally, Spanish reinforcements arrived. The rebels retreated, leaving behind 150 of their men dead or wounded, a tractor, a machine gun and two cannons. To the dismay of the Italians, the injured were quickly finished off. One was found to be carrying a noose, intended for any Italian captive. Carlo had been nicked by a bullet, but the wound, he wrote to Marion, was clean and did not hurt; at the bottom of the letter, Calosso added a postscript: the injury 'was very very small'.

With Angeloni dead, Carlo took sole command and directed his men to dig trenches and build shelters, while he organised food and liaised with the Spanish militia. 'I am doing magnificently,' he told Marion, urging her not to make too many 'alarming mental visits' to Aragon, and saying that he had become extremely fit, walking for hours in the high mountains without getting tired. Letters were collected and delivered by a motorcyclist who came up to the front twice a week from Barcelona. The Italians' triumphant stand at Monte Pelato militarily signified little, but their morale was high: they had proved themselves against a vastly larger and better equipped enemy. It rose still further when, a few days later, a night patrol returned at dawn with nineteen nationalist prisoners.

'After the Russian revolution, the Spanish revolution is the greatest epic of modern times,' Carlo wrote to Marion. 'A new world is being born ... I am experiencing moments of beauty and purity such as I have felt only a couple of times in my life, for which it is worth sacrificing the pleasures and even the calm happiness of normal life.' He would return home, he told her, 'enriched, fortified, rejuvenated', and he begged her to believe in the 'really immense usefulness' of what he was doing. If Marion had her doubts, she does not appear to have voiced them.

Léon Blum, now head of the Popular Front in France, had initially agreed to send aircraft and artillery to help the Republicans against Franco's forces. Coming under pressure from members of his own cabinet, as well as from Stanley Baldwin and Anthony Eden in Britain, he changed his mind. Representatives from twenty-seven nations met in London to discuss reactions to the war, and, after some bickering over details and terms, a pact of non-intervention was signed. But it contained no proper system for enforcing an embargo on weapons and military support and, behind its slippery declarations, the three dictators, Hitler, Mussolini and Stalin, were soon stepping up their involvement. While Britain and France sat by and watched, Mussolini strengthened his ties with Germany. Carlo, who had always liked Blum and was grateful to him for helping him stay in France, raged against his cowardice over Spain, saying that the Frenchman had been imprisoned by his 'usual doubts and timidity' and that his speech on collective security was 'nothing but an infernal circle of feebleness and deals'. He wrote crossly to Marion: 'Our theory that the old socialists are finished, miserably finished, is true.'

In October, after a meeting between Hitler and Ciano at Berchtesgaden, Germany and Italy increased their aid to Franco; an entente was declared, 'an axis', as Mussolini announced, 'around which can unite all those European countries who believe in collaboration and peace'. Hitler sent more Junker planes and raised the Condor Legion; Mussolini signed a secret agreement with the rebels and opened a recruiting office in Rome's Piazza Navona for 'volunteers' to fight alongside Franco's soldiers. Russia too was busy sending military advisers to Spain to help the Republicans; fighter planes, trucks and tanks would follow. The war was settling in. More Catholic priests were murdered, more Republican supporters shot, more old scores paid off. On 1 October, Franco was named head of state and installed in Burgos; his troops advanced to the southern and western suburbs of Madrid.

In Aragon, more Italians kept arriving to join the Ascaso, but the mood of comradeship was turning sour. Faced by the reality of the scorching and dusty plain, the anarchists among Carlo's men were quarrelsome and surly. He spent much of his time trying to keep the peace. Nothing was made easier by the fact that the Catalan militia behaved like conquering occupiers, laying waste to the countryside, executing their captives and looting what little the local people still possessed. His friends remarked on how very patient Carlo remained, 'which indeed I am', he wrote to Marion. 'One has to keep one's mind fixed firmly on the essential objective.' What he did not know was that Enrico Brichetti, an unkempt, bespectacled friend from Paris, who had come to join the anti-fascists in Spain, was in fact sending back secret reports to Bocchino.

Carlo was in Barcelona in early November when he was asked to broadcast to Italy on behalf of the Republicans. He managed to send a message to Nello giving both the time and the radio frequency of his talk, and in Forte dei Marmi, where the Rossellis had gone on holiday to a little hotel among the pine trees, they gathered to listen to him. Carlo spoke with passion, and his pauses, timing and repetitions were those of a skilled orator. 'Companions, brothers, Italians,' he began, 'listen. An Italian volunteer is speaking to you from Barcelona ... The revolution in Spain is triumphant ... a new order has been born, based on liberty and social justice.' Soon it would spread to Italy. But, he went on, Italian fascist planes were dropping Italian fascist bombs every day on to innocent women and children, and Italians needed to wake up and bring an end to such shame and dishonour. 'Italians, help the Spanish revolution. Free men, rise up! Today in Spain, tomorrow in Italy.' It was an echo of the phrase that ends the Passover Seder: 'Next year in Jerusalem'. His words were picked up, reported, printed all over the world.

Four days later, a police report was placed on Ciano's desk in Rome. Rosselli, it said, had become the most prominent of the Italian anti-fascists fighting in Spain, and he enjoyed 'great popularity'. What was more, his name was being mentioned as the 'only possible successor to Mussolini'. For Ciano, there was only one heir to the Duce: Ciano himself.

In public Carlo kept insisting that the war was going well, that the Catalan soldiers were disciplined and his own men well armed. In private he was struggling, bumping over the dirt tracks from one ill-tempered meeting to another in an old Chevrolet car he had got hold of. He was wearing a discarded airman's uniform, with pockets on the knees which made him think of letter boxes, and he looked, he told Marion, 'like a cross between an old revolutionary and a tramp, but more tramp than revolutionary'. Italian anti-fascists were now fighting in several different units, and his old friend and collaborator Pietro Nenni was in Spain, the socialists and communists in Paris having overcome their resistance to joining the Republicans. Casualties among them were mounting. Fernando de Rosa, the young man who had fired a shot at Prince Umberto, was dead, killed by a bullet while trying to regroup his men.

On 20 November, the Ascaso went into battle at Almudévar, but the attack failed through lack of coordination, even though Carlo, covered in mud, scrambled around, radiating energy and confidence. His men had fallen out among themselves, with the anarchists refusing any kind of military discipline. He was beginning to think in terms of a new group, without any anarchists, better organised and trained; he wanted to call it the Battaglione Matteotti. By early December, the Ascaso was in full crisis.

The autumn had brought cold and rain and the men were camped in a field between olive trees and vines; Carlo, in his letters home, remained determinedly cheerful. 'I feel that I have reached a state of equilibrium and understanding that I never had when I was young,' he told Marion. He made little of the fact that his wound had brought back his old phlebitis, which had kept him in bed so often as a boy, and that he had been forced to go for treatment to the Swiss field hospital. Relations between the anarchists and the other men grew worse. Carlo was blamed for the failures and sidelined by the anarchists. He wrote to Cianca angrily that they had taken advantage of his absence and indulged in jealousies and idiotic intrigues; his views on them had changed and he now considered them 'totally useless'.

On 6 December he decided that there was no longer a role for him and he resigned. 'I have realised', he wrote sadly, 'that I love humanity in the abstract and individuals concretely, but that groups, other than in exceptional circumstances, seem to me every day more impossible and sometimes even unbearable.' The pain in one leg had now spread to the other, and he had developed sciatica.

The anarchists drifted off; fighters were being recruited for the International Brigades and assigned to units according to their experience and origins. Carlo did not regret his first impulse to come to Spain, because he had shown solidarity at a time when his Republican comrades were without many other foreign friends, and he felt that he and his companions had fought valiantly. He took pleasure in the popularity of his Italian recruits, portrayed by one reporter as combining 'a passionate chivalry and devotion with supreme courage and resourcefulness and discipline', though this was not how Carlo would have described the anarchists among them. (The Swiss volunteers, by contrast, were seen as dour and impatient, the Poles as dashing and fearless, the Americans as sober and intelligent.)

He was recovering only very slowly, however, and he had to keep delaying his return to Paris. To the children he wrote a charming letter, asking Mirtillino, who was learning fractions, to devote a fraction of every third day to writing him a letter, and including a story for Aghi and Melina about a clock that ran backwards, so that the man who owned it was forced also to do everything backwards. 'How sick I am of feeling such constant anguish about him,' Marion wrote to Amelia from Montreux, where she had taken the children for a holiday. 'Do you think it possible that this torment may perhaps be over?'

Having been away for almost six months, apart from a quick week-long visit in October, Carlo reached home on 7 January 1937.

Though he arrived looking thin and ill, with his leg continuing to ache, and though Marion and his doctors tried to make him rest, Carlo immediately resumed his customary frenetic pace. On 18 December, the first Italian fascist troops had sailed to join Franco's forces in Spain. The newly formed Italian anti-fascist battalion, the Garibaldi, needed men. Determined to help recruit them, he told a group of volunteers assembled in Argenteuil at the beginning of February that in Spain they would be able to dispel for ever the notion that anti-fascists were not true fighters. The Spanish Civil War was something for which, if necessary, it was worth dying. And then he repeated the words that he had used on Ràdio Barcelona: 'Today in Spain, tomorrow in Italy.'

Marion's health was slightly better and she wrote to Amelia that she and Carlo were making plans for trips. 'I am full of longings these days, for journeys, for new clothes, even for a bit of Tuscany.' She told Amelia how grateful she was for the interest that her mother-in-law took in the minutiae of their domestic lives, but as both women knew, there was not much else they could safely discuss in their letters. Melina, she reported to Amelia, remained as impossible as ever to reason with, but responded better if dealt with gently. Pleasure for the little girl was not so much enjoyment as passion.

In March came news that the Garibaldi Battalion had played a decisive part in the Battle of Guadalajara, the first in which Italian fascists and anti-fascists fought against each other. Mussolini's Lupi di Toscana were routed, 500 men taken prisoner and tanks, trucks, machine guns and cannons lost to the Republicans. Communist planes had strafed the Italian fascist troops as they fled 'because no one fired back, and all were running, and most of all the many officers'. Though the cold, the lack of hot food, the fear of being captured by an enemy known to torture and kill its captives were all blamed, the defeat for Mussolini was ignominious. In Paris, *L'Oeuvre* carried a headline: 'The Italians are showing their heels'. From Rome, Ciano gave orders that while the Spaniards taken prisoner should be treated correctly, all Italian mercenaries should be shot.

Carlo was jubilant. In the next Giustizia e Libertà *Quaderni* he gave full coverage to the battle, printing photographs of the rout and of the Italian soldiers taken prisoner or who had deserted. Many of these men, he wrote, had only joined out of economic necessity, and had never been told where they were being sent. Forty-nine thousand Italian soldiers had already been despatched to support Franco.

Carlo's revelations received much international attention. The spies in Paris reported that he was in an excellent mood, telling everyone that the way things were going it was likely he himself would be back in Italy by the summer. Mussolini cut short a trip to Libya to deal with the disaster, and wrote in *Il Popolo d'Italia* that the anti-fascists were 'hyenas in human form', feasting on the pure blood of Italian youth 'as if it were whisky'. One thing was certain, he wrote, and that was that those who died at Guadalajara would be 'vindicated'. Carlo kept up the attack. He published the secret orders from Mussolini to the Italian press, demonstrating how servile it had become, and how obediently it printed lies. Then he had his article translated into French and circulated it to foreign newspapers.

Even if not everyone agreed with his views, Carlo's place as the most prominent leader of the non-communist anti-fascist opposition was now uncontested. He continued to argue passionately for the involvement of the young, and was thinking of bringing out a French edition of the *Quaderni*. He told Salvemini that he was beginning to understand that his real function was to 'serve as the yeast with which others will bake the bread, both intellectually and practically'. Personally, he had been moving towards the left; he had not lost his hostility towards what he saw as the rigidity and sectarianism of the USSR, but had come to appreciate its discipline and efficiency. What he felt about their brutality in Spain he did not say. While he continued to press, as he always had, for a united movement of all the anti-fascists, whatever their politics, he felt little sympathy for the socialists and their obsessive desire to hold on to the past. Sometimes, now, he sounded a little weary. He spoke wistfully of humanity, humanism, the 'religion of man, of the human being, man as a morally superior being'.

After several short-tempered brushes, Salvemini and Carlo were again on affectionate terms. Salvemini had settled in the US and was based at Harvard, where Ruth Draper had endowed a chair in European history in de Bosis' name, and he had become its first incumbent. He longed for Europe, but saw no other way of earning his living. 'As for America,' he had told Carlo, 'I am going there as to a prison.' But at least he was far from a country in which people were 'driven mad by fear'.

Despite their resolve to carry out no more flights, Carlo, Tarchiani and Cianca were now planning another sortie, going as far as to buy a plane, print leaflets to drop over Milan and Turin, and recruit a pilot. Every step of this was known to Bocchini in Rome, who received regular updates from a new spy, Alfredo

Zanella, who had wormed his way so effectively into Carlo's trust that he had been made administrator for Giustizia e Libertà. The mission ended when the plane was seized by the French police in Grenoble.

Carlo's dossier in Rome was growing fat. Surveillance had become 'massive and extremely efficacious'. There were said to be some 100 OVRA men stationed in Paris alone, some of them grouped under a Baron Fassini, a personal friend of Mussolini's. Report after report spoke of how dangerous, ruthless and single-minded Carlo was. Another of Bocchini's recruits, passing himself off as a smuggler and therefore able to cross in and out of Italy without fear of capture, had become so close to Carlo that he was put in charge of all Giustizia e Libertà's plans for Italy, where Carlo was trying to help organise a new clandestine network. He had also given Antonio Bondi – 'Arsace', number 693 – the job of printing the new membership cards. Bocchini thus had the names and addresses of all Carlo's Italian contacts. Of the few women among the Italian spies, Elisabeth Schulz was 'dark-haired, very elegant and very distinguished', spoke four languages and stayed at the Negresco when in Nice. Another, Graziella Roda, former mistress of the anarchist Assunto Zamboni, was a manipulative and clever young woman, an excellent actress, venal and boastful. 'Do you want to get rid of Lussu, Bassanesi?' she wrote to Rome. 'I can get it done.'

After Carlo's return from Spain, his friends begged him to be more wary and watchful, but he remained stubbornly trusting towards those who approached him with stories of fascist persecution. Mirtillino would later remember how even total strangers would invariably be welcomed warmly to the house. As Pitigrilli observed: 'Rosselli lets himself be approached by everyone.'

In Florence, Nello, Maria and Amelia continued to be followed and watched, but spies reported that none of them was showing any signs of political activity. Intercepted letters were about presents of snowdrops and carnations, and the need for galoshes for Parisian trips. Maria was seven months pregnant with her fourth child and it had not been an easy pregnancy. The family spent as much time as possible at L'Apparita, where Nello rose early to do gymnastics, in order 'to put a brake on my stomach, which grows at a terrifying rate every day'. He had sent his manuscript on British and Italian diplomatic relations to Volpe, and was thinking of writing a life of Giuseppe Montanelli, the Tuscan law professor who fought for the unification of Italy and helped Verdi with the libretto for *Simon Boccanegra*. Montanelli, Nello told Einaudi, was a much misunderstood and neglected hero, and he would write his book along the lines of an English biography, telling his story through his character as much as through his times. He had also amassed some 800 pages of notes towards a new history of Italy, to cover the years 1870 to 1930, but was unsure how to proceed. For all his chronic self-doubt, and fears about what he kept insisting was his own 'superlative social unusefulness', Nello was a highly competent researcher, with a clear, lively style and a total disregard for hyperbole, and was much admired by fellow historians. Surreptitiously, he continued to keep in touch with friends such as Barbara Allason, and to send money to Ernesto Rossi and Traquandi in prison.

Florence itself had become an uneasy place, particularly for the Florentine Jews, who for the first time worried about their own safety. Mussolini's views on Italy's tiny Jewish population – no more than 50,000 people – had always been contradictory, as was so much else of his thinking, and he had rapidly backed off when some of his diatribes against Judaeo-Masonic-Bolshevik conspirators fell on deaf ears. Jews had played a significant part in the rise of fascism – 230 had taken part in the March on Rome, and were thus described as 'fascists of the first hour' – but like the Freemasons, they were guilty of having competing loyalties. As long as he considered his role to be a mediator between Germany and the European democracies, Mussolini's policy towards the Jews remained ambiguous, willing on the one hand to take in those persecuted by the Nazis and to ridicule Hitler's social theories, referring to them as 'anti-scientific drivel', while on the other hand encouraging anti-semitic campaigns. Lists of all known Italian Jews had already been drawn up.

In Florence, those Jews who had made a show of supporting the fascists spoke of 'washing out the shame' of those who had not, and a militant new Jewish movement, with its own paper,

La Nostra Bandiera ('Our Flag'), made it clear that Italy's Jews were among the regime's most loyal supporters. During Italy's Day of Faith, when women had given their wedding rings to be melted down for the war in Abyssinia, 'Giovinezza' had been played in virtually every synagogue.

In Florence, fascist literary circles had taken on a definite tone of anti-semitism, not least because their members identified Jews with all that they most disliked about cosmopolitan, modern life. Early in 1937, Paolo Orano, rector of Perugia university, produced what purported to be a history of the Jews of Italy, but was in fact a vitriolic attack on Zionism. Angiolo Orvieto, one of Amelia's very few remaining friends still in Italy, had been forced out of his presidency of the Leonardo, and had retired to spend his days studying Judaism and doing crossword puzzles. His wife Laura had a chapter with the title 'The King is Jewish' removed from one of her successful children's books. Amelia herself had long since stopped attending the Lyceum, where some of the more openly anti-semitic ladies made little effort to conceal their distaste for all things Jewish. Amelia's own position on her religion had never wavered: she was, she would say to anyone who asked her, Italian first and Jewish second. (Fascist Jews had been heard to say that they were fascist first and Jewish second.) The notion that she might not be considered a real Italian was so absurd to her as to be unthinkable.

On 1 May, Maria gave birth to Nello and her second son. They named him Alberto, Carlo's middle name, and a telegram with loving messages arrived from '*i Parigini*' to the '*Apparitini*'. Carlo wrote a little ruefully to his mother about what appeared to him to be the calm harmony of Nello's household, while his own seemed so chaotic. In their small apartment in the 6ième, Melina and Aghi upset Marion with their boisterousness.

News reached Carlo in Paris of the death of Antonio Gramsci. He had recently been released, ill, after eleven years in prison. A memorial was held in the Gymnase Huyghens in the 14ième, where Carlo spoke of his admiration for the 'most noble' and highly intelligent man, who had devoted his life to serving not himself but an ideal, and had been relegated to the margins of the Communist Party for refusing to go along with orthodox Stalinism. 'And perhaps', he told his listeners, 'it is better to die with the simplicity of a Gramsci rather than to live and lose all reason for living.' In the next issue of *Quaderni*, under the headline 'A Slow Assassination', Carlo called Gramsci's death the greatest crime carried out by the fascists since the murder of Matteotti. He compared the 'reserved, rational, severe' Gramsci, 'an enemy to rhetoric and to the facile, faithful to the working class in good times and bad', to the 'noisy, irrational, demagogic' Mussolini.

All through the spring of 1937 Carlo's leg continued to give him trouble. There was talk of him going for a cure to Bagnoles-de-l'Orne, a spa in Normandy renowned for the healing properties of its waters. He was extremely reluctant to take any time away from Paris but Amelia wrote sternly from Florence that he should delay no longer, and that she would join him there. 'You <u>must not</u>', she wrote, 'give up going at any cost.' Bellavia reported to Bocchini that Carlo was in a cross and irritable mood, and that he had been telling friends: 'As for Italy, there is one absolutely necessary thing that we must do first: and that is to <u>kill Mussolini</u>.' The last two words were underlined.

At last, still protesting, Carlo agreed to spend a few weeks at Bagnoles; Marion said that she would go with him. Amelia was not well, and reluctantly agreed not to join them after Nello offered to take her place. Maria, Silvia, Paola, Aldo and the one-month-old Alberto remained in Florence. Nello applied for a passport to leave Italy, and it came through immediately, but when he bumped into Piero Calamandrei in the street, and told him how quickly it had been issued, Calamandrei begged him not to make the journey, saying there was something suspicious in the speed and lack of questions. But Nello had not seen Carlo for many months and there was much the two brothers wanted to discuss. Their years apart had done nothing to lessen the intense closeness of their relationship. Before leaving, Nello met Benedetto Croce, and they drove around the city talking.

Before setting out for Normandy himself on 27 May, Carlo had a fond meeting with Lussu, just back from the Haute-Savoie and on his way to Spain. Then he took Marion away for a few days to Beaulieu-sur-Mer. Writing to Zia Gì, Marion described it as another 'honeymoon'. It was, she said, 'very *dolce*'.

The French political world of the mid-1930s was extremely unstable. There was much talk of bombs, conspiracies and assassinations, and the newspapers often carried pictures of explosive devices, projectiles and the clocks designed to detonate them. After the first election of a coalition of left-wing parties in 1934, a number of extreme right-wing organisations had found willing members among disaffected military officers, monarchists, nationalists, adventurers, anti-semites and petty criminals. One of these conspiracists was a decorated hero of the war, Eugène Deloncle; with his glaring eyes, strong chin and large, pale face, he looked a little like Mussolini. Deloncle was an engineer by training, and an ambitious, energetic and secretive mythomaniac. He had a childhood friend, as drawn to clandestinity as himself, called Aristide Corre, a womaniser and compulsive diary-writer, who acted as his faithful lieutenant. Deloncle and his followers considered Léon Blum the very epitome of Jewish radicalism. During the funeral of an academician early in 1936, a group of these extremists ambushed Blum's car, smashed its windows, punched him and would have done a great deal more damage had policemen not arrived on the scene and taken Blum to hospital. Later, his bloodstained hat and tie were put on display as trophies in their headquarters.

After Blum's Front Populaire returned to power in April 1936, all extremist paramilitary organisations were banned. But against a backdrop of strikes, factory occupations and much talk of Bolshevism, Deloncle founded a new group of militant extremists; since its members, like the Ku Klux Klan, wore a pointed hood, they called it by the French name, La Cagoule. Cagoulards swore an oath of secrecy, considered all communists, Freemasons and Jews their bitter enemies, and undertook to take up arms in the case of a Bolshevik uprising. At their ceremonies were many displays of flags, daggers, crosses and entwined serpents. Each Cagoulard was given an alias and a number, then formed into cells of between 7 and 12 men; 3 cells became a fighting unit; 3 units a battalion; 3 battalions a regiment, and 2 regiments a brigade. In Paris, there were 6 active brigades and 1 held in reserve, in all some 2,000 men. Deloncle had no trouble finding both rich backers and eager recruits. The very young François Mitterrand had friends among these right-wing activists: his brother Robert had just got engaged to Deloncle's sister-in-law.

Deloncle himself was alert to threats of a communist takeover. Impressive stashes of weapons – dynamite, machine guns, revolvers – were hidden in strategic spots around Paris. Other groups were formed in Clermont-Ferrand and Nice, and spies were planted in the French secret services and in the regular army. By 1937, they had recruited a small, muscular killer called Jean Filliol, the twenty-eight-year-old brawling, heavy-drinking son of a post-office worker from Bergerac, who had already murdered a Russian bank director. Sometimes Filliol and his men dressed as policemen and stirred up violence at the already inflammable political marches and demonstrations.

One of the Cagoule's dreams was to see the Third Republic replaced by a monarchy; another was for the organisation to find its place among other extreme right-wing groups in Germany, Spain, Italy and Britain. Mosley's Blackshirts were not faring well, but ties with Franco's Falangists and Mussolini's *squadristi* seemed promising. In 1936, Deloncle had been to Rome to meet Ciano, widely regarded as the most powerful man in Italy after his father-in-law. Ciano was now thirty-four, slippery, lazy and ambitious. For the past ten years or so, his closest friend had been a journalist called Filippo Anfuso, a smooth man-about-town and the author of several volumes of poetry and short stories. The two men had been in China together in 1932, when Ciano served as minister plenipotentiary to Shanghai and Anfuso was his first secretary. After Ciano was appointed minister for foreign affairs, he made Anfuso his chef de cabinet. Of the two, the older, more cultured, more clear-headed Anfuso was the dominant character. It was to him that Ciano entrusted all his most delicate missions.

Anfuso was Sicilian; he too had a close friend, a forty-three-year-old lieutenant colonel in the carabinieri called Santo Emanuele, who was in charge of one section of military intelligence. Emanuele, also Sicilian, was unscrupulous, quick on his feet, profoundly greedy for promotion and much liked and trusted by Bocchini, though not by his fellow carabinieri. Through Anfuso, he had performed a number tasks for Ciano, such as sneaking into the foreign embassies in Rome late at night to copy useful documents. Anfuso said of him that he possessed the zeal of a Domenican friar and the obedience of a dog.

In January 1937 a meeting took place in San Sebastian in northern Spain between the Cagoule and Franco's men to discuss mutually advantageous deals and weapons. Another was held with Italian counter-espionage about destroying networks of anti-fascists in France; a captain serving with the military secret services in Turin was given the task of exploring the suppression of 'trouble-some people'.

On 3 February, Emanuele noted: 'Rosselli affair: goal: to elim-inate him.' Anfuso and Ciano discussed what became code-named *'l'affaire Rossignol'* – The Nightingale Affair. Mussolini gave the go-ahead to deal with the French.

In Paris, the Cagoule agreed to see to the assassination, but asked for 100 semi-automatic Berettas as a gesture of good faith. The Italians demurred; the guns would be handed over, they said, once the job was done. The Cagoule also asked for more weapons for its own arsenal, and for a safe house in Italy. There was another meeting, and to this the Cagoule brought Joseph Darnand, later the head of the French fascist Milice under the Vichy gov-ernment, and eager to clean out the Italian anti-fascists in France. Late in May, Emanuele went back to Paris to meet the chief spy, Bellavia, who confirmed that Carlo was going to Bagnoles. 'Where is Bagnoles-de-l'Orne?' Bocchini's head of the political police, Di Stefano, cabled his man Antonini – *'Urgentissimo'*. Antonini sent back word that Carlo had originally invited him to visit him in Bagnoles, but later cancelled the invitation, saying that he was expecting his brother Nello, with whom he wanted to spend as much time as possible.

According to the secret diary kept by Deloncle's lieutenant, Aristide Corre, which only came to light many years later, every detail was gone over many times. There were eight conspirators. One was the twenty-year-old son of fanatical monarchists, Jean-Marie Bouvyer, who had already been keeping watch on Carlo, and who was a skilled shot. Then there was Louis Huguet, a former boxer, who had earlier been sent to ring on the Rossellis' door to see if their apartment offered possibilities for assassination; Corre's mistress, Hélène d'Alton; Filliol and his girlfriend Alice Lamy; a jack-of-all-trades called Fernand Jakubiez, who sometimes acted as Deloncle's personal driver; Jacques Fauran, a schoolfriend of Bouvyer's who owned an open two-seater red Oldsmobile; and twenty-five-year-old François Baillet, a burly sometime pastry chef from Burgundy, good at street-fighting. The six men – all long-term members of the extreme far-right – and the two women, about whom little is known, were to travel by different means and rendezvous in Normandy. They took with them two cars, one of them the red Oldsmobile.

Bagnoles-de-l'Orne, the only spa town in north-west France, had become popular during the late 1880s, when fashionable belle-époque Parisians came to take the waters for their rheumatic conditions and to stay in the elegant hotels around its little lake, with its fountains, marble pavilions and decorative swans and ducks. A casino had been built, and villas with striped facades and bow windows, their terraces covered in hydrangeas and dahlias. During the thermal season there were concerts and horse-racing on a track nearby. The area was densely wooded and in its green forests Lancelot was said to have sung his ballads to Queen Guinevere. Bagnoles had fallen on quiet times during the First World War, but in the 1920s and 1930s its fortunes revived. Carlo and Marion arrived on the evening of 27 May, after a drive of almost 300 kilometres in their rickety black Ford, veteran of the Spanish Civil War. They had booked adjoining rooms with balconies, numbers 60 and 61, in the Hotel Cordier, an imposing six-storey mansion with a large glass-fronted veranda overlooking the forest, a few minutes' walk from the spa.

They soon fell into a pleasant routine. Carlo took the cure in the mornings and worked in the afternoons. Around 5 o'clock, they explored the countryside; Marion was charmed by its orchards and fields full of cows. Carlo was writing an article attacking France and Britain for sitting by while Germany, Spain and Italy acted. 'This is dangerous from every point of view,' he warned, with poignant accuracy; 'Possibly even mortally so.'

He was, as ever, restless and Marion wrote to Zia Gì that the 'maritino', the little husband, was starting to get bored. On their afternoon drives, she said, they often stopped to eat the local

Carlo and Marion at Bagnoles-de-l'Orne, May 1937

delicacy, meringues and honey. Carlo was no longer wearing a bandage on his leg and she was wondering whether she really needed to return to Paris on 9 June, to celebrate Mirtillino's birthday, since it was so restful here. They bought a loaf of the sweet *pain de mie* and posted it to the children. On 6 June, Carlo wrote to them that he was just off to collect Nello from the station and that he was spending his days eating meringues and being hosed down and massaged with brushes.

The reunion between the two brothers was extremely happy; before they had even left the station they had resumed their life-long intimate conversation. Photographs show the three of them, Marion in a high-necked muslin dress, the two men in sober dark jackets and ties, sitting in deckchairs, smiling. Carlo wears a trilby. They look remarkably alike, two bespectacled, round-faced, solid men with genial expressions. They told each other, teasingly, that they had both managed to put on yet more weight since their last meeting.

The brothers together at last in Normandy

In the evenings, Carlo and Marion rang the flat in Paris and talked to Bruna, the nanny they had left in charge. Carlo's letters to the children were comic and teasing. On 7 June, the children wrote back. 'Do you realise that I am about to be 10?' asked Mirtillino. Melina reported that she could now write with ink. Andrea sent 'a train full of kisses'. Mirtillino, who had always been rather shy and withdrawn, was now at the prestigious Lycée Montaigne and becoming more gregarious. Carlo and Nello sent him a telegram: '35 kisses and 47 happy birthdays. Uncle Nello and Daddy'. Amelia wrote to say that Nello's new baby was putting on weight, that Florence was unbearably hot, and that she had just been to a Pirandello play and had been much struck by its message that anyone not interested solely in material things was doomed to solitude.

On 4 June, the prefect of Florence had reported to the Ministry of the Interior in Rome that Nello was 'currently staying in the Hotel Cordier, in Bagnoles-de-l'Orne'. This fact was already well known to the Cagoule. By now, the ex-boxer Louis Huguet had taken a room in the same hotel, while the marksman Jean-Marie Bouvyer was keeping watch from the nearby Hotel Bel-Air. Both men, at different times, returned to Paris to report to Corre, pick up money and get further instructions.

On Wednesday 9 June, two cars, a Peugeot 402 carrying Filliol, Alice Lamy and François Baillet, and Fauran's red Oldsmobile with Jakubiez on board, met on the road between Alençon and Domfront, a few kilometres from Bagnoles. Bouvyer arrived separately, by train. At 1.30 p.m., four of the men went to eat in the restaurant where Carlo, Nello and Marion were having lunch. Marion had decided to catch the 4 p.m. train to Paris. How happy Mirtillino 'will be to have you there', Amelia wrote to Marion. Marion planned to return to Bagnoles two days later.

Dinner at the Hotel Cordier was not until late so, after dropping Marion at the station, the two brothers drove on to Alençon, visited the fourteenth-century Gothic church of Notre-Dame, bought postcards and sat writing them in a café. Nello bought some embroidered handkerchiefs for Maria. At 6.45 p.m., while the sun was still high, Alice Lamy, who had been watching them from a street corner, gave the signal that Carlo and Nello were leaving.

Towards 7 p.m., the Peugeot overtook Carlo's Ford and soon after stopped at the roadside near the Château de Couterne, a few kilometres from Bagnoles. It was a deserted, thickly forested spot, giving excellent cover. When Carlo drove around the corner and saw the parked Peugeot and a group of men ostensibly about to change a tyre, he pulled over; Nello got out to see whether he could help. Heedless as ever, neither brother seems to have given any thought to the possibility of an ambush.

Filliol took out his revolver and fired. Nello staggered, tried to protect himself, was punched and fell over. Jakubiez attacked him with a dagger, stabbing at Nello's chest, right arm and neck; in all, he delivered seventeen wounds. Carlo, scrambling out of the car to come to his brother's help, was shot and then stabbed. There was blood everywhere. The killers searched Carlo's pockets and took his wallet and various documents; they left Nello's money untouched.

At this moment a young hairdresser, Hélène Besneux, cycled

past: seeing a pool of blood and a group of men, she hastened on, pedalling as fast as she could. Filliol and Jakubiez got into Carlo's car and drove it to a secluded spot close by, where they tried, but largely failed, to set it on fire using a Nestlé tin full of explosive. Before they left, they dragged the two bodies into the woods, where they lay, Carlo half covering Nello, their arms stretched out, a dagger by their side.

In Paris, when the Cagoule heard the news, Aristide Corre wrote in his diary: 'Our *affaire Rossignol* is finally concluded. Here is one matter that won't be giving us any more trouble.'

CHAPTER NINETEEN

A Corneillian Tragedy

It was not until 2 o'clock on the Friday afternoon that Marion, having heard nothing from Carlo, telephoned the Hotel Cordier. A surprised concierge told her that her husband had not been seen since the previous day. Soon after, a reporter rang the bell of the flat in Rue Notre-Dame-des-Champs. On seeing his expression, Marion began to cry. The maid quickly pushed the reporter out of the door, saying that Marion had a bad heart. The man went round to the offices of Giustizia e Libertà, found Cianca, and told him that he had heard that Carlo was dead. Cianca hurried round to see Marion. Mirtillino, hearing agitated talk and then seeing his mother's anguished face, thought at first that it was about money, because he had often heard his parents exchange angry words about the amount that Carlo was spending on the anti-fascists. Normally, she spoke to him in Italian. Now she said, in English, 'Darling, Babbo has been killed.'

In Bagnoles, the bodies had not been discovered for some time. Two men returning home from the fields had come across the half-burnt car in the ditch, seen what looked like a bloodstained glove on the seat and reported it to the local mayor. A carthorse had been sent to pull the car back on to the road. But it was only on the Friday morning that a blacksmith called Henri Jarry, stopping to relieve himself by the side of the road as he cycled towards Bagnoles, spotted the two corpses. In the police report, Carlo was described as lying on his back, his left shoe and right glove missing; Nello was said to have his face pressed into the earth, his trouser legs pulled up to his knees. The autopsy confirmed signs of struggle, and many knife and bullet wounds. The dagger was found lying nearby. On Saturday 12 June, Marion arrived to identify the bodies. Inadvertently, Mirtillino later saw the photograph of his dead father and uncle; his first thought was that their bodies looked alien and somehow shrunken.

The first telegram that reached Florence was unclear: 'Serious accident, come at once'. Amelia assumed that there had been some kind of car crash in Normandy, and that both Carlo and Nello had been injured. Maria, who was breastfeeding Alberto, was staying with Zia Gì at Il Frassine, but Amelia asked for a passport and was given one at once – Bocchini later told Mussolini that he thought this a sensible move – and she left by train for Paris. Aldo Forti, their close friend and tenant in the top flat in Via Giusti, insisted on accompanying her; his wife, terrified for his safety, made him promise to take the train straight back. What Amelia spent the long night thinking, as the train wound its slow way northwards, one can only imagine. Whatever desperate hopes she may have clung to were dispelled as soon as she reached the Gare de Lyon. On the platform were many reporters and photographers. It was enough to see their faces.

Amelia was already on the train when Marion telephoned Zia Gì to tell her what had happened. Fearing Maria's despair, Zia Gì asked the local doctor, a close family friend, to break the news. Nello's two boys, Aldo and Alberto, were too young to understand, but Silvia was now nine and Paola seven. Nothing was said to them. No one could quite bear to. Their grandmother Luisa arrived to collect the girls and take them to her house in Mugello. Days passed. When after a month the girls were finally collected by Zia Gì, Silvia asked: 'How is Babbo?' 'Well,' replied Zia Gì, 'he has a bit of a cold.' They found their mother in bed. She had decided to see them in her nightdress, to conceal her black mourning clothes. She started to speak, stopped, cried, then said that Nello had gone off on a long journey and would be away for some time. When one of the girls said: 'I do hope that Babbo will be back soon,' Maria faltered and replied that he was very ill.

It was Zia Gì, when they went to Il Frassine, who told them the truth. Silvia asked: 'So is our mother a widow?' Zia Gì said that she was. Paola said: 'So we are orphans.' Then Silvia asked: 'And Mellina and Andrea too?' The girls were relieved when Zia Gì agreed: it made them feel less alone. But though they knew that their father was dead, when they saw Nello's car driven back to the house, they thought that it was their father coming home.

News of Carlo's death reached the Italian anti-fascists fighting in Spain on the evening of 15 June. Pietro Nenni wrote in his diary: 'It was as if something broke inside us. I can't sleep ... Rosselli, Matteotti's torch bearer.' In Regina Coeli prison in Rome, Rossi and Bauer overheard the guards talking. Rossi said: 'The future has suddenly become darker.' To his mother, he wrote that the Rosselli brothers were part of his spiritual family, composed nowadays 'almost all of the dead', but who nonetheless felt more real and alive to him than the cell in which he lived. He and Bauer smuggled out a message written on cigarette paper saying that they would avenge Carlo and Nello's deaths, but Salvemini, who was on a visit to Paris, decided not to make it public, on the grounds that it would only cause them more trouble, and they had enough of it already.

When the bodies were released by the police in Normandy and brought back to Paris, the coffins were taken to Rue Notre-Dame-des-Champs for the wake. The many visitors, French and Italian, who came to pay their respects were received by Amelia and Marion, both of them grimly self-contained. They insisted on sitting all night by the bodies. The two coffins were draped in dark-red velvet, Carlo's with the words 'Giustizia e Libertà' in black. The Rosselli cousins Sandro Levi and Sarina Nathan arrived from London. At some point during the long hours of darkness, Amelia said, in a low voice: 'At times I seem to feel the cuts of the knife in my own flesh.'

Of all the close friends, only Lussu, who had hastened back from Spain when he heard the news, did not wish to see the bodies. Writing about Carlo later, he said that he could not bear to 'see so much physical power destroyed'. He preferred to remember his friend, the man to whom he had talked almost every day for the last ten years, as he had known him, 'youthful, smiling, his eyes kind and, after the war in Spain, more thoughtful and penetrating'. Later, Guglielmo Ferrero said that Aldo, Carlo and Nello had as boys represented everything that was best in the Italian tradition: a hunger to learn, respect for intelligence and morality, a liberal spirit, humane ideals, simplicity of manner and seriousness about life. 'I feel lost,' Amelia wrote to Maria of Nello.

'I don't know where to be. I want to stay where he is, I want to hear people talking about him, and yet I also want to flee. Far away from everyone.' What haunted her was the memory of saying to Nello, when he offered to take her place and go to meet Carlo in Bagnoles: 'Of course.'

The funeral took place on Saturday 19 June. Before leaving for Spain, Carlo had requested that Beethoven's *Seventh Symphony* be played in case of his death at the front. Marion had got to know Toscanini during his occasional visits to Paris and she now asked him whether he would come to conduct at the funeral; he was not able to get away from London, but sent affectionate messages. The bodies had been taken to the hall of the Maison des Syndicats and here, before an enormous crowd, an orchestra played the Beethoven symphony. The street outside was lined with wreaths and summer flowers. As she listened to the first bars, Marion, who had been staunch and composed, put her face in her hands and began to cry. She was heard to say softly: 'Addio, Carlo.' Speaking of Carlo in his funeral address, Cianca made a promise: 'In your name, we will continue the fight ... We will commemorate you every day, your spirit living on in our actions. This is not a farewell. It's a vow.'

Every Italian anti-fascist organisation, every left-wing French newspaper, every group of foreign exiles had called on people to follow the coffins to the cemetery of Père Lachaise. Some 200,000 people did. Many were in tears, but along with the sadness there was also considerable anger. At the front walked Marion, Cianca, Tarchiani, Lussu, all Carlo's close friends in exile. One carried the beret that Carlo had worn in Spain. Behind them walked a long, largely silent crowd of men and women in their dark clothes: trade unionists, writers, members of Blum's government, French intellectuals, and many friends. Nello and Carlo were buried side by side, in a plot in the middle of one of Père Lachaise's northernmost sections, not far from Gobetti, Treves and Turati. A bunch of white hydrangeas had been laid on the coffins, with the words '*La Mamma*'. A photographer had followed the cortege, taking pictures of the principal mourners. Copies were soon on their way to Bocchini, the names of the most important anti-fascists neatly transcribed by Antonio Bondi on sheets of tracing paper carefully pasted on top.

Amelia did not join the cortege. For days, she had been ferociously self-contained. But as the coffins with her two sons were
carried down the stairs, she let out a low moan of pain and horror. It was like that of a wounded animal. For the two days that
they had lain together in the flat, she had been able to think of
Carlo and Nello as boys, sleeping, side by side. Watching them
go, she knew that she had lost them for ever.

It took some time for the truth about the killings to emerge. In
Italy, Mussolini's skilled propaganda machine put out a story that
Carlo, a 'little and ridiculous dictator', had fallen foul of his
left-wing associates, angry because he was making peace with the
fascists and intended to return to Italy. His murderers were vari-
ously said to be Spanish anarchists, the Russian secret services or
even the *giellisti* themselves. Giovanni Ansaldo, Carlo's former
friend and now editor of *Il Telegrafo* – and branded not long
before by Carlo as 'obscene' and a 'prostitute' for having gone
over to the fascists – wrote that Carlo was an unscrupulous,
ambitious, ridiculous 'despiser of men', and that he had probably
been killed because he had approved the death of Berneri, murdered recently in Barcelona. These rumours were so deftly
circulated that even the London *Times* ran a story speculating
that these were the reasons for the murders.

But the Rossellis had many friends, both in England and in
France. In London, several prominent writers and politicians
signed a letter to *The Times*, calling these allegations 'monstru-
ous'. Two days later, evidently embarrassed by its earlier incorrect
stories, the paper published a second letter, this time from Marion,
who wrote that Carlo had been faithful to the end to his 'ideal
of truth and liberty', and that to say otherwise was 'worse than
a crime'. In France, while a few of the more rabid right-wing
papers referred to Carlo as a terrorist and urged the government
to rid itself of this kind of 'leprosy' – and a cartoon showed
Mussolini addressing an officer with the words 'And you can add
Bagnoles-de-l'Orne to the list of our victories!' – there was an
outpouring of anger and grief.

In a letter carried by most of the mainstream papers, Pablo
Picasso and André Breton were among a group of intellectuals
who wrote that if the death of Matteotti had signalled the death

of liberty in Italy, that of the Rosselli brothers had signed its death warrant in the whole of Europe. In letter after letter, article after article, Carlo's intelligence, lucidity, erudition and courage were warmly praised. He had been, said Tarchiani, 'the supreme physical and spiritual force of the second Italian Risorgimento'. It was by becoming such an evident future leader of Italy, said Carlo's friends, that he had signed his own death warrant. Even Palmiro Togliatti, leader of the communists, who had been so critical of Carlo, declared that his party would 'dip our flag in memory of Carlo and Nello, promising that we will do all that we can to avenge them'. Carlo himself had had a keen understanding of the powers of the press, and his own use of it – exposing Mussolini's lies about Spain and printing the unhappy letters of the so-called volunteers – had unquestionably played a part in the decision to have him killed.

In Paris, the government remained uneasily silent. They had no wish to stir up trouble with the Italians. In any case, ten days later, Blum fell, to be replaced by another short-lived parliament.

Bocchini had boasted on several occasions that the anti-fascists had been crushed. Each time he had been proved wrong. But Carlo's murder threw the exiles into paralysis and disarray, and even though Lussu and Cianca kept Giustizia e Libertà alive, it had been seriously weakened. It was certain that the fascists had intended to silence their opponents' most visible and effective leader; but they were not sorry to get rid of Nello either, slowly emerging as one of Italy's most impressive and independent-minded historians. The killings sent a useful message that the fascists were organised, powerful, dangerous and had a very long reach. On Carlo's dossier in the Rome police archives was stamped the word 'Morto' in large, bold, purple lettering.

Of all the Rossellis' friends, Salvemini, who had loved them like sons, was the most tenacious at getting to the truth. In July, he wrote an article for I Quaderni, under the headline 'Il Mandante', 'The Principle'. In it, he formally accused Mussolini of having given the order for their deaths. It was already perfectly clear to him and Lussu that French assassins had been hired by the fascists and that Nello had been killed only because he happened to be with Carlo at Bagnoles at the time. As Marion said, it was absurd to imagine that Mussolini and Ciano had not known precisely what was going on.

The French police had not been idle either. The search for the killers had set off in several different directions. Anyone known to have been in recent touch with Carlo was tracked down and interrogated. Car-drivers in the locality who spoke Italian were questioned. Appeals went out to trace a 'big, swarthy' man with brown hair swept back, seen at the Hotel Cordier. Names of possible assassins were bandied about.

The Cagoule had been clumsy: they had left several obvious traces. Hélène Besneux, the young girl who had cycled past the murder scene, remained bold and uncowed in her testimony, even after receiving anonymous threatening letters. In due course, Filliol, Bouvyer and Jakubiez were picked up, and Marion remembered Jakubiez's face from the time he had called at the flat, posing as a travelling carpet salesman. Then a senior figure in the Cagoule confessed that the organisation had indeed been responsible for the assassinations. More names were produced. In February 1938, the police staged a reconstruction, with Carlo's car, and Hélène Besneux cycling past. Various alibis foundered; more confessions followed. It would be another year before seventy-one people from the extreme right were charged with a variety of crimes, among them the murders of Carlo and Nello, but by now there was little doubt in anyone's mind about where the orders for the killings had come from.

As for the Italian spies in Paris, several were unmasked during the course of the French investigations. Bellavia was briefly arrested, then went back to Italy to work for OVRA in Turin. Others disappeared. A few were put to work under a new boss who gave them new names and identities. But with Carlo gone, something of the urgency had gone too. Bocchini turned his attention back to what was going on in Italy, and mopped up Pentecostalists and members of the Salvation Army.

From Alberto Moravia, Amelia's much-loved nephew, there was total silence. No telephone call, no letter, no flowers. She did not take it well.

'Everything still seems to me impossible,' wrote Amelia to Gina Lombroso soon after the funeral. 'Nothing is real, I can't take anything in, I am like a robot, I can understand nothing except for the fact that my life is finished.'

She stayed on in Paris to help Marion, whose heart troubles had intensified, though she kept worrying that she should go back to Florence to be with Maria. The only thing that made life bearable, she told her Italian daughter-in-law, whom she had always found easier to love than Marion, was that they had descended together into the abyss, and that together, in these black and despairing depths, they would discover the strength to live. Marion's grief was so extreme, so entirely focused on herself, that even Amelia felt irritated, telling Zia Gì that she found the degree of egoism 'unbelievable'. It was beginning to dawn on her that, though she was sixty-eight, it would be up to her to look after the two widows and their seven children, decide where to live and how, and that whatever they all did, they would have to do

Andrea, Silvia, Paola (back row) and Aldo and Melina
(sitting) in Switzerland

it together. Amelia, wrote Sandro Pertini later, was like 'the heroine in a Corneille tragedy'.

Her first decision was that neither she nor Carlo's children would set foot inside Italy again while Mussolini remained in power. Towards the end of 1937, Amelia rented a house in Villars, above Montreux in Switzerland, not far from the Ferreros in Geneva. Maria and her four children joined her and the older ones went to Swiss schools, where they were soon speaking good French. In the evenings, Amelia read to them in Italian, so that they should not forget their native language. To counter what she described to her friend Max Ascoli as their 'torment of grief', the two women threw themselves into plans for publishing all Nello's writings.

Marion, restless, frantic, uncertain, stayed on for a while in Paris, then paid a brief visit to Villars. It was the first time the sisters-in-law had met since the murders. Amelia worried about how they would get on, knowing how very different the two young women were, and conscious that she had long managed with a different voice, a different way of being, with each of them. She told friends that she felt the pain three times over, for all three of them, and was comforted only by the thought that she herself would not survive long. Slowly, mourning together, dressed in black, the three women forged a shared bond in sadness.

They were there when, in Catalonia, the communists, anarchists and socialists created a nightmare of confusion and disagreement, spies and commissars carrying out brutal purges, unleashing a civil war within a civil war; and later when the Spanish Republic disbanded all foreigners fighting with them. It was in some ways a relief that Carlo had not lived to see his friends reduced to murderous in-fighting and the Republic fail to transform the Spanish Civil War into a global crusade against fascism.

The house in Villars was remote, and they saw very few people. Later, Silvia and Paola would remember their mother and grandmother listening to Beethoven's *Seventh* with tears in their eyes. The solitude was such, Amelia wrote to Zia Gì, that 'I no longer think that I belong to the species of sociable animals.' She could find no religious faith to fall back on and reported that even the pleasure in books seemed to have deserted her. 'The word future', she wrote, 'has no meaning for me. In fact, it frightens me. I go

Amelia at Quainton in Buckinghamshire

Nello's four children at Quainton

forwards, looking backwards.' But Amelia was made of strong stuff, and she needed more than the silent Swiss mountains could provide. Switzerland was indeed peaceful, but it was peaceful intellectually too, and living so far from 'the great universal problems, from great ideas' was not good enough. What was more, it was not good enough for the children either, for whom she wanted 'a country with wide horizons, a long history, intellectual richness'.

Maria had decided that England would suit them all better, and in October 1939, when the Swiss refused to renew the children's visas on the grounds that they had enough Italian exiles already, they moved first to Eastbourne and then to the little village of Quainton in Buckinghamshire. But here the house was unheated and the pipes froze and, accustomed to the warmth of Italy, the women found the cold unbearable. There was no good local school so the girls had to be sent away as boarders, to a school where the windows were kept open at night all through the winter and Silvia was bullied until she learnt to hide her feelings and made the other pupils laugh with imitations of Mussolini.

Marion did not stay with them long. She roamed, unable to settle. 'She sought vengeance,' Mirtillino wrote later. 'She hated.' For a while, she went back to Paris, took classes in biology at the Sorbonne, but she felt too agitated to study. 'There is no good reason for me to be in one place rather than another,' she wrote sadly. She made herself more ill, and her tormented undecidedness maddened Amelia and Maria. She tried Cambridge, then decided that there was something about England she could no longer adjust to, so returned to France, this time to Nantes, to stay with her friends Françoise and Louis Joxe. It was while she was here that she had a stroke. It left her briefly paralysed and though her movement and speech came back, her hand shook and her words sounded blurred; she never spoke to the children in Italian again. Marion and the children were still in Nantes when the Germans invaded France in the early summer of 1940. The Joxes drove them to Saint-Malo, where they caught the last ferry to Southampton. They docked on the day that Italy entered the war.

Maria and Amelia fretted that the Germans, having occupied France, would invade England. Being Jewish and anti-fascists, they would not be safe. The news from Italy was not good, and though their friends the Cividallis had managed to emigrate to Palestine, Maria's parents and many relations were still in Italy. Mussolini's race laws – barring Jews from professions and their children from school – had been passed in November 1938. That same year, the pseudo-scientific Manifesto of Racial Scientists had asserted that 'Jews do not belong to the Italian race.' The goose-step had been formally adopted, and Mussolini was talking about setting up 'concentration camps' for dissident Masons and Jews, or resettling them in Somalia, where, with luck, they might be eaten by sharks.

Amelia, Maria wrote to the Cividallis, was as ever extremely strong and determined but she was, 'alas, much aged'; her face was thinner, more deeply lined and she seemed worn out. Max Ascoli and Salvemini had been pressing the family to join them in the States. Maria was eager; Marion, ill, agreed. Visas were slow in coming, but Max Ascoli's second wife, Marion Rosenwald, had well-placed connections and Eleanor Roosevelt intervened to speed up the permissions. In August 1940 they set sail for Montreal on a ship guarded by a convoy, in the last two cabins, just beside the engines, constantly mindful of the possibility of German submarines. The sea was very rough; Maria had bought leashes for the two smallest boys in case the boat was hit and they got lost. Amelia was now seventy. The eldest of the seven children, Mirtillino, was thirteen; the youngest, Alberto, three. 'Everything unknown before us,' Amelia wrote to Ascoli before embarking. 'It's like playing lotto.'

As Italian enemy-aliens, Amelia, Maria and her children were detained for a short while by the Canadian customs officers, while the English Marion, Mirtillino, Melina and Aldo wandered around Montreal waiting for them to be freed. Then they caught a night train to New York. Max Ascoli and his wife boarded their train as it passed through Croton, on the Hudson. They took them to have breakfast in the dining car, where they were given bacon, cornflakes and grapefruit, which none of the children had ever seen before.

Early in May 1921, eighteen months before the March on Rome, Mussolini had received a telegram from a group of Italians in New York, most of them members of a shooting club. 'The first

Italian *fascio* in the United States', it said, 'today salutes the *fasci* of Italy!' The 1920s and early 1930s saw a flowering of pro-Mussolini associations and newspapers among the four and a half million Italians living in the US, eager to celebrate their *italianità* and to praise the man they held responsible for saving from the Bolsheviks a homeland they remembered with sentimental nostalgia. Many were ultra-Catholic, hostile to newcomers, ignorant about what Italy had turned into since they emigrated, and delighted to abandon, as instructed, 'barbaric dialects, worthy of Harlem negroes or the slum dwellers of London'. Italian consulates across the country acted as cover for Bocchini's men, while Italo-American businessmen and bankers, who had done well in their adopted country, willingly put money into training their young to march, sing 'Giovinezza' and raise their arms in the fascist salute. In New York, 'well born' Italian ladies joined a women's *fascio*. The Duce himself was described by a reporter sent by *McCall's* magazine to Italy, as a 'despot with a dimple'.

Arrival in the United States

When Rudolph Valentino died in 1926, *squadristi* formed a guard of honour round his bier, on which had been placed a garland with the name of Mussolini on it. Not all this adoration was peaceful. The 1920s and 1930s also saw brawls between Blackshirts wielding *manganelli* and their opponents in the streets of Boston and New York.

By the time Amelia and her two grieving families reached America, however, much of this noisy confrontation had quietened down. The anti-fascists were now a considerably larger group, their numbers increased by successive waves of people driven into exile. New York, rather than Paris, had become the capital of the Italian *fuoriusciti*. Max Ascoli had turned the New School for Social Research in New York into a haven for many of the professors among the refugees, saying that they were a 'small group of survivors of what was European civilisation' and represented the many others who had been murdered or silenced.

Waiting for them in New York, the Rossellis found Lussu, Cianca, Tarchiani, Parri and Don Sturzo. And, of course, Salvemini, a little older, a little balder, with his round black-framed glasses and his neat beard and moustache, his look knowing and benign. Salvemini had spent his years of exile in a fever of work, putting out book after book on fascism, full of scholarly research and statistics, writing fast and well, lecturing all over the country in his erratic English about the 'suffocation and paralysis' inflicted by Mussolini and his men. Time had done nothing to temper his passion or his strong, impatient views, and he was much attacked as a 'drifting shipwreck', filled with 'mad, bitter hatred . . . and a macabre obsession'. Salvemini liked the language of the American liberals and their commitment to justice but grumbled that they were too obsessed by Nazis and communists to pay proper heed to the dangers of Italian fascism.

Amelia and Maria still had an income from shares in Italy and, for $80 a month, they took a small mock-Victorian house in Larchmont, Westchester, a forty-minute train ride from Grand Central Station. It was not elegant but it was comfortable and the local schools were good. Ruth Draper and Max Ascoli, who said that Carlo and Nello had been his closest friends and that their children would want for nothing, helped with the fees. Amelia, who had once had cooks, maids and menservants, presided over the running of the house with the help of a single part-time maid; Maria cooked and organised the children's lives. Marion, ever restless and uneasy, rented a second house nearby. Soon after moving in, they received a visit from a neighbour who assured them that one of Larchmont's attractions was that it was 'free of negros and Jews'. But we, said Amelia coldly, 'are Jews'. Next day, a large bunch of flowers was delivered.

If Amelia worried that Silvia and Paola would lose their 'beautiful simplicity' among the American schoolgirls she considered 'painted, permed, playing at being women', she was also deeply grateful for the security in which they now found themselves. Every morning after breakfast she retired to her bed and did her correspondence, writing and receiving dozens of letters, in French, Italian and English, from all over the world, and making arrangements for the publication of her sons' works. More than either of her daughters-in-law, she approached the New World with curiosity and openness and, determined to make the most of what it had to offer, regularly took the children into New York to visit museums and go to concerts. They went to Niagara Falls and to the Oyster Bar at Grand Central Station. For Alberto's sixth birthday, she gave him a violin.

For the children, Amelia had rapidly become their main figure of authority, imparting a certain old-fashioned code of behaviour which revolved around truthfulness and justice, and she would brook no dissent. She regarded her own role as one of providing stability in a country in which they were Jews among Protestants, Italians at a time of war with Italy, and a household of women without men. Stability and love: none of the children would ever forget the solidity of the love she surrounded them with. Mirtillino, Silvia and Paola were excellent students, but Melina remained volatile and awkward. Maria clung to Alberto, the baby born so soon before Nello's death, and Aldo showed signs of depression. It took Amelia a long time to coax Maria out of her black mourning clothes, persuading her to wear a little white collar. There was always a sense of waiting – waiting to go home, waiting to resume real life. Amelia would tell friends that she felt herself to be profoundly an exile, too old to put down new roots.

When visitors came to call, they found Amelia sitting very upright in a high-necked blouse, her white hair parted in the middle and piled high on her head; they addressed her as Signora Amelia and used the formal '*Lei*'. One recent Italian arrival came to pay his respects on a particularly hot summer day, and asked whether he might take off his jacket. 'No,' she replied. Amelia never complained; complaining was not in her nature, though her letters to Italian friends were sometimes despairing. 'How can one explain', she wrote to Gina Lombroso, 'all this terrible suffering and bloodshed, the collapse of all those spiritual values which were once our reason for living?' Whenever he could get away, Salvemini came to see them. The two old friends approached each other with a sort of tenderness and clasped hands, murmuring '*Che piacere, che piacere*', 'What a pleasure'. '*La vecchia Signora Amelia*', he wrote to Ernesto Rossi, '*è meravigliosa*.'

Amelia, Marion and Maria were endlessly busy. Maria had emerged as a strong and capable woman, and started a charity shop in Larchmont to raise money for Italian refugees. All three women were involved in the Mazzini Society, set up by Salvemini and Ascoli in September 1939 to inform the American public about Italian fascism, to counter fascist propaganda and to help the newly arrived refugees settle. It was not an altogether easy enterprise, its members split between those who saw themselves as Americans of Italian origin and those who, like Lussu, Cianca and Parri, were simply waiting for the moment they could go home. Over time, schisms developed and acrimonious exchanges led to resignations. There were moves to expel the 'intransigent and quarrelsome' Salvemini. Amelia was among those who stepped down, saying that she refused to take sides. She seemed to age and to grow frailer, telling friends that it required ever more courage to go on living, but she was never, at any point, as Silvia remembered much later, 'what you might call an ordinary grandmother'.

In the summer of 1943, after most of the Grand Council voted against him, Mussolini was ousted from power and Pietro Badoglio made head of state. When Italy joined the Allies in September and the Germans moved to occupy the whole country, Lussu, Tarchiani and Cianca hurried home to meet up with Carlo Levi, Rossi, Bauer and Ginzburg – all now freed from the *confino* – to see if they could serve with the partisans, and to start drawing up plans for the governance of post-war Italy.

Having been imprisoned in the Gran Sasso, Mussolini was rescued by German forces and installed in the town of Salò to preside over a corrupt and incompetent puppet state known as the Italian Social Republic. In the mountains in the north, groups of partisans, taking the name Partito d'Azione and some under the banner of the Rosselli Brigades – Primo Levi among them – were fighting bitter battles against the retreating Germans. As a 'gypsy people gone to rot', declared the Germans, the Italians would have to pay heavily for their treachery.

For months on end in Larchmont, there was no news of the fate of Amelia's friends or of Maria's family, as Jews in grave danger now of arrest and deportation by the Germans. Maria's five-year-old niece Gianna had been given a different name, Pallina, and put for safety into an orphanage; her parents Max and Luisa were being hidden in clinics in different parts of the city. The house in Via Giusti and L'Apparita, to protect them from being seized as Jewish property, had been nominally sold to Maria's Catholic sister-in-law. They heard that Zia Gì was safe, but had taken refuge in the house of the parish priest after the Germans looted Il Frassine at gunpoint.

Finally came word that the 3rd, 4th and what remained of the 2nd Rosselli Brigades – for there had been many casualties – were among the first men to liberate Florence. 'Does this not seem to you a dream?' Amelia wrote.

In September 1944, after the liberation of Rome, an investigation was launched into the murders of Carlo and Nello. Ciano was by now dead, shot on his father-in-law's orders in January for having voted against him the night that he was removed from power; in his diaries – from which various pages had vanished – he had said nothing on the subject of Carlo or Nello. Santo Emanuele implicated Anfuso, currently still Mussolini's ambassador to Berlin. A former head of military intelligence, General Giacomo Carboni, testified that Ciano had once said to him that Emanuele's great merit lay in 'having been the author of the elimination of the Rossellis', but that Ciano later regretted their murders, for Carlo 'could have done good for Italy'. Anfuso admitted to having been in touch with the Cagoulards, but said that it had been Emanuele's idea to get rid of the two brothers.

A first trial opened on 29 January 1945, with witness statements by Lussu, Garosci and Calamandrei. By the time the conspirators had finished changing their statements and accusing each other, Anfuso, on the run, had been sentenced to death for collaboration and life for the Rosselli killings, and Emanuele to life imprisonment. In 1946, Anfuso's sentence was lifted, and even Emanuele was granted amnesty in 1947. In 1949, the Court of Appeal opened a new hearing, which either absolved the accused, or dropped the charges on the grounds of lack of evidence.

Had Mussolini ordered the killings? As with Matteotti, it was impossible to be certain. By the end of April 1945, he was dead, stopped by partisans near Lake Como as he fled to Switzerland, then shot with his mistress, Clara Petacci, and their bodies hanged from meat hooks in a square in Milan. Salvemini was only one of many who believed that, even if he had not given a direct order, Mussolini certainly knew what was happening. As for Ciano, he was beyond doubt complicit.

In France, there was also a further inquiry into the killings. But Charles Tenaille, the Cagoule leader, was dead, fighting for the Nazis on the Russian front, and Deloncle had been killed by the Gestapo. Filliol, Bouvyer, Huguet and Fauran were all condemned to death – in absentia. Alone of the principal murderers, Jakubiez was sentenced to life with hard labour. In the court, he admitted that he had taken a hand in the murders, and said that while Carlo was 'killed in an instant', Nello had fought back, been stabbed again and then finished off with a pistol.

Amelia never believed that she would live to go home. But in June 1946, having delayed their return to wait for Marion, who had suffered a second stroke, the family boarded the *Vulcania*, bound for Naples and Genoa. Marion had not set foot in Italy for fifteen years; the others had been away for seven. Alberto, who had no memory of Italy, was now ten. All the children spoke better English than Italian.

In their absence, their fathers had become heroes.

When they docked in Naples, friends boarded the ship to tell them that the royal train had been sent to meet them. As they travelled north they looked out of the windows at the devastation of the Italian landscape. At every stop, people were waiting with flowers. At Rome, they were taken to spend the night in a suite in the Grand Hotel, and next morning, while the three women met the new political leaders of Italy, many of them old friends, the children were given a tour of the city in a horse and carriage. Florence was dark and silent; in the enclosed carriage sent to meet them at the station, they listened to the clip-clop of the horse's feet. In the house in Via Giusti, Maria's parents were waiting; her father Max was wearing a white suit and a panama hat. There were so many flowers that it looked like a garden. They ate figs, melons and prosciutto.

None of them found arriving home easy. They learnt that Carlo Pincherle, Amelia's brother, had died, as had her dear friends Guglielmo and Gina Ferrero. It shocked them to realise how many of their friends and acquaintances had willingly cooperated with Mussolini and the fascists. Perhaps saddest of all, for Amelia, was her nephew Alberto Moravia's behaviour. Early in 1945, he had written to say that, since he had been so closely watched by spies, he had thought it prudent to wait until then before telling her how much he had minded the deaths of his cousins, Carlo and Nello. 'But I was close to you in your grief.' Amelia did not reply. Moravia had acted, she said, 'out of opportunism, or, at its most charitable, out of weakness'.

But then Moravia chose to write a novel, *Il conformista*, closely based on Carlo's story, in which his murder is described in gruesome detail; instead of Nello it is Marion who is murdered, sensual and shapely in death. Carlo – Quadro – is portrayed as cynical, imprudent, didactic and pompous, and Marion – Lina – as a woman who is sexually aroused by other women. Prepared to sacrifice young friends with a 'cruel indifference to human life', Quadro, urged his converts to 'bold and dangerous undertakings which were almost always disastrous'. Though the novel received almost uniformly bad reviews, and the rest of the family refused to have anything more to do with Moravia, Amelia was surprisingly forgiving. Moravia himself never expressed the slightest hint of remorse, nor explained why he had chosen to write as he had. If asked about the Rosselli brothers in interviews, he would produce a few vague anecdotes about their childhood. It was as if the past held little interest for him.

Of the three women, Marion found return to Italy the hardest. She was bewildered and appalled by the changes, saying that nothing in post-war Italy seemed to reflect the values that Carlo and Nello had fought for, nor the sacrifices they had made. Amelia and Maria set up house together in Via Giusti, and often went up to L'Apparita, where a kind neighbour had saved Nello's library. Silvia and Paola got engaged to two brothers, Francesco and Marco Forti, the sons of Aldo Forti, who had accompanied Amelia on the terrible train journey to Paris in June 1937. Maria took the girls to Paris to visit the graves in the Père Lachaise Cemetery.

Marion stayed on for a while in Florence, but she found the stairs in Via Giusti too hard, and felt excluded on the ground floor from the rest of the family above. Amelia's devotion and closeness to Maria were sometimes difficult for Marion to bear. Soon, she drifted back to England, where Mirtillino was doing his military service after graduating from Swarthmore College in the US. He was always the child she loved the most – *'il mio adorato Mirtillino'* – and with Melina, who was often moody and prone to depression, she continued to have a difficult time. Andrea had a solitary childhood.

On 13 October 1949, by now so breathless that she found it hard to walk, Marion died in a hospital in West Isleworth. She was fifty-two. 'I loved her like, and perhaps more than a daughter,' Amelia wrote to Mirtillino. 'She represented for me the presence of your father, and all that life of excitement and passion of which I too was a part.' Speaking at a memorial service, Salvemini, who was back in his old job at Florence university, said that Marion had never recovered from the loss of Carlo and that the rest of her short life had been marked by a lonely, remorseless decline. Not long before she died she had told him that there was no day on which she did not miss Carlo. The Rosselli heroes left sad family legacies of depression and troubled minds. Melina, in particular, suffered from her family history. She became a talented and successful poet, but would commit suicide by throwing herself out of her attic window near the Piazza Navona on 11 February 1996, the anniversary of the death of Sylvia Plath, whose work she had translated.

Every one of Mussolini's boasts and slogans proved illusory. Fascism had brought not stability, prosperity and victory, but war, humiliation, penury and foreign occupation. The 'Corporative

State' had been expensive, cumbersome and useless to the economy. Some 13,000 people, among them a generation of Italy's cleverest and most promising men, had spent many years on the penal islands, where dozens had died and many more seen their health permanently destroyed by malnutrition, untreated diseases and lack of all proper sanitation. Bassanesi, the dreamer who had dropped leaflets from his plane over Turin and Milan, was in a lunatic asylum.

Bocchini was dead by 1940, after a Lucullan feast in a Roman restaurant (both Himmler and Heydrich had attended his funeral). The Futurist Marinetti had died fleeing the partisans at Salò. Both Farinacci, the brutal *ras* who had been responsible for so much violence, and Gentile, who had given fascism such legitimacy, were shot. Some 10,000–12,000 active fascists were pursued and killed by the partisans at the moment of liberation. In July 1944 a High Commission for Sanctions against Fascism was set up in Rome, in order to purge the administration of fascists, prosecute those guilty of crimes and to retrieve stolen property, but many were soon granted amnesty, for without them Italy would have had few civil servants, teachers or policemen. The commission found over 130,000 dossiers on fascist suspects in the archives. A list of 622 of the most egregious spies and informers was published, and they were generally ridiculed, but few suffered more than passing shame. There had of course been many more – the historian Mauro Canale puts the number at 815 Polpol men, but if you include all those who worked for them, and all OVRA's operatives, the figure was probably close to 10,000. One way or another, most wriggled out of censure.

It became known that forty-two separate individuals, at one time or another, spied on Carlo.

Ferruccio Parri, the man whom Carlo had loved as a brother, became the first post-war Italian prime minister, presiding over a radical democratic party, the Partito d'Azione, with the same political creed of justice, liberty, federalism and republicanism that had inspired Carlo's *Socialismo Liberale*. Both Lussu and Rossi served in it; Tarchiani was made Italian ambassador to the US. But Italy was in a turbulent state and neither Parri's uncompromising nature, nor the Partito d'Azione's lofty ideals were a match for the canny new Christian Democrats under Alcide de Gasperi. They were out of power within a year. Piero Calamandrei, who became rector of Florence university and took on something of Carlo's mantle in post-war Florence, later wrote that fascism had dealt such a devastating blow to Italy because it struck down 'the best men, who had to be assassinated one by one, only to leave behind them desolation and a desert in our political life'. Mussolini had been shrewd in knowing whom to murder. Matteotti, Amendola, Gobetti, Gramsci, Carlo and Nello would all have made future leaders.

But, Calamandrei went on, the battle for the liberation of Italy had shown that there were still young men and women faithful to the spirit of the Rosselli brothers, conscious of duty and responsibility, ready to defend the ideals of Mazzini and the Risorgimento that they had held so dear. It was no accident that many had taken the name Rosselli for their partisan groups, for they, too, believed in liberty and justice. Carlo and Nello, his two smiling young friends, would live on, alive and very present, symbols of what it meant to *non mollare*. For himself, he wanted to remember them 'when they were still men of this world', standing side by side, as in a portrait, Carlo in front, Nello at his shoulder, a little in the background, but illuminating the 'poetic secret of the whole picture'.

As for Amelia, she lived on, as upright and uncomplaining as she had always been, apparently serene, slightly remote, a little daunting in her elegant mauve and pale grey high-necked blouses, loving and watching over the children, worrying about Melina, sharing her life with Maria, who grew stronger and more decisive as the years passed. Amelia died the day after Christmas 1954, at the age of eighty-four, leaving life, as a friend said, on the tips of her toes, without fuss, giving no trouble, slipping very quietly away. 'Addio for today,' she had written a few days before to Mirtillino. 'There is so much that I would like to write to you, but I am rather weary ... I kiss you tenderly. Nonna.'

Postscript

In April 1951 Carlo and Nello's bodies were exhumed from Père Lachaise in Paris and brought home to Florence by train in a special carriage. Here they lay in state in the vast panelled and frescoed Salone dei Cinquecento in Palazzo Vecchio under the banners of the city and the flags of the Rosselli partisan brigades. Trumpeters played. Maria laid a wreath of red flowers. Salvemini, now in his late seventies, had been asked to give the address, and there was some anxiety that he might go too far in criticising the recent not-guilty verdicts handed down to their killers. In the event, in the presence of Luigi Einaudi, President of the Republic and Carlo's early mentor and supporter, and many of the men who had fought alongside them for a better Italy, Salvemini said only that it would be 'infantile' not to think that the order for 'this monstrous crime' had not come from Mussolini. Much of the rest of his ovation was devoted to Carlo's dreams for a united Europe.

Maria and her four children, Silvia, Paola, Aldo and Alberto, were there, along with Carlo's Mirtillino, Melina and Andrea, as were Ernesto Rossi, Nello Traquandi, Emilio Lussu, Ferruccio Parri and even Gioacchino Volpe, the historian who had walked a thin line with the fascists but done so much to help Nello. At 11.30 a.m., as the coffins were carried out of the Palazzo Vecchio by former partisans and the Florentine city police, to make their way first to the university for another ceremony, then up to the cemetery of Trespiano in the hills overlooking the city, an orchestra played Beethoven's *Seventh Symphony*. The music flowed out into the Piazza della Signoria, where thousands of Florentines had gathered.

Mirtillino and Ferruccio Parri during the ceremony at the
cemetery above Florence

In Trespiano, Carlo and Nello were put to lie under a grey
marble tombstone, in a secluded corner of the cemetery surrounded
by cypresses, where Salvemini, Rossi and Traquandi would later
join them. Thinking back to the long struggle, to the love that
had bound them so close for so many years, Salvemini said: 'These
young men were my youth . . . they were my masters in life.'

'Carlo and Nello Rosselli', read the words engraved on the
stone, 'Giustizia e Libertà. For this they died. For this they live.'

Acknowledgements

This is a book which could not have been written without the extremely kind support, encouragement and help of the Rosselli family, who put at my disposal letters, diaries, papers and photographs and who talked to me about the lives of their grandmother and fathers. I thank Silvia, Paola, Aldo, Andrea and David very much indeed, as I do their cousin, Elissa Benaim.

Several historians were also extremely helpful. I should like to thank in particular Mimmo Franzinelli, Mauro Canali, Luca Michelini, Simone Visciola, Zeffiro Ciuffoletti and Stanislao Pugliese. In Lipari, Nino Paino and Giuseppe la Greca provided me with much local background and history; in Ustica, Vito Ailara found me very useful material in the Centro Studi. I thank them both very much. My thanks are also due to Marina Calloni, Isabelle Richet, Marcello Sorgi, Anna Chimenti, Diego Gambetta, Monica Miniati, Lionella Viterbo and Sonia D'Ambra.

Most of the research for this book was done in libraries and archives. I would like to thank Anna Mereu and Daniela Italia of the Fondazione Rosselli in Turin; Valdo Spini and the Fondazione Circolo Fratelli Rosselli in Florence; Simone Neri Serneri and Marta Bonsanti of the Istituto della Resistenza in Toscana; Gian Luca Corradi and the Biblioteca Nazionale Centrale di Firenze; Raffaella Barbacini and the Archivio Centrale dello Stato in Rome; Caterina del Vivo and the staff of the Gabinetto, G. P. Vieusseux; the Biblioteca Marucelliana; the Archives Nationales in Paris; the London School of Economics; the University of Reading Library; the National Archives in London; and the British Library.

Finally my thanks go to my travelling companions, Patricia

Williams and Kathy van Praag, and to Paul Corner and Anne Chisholm, who read the book in manuscript. As always, I am most grateful to my wonderful editors, Penny Hoare, Poppy Hampson, Jennifer Barth and Pamela Murray, to my copy-editor Eugenie Todd and my proof reader Sarah Barlow, and to my equally wonderful agent, Clare Alexander.

All the Italian translations are mine.

List of Illustrations

BNCF – Biblioteca Nazionale Centrale di Firenze, Fondo Pannunzio
ISRT – Istituto Storico della Resistenza in Toscana

p.vi   Carlo and Nello (courtesy of BNCF)

p.xvi Amelia and her sons (family collection)

p.9   Amelia Pincherle at the time of her marriage (courtesy of ISRT)

p.12   Amelia and her husband Joe Rosselli (courtesy of ISRT)

p.29   Carlo, as a boy in Florence (courtesy of ISRT)

p.54   Amelia and Aldo, in military uniform (courtesy of ISRT)

p.76   A post-war occupation of the factories in Piedmont (Wikimedia Commons)

p.77   A band of *squadristi*, off on a 'punitive raid' (Wikimedia Commons)

p.86   Mussolini and his followers, during the March on Rome (Wikimedia Commons)

p.91   Filippo Turati and Anna Kuliscioff (Centro Espositivo Sandro Pertini)

p.94   Piero Gobetti (Wikimedia Commons)

p.97   Gaetano Salvemini (courtesy of BNCF)

p.106 Salvemini, Carlo Levi and Carlo at the Fabian summer school (courtesy of ISRT)

p.113 Mussolini addresses his supporters from a balcony in Rome (Keystone-France\Gamma-Rapho via Getty Images)

p.115 Giacomo Matteotti (Wikimedia Commons)

p.116 The Lancia car in which Matteotti was kidnapped (Wikimedia Commons)

p.128 The Disperata, one of Florence's most brutal *squadre* (Wikimedia Commons)

p.130 A 'punitive expedition' against a socialist trade-union headquarters (Wikimedia Commons)

p.132 Nello in his early twenties (courtesy of BNCF)

p.133 Carlo in his early twenties (courtesy of BNCF)

p.144 Giovanni Améndola (Wikimedia Commons)

377

p.145 Giovanni Becciolini (Rito Simbolico Italiano)

p.163 Arturo Bocchini (Wikimedia Commons)

p.168 Lorenzo da Bove, Turati, Carlo, Sandro Pertini and Ferruccio Parri in Calvi (Centro Espositivo Sandro Pertini)

p.172 Nello in Venice with Maria (family collection)

p.179 Small boys marching in their Balilla uniforms (Luana Allevi)

p.180 Mussolini inspects a group of young fascist girls (Universal History Archive/UIG via Getty Images)

p.183 Carlo's wife Marion and their first child Giovanni (courtesy of BNCF)

p.194 Nello's house on Ustica with a crowd of *confinati* (courtesy of Centro Studi e Documentazione Isola di Ustica)

p.217 Nello and his second daughter, Paola (courtesy of ISRT)

p.217 Maria with Paola and Silvia (family collection)

p.224 The Club della Fuga on Lipari (courtesy of ISRT)

p.233 Francesco Fausto Nitti, Carlo and Emilio Lussu (courtesy of ISRT)

p.241 Mussolini's love of Roman antiquity (Ullstein Bild/Ullstein Bild via Getty Images)

p.244 L'Apparita, the Rosselli house at Bagno a Ripoli above Florence (family collection)

p.246 Filippo Turati and the Italian exiles in Paris (Centro Espositivo Sandro Pertini)

p.256 Giovanni Bassanesi (courtesy of ISRT)

p.272 Mussolini with his wife Rachele and their five children (Everett Collection Historical / Alamy Stock Photo)

p.286 Ernesto Rossi and his mother Elide (courtesy of ISRT)

p.288 Umberto Cevo with his youngest child (courtesy of ISRT)

p.298 Salvemini with Mirtillino (courtesy of ISRT)

p.300 Turati (courtesy of ISRT)

p.307 Zio 'Giù' Zabban (courtesy of ISRT)

p.307 Marion, Zia Gì and Mirtillino (courtesy of ISRT)

p.314 Mussolini, Hitler and the King and Queen of Italy (Everett Collection Historical / Alamy Stock Photo)

p.324 Marion, Mirtillino and Carlo (courtesy of ISRT)

p.325 Nello and Carlo with two of their children (courtesy of ISRT)

p.347 Carlo and Marion at Bagnoles-de-l'Orne, May 1937 (courtesy of BNCF)

p.348 Carlo and Nello (family collection)

p.358 Andrea, Silvia, Paola, Aldo and Melina (family collection)

p.360 Amelia at Quainton in Buckinghamshire (family collection)

p.360 Nello's four children at Quainton (family collection)

p.363 The family in the United States (family collection)

p.374 Mirtillino and Ferruccio Parri (courtesy of ISRT)

Sources and Select Bibliography

The Rossellis were a family of letter-writers. For the lives of Amelia, Carlo, Nello, Marion and Maria and their friends, the best sources are to be found in the many thousands of letters they wrote to each other all through their lives; these are currently held in the Fondazione Rosselli in Turin. Two selections of these letters have been edited by Professor Ciuffoletti (Zeffiro Ciuffoletti, *Epistolario familiare* and *Nello Rosselli*). A collection of letters written by Carlo Rosselli during his many periods abroad is to be found in Carlo Rosselli, *Scritti dall'esilio*. Amelia's memoirs, published in 2001 (*Memorie*), are also essential reading, as are two volumes put out by the Direzione Generale per Gli Archivi: *Lessico familiare* and *Un'altra Italia nell'Italia del fascismo*. In the Archivio Nazionale dello Stato the following files are especially valuable: CPC.b.1205.fasc.Cave Marion; CPC.b.4421. fasc.Rosselli Carlo; CPC.b.4422.fasc.Rosselli Sabatino; PP.Personali.b.79/A. fasc.Rosselli Carlo; PP.Personali.b.78/A.fasc.Rosselli Carlo; PP.Personali.b.80/A.Rosselli Sabatino; Confinati,b.883.fasc.Rosselli Carlo.

There are a number of biographies of Carlo and Nello, most of them in Italian: the best are by Stanislao Pugliese (*Carlo Rosselli*), Giovanni Belardelli (*Nello Rosselli*), Giuseppe Fiori (*Casa Rosselli*) and Aldo Garosci (*La vita di Carlo Rosselli*).

There are many excellent biographers and historians of Mussolini and Fascist Italy. For this book, I drew extensively on the work of R. J. B Bosworth, Paul Corner, Franco Antonicelli, Charles F. Delzell, Denis Mack Smith, and Gaetano Salvemini (*The Fascist Dictatorship in Italy*; *Under the Axe of Fascism*).

Two Italian historians have explored in depth Mussolini's secret services: Mauro Canali (*Le spie del regime*), and Mimmo Franzinelli (*Delatori*; *I tentacoli dell'OVRA*, and *Squadristi*). Their work is invaluable to anyone interested in this field.

Select Bibliography

Adamson, Walter L., *Avant-Garde Florence: From Modernism to Fascism*, London, 1993

Addis Saba, Marina, *Anna Kuliscioff: Vita privata e passione politica*, Milan, 1993

Alatri, Paolo, *L'antifascismo Italiano*, Rome, 1975

Allason, Barbara, *Memorie di un'antifascista 1919–1940*, Florence, 1976

Anni della Resistenza. Lezioni e testimonianza sul fascismo, Naples, 1975

Ansaldo, Giovanni, *L'antifascista riluttante: Memorie del carcere e del confino, 1926–1927*, Bologna, 1992

Antonicelli, Franco (ed.), *Trent'anni di storia italiana (1915–1945)*, Turin, 1961

Armani, Giuseppe, *La forza di non mollare: Ernesto Rossi dalla grande guerra a Giustizia e Libertà*, Milan, 2004

Arrighi, Paul, *Silvio Trentin: Un Européen en résistance 1919–1943*, Portet-sur-Garonne, 2007

Ashby, Charlotte, Tag Gronberg and Simon Shaw-Miller (eds), *The Viennese Café and Fin-de-Siècle Culture*, New York, 2013

Attanasio, Sandro, *Gli italiani e la guerra di Spagna*, Milan, 1974

Bagnoli, Paolo (ed.), *Una famiglia nella lotta: Carlo, Nello, Amelia e Marion Rosselli dalle carte dell'archivio dell'Istituto Storico della Resistenza in Toscana*, Florence, 2007

Baldoli, Claudio, 'L'Italia Nostra and the Creation of a little Fascist Italy during the 1930s', *London Journal*, Vol. 26, 2001

Banchelli, Umberto F., *Le memorie di un fascista*, Florence, 1922

Bardi, P. M., *15 giorni a Parigi fra i fuoriusciti*, Milan, 1932

Barea, Ilsa, *Vienna: Legend and Reality*, London, 1966

Barilli, Caterina, *Un uomo e una donna: vita di Ernesto e Ada Rossi*, Rome, 1991

Battini, Michele, 'Carlo Rosselli, Giustizia e Libertà and the Enigma of Justice', *Journal of Modern Italian Studies*, Vol. 17, 2012

Bechelloni, Antonio (ed.), *Carlo e Nello Rosselli e l'antifascismo europeo*, Milan, 2001

Belardelli, Giovanni, *Nello Rosselli*, Rome, 2007

Bennett, Arnold, *Florentine Journal: 1 April–25 May 1910*, London, 1967

Benzoni, Giuliana, *La vita ribelle*, Bologna, 1985

Bernabei, Alfio, *Esuli ed emigrati italiani nel Regno Unito 1920–1940*, Milan, 1997

Bianda, Renata, et al. (eds), *Atleti in camicia nera: lo sport nell'Italia di Mussolini*, Rome, 1983

Blasi, Jolanda de, *Romanità e germanesimo*, Florence, 1941

Blatt, Joel, 'The Battle of Turin: Carlo Rosselli, Giustizia e Libertà, OVRA and the Origins of Mussolini's Anti-semitic Campaign', *Journal of Modern Italian Studies*, Vol. 1, 1995

Bosis, Lauro de, *Storia della mia morte e ultimi scritti* (ed. Francesco De Silva), Turin, 1948

Bosworth, R. J. B., 'The British Press, the Conservatives and Mussolini', *Journal of Contemporary History*, Vol. 5, 1970
   Italy and the Wider World 1860–1960, London, 1996
   Mussolini, London, 2002
   Mussolini's Italy: Life under the Fascist Dictatorship 1915–1945, London, 2005

Brown, Horatio, *Life on the Lagoons*, London, 1884

Bullock, Ian, and Richard Pankhurst, *Sylvia Pankhurst: From Artist to Anti-Fascist*, London, 1992

Busoni, Jaurès, *Confinati a Lipari*, Milan, 1980

Calamandrei, Piero, *Uomini e città della resistenza*, Rome, 1977
   'Ricordo di Nello', *Il Ponte*, Anno 1, No. 1, 1945

Calimani, Riccardo, *The Ghetto of Venice*, New York, 1985

Calloni, Maria, and Lorella Cedroni, *Politica e affetti familiari: lettere dei Rosselli ai Ferrero*, Milan, 1997

Camurri, Renato, *Max Ascoli: Antifascista, intellettuale, giornalista*, Milan, 2012

Canali, Mauro, *Le spie del regime*, Bologna, 2004
   'The Matteotti Murder and the Origins of Mussolini's Totalitarian Fascist Regime in Italy', *Journal of Modern Italian Studies*, Vol. 14, 2009

Cannistraro, Philip V., and Brian R. Sullivan, *Il Duce's Other Women*, New York, 1993
   'Per una storia dei fasci negli Stati Uniti 1921–1929', *Storia Contemporanea*, December 1995

Cantagalli, Roberto, *Storia del fascismo fiorentino 1919–1925*, Florence, 1972

Caretti, Stefano (ed.), *Matteotti il mito*, Pisa, 1994

Casucci, Costanzo (ed.), *Carlo Rosselli: Scritti dall'esilio*, Turin, Vol. 1, 1982; Vol. 2, 1988

Centro Studi e Ricerche di Storia e Problemi Eoliani, *Il confino politico a Lipari*, Atti di Convegni 17 April 1983 e 24 May 1985, Marina di Patti, 1990

Ceva, Bianca, *1930: Retroscena di un drama*, Milan, 1955

Ciano, Galeazzo, *Diary 1937–1943*, London, 1947

Ciuffoletti, Zeffiro (ed.), *Nello Rosselli: Uno storico sotto il fascismo. Lettere e scritti vari (1924–1937)*, Florence, 1979
   Epistolario familiare: Carlo, Nello Rosselli e la madre (1914–1937), Milan, 1997

Colombo, Arturo, *Riccardo Bauer*, Bologna, 1979

Copsey, Nigel, *Anti-Fascism in Britain*, London, 2000

Corner, Paul, *The Fascist Party and Popular Opinion in Mussolini's Italy*, Oxford, 2012

Corno, Nicola Del (ed.), *Carlo Rosselli: gli anni della formazione e Milano*, Milan, 2010

Cullen, Niamh, *Piero Gobetti's Turin: Modernity, Myth and Memory*, Oxford, 2011

Degl'Innocenti, Maurizio, *L'emigrazione nella storia d'Italia dal 1914 al 1975*, Florence, 1978

Delzell, Charles F., *Mussolini's Enemies: The Italian Anti-Fascist Resistance*, Princeton, 1961

Diggins, John P., *Mussolini and Fascism: The View from America*, Princeton, 1972

Dilettoso, Diego, *La Parigi e la Francia di Carlo Rosselli*, Milan, 2013

Dogliani, Patrizia, 'Sport and Fascism', *Journal of Modern Italian Studies*, Vol. 5, 2000

Dollmann, Eugen, *The Interpreter*, London, 1967

Duggan, Christopher, *Fascist Voices, An Intimate History of Mussolini's Italy*, London, 2012

Edwards, P. G., 'The Foreign Office and Fascism 1924–1929', *Journal of Contemporary History*, Vol. 5, 1970

Eleonora Duse e Firenze, Catalogue of Conference, October/November 1994, Florence, 1994

L'Esercito italiano nella grande guerra, Vol. III: Le operazioni del 1916, Ministero della Difesa, Rome, 1931

Fedele, Santi, *E verrà un'altra Italia: Politica e cultura nei* Quaderni di Giustizia e Libertà, Milan, 1992

Ferrero, Leo, *Diario di un privilegiato sotto il fascismo*, Turin, 1946

Ferro, Giovanni, *Milano capitale dell'antifascismo*, Milan, 1985

Festorazzi, Roberto, *Mussolini e l'Inghilterra 1914–1940*, Rome, 2006

Fiori, Giuseppe, *Il cavaliere dei Rossomori: Vita di Emilio Lussu*, Turin, 1985

   Casa Rosselli: Vita di Carlo e Nello, Amelia, Marion e Maria, Turin, 1999

Flora, Francesco, *Ritratto di un ventennio*, Florence, 2003

Fornari, Harry, *Mussolini's Gadfly: Roberto Farinacci*, Nashville, 1971

Franzinelli, Mimmo, *I tentacoli dell'OVRA: Agenti, collaboratori e vittime della polizia politica fascista*, Turin, 1999

   Delatori: Spie e confidenti anonimi: l'arma segreta del regime fascista, Milan, 2001

   Squadristi: Protagonisti e tecniche della violenza fascista 1919–1922, Milan, 2003

   Il delitto Rosselli: 9 giugno 1937: Anatomia di un omicidio politico, Milan, 2007

Frullini, Bruno, *Squadrismo fiorentino*, Florence, 1933

Fucci, Franco, *Ali contro Mussolini*, Milan, 1978

   Le polizie di Mussolini: La repressione dell'antifascismo nel 'ventennio', Milan, 1985

Galante Garrone, Alessandro, *Zanotti-Bianco e Salvemini: Carteggio*, Naples, 1983

Gandolfo, Andrea, *Sandro Pertini: Dalla nascita alla resistenza 1896–1945*, Rome, 2010

Gariglio, Bartolo (ed.), *L'autunno delle libertà: Lettere ad Ada in morte di Piero Gobetti*, Turin, 2009

Garosci, Aldo, *Profilo dell'azione di Carlo Rosselli e di Giustizia e Libertà*, Turin, 1945
   La vita di Carlo Rosselli, Florence, 1948

Gentile, Emilio, 'La politica estera del partito fascista 1920–1930', *Storia Contemporanea*, Vol. 26, 1995

Ghini, Celso, and Adriano dal Pont, *Gli antifascisti al confino 1926–1943*, Rome, 1971

Giacone, Alessandro, and Éric Vial (eds), *I fratelli Rosselli: l'antifascismo e l'esilio*, Rome, 2011

Gilmour, David, *The Pursuit of Italy*, London, 2011

Ginzburg, Leone, *Lettere dal confino 1940–1943*, Turin, 2004

Giorgi, Giuliana Segre, *Piccolo memoriale antifascista*, Turin, 1994

Giovana, Mario, *Giustizia e Libertà in Italia: Storia di una cospirazione antifascista 1929–1937*, Turin, 2005
'*Giustizia e Libertà nella lotta antifascista e nella storia d'Italia: Attualità dei fratelli Rosselli a 40 anni del loro sacrificio*', conference, 10–12 June 1977, Florence, 1978

Goad, Harold E., *What is Fascism?*, Florence, 1929

Grasso, Giovanni (ed.), *Luigi Sturzo e i Rosselli tra Londra, Parigi e New York: Carteggio, 1929–1945*, Soveria Mannelli, 2004

Grazia, Victoria de, *The Culture of Consent: Mass Organisation of Leisure in Fascist Italy*, Cambridge, 1981
   How Fascism Ruled Women: Italy 1922–1945, Berkeley, 1992

Gronberg, Tag, *Vienna: City of Modernity, 1890–1914*, Bern, 2007

Guerri, Giordano Bruno, *Galeazzo Ciano: Una vita 1903–1944*, Milan, 1979

Hainsworth, Peter, 'Florentine cultural domination under fascism: *Il Bargello*', *Modern Language Review*, Vol. 95, 2000

Hibbert, Christopher, *Rome: The Biography of a City*, London, 1985
   Florence: The Biography of a City, London, 1994

Hughes, Robert, *Rome*, London, 2011

Hughes-Hallett, Lucy, *The Pike: Gabriele d'Annunzio, Poet, Seducer and Preacher of War*, London, 2013

Istituto Socialista di Studi Storici, *L'Emigrazione socialista nella lotta contro il fascismo*, Florence, 1982

Johnston, William M., *The Austrian Mind: An Intellectual and Social History 1848–1938*, London, 1972

Kasevich, Charles, 'The British Labour Press and Italian Fascism 1922–1925', *Journal of Contemporary History*, 1975

Kaspi, André, and Antoine Marès (eds), *Le Paris des étrangers depuis un siècle*, Paris, 1989

Koon, Tracy H., *Believe, Obey, Fight: Political Socialisation of Youth in Fascist Italy, 1922–1943*, London, 1985

Lamb, Richard, *Mussolini and the British*, London, 1997

Lessico familiare: Vita, cultura e politica della famiglia Rosselli all'insegna della libertà, Direzione Generale per Gli Archivi, Florence, 2002

Leto, Guido, *OVRA: Fascismo – Antifascismo*, Bologna, 1951

Levi, Alessandro, *Ricordi dei fratelli Rosselli*, Florence, 2002

Lombroso, Gina, *The Soul of a Woman*, London, 1924

Luna, Giovanni di, *Donne in oggetto: L'antifascismo nella società italiana 1922–1939*, Turin, 1995

Lussu, Emilio, *Per l'Italia dall'esilio*, Cagliari, 1978

    Lettere a Carlo Rosselli e altri scritti di Giustizia e Libertà, Sassari, 1979

    Autobiographical Account by a Leading Sardinian Republican Politician of Resistance to Fascism in Sardinia 1918–1930, Rome, 1992

Lussu, Emilio, and Joyce Lussu, *Alba rossa*, Ancona, 1994

Lyttelton, Adrian, 'Fascism in Italy: The Second Wave', *Journal of Contemporary History*, Vol. 1, 1966

Mack Smith, Denis, *Mussolini*, London, 1981

    Mazzini, London, 1994

Mangilli-Climpson, Massimo, *Men of Heart of Red, White and Green: Italian Antifascists in the Spanish Civil War*, New York, 1985

Mantelli, Brunello, and Nicola Tranfaglia, *Il libro dei deportati Vol. II: Deportati, deportatori, tempi, luoghi*, Turin, 2010

Mariani, Laura, *Quelle dell'idea: Storie di detenute politiche 1927–1948*, Bari, 1982

Marzo, *Le cronache di una vita*, Genoa, 1983

Il Marzocco: Carteggi e cronache 1887–1913, Florence, 1984

Milza, Pierre, *Italie fasciste devant l'opinion française*, Paris, 1967

    Le fascisme italien et la presse française: 1920–1940, Paris, 1967

Milza, Pierre (ed.), *Les italiens en France de 1914 à 1940*, Rome, 1986

Miniati, Monica, *Le 'emancipite': le donne ebree in Italia nel XIX e XX secolo*, Rome, 2003

Modigliani, Vera, *Esilio*, Florence, 1946 (privately printed)

Monti, Augusto, 'Leone Ginzburg', *Il Ponte*, July 1948

Monticone, Alberto, *Il fascismo al microfono: Radio e politica in Italia 1924–1945*, Rome, 1978

Moravia, Alberto, *Gli indifferenti*, Milan, 1933

    Il conformista, Milan, 1951

    Lettere ad Amelia Rosselli con altre lettere familiari, Milan, 2009

Morris, Jan, *Venice*, London, 1993

Morro, Umberto, et al., *Per Gobetti: Politica, arte, cultura a Torino 1918–1926*, Florence, 1976

Moseley, Ray, *Mussolini's Shadow: The Double Life of Count Galeazzo Ciano*, London, 1999

Myers, David N., et al. (eds), *Acculturation and Its Discontents: The Italian Jewish Experience Between Exclusion and Inclusion*, Toronto, 2008

Nitti, Francesco Fausto, *Escape*, London, 1930

Non a Ustica sola ... Atti del convegno ... Ustica, 28–29 August 2000, Florence, 2002

Norwich, John Julius, *Paradise of Cities: Nineteenth-Century Venice Seen through Foreign Eyes*, London, 2003

Origo, Iris, *A Need to Testify*, London, 1984

Orvieto, Laura, *Storia di Angiolo e Laura*, Florence, 2001

Pagano, Alessandra, *Il confino politico a Lipari*, Milan, 2003

Pajetta, Giancarlo (ed.), *Lettere di antifascisti dal carcere e dal confino*, Rome, 1975

Palla, Marco, *Firenze nel regime fascista 1929–1934*, Florence, 1978
    (ed.), *Storia della resistenza in Toscana*, Bari, 2006

Pankhurst, Richard, 'Sylvia Pankhurst and the Italian Anti-fascist Movement', *Socialist History*, Vol. 19, 2001

Parri, Ferruccio, *Scritti 1915–1975* (eds Collitti el al.), Milan, 1975
    La coscienza della democrazia, Milan, 1985

Pickering-Iazzi, Robin (ed.), *Mothers of Invention: Women, Italian Fascism, and Culture*, Minnesota, 1995

Picture Post: Italy Special, Vol. 20. No. 7, 14 August 1943

Pieroni Bortollotti, Franca, *Femminismo e partiti politici in Italia, 1919–1926*, Rome, 1978

Pirastu, Salvatore, *Fuga dal confino*, Cagliari, 1999

Pont, Adriano Dal, *I lager di Mussolini: L'altra faccia del confino nei documenti della polizia fascista*, Milan, 1975

Pont, Adriano Dal, Alfonso Leonetti, Pasquale Marello and Lino Zocchi, *Aula IV: processi del Tribunale Speciale Fascista*, Rome, 1975

Pretelli, Matteo, *Il fascismo e gli italiani all'estero*, Bologna, 2010

Pugliese, Stanislao, *Carlo Rosselli: Socialist Heretic and Antifascist Exile*, London, 1999
    Fascism, Antifascism and the Resistance in Italy, 1919 to the Present, Oxford, 2004

Quaderni del Circolo Rosselli, 'Amelia Pincherle Rosselli', Florence, No. 3, 2006

Quazza, Guido, et al., *Ferruccio Parri: Sessant'anni di storia italiana*, Bari, 1983

Renard, Isabelle, *L'Institut français de Florence 1900–1920*, Paris, 2001

Rijtano, Rosita, 'Confino politico a Lipari: La fuga di Carlo Rosselli', thesis, Messina, 2009–10

Roeck, Bernard, *Florence 1900: The Quest for Arcadia*, New Haven, 2009

Rosengarten, Frank, *The Italian Anti-fascist Press 1919–1945*, Cleveland, 1968

Rosselli, Amelia, and M. Calloni, *Memorie*, Bologna, 2001

Rosselli, Aldo, *La famiglia Rosselli: Una tragedia italiana*, Milan, 1983

Rosselli, Carlo, *Oggi in Spagna, domani in Italia*, Paris, 1938
    Scritti dall'esilio, Turin, 1988

Scritti politici e Autobiografici, ed. Gaetano Salvemini, Naples, 1944

Rosselli, Nello, *Carlo Pisacane nel Risorgimento Italiano*, Turin, 1977

Rosselli, Silvia, *Gli otto venti*, Palermo, 2008

Rossi, Cesare, *Personaggi di ieri e di oggi*, Milan, 1960

Rossi, Ernesto, *La pupilla del Duce*, Parma, 1956

    'I falsari dell-antifascismo', *Il Ponte*, Maggio, 1957

    Un democratico ribelle: cospirazione antifascista, carcere, confino, Milan, 2001

    (ed.) *Una spia del regime*, Milan, 1955

    (ed.), *No al fascismo*, Turin, 1957

    (ed.), *Non Mollare*, Florence, 1955

Rossi, Ernesto, and Gaetano Salvemini, *Carteggio: Dall'esilio alla Repubblica: Lettere 1944–1957*, Turin, 2004

Rossi, Laura (ed.), *Politica, valori, idealità: Carlo e Nello Rosselli: maestri dell'Italia civile*, Rome, 2007

Salvemini, Gaetano, *The Fascist Dictatorship in Italy*, London, 1928

    Under the Axe of Fascism, London, 1936

    Carlo and Nello Rosselli: A Memoir, London, 1937

    'The Origins of Fascism in Italy', *Il Ponte*, April 1952

    Memorie di un fuoriuscito, Milan, 1960

    Italian Fascist Activities in the United States, New York, 1977

    Carteggio 1921–1926, Rome, 1985

Salvoni, Elena, *Elena: A Life in Soho*, London, 1990

Scaffidi, Barbara, 'Contravenzioni al confino Lipari 1926–1932' (Thesis), 1997–8

Scalarini, Giuseppe, *Le mie isole*, Milan, 1992

Schiavi, Alessandro, *Esilio e morte di Filippo Turati 1926–1932*, Rome, 1956

Segre, Dan Vittorio, *Memoirs of a Fortunate Jew*, London, 1987

Shaw, Bernard G., *The Fabian Society: Its Early History*, Fabian Tract No. 41, London, 1892

Signori, Elisa (ed.), *Fra le righe: carteggio fra Carlo Rosselli e Gaetano Salvemini*, Milan, 2009

Snowden, Frank M., *The Fascist Revolution in Tuscany 1919–1922*, Cambridge, 1989

Soldani, Simonetta, *La Toscana nel regime fascista 1922–1939*, Florence, 1971

Sorgi, Marcello, *Edda Ciano e il comunista*, Milan, 2009

Spiel, Hilde, *Vienna's Golden Autumn*, London, 1987

Spini, Giorgio, and Antonio Casali, *Firenze*, Rome, 1986

Stille, Alexander, *Benevolence and Betrayal: Five Italian Jewish Families under Fascism*, London, 1992

Tannenbaum, Edward R., *Fascism in Italy: Society and Culture 1922–1945*, London, 1973

Thompson, Mark, *The White War: Life and Death on the Italian Front 1915–1919*, London, 2008

Tindaro, Motta, *A Lipari con la carta di permanenza durante il regime fascista*, Naples, 1971

Tombaccini, Simonetta, *Storia dei fuoriusciti Italiani in Francia*, Milan, 1988

Tranfaglia, Nicola, *Carlo Rosselli: dall'interventismo a Giustizia e Libertà*, Bari, 1968

'*Trent'anni dopo la marcia su Roma*', Il Ponte, October 1952

Treves, Claudio, *Il fascismo nella letteratura antifascista dell'esilio*, Rome, 1953

Treves, Paolo, *What Mussolini Did to Us*, London, 1940

Turati, Filippo, and Anna Kuliscioff, *Carteggio 1: May 1898–June 1899*, Turin, 1949

Visciola, Simone, and Giuseppe Limone (eds), *I Rosselli: eresia creativa, creatività originale*, Naples, 2005

Vito, Luca di, and Michele Gialdroni, *Lipari 1929: Fuga dal confino*, Rome, 2009

Vivarelli, Roberto, 'Le ragioni di un comune impegno: Riccordando Gaetano Salvemini, Carlo e Nello Rosselli, Ernesto Rossi,' Rivista Storica Italiana, Vol. 3, 1988.

Viviani della Robbia, Maria Bianca, 'Ricordo di Amelia Rosselli', *Il Vieusseux*, Florence, Jan–April 1990

Waterfield, Lina, *A Castle in Italy*, London, 1961

Zani, Luciano, *Italia Libera: il primo movimento antifascista clandestino*, Bari, 1975

Zogami, Leopoldo, *Confinati politici e relegati comuni a Lipari*, Messina, 1970

Zorzi, Alvise, *Venezia Scomparsa*, Milan, 1984

Zucàro, Domenico, Il Quarto Stato *di Nenni e Rosselli*, Milan, 1977
    Lettere di una spia, Milan, 1978

Zuccotti, Susan, *The Italians and the Holocaust: Persecution, Rescue and Survival*, London, 1987

Notes

All the Rosselli family letters belong to their personal archive.

Chapter One: A Watery Childhood

p1 'Amelia Pincherle ...' The best account of Amelia's childhood comes from Rosselli and Calloni, 2001.
p2 'By the nineteenth century ...' see Calimani, 1985
p3 'When, in 1859 ...' see Gilmour, 2011; Mack Smith, 1994
p6 'In the autumn of 1881 ...' see Zorzi, 1984
'Though D. H. Lawrence ...' Norwich, 2003, p. 96
'The launch of the ...' Brown, 1884, p. 292
p7 'A regular line ...' The Knapsack: Guide for Travellers in Italy, London, 1865
p8 'In 1872, the year ...' see Hibbert,1985; Robert Hughes, 2011
p10 '"My dear Papa ..."' Letter, 17 June 1914
'sciences were "odious" ...' Letter, 30 November 1913
'In the 1830s in London ...' see Mack Smith, 1994
p12 'Whether Joe felt ...' Aldo Rosselli, 1983
p13 'Come here ..."' letter, 23 June 1891
p14 'By the late 1870s ...' Johnston, 1972, p. 133; Spiel, 1987
'Coffee houses ...' Gronberg, 2007
p15 'Behind all the exuberance ...' Barea, 1966, p. 269
'She turned her thoughts ...' *Quaderni*, 2006
p16 'In the years ...' Gilmour, 2011, p. 255

Chapter Two: *Donne Emancipate*

p19 'The Florentines loved ...' Calamandrei, *Il Ponte*, 1945
'There was a word ...' Roeck, 2009, p. 59
'They arrived in 1903 ...' Rosselli and Calloni, 2001
p21 '"Charley and Nino ..."' Letter, undated
'Edward Lear ...' Hibbert, 1994, p. 275

'Marmalade, digestive biscuits ...': Baedeker, 1868
p22 'As Arnold Bennett ...' Bennett, 1967
p23 'Having travelled ...' Orvieto, 2001
p24 'Eleonora Duse ...' *Eleonora Duse e Firenze*, 1994
p25 'Better still, Amelia ...' Silvia Rosselli, conversation with author
'*Il Marzocco* ...' Carteggio e cronache 1887–1913, 1985, Florence
p26 'She asked the Orvietos ...' Visciola and Limone, 2005
p27 'At home, Amelia ...' Rosselli and Calloni, 2001
p31 'For all her success ...' *Quaderni*, 2006, p. 103
'I am a little ...' Letter, 25 March 1909
'she gave off a feeling ...' Orvieto, 2001, p. 109
'She described Amelia ...' Viviani della Robbia, 1990

Chapter Three: Defining *la Patria*

p32 'There were many ...' Roeck, 2009, p. 113
p33 'With his lover ...' Addis Saba, 1993; see also Turati and Kuliscioff, 1949
'But Italy was awash ...' for good historical accounts of Italy at this period, see Bosworth, 1996, 2002, 2005, Corner, 2012 and Duggan, 2012
p34 'As the poet Carducci ...' Gilmour, 2011, p. 279
'Among Giolitti's ...' see Adamson, 1993
'Born in Molfetta ...' see Origo, 1984
p36 'What he shared ...' see Caretti, 1994
'Another was a blacksmith's son ...' For biographies of Mussolini, see Bosworth, 2002; Mack Smith, 1981; Cannistraro and Sullivan, 1993
p37 'But as the century ...' There is a large literature on women under the fascists. See in particular Luna, 1995; de Grazia, 1992; Pickering-Iazzi, 1995
p38 'Gina was a successful ...' Lombroso, 1924
p39 'In the middle ...' *Quaderni*, 2006, p. 83
'Somewhat to Amelia's discomfort ...' Rosselli and Calloni, 2001, p. 128
p40 'Amelia said that music ...' ibid., p. 127
'When they were bad ...' Letter, February 1911
'"I must now do ..."' Aldo to Amelia, 7 January 1911
p41 'Nello wrote to her ...' Nello to Amelia, July 1911
'Florence was gradually ...' see Hainsworth, 2000
p42 'It was important ...' Roeck, 2009, p. 244
'"we will glorify ..."' Gilmour, 2011, p. 280
p43 'The war in Libya ...' see Bosworth, 2002
p44 '"Dearest, don't you ..."' Laura to Amelia, 19 July 1909
p45 'She would look back ...' Rosselli and Calloni, 2001, p. 122
'Some time in 1912 ...' *Quaderni*, 2006, p. 105

p46 '1911 and 1912 ...' see Bosworth, 2002
At a Futurist *grande serata* ...' See Adamson, 1993
p47 '"You know perfectly ..."' Amelia to Carlo, 6 August 1914
p48 'He was, she wrote ...' Rosselli and Calloni, 2001, p. 138
p49 'In October 1914 ...' Adamson, 1993, p. 197
p50 '"What I do ..."' Amelia, 20 December 1914

Chapter Four: Becoming a Man

p51 'On 23 May ...' see Thompson, 2008
p52 'Angiolo Orvieto ...' Orvieto, 2001, p. 91
p53 'Even now, seven ...' see Origo, 1984
p55 '"If I were told ..."' Levi, 2002, p. 15
p56 'Even so, a senior ...' see *L'Esercito italiano nella grande guerra*, 1931
'"literally a field of filth"...' Thompson, 2008, p. 150
p57 'Three days of silence ...' Rosselli and Calloni, 2001, p. 153
p58 '"I am living ..."' Amelia Rosselli, 22 May 1916
'What terrified her ...' Rosselli and Calloni, 2001, p. 155
p59 'Fuel was rationed ...' see Waterfield, 1961
p61 '"No, dear Carlo ..."' Zio Giù to Carlo, 9 August 1917
p62 '"The more the days ..."' Amelia to Carlo, 4 November 1917
'Here she recreated ...' see Aldo Rosselli, 1983
p63 'They talked about ...' Amelia to Carlo, 1 December 1917
'*terribilmente gelato* ..."' Nello to Amelia, 1 December 1919
p64 'There was talk ...' Adamson, 1993, p. 227
p65 'He told Zio Giù ...' Carlo to Zio Giù, 28 November 1918
'"I see the sail ..."' Amelia to Carlo, 16 December 1918

Chaper Five: The Dark Seraphim

p66 'As Salvemini would say ...' Salvemini, 1928, p. 16
'The young diplomat Harold ...' Lyttelton, 1966, p. 462
p67 'Twisting and turning ...' Koon, 1985, p. 23
p68 'The cry of the *Arditi* ...' see Franzinelli, 2003
'The Belgian poet ...' Hughes-Hallett, 2013, p. 520
'Mussolini told them ...' Bosworth, 1996, p. 115
'those they considered "degenerates" ...' see Banchelli, 1922
p69 'Leninism, he warned ...' Adamson, 1993, p. 227
'Just as Amelia was moving ...' see Rosselli and Calloni, 2001
p70 '"Enjoy yourself ..."' anonymous correspondent, 5 March 1919
'As Amelia said ...' see *Quaderni*, 2006
p73 'Salvemini, back ...' Caretti, 1994, p. 136; see also Origo, 1984
'Nello, still in uniform ...' Alatri, 1975, p. 54; see also Belardelli, 2007

p75 'As Carlo saw it ...' *La Vita*, 20 May 1919
'The new government was ...' Amelia to Carlo, 20 January 1919
p76 '"We need so badly ..."' Amelia to Carlo, 28 January 1919
p77 'Though the epicentre ...' see Franzinelli, 2003
p79 'He told his mother ...' Tranfaglia, 1968, p. 43
p81 'the new fascist members ...' Waterfield, 1961, p. 194
'Writing to his mother ...' Ciuffoletti, 1979
'a more Machiavellian ...' see Spini and Casali, 1986
p82 'It was becoming ...' Snowden, 1989, p. 194
'Burning down left-wing ...' Frullini, 1933, p. 268
p83 'The culprits were ...' Franzinelli, 2003, p. 111
'"Today", he wrote ...' Carlo to Amelia, 18 January 1921
p84 'Mussolini spoke of ...' Rosengarten, 1968, p. 17
'In one place ...' Salvemini, *Il Ponte*, 1952
p85 '"Either you give me ..."' see Garosci, 1948
'Other cities ...' Gilmour, 2011, p. 231; see also Snowden, 1989, and Alatri, 1975
p87 'Mussolini, shrewdly ...' Bosworth, 2002, p. 169
'Rome was described ...' Mack Smith, 1981, p. 56
'It was to be another ...' Pickering-Iazzi, 1995, p. 19
p88 '"on the verge of madness ..."' Salvemini, *Il Ponte*, April 1952

Chapter Six: Planting a Tree

p89 'Mussolini could now ...' Mack Smith, 1981, p. 57
'*The Times* was more ...' Bosworth, *Journal of Contemporary History*, 1970
'Even the legendary ...' *Observer*, 6 May 1923
p90 'This was a man ...' see Lamb, 1997
'"The Italians seem ..."' Bosworth, 2002, p. 184
'He was still a bit ...' Mack Smith, 1981, p. 61
'both shared ...' the US *Daily Express*, 4 January 1923
p91 '"What can save ..."' Anna Kuliscioff to Turati, 28 February 1923, Turati and Kuliscioff, 1949
p92 'October 1922 ...' Waterfield, 1961, p. 189
'"An enormous black ..."' Carlo to Amelia, 28 February 1923
'In the Circolo ...' Ernesto Rossi, 1957
p93 'As Rossi said ...' Garosci, 1948
'Having played ...' Cullen, 2011
p94 'Carlo had heard ...' Allason, 1976
'When he spoke ...' letter to Ada Gobetti in Morro et al., 1976
p95 'Youthful, enthusiastic ...' see Cullen, 2011
p96 'Carlo met Gobetti ...' Paolo Treves, 1940, p. 24
'Another frequent visitor ...' see Garosci, 1948
p98 '"He was planting ..."' Pugliese, 1999, p. 31

p100 ' "At that moment . . ." ' Marion to Aldo Garosci, n.d.
'Three days later . . .' Carlo to Amelia, 2 March 1923
'Carlo, said Salvemini . . .' see Garosci, 1948

p101 'But once he had . . .' Carlo to Amelia, 25 July 1923

p103 'In the winter of . . .' Gentile, *Storia Contemporanea*, p. 961

p104 ' "What, then, is . . ." ' *Il Commento*, 30 September 1923

p105 'The weather was . . .' Fabian Summer School Log Book, 1923 London,
LSE

p107 'The only blight . . .' Carlo to Amelia, 6 August 1923
' "If you but knew . . ." ' Salvemini to Umberto Zanobbi Biano, 4
September 1923

p108 ' "Do they not realise . . . ?" ' Carlo to Amelia, 2 September 1923

Chapter Seven: Moral Choices

p109 'Amendola, the principled . . .' see Salvemini, 1928
'though he insisted . . .' Cesare Rossi, 1960, p. 191
'The stairs and corridors . . .' see Origo, 1984

p110 'Moravia would later . . .' Moravia, 2009, p. 15
'I am a supporter . . .' *Il Popolo d'Italia*, 12 November 1922

p111 'They needed, the organisation . . .' Pickering-Iazzi, 1995, p. 33
'He was also working . . .' see Belardelli, 2007

p112 'He was asked . . .' Tranfaglia, 1968, p. 219
'the London *Times* . . .' Lamb, 1997, p. 62

p113 'The fascist ticket . . .' Bosworth, 2002, p. 91

p114 'The "new politics" . . .' Antonicelli, 1961, p. 77

p115 'Carlo called him . . .' Pugliese, 1999, p. 41
'In the late spring . . .' *Daily Herald*, 12 February 1924

p117 'When it refused . . .' Alatri, 1975, p. 115
' "Time is working . . ." ' Turati to Anna Kuliscioff, 24 June 1924
' "The enemy has caught . . ." ' *ibid.*, 13 July 1924
'With the death of . . .' Allason, 1976, p. 45

p118 'Was Mussolini . . .' Canali, *Journal of Modern Italian Studies*, 2009
'Mussolini clung on . . .' Bosworth, 2002, p. 20
'Matteotti, he said . . .' Lamb, 1997, p. 65
'It was their duty . . .' see Ernesto Rossi, 2001

p119 'Post-war Italy . . .' see Caretti, 1994, p. 141
an energetic, youthful . . . *Giustizia e Libertà*, 8 June 1934

p120 ' "We do not wish . . ." ' Alatri, 1975, p. 379

p121 'A young supporter . . .' Enrico Bocci, *Una vita per la libertà*
p. 46, Florence, 1969
'A "Friends of Italian . . ." ' see Bernabei, 1997

p122 'As *The Times* . . .' *The Times*, 21 June 1924
'Closely following . . .' Tranfaglia, 1968, p. 180
' "For me, at least . . ." ' Carlo to Amelia, 15 September 1924

'Would his mother ...' Carlo to Amelia, 9 October 1924
p123 'The inspector, seeing ...' Waterfield, 1961, p. 214
p125 'By late 1924 ...' see Canali, 2004
p126 '"We live", wrote ...' Addis Saba, 1993
'As Salvemini wrote ...' Salvemini, 1928, p. 381
'But the *squadristi* ...' Bosworth, 2002, p. 199
'As Ernesto Rossi would ...' see Ernesto Rossi (ed.), 1955

Chapter Eight: '*Non Mollare*'

p127 'Just as the city ...' Palla, 2006, p. 120–21
p128 'Of the several different ...' see Cantagalli, 1972
p129 'A small plane ...' see Ernesto Rossi, 2001
p130 'In Pisa the damage ...' see Alatri, 1975
'It was known as ...' see Franzinelli, 2003
p131 'Matteotti was, lamentably ...' Mack Smith, 1981, p. 85
'It was now a question ...' Lamb, 1997, p. 70
'When the Chamber ...' Garosci, *Il Ponte*, July 1957, p. 1024
'It was indeed ...' Lyttelton, *Journal of Contemporary History*, 1966, p. 197
p132 'Across Italy ...' see Fornari, 1971
p133 'Then Nello ...' Belardelli, 2007, p. 42
p134 '"I sense", wrote ...' Carlo to Salvemini, 12 January 1925
'What both statements ...' Fiori, 1999, p. 47
p136 'Hearing that he had been ...' Segreteria Particolare del Duce, Carteggio Riservato Busta 48
p137 'In his diary ...' Nello Rosselli, Diary, 8 April 1925
'Whenever he was alone ...' Nello to Amelia, 10 June 1925
'"It seems to me ..."' Nello to Amelia, 23 May 1925
'"It was enough ..."' Calamandrei, *Il Ponte*, 1945
p138 '"Things are going ..."' Carlo to Amelia, 4 May 1925
p139 '"To such provocations ..."' Alatri, 1975, p. 396
'For the first few weeks ...' Origo, 1984, p. 216
'The judge ...' see Ernesto Rossi (ed.), 1955
p140 'Amelia was with ...' Fiori, 1999, p. 52
'next morning ...' Rosselli and Calloni, 2001
p142 '"But I feel extremely ..."' Nello to Maria, 23 July 1925
'There was now a thought ...' Origo, 1984, p. 218
p143 'In *Critica Fascista* ...' *Critica Fascista*, 1 May 1925
'The prefect did ...' Salvemini, 1928, p. 295
Friends who saw ... see Allason, 1976
p144 '"This time ..."' Zani, 1975, p. 183
Working ever more ... Franzinelli in Ernesto Rossi (ed.), 1955 p. 22
p146 'From his headquarters ...' Salvemini, op. cit., p. 270

'Just after midnight ...' see Barilli, 1991
p147 'In the streets ...' Palla, 2006, p. 142
When Amelia ... Rosselli and Calloni, 2001
p148 'Mussolini announced ...' *Gerarchia*, October 1925
p149 'Marion Cave, writing ...' Marion to Salvemini, 20 October 1925
'Rossi had become ...' Salvemini, 1985
p150 'Turati had to be ...' see Paolo Treves, 1940
'Next to die ...' see Gariglio, 2009
p151 'At a memorial ...' Antonicelli, 1961, p. 134
'"I weep for you ..."' Carlo to Ada Gobetti, 7 April 1926

Chapter Nine: Breaking Free

p152 'Nello told Maria ...' Nello to Maria, 7 November 1925
p153 '"The only man ..."' Carlo to Salvemini, 29 September 1925
'Telling his friend ...' Salvemini to Calamandrei, 19 September 1925
'They were singing ...' Rosselli and Calloni, 2001, p. 197
p154 'Carlo was convinced ...' Garosci, *Il Ponte*, July 1957
'Unlike most ...' Zucàro, 1977, p. 10
p155 'Then they would navigate ...' Visciola and Limone, 2005, p. 84
'In April ...' ACS Min Interno, Dir Gen, PSA.ge.r 1926
'"I too have ..."' Garosci, *La vita di Carlo Rosselli*, p. 48
p156 'Perhaps choosing ...' Carlo to Amelia, 26 April 1926
p157 'Carlo was described ...' Fiori, 1999, p. 61
p159 '"I beg you ..."' Amelia to Carlo, 20 September 1926
'Mussolini called 1926 ...' Zucàro, 1977, p. 18
'The first attack ...' Frances Stonor Saunders, *The Woman Who Shot Mussolini*, London, 2010
p160 'The third event ...' Bosworth, 2002
p162 'The task of implementing ...' Dollmann, 1967
p163 'What obsessed ...' Franzinelli, 1999
'Soon, Bocchini's ...' Fucci, 1985, p. 87
p164 'Another casualty ...' Rosengarten, 1968
'Carlo, wrote another friend ...' Paolo Treves, 1940
'The fact that ...' Salvemini, 1937, p. 18
p165 'One night ...' Rosselli and Calloni, 2001, p. 200
'Two routes ...' Barilli, 1991
p166 'He found the perfect ...' Fiori, 1999, p. 72
p169 'Turati, standing ...' Schiavi, 1956

Chapter Ten: Defying the Barbarians

p170 'In Milan, where the train ...' Levi, 2002
'Carlo was "noisy ..."' Ernesto Rossi, 2001, p. 89
171 'A note from the prefect ...' ACS Confinati politici, Busta 883

p173 'Like Carlo ...' Nello to Amelia, 11 June 1927

p178 'The time for history ...' Koon, 1985, p. 7
'In theory, freedom ...' Flora, 2003, p. 35
'In order for ...' Salvemini, 1936

p179 'Under the Dopolavoro ...' de Grazia, 1981, p. 173
'Toscanini, who had ...' Bosworth, 2005, p. 197
'A new sport ...' Mack Smith, 1981, p. 116
'The new Italian ...' Koon, 1985, p. 12 and p. 30

p181 'Two of his mistresses ...' Mack Smith, 1981, p. 114
'Content, declared ...' de Grazia, 1981, p. 225
'With the laws ...' Flora, 2003

p182 'But in 1927 ...' Canali, 2004, p. 70
'On 26 May ...' Franzinelli, 1999, p. 33

p183 'What quickly became known ...' for the best accounts of the Savona trial, see Pugliese, 1999; Levi, 2002; Salvemini, 1937.

p184 'Carlo was well ...' Marion to Amelia, 9 September 1927

p185 'Parri's lawyer ...' Fiori, 1999, p. 83

Chapter Eleven: *Il Confino*

p188 'To the Italians ...' see Dal Pont, 1975; Mantelli and Tranfaglia, 2010; Dal Pont et al., 1975; Vito Modugno e Massimiliano de Pace. 'Lipari' (thesis)
'In 1926 ...' see Scaffidi, 1997–8
'"We will remove ..."' Mussolini, speech on 26 May 1927

p189 'Soon, there were well ...' see Ghini and Pont, 1971

p190 'Nello reached Ustica ...' *Il Ponte*, 1946, No. 4

p191 'One of the first ...' Pino del Greco, conversation with author

p192 '"We read, we discuss ..."' Nello to the Ferreros, 18 July 1927
'It was, he said ...' Nello to Lella Ramonino, 20 July 1927

p193 'The clock in the square ...' see *Non a Ustica sola* ... , 2000
'Nello was captivated ...' Belardelli 2007, p. 86

p194 'To his mother-in-law ...' Nello to Luisa, 3 August 1927

p195 '"You might say ..."' Nello to Amelia, 11 September 1927
'"Bring what you ..."' Giulio Montaleci to his family, March 1927

p196 'Nello, Amelia wrote ...' Amelia to Zia Gì, 2 October 1927
'This was, wrote Nello ...' Nello to Zia Gì, 29 November 1927

p197 'The prefect warned ...' prefect to police in Rome, 25 September 1927

p198 'Though it took some months ...' ACS PS.1928.Kl.b.20, Palermo

p199 'His facial expression ...' Rosselli and Calloni, 2001, p. 225
'To his uncle ...' Nello to Gabriele, 17 January 1928
'Boselli duly wrote ...' Boselli to Mussolini, 9 January 1928

p200 'As the boat pulled ...' *Il Ponte*, 1946

p201 'Against all the odds ...' Nello, diary p. 22, personal papers
'Later, he wrote ...' Nello to Enrico Greppi, 21 February 1928

Chapter Twelve: The Island of Winds

p202 '"I arrived ..."' Carlo to Amelia, 29 December 1927
'The port of Lipari ...' Carlo to Amelia, 31 December 1927
'Within days ...' Fiori, 1999
'It had a terrace ...' Pino del Greco, conversation with author
'Writing to Parri ...' Carlo to Parri, 6 January 1928; see also Parri, 1975

p204 'Anything with the word ...' see Tindaro, 1971; Pagano, 2003
'At dusk ...' Scaffidi, 1997–8
'On Lipari the most ...' Zogami, 1970

p205 '"The desire to ..."' Ernesto Rossi, 1957
'Carlo had few ...' Carlo to Max Ascoli, 20 February 1929

p206 'Another new friend ...' Fiori, 1985; see also Lussu, 1992

p207 'He longed only ...' Nitti, 1930, p. 186
'"Dolci does ..."' Vito and Gialdroni, 2009, p. 32
'The Liparesi continued ...' Rijtano, 2009–10

p208 'Among the newcomers ...' Busoni, 1980
'And among the political ...' ACS Confinati politici 904; see also Mariani, 1982

p209 'Vera Santoni ...' ACS Confinati politici 912

p210 'Binazzi was ...' Busoni, 1980
'"I believe that ..."' Carlo to Amelia, 15 March 1928

p211 'Carlo was taking ...' Carlo to Amelia, 16 February 1928
'Carlo, she said ...' Marion to Zia Gì, 16 February 1928

p212 'The days passed ...' Carlo to Amelia, 7 March 1928
'In the evenings ...' ACS Confinati politici, Busta 883

p213 'Politics was the ...' Ghini and Dal Pont, 1971

p214 '"What we were looking ..."' Parri, *Il Ponte*, 1957
'Nello, ostensibly free ...' *Non a Ustica sola*, 2002

p215 '"There's no place ..."' Nello to Amelia, 18 June 1928

p218 'Carlo found ...' Carlo to Amelia, 13 December 1928

p219 'but his need ...' Carlo to Amelia, 16 September 1928
'Carlo told Zia ...' Carlo to Zia Gì, 28 July 1928
'Late one night ...' Carlo to Nello, 22 July 1928

p220 '"Monotony, monotony ..."' see Vito and Gialdroni, 2009

Chapter Thirteen: Not Even the Flies Escape

p221 'Giovanni Ansaldo ...' see Marzo, 1983
'When Parri's ...' ACS Confinati politici. Busta 755

p222 'A young Tuscan ...' see Zogami, 1970; Pirastu, 1999
'All four men ...' Vito and Gialdroni, 2009, p. 66; see also Carlo Rosselli, *Fuga in Quattro Tempi*, 1944

p223 '"Have you ever ..."' Carlo to Amelia, 6 February 1928

p225 'Bruna Pagani ...' 'Il mio amico Emilio Lussu', *La Catena*, Paris, 1930

'he described a long-term ...' Carlo to Amelia, 13 December 1928
p226 'On 6 October ...' Vito and Gialdroni, 2009, p. 274
'Music brought ...' see Sorgi, 2009
p228 'Carlo had scratched ...' see Pugliese, 1999; Salvemini, 1937
p229 'The almanac showed ...' see Nitti, 1930
p235 'The Lipari "raid" ...' Vito and Gialdroni, 2009, p. 358

Chapter Fourteen: To Be an Exile

p236 'On 29 July ...' Vito and Gialdroni, 2009
p237 '"They have arrived! ..."' *La Libertà*, 11 August 1929
p238 'Much was made ...' Pirastu, 1999
p239 'An official told ...' *Italy Today* 1929
'his friends told him ...' Laura Rossi, 2007, p. 48
'"The persecution ..."' Amelia to Nello, 13 August 1929
p241 'Cremonesi was ...' Busoni, 1980
'On 27 August ...' Ernesto Rossi, 2001, p. 174
p242 'As he wrote ruefully ...' Nello to Gina Lombroso, 24 September 1929
'However, Ponza ...' Franzinelli, 2007, p. 38
p243 '"It is certain ..."' Carlo Levi to Nello, 20 August 1929
p245 'She carried ...' Silvia Rosselli, 2008
'Long before ...' Tombaccini, 1988
p246 'Many of these refugees ...' Giorgi, 1994
p247 'The exiles lived ...' Modigliani, 1946; see also Bardi, 1932
'To every new arrival ...' Cesare Rossi, 1960, p. 146
'Turati, who ...' Tombaccini, 1988, p. 66
p248 'In the French ...' *L'Oeuvre*, 7 August 1929
'As he wrote to Amelia ...' Carlo to Amelia, 14 August 1929
'Within two weeks ...' Fiori, 1999
p249 'After much debate ...' *Giustizia e Libertà*, No. 1, November 1929
'Carlo was indefatigable ...' Salvemini, 1937
p250 'The new Italy ...' *Manchester Guardian*, 4 December 1929
'Il Popolo d'Italia ...' 11 December 1929
p251 'Now Mussolini announced ...' Francesco Lefebvre D'Ovidio, *Nuova Rivista Storica*, May 2012, p. 467
'In theory, these men ...' Franzinelli, 2001, p. 148; see also Canali, 2004
p252 'His "principles" ...' Min Int Dir Polpol Rosselli,C. A., 4 Sep 1929
'On Carlo's personal ...' ACS Min Int Casellario Pol Centrale 4421
'The Rossellis were reported ...' Pugliese, 1999, p. 126
'Since the French ...' Archives Nationales F/7/13250, 'Antifascistes en France'
'As Lussu wrote ...' Emilio Lussu, *La Catena*, p. 39
p254 'His trial ...' Ernesto Rossi, 1957, p. 147
p255 'The new plot ...' Fucci, 1978

Chapter Fifteen: Just One Heart

p259 'As Piero Calamandrei ...' *Il Ponte*, Anno 1, 1945

p260 'He, like Carlo ...' Nello to Max Ascoli, 20 February 1928
'"I am wonderfully ..."' Nello to the Zabbans, 9 July 1930

p261 'Salvemini, noted Mussolini ...' Vito and Gialdroni, 2009
'Mindful of their ...' *Il Popolo d'Italia*, 12 November 1927

p262 '"You made me ..."' Nello to Salvemini, 4 November 1930
'Word went out ...' HO 144/22561
'a firm hand ...' *Journal of Contemporary History*, Vol. 15, 1970, p. 156

p263 'But the Italian ...' Baldoli, 2001
'Ever slippery ...' Cannistraro and Sullivan, 1993, p. 336
'Carlo, who had ...' Fiori, 1999, p.103
'Amelia disliked its ...' Amelia to Zia Gì, 25 November 1930
'"Madonna, what a ..."' Nello to Amelia, 20 July 1930

p264 'Mussolini had granted ...' see Ciuffoletti, *Nello Rosselli*, 1979
'One of his first ...' Amelia to Carlo, 23 December 1931
'Even when softened ...' Belardelli, 2007, p. 130
'What they did not ...' Min dell'Int Divisione Polizia Politica, Rosselli, Carlo Alberto

p265 'Amelia too was ...' Min dell'Int. Divisione Polizia Politica, Rosselli, Carlo Alberto

p266 'The early 1930s ...' see Bosworth, 1996
'As Mussolini declared ...' 'La Toscana nel regime fascista', *Convegno di Studi*, 1969, p. 544
'In return, the Vatican ...' see Delzell, 1961

p267 'In reality, much of ...' Gilmour, 2011, p. 317

p268 'Pot-bellied ...' de Grazia, 1981, p. 76
'As for girls ...' Koon, 1985, p. 97; see also Tannenbaum, 1973
'The fascists wanted ...' Dogliani, 2000

p269 'Action, not thought ...' see Flora, 2003
'Of all activities ...' see Bianda et al., 1983

p270 'At the Holy Palate ...' Hughes, 2011, p. 479

p271 'He would later say ...' Mack Smith, 1981, p. 109
'In April 1930 ...' see Guerri, 1979
'As important to ...' see Bosworth, 2005

p273 '"The more Italians ..."' speech of 26 May 1927
'"We want ..."' Fucci, 1985, p. 147
'But the secret services ...' see Franzinelli, 1999

p274 'When Nello managed ...' see Benzoni, 1985

p275 'It would include articles ... Belardelli, 2007, p. 146
'"When I am with ..."' Nello to Carlo Silvestri, 7 January 1932

p276 '"Eroticism" was to be ...' Palla, 1978, p. 364
'Nello's "moral ..."' ACS CPC 4422 Rosselli S.
'"We deluded ourselves ..."' *Il Ponte*, No. 1, 1945

p277 '"How sad, my dear ..."' Nello to Salvemini, 17 August 1933

Chapter Sixteen: Dancing for Liberty

p278 '"I am not living ..."' Carlo to Amelia, 30 December 1930
'He was everywhere ...' Fiori, 1999, p. 118

p279 '*Socialismo Liberale* ...' for a good account of Carlo's ideas, see Pugliese, 1999
'There was more ...' Carlo Rosselli, 1944, XLV
'Carlo had sent ...' Nello to Carlo, 19 June 1930
'But he was not prepared ...' Tombaccini, 1988, p. 142

p280 'Croce, who joined ...' Pugliese, 1999, p. 114
'The few young anti-fascists ...' Corno, 2010
'In Milan, there were ...' Colombo, 1979
'For a while, there ...' Gandolfo, 2010

p283 'Another useful man ...' Franzinelli, 1999, p. 120
'one of OVRA's most ...' ACS CPC Fascicoli personali Vincenzio Bellavia
'One report spoke ...' ACS Segreteria Particolare del Duce.Carteggio Ris. Busta 77, Carlo e Nello Rosselli
'Another named Lussu ...' ACS Segreteria Particolare del Duce. b71 fascio H/R Lussu Emilio

p284 'Carlo del Re was ...' ACS.MI DGPS.DPP Materia, bb104 and 105

p285 'Despite Ceva's ...' Barilli, 1991, p. 70

p287 'Ernesto Rossi, meanwhile ...' see Ernesto Rossi, 1955, and 2001

p289 'the "Trial of the intellectuals" ...' *Italy Today*, June 1931

p291 'To a friend she wrote ...' Pajetta, 1975
'An informer reported ...' ACS Min dell'Int Divisione Polizia Politica, Rosselli, Carlo

p293 'With their friends in jail ...' Carlo to Marion, 10 May 1931
'At 8 o'clock ...' Origo, 1984, p. 87

p294 'The problem, he wrote ...' Bosis, 1948

p296 '"When I am free ..."' Carlo to Marion, 20 November 1931

Chapter Seventeen: A World of Moral Richness

p297 'Amelia, Nello and Maria ...' Silvia and Paola Rosselli, conversation with author
'The Italian embassy ...' ACS Min dell'Int. Divisione Polizia Politica, Rosselli, C. A.

p298 'Nothing about the refugees ...' *Le Petit Bleu*, 9 May 1932
'Though some of the exiles ...' Modigliani, 1946
'A new young friend ...' Dilettoso, 2013

p299 'she was heckled ...' Archives Nationales F/7/13250, 'Antifascistes en France'

p300 '"We have to get out ..."' Schiavi, 1956, p. 463
'"I understand that it ..."' Salvemini to Carlo, 16 January 1933
'Hoping to rise ...' Fedele, 1992

p301 'Marion wrote ...' Marion to Amelia, 8 June 1933
p302 '"La guerra che torna" ...' Garosci, 1948, p. 86
p303 'In this too ...' *Giustizia e Libertà*, 17 May 1935
    'On Christmas Eve ...' Hibbert, 1985, p. 289
    'Some four million ...' Waterfield, 1961, p. 225
p304 'Dedicating one room ...' Franzinelli, 2003, p. 170
    'Mussolini's stranglehold ...' Pretelli, 2010
    'To many Italians ...' Hughes, 2011, p. 487
p305 'But Velia had ...' Caretti, 1994
    'Carlo, with Salvemini's ...' Pankhurst, 2001
p308 'Which was not ...' Belardelli, 2007, p. 160
p309 'He told his friend ...' Carlo to Leone Ginzburg, 3 August 1934
p311 'As Lussu would later ...' Fiori, 1985, p. 156
p312 'Carlo, he reported ...' ACS Segreteria Particolare del Duce. Carteggio riservato Busta 77
    'A police trap ...' see Segre, 1987
    'The women among them ...' see Allason, 1976
    'a Jewish conspiracy ...' Stille, 1992, p. 101
    'Nello's good fortune ...' Belardelli, 2007, p. 176
p314 'On 14 June ...' Lamb, 1997, p. 105
p315 'Italians, he told ...' Hughes, 2011, p. 488
p316 '"For fascism ..."' Franzinelli, 2007, p. 43
    'An unnerving incident ...' see Salvemini, 1937
p317 'The delegate of the ...' Caroline Moorehead, *Dunant's Dream*, New York, 1999, p. 310
    'In England ...' Bernabei, 1997, p. 130
    'As one English ...' ACS Min DGPS.AGR C1b14
p318 '"The war in Africa ..."' Segreteria Particolare del Duce, Carteggio riservato Rosselli, Carlo and Nello, Busta 77
    A new pact of unity ... Bechelloni, 2001, p. 98
p319 'Carlo was also having ...' (ed.) Grasso, 2004, p. XXXIV
    'One of the many ...' see Bardi, 1932
p320 'What Carlo did not know ...' ACS Min Int Direzione Polizia Politica Fasc b 141 K/10
    'With the bickering ...' Carlo to Dolci, 17 September 1935
    'It was time for ...' *Quaderni di Giustizia e Libertà*, 12 January 1935
    'He wanted, he said ...' (ed.) Bagnoli, 2007, p. 16
p321 '"In our life ..."' Marion to Carlo, 18 July 1934
p322 'Bellavia, spy no. ...' ACS Min Int Direzione Polizia Politica, Rosselli C. A.
p326 'As a present ...' ACS Min Int Casetta Politica centrale, Busta 1205
    'There were walks ...' Silvia and Paola Rosselli, conversation with author
p327 '"Otherwise, tell me ..."' Amelia to Marion, 5 October 1935

Chapter Eighteen: A Free Man Again

p328 'Ciano, newly elected ...' see Bosworth, 2002, see also Attanasio, 1974; Mangilli-Climpson, 1985
p329 '"We declare ..."' *Giustizia e Libertà*, 31 July 1936
p330 'Borrowing a white ...' see Carlo Rosselli, 1988
p333 'He would return ...' Carlo to Marion, 31 August 1936
'While Britain and France ...' *Giustizia e Libertà*, 3 July 1936
p334 '"Companions, brothers ..."' Carlo Rosselli, 1938
'Four days later ...' Guerri, 1979, p. 249
p336 '"Do you think ..."' Marion to Amelia, 4 January 1937
p337 'Mussolini cut short ...' *Il Popolo d'Italia*, 19 June 1937
p338 'He spoke wistfully ...' Carlo Rosselli, 1944, p. LXVIII
p339 'Carlo's dossier ...' Franzinelli, 2007, p. 427
'Report after report...' Archives Nationales, F/7/14747, 'Organisations italiennes'
'In Florence ...' ACS Rosselli, Sabatino, Enrico, CPC4422
p340 'For all his chronic ...' Fiori, 1999, p. 193
p341 'In Florence, fascist ...' Hainsworth, 2000
p342 'He compared the ...' Pugliese, 1999, p. 211
p343 'The French political ...' Archives Nationales, F/7/14683–4
p346 'Carlo was writing ...' *Giustizia e Libertà*, 9 June 1937
p348 'On 4 June ...' ACS Min Int Casellare Politico Centrale 4421
p349 'On Wednesday ...' see Franzinelli, 2007

Chapter Nineteen: A Corneillian Tragedy

p351 **Mirtillino, hearing** ... John Rosselli, 'Death of My Father', August 1960, private papers
p352 **The first telegram** ... Silvia and Paola Rosselli, conversation with author
p353 'In Regina Coeli ...' Ernesto Rossi, 2001, p. 157
'Writing about Carlo ...' Emilio Lussu, *Il Ponte*, June 1947
p354 'The funeral ...' Levi, 2002, p. 208
p355 'These rumours ...' *The Times*, 12 June 1937
p356 'In letter after letter ...' Milza, *Le fascisme italien*, p. 335
'It was by becoming ...' Max Ascoli, *The Nation*, July 1937
p357 'From Alberto Moravia ...' Silvia and Paola Rosselli, conversation with author
p359 'Amelia, wrote Sandro ...' Pugliese, 1999, p. 221
'Her first decision ...' Amelia to Gina Lombroso, 26 June 1937
'She told friends ...' Amelia to the Ferreros, 28 August 1938
p361 '"She sought vengeance ..."' John Rosselli, op. cit.
'"There is no good ..."' Marion to Max Ascoli, 22 February 1939
p362 'Early in May ...' see Cannistraro and Sullivan, 1995
p363 'The Duce himself ...' Diggins, 1972, p. 62

p364 'Max Ascoli had turned ...' Max Ascoli papers, Howard Gotlieb Archival Research Centre, Box 203, Folder 1
'Salvemini had spent ...' Salvemini, 1936, p.xii
p365 'If Amelia worried ...' Marion to Cividallis, 10 October 1940
'She regarded her own ...' see Aldo Rosselli, 1983
p366 'Over time, schisms ...' *Guistizia e Libertà*, IRT, sezione V1, Fasc.1, Scatola 13
p367 'In September 1944 ...' see Moseley, 1999
p369 'But then Moravia ...' Moravia, 1951, p. 250
Prepared to sacrifice ... Moravia, 1951, p. 217
p370 'Every one of ...' Gilmour, 2011, p. 305
p372 'But, Calamandrei ...' Calamandrei, 1977, p. 73

Index

Italic page numbers refer to illustrations

Abyssinian wars: (1895–96) 17, 35, 43; (1935–36) 315–18, 328, 341
Acerbo, Giacomo 113
Acerbo Law 113, 114
Acton, Sir Harold 60
Ada (cook) 140–41, 146
Addis Ababa 316, 318
Addis Ababa, Treaty of (1896) 17
Adowa, Battle of (1896) 17, 43
Aeolus, King of Winds (mythological figure) 203
aeronautics see aviation
Albania 50, 108
Albertini, Luigi 88, 164
Albini, Ettore 167, 210
Alençon, France 349
Alfonso XIII, King of Spain 292
Allason, Barbara 310, 312, 340
Alleanza Nazionale 293
Almanacco della Donna Italiana, prize-giving committee 110
Almudévar, Spain 335
Alpini military corps 53, 55–7, 74, 120, 330
Amendola, Giovanni: appearance and character 36, 117, 144; rising political star 36; attacked by Mussolini's supporters 109, 124; Aventine Secession 116–17; Unione Nazionale movement 118; publication of memorandum on Matteotti murder 134; further violent attacks by fascists 143–4; death 150; reactions and aftermath 155, 177, 319
Amsterdam, Olympic Games (1928) 268
Ancona 46, 85
Andermatt, Switzerland 257
Andrea Doria (warship) 67
Anfuso, Filippo 344–5, 367–8
Angeloni, Giale 209
Angeloni, Mario 209, 330, 332
Anima (play; Amelia Rosselli) 15–16, 17–18, 20, 27, 38
Ansaldo, Giovanni 165, 166, 170, 174, 221, 355
anti-clericalism 32, 36, 49
anti-semitism 9, 15, 85, 111, 297–8, 312, 340–41, 362, 367; in France 297–8, 343; in Germany 137, 340
Antibes, France 323
Antonini, Giacomo 318, 330, 345
Aosta 237, 238
Aosta, Prince Amadeo, Duke d' 34, 88, 90, 180
Arditi (Italian army special force) 67, 68, 78, 83, 225
Arezzo 82, 130
Arpinati, Leandro 160
Arturo (gardener) 141
Ascaso column (Spanish Civil War militia) 330–32, 334, 335
Ascoli, Max 359, 362, 364
Asquith, H.H. (later 1st Earl of Oxford and Asquith) 122
Assunta (housekeeper) 30, 31, 41, 59

Astor, Nancy, Viscountess 250
Atatürk, Mustafa Kemal 89
Atlantic Monthly (magazine) 240
Augustus, Roman Emperor 271
Austria, Republic of 314–15
Austro-Hungarian Empire: control of Venice 2–3, 6, 45; Italian War of 1859 3; under Emperor Franz Joseph 14–15; anti-Austrian feeling in Italy 45, 49; First World War 47, 48–9, 51–2, 61, 63; surrender 63; dismantled 67; *see also* Vienna
Avanti! (newspaper) 26, 33, 154, 161, 167, 193; Mussolini's editorship 36–37, 46, 49
Aventine Secession 116–17, 118, 122, 125, 131, 161, 208
aviation 257, 269–70, 304, 329; *see also* leafleting flights
Azaña, Manuel 292

Baden-Powell, Robert, 1st Baron 180
Badoglio, Pietro 366
Bagno a Ripoli 59, 73; L'Apparita 243, 244, 306, 339–40, 367, 370
Bagnoles-de-l'Orne, France 342, 345, 346–52, 357
Baillet, François 346, 349
Bakunin, Mikhail 73, 111, 136, 174, 260
Balabanoff, Angelica 181
Balbo, Italo: *ras* of Ferrara 84–5, 148; aviation minister 131, 269–70, 284
Baldwin, Stanley (*later* 1st Earl Baldwin of Bewdley) 333
Balilla (fascist youth organisation) *see* Opera Nazionale Balilla
Banchelli, Umberto 82–3
Bandinelli, Napoleone 145
Barbusse, Henri 70
Barcelona 292, 329, 330, 334, 355
Bari 85, 267
Barzini, Luigi 267
Bassanesi, Giovanni: appearance and character 255, *256*, 296; background and early life 255; leafleting flight over Milan 255–8, 274, 294; secret police reports on 284, 294; visits Spain following

establishment of Second Republic 292; arrested attempting further leafleting flight 294, 295, 296; later life 296, 339, 371
Basso, Luigi 208
Battaglie Fasciste (newspaper) 136, 144–5
Bauer, Adele 286
Bauer, Riccardo: appearance and character 97, 164, 280; academic career 97; editorship of *Il Caffè* magazine 97, 143; distribution of *Non Mollare* underground newspaper 134; role in escape network 164, 166; capture and imprisonment 166, 170, 193; released 216, 280; resumed anti-fascist operations 216, 280–82, 285; caught in secret police trap 285–6; trial and imprisonment 289–91, 319, 353; reaction to Rosselli brothers' deaths 353; released 366; serves with partisans during wartime 366
Beaulieu-sur-Mer, France 343
Becciolini, Giovanni 145, *145*
Becco Giallo, Il (Italian exiles' newspaper) 247
Bedford College, London 99
Beethoven, Ludwig 298; *Fifth Symphony* 326; *Seventh Symphony* 297, 354, 359, 373
Bellavia, Vincenzo 283, 322, 329, 342, 345, 357
Benda, Julien 322
Benedict XV, Pope 50
Bennett, Arnold 22
Berenson, Bernard 60, 142
Berenson, Mary 142
Bergamo 281
Berlin 136–7, 142
Berneri, Camillo 252, 254, 329, 330, 355
Bertollini, Agata 209
Besneux, Hélène 349–50, 357
biennio rosso (1919–20) 76, 93–4
Binazzi, Pasquale and Zelmira 210
Bini, Livio 283
Birmingham 107
Bizerta, Tunisia 236
blackshirts *see squadristi*

Blum, Léon 297, 333, 343, 356
Boccherini, Luigi 2
Bocchini, Arturo: appearance and character 162–3, *163*; background and early life 162; Mussolini's appointment as chief of police 162; protection of Mussolini and implementation of public security measures 162–3, 280; attempts to stop Filippo Turati's escape 167; reorganisation of state police and establishment of OVRA 182, 273–4; treatment of *confinati* 190, 209, 234, 240; surveillance of Italian exile communities 250–53, 282–4, 311–12; and bombing of Milan trade fair 274, 282; targeting of Giustizia e Libertà movement 282–9, 310; orders surveillance of Matteotti family 305; thwarts further assassination attempts on Mussolini 310–311; deployment of spy 'Pitigrilli' 311–14; continued surveillance of Carlo Rosselli 334, 338–9, 342, 345; reaction to deaths of Rosselli brothers 352, 354, 356, 357; death 371
Bocconi University, Milan 68, 101, 111–12, 157, 158
Bologna 4, 63, 84, 85, 109, 160, 161, 268, 273
Bolshevism 69, 75–6, 88, 105, 177–8, 343
Bondi, Antonio (agent 'Arsace') 283, 339, 354
Bongiorno, Edoardo 226, 229, 234
Bonomi, Ivanoe 89, 247
Bonservizi, Nicola 247–8, 253
Bordeaux 13
Bordello, Antonio 193
Bordiga, Amadeo 198
Borella, Aldo 283
Borgo San Lorenzo 306
Boselli, Paolo 199–200
Boston 364
Bouvyer, Jean-Marie 345–6, 349, 357, 368
Bove, Lorenzo da 168
boxing (sport) 179
Breton, André 355–6
Briand, Aristide 168, 248

Brichetti, Enrico 334
British Empire Exhibition (1924–25) 121
Browning, Elizabeth Barrett 25
Browning, Robert 7, 21
Bruna (nanny) 348
Brussels 253
Bubi (terrier) 276
Buemi, Michele 197–8
Burgos, Spain 333
Buvone, Domenico 311
Byron, George, 6th Baron 7

Cabiati, Attilio 101
Cadorna, Luigi 51, 61
Caffè, Il (magazine) 97, 143, 164
Cagliari 206
Cagoule, La (French fascist group) 343–4; assassination of Rosselli brothers 345–6, 349–50, 357, 368, 369
Calamandrei, Piero 74, 83, 93, 137, 161, 276, 342, 368, 371–2
Calosso, Umberto 331, 332
Calvi, Corsica 168–9
Cambridge 361
Campolini, Carlo 138
Canale, Mauro 371
Cannata, Francesco 210, 226, 230, 231, 234
Cannes 135, 150
Cantoni, Laura *see* Orvieto, Laura
Cap d'Antibes, France 292
Cap Ferrat, France 323
Caporetto, Battle of (1917) 61, 64, 84
Capponi, Contessa Luisa 72
Carboni, Giacomo 367
Carducci, Giosuè 34
Carlo Pisacane nel Risorgimento Italiano (Nello Rosselli) 243, 264, 275
Carlyle, Thomas 79; *History of the French Revolution* 204
Carnia 54, 55
Carrara 85, 160, 169
Carter, Barbara 185–6, 238
Casavolta, Nicola 316
Caserta 60, 61
Casina di Aldo, La (children's home) 58–9, 62, 72

castor oil, forcible administration of xiii, 78, 82, 84

Catholic Church: and fascist regime 88, 91, 113, 116, 117, 266–7, 273, 320–21; and Spanish Civil War 328; *see also* papacy

Cattaneo, Carlo 143

Cave, Ernest 99, 224, 229

Cave, Marion: appearance and character 99–100, *183*, 291, *324*, *347*, *363*; background and early life 99; ill health 99, 149, 175, 218, 238, 250, 291–3, 323, 326, 358, 361; travels to Italy 99, 240; joins Circolo di Cultura group in Florence 99–100; involvement in Italia Libera movement 120, 121, 123, 138–9; works for *Non Mollare* underground newspaper 134; at Gaetano Salvemini's trial 139; courtship with Carlo Rosselli 149, 150, 156; marriage and honeymoon 158, 172; travels to Stresa and Portofino with Carlo 158–9; early married life in Milan 159, 164, 165; first pregnancy 165, 175; assists Carlo's escape network 166; Carlo's arrest and imprisonment 170, 174–5; birth of son Giovanni ('Mirtillino') 177, *183*; Carlo's trial 171, 184, 185, 186; joins Carlo during *confino* on Lipari 203, 210–214; visits England with son 218; returns to Lipari 218, 220, 225–6; assistance with Carlo's escape plans 223, 224, 230, 238; second pregnancy 230, 231, 237, 250; leaves Lipari 230; arrest and imprisonment following Carlo's escape 237; successful campaign for release 237–9; family establishes home in Paris 249–50; secret police's surveillance of 252, 284, 299; birth of daughter Melina 255; refused passport to visit London 262; third pregnancy 263, 278; family life in Paris 278, 291, 299, 321–3, 326, 337, 341; birth of son Andrea 291–2; recuperation in south of France 292–3; Carlo arrested and imprisoned during attempted leafleting flight 295–6; deaths of Filippo Turati and Claudio Treves 301; family holidays 310, 323–7, *324*, 336; in Paris while Carlo fights in Civil War in Spain 329, 330, 333; cares for Carlo on return from Spain 336; last holiday with Carlo 342–3; with Carlo on convalescence trip to Bagnoles 342, 346–8, *347*; returns to Paris alone 349; learns of Carlo's death 351; travels to Normandy 351–2; identification of body 352; at Carlo and Nello's wake and funeral 353, 354; life as widow in Paris 355, 356–7, 358–9; stays with sister-in-law in Switzerland and England 359, 361; suffers strokes 361, 368; family leaves Europe for United States following outbreak of war 361, 362, *363*; life in New York 365–6; returns to Italy after war 368–70; death 370

Cavour, Camillo Benso, Count of 3, 10

Ceruti (*confinato* on Lipari) 209

Ceva, Elena 288, 289

Ceva, Umberto 280, 285–6, 287–9, *288*

Chamberlain, Sir Austen 316

Charles-Roux, François 87

Christian Democratic Party 371

Churchill, Sir Winston 181, 316

Cianca, Alberto: appearance and character 248–9; journalism career 247; in exile in Paris 247, 254; founder member of Giustizia e Libertà movement 248–9, 335; involvement in plots and stunts 254, 255, 338; learns of Rosselli brothers' deaths 351; at their funeral 354; continues work at Giustizia e Libertà 356; in New York during wartime 364, 366; returns to Italy to serve with partisans 366

Ciano, Edda (*née* Mussolini) 37, 271, 272

Ciano, Galeazzo: background, appearance and character 271, 344; marriage to Edda Mussolini 271; early political career 271, 321, 344; foreign minister 328, 333, 344, 345; and Spanish Civil War 328, 333, 337; surveillance of Carlo Rosselli in Spain 334; as potential successor to Mussolini 334, 344; and assassination of Rosselli brothers 344, 357, 367, 368; death 367

Circolo di Cultura (intellectual cooperative group) 75, 83, 92, 93, 98–100, 111, 129–30

Civadalli family 59, 362

Civadalli, Gualtiero 59

Civitavecchia 85, 210

Clerkenwell, London 102, 103

Clermont Ferrand, France 344

Cocteau, Jean 322

Cole, G.D.H. 102

Colle Isarco 177

Commento, Il (newspaper) 104, 121

Communist Party (Italian) 80, 87, 113, 162, 246; members sent to internal exile 189, 192–3, 198, 208, 213–14, 273

Como, San Donnino prison 170, 174, 175, 213

concentration camps 302, 362

Concentrazione Antifascista (exile organisation) 246–8, 278, 299–300, 318–19

Condor Legion (German military unit) 333

confino, il (internal exile) 161, 176, 188–90, 207–210, 371; pardons 221; *see also* penal islands

Consiglio Nazionale delle Donne (fascist women's organisation) 111

Consolo, Gustavo: arrest and trial 135, 136; murdered 146, 147, 149, 185

Conti, Antonio 99

contraception 91, 180

Corfu incident (1923) 108

Cornellia Africana 211

Corre, Aristide 343, 345–6, 350

Corriere della Sera (newspaper) 45, 88, 164, 223, 257, 267

Corriere Italiano (newspaper) 118

Corsica 167, 168–9, 294

Cortina d'Ampezzo 110, 158

Cortona 135, 146

Costa, Andrea 177

Courmayeur 237

Couterne, Château de, France 349

Cremona 85, 131

Cremonesi, Filippo 241

Crispi, Francesco 16–17, 188

Critica, La (magazine) 274

Critica Fascista (journal) 143, 154

Critica Sociale (journal) 33, 36

Croce, Benedetto 36, 183, 215, 274, 275, 280, 289, 308, 310, 342; drafting of *Manifesto of Antifascist Intellectuals* 161, 162

Cronaca, La (newspaper) 103–4

Croton-on-Hudson, New York 362

Cultura, La (magazine) 310

Curzon, George, 1st Marquess Curzon of Kedleston 66

Cyrenaica *see* Libya

da Ponte, Tommaso 234

DAGR (Divisione Affari Generali e Riservati) 182

Daily Express (London newspaper) 238

Daily Express (New York newspaper) 90

Daily News (New York newspaper) 238

d'Alton, Hélène 346

D'Annunzio, Gabriele 22, 23–4, 67–8, 73, 75, 77, 87, 209, 293

Dante Alighieri 3, 29; *Divine Comedy* 209, 269

Darnand, Joseph 345

Dayton, Katharine, interview with Mussolini 240

De Bono, Emilio 114

de Bosis, Lauro 293–4, 295, 338

de Gasperi, Alcide 371

De Martino, Giacomo 103

de Rosa, Fernando 253–4, 335

death penalty: reinstatement of 161, 162; implementation of 289

Decalogue of Moral Hygiene (fascist) 276

dei Cas, Rina 282

del Re, Carlo 284–7, 289, 290

Deloncle, Eugène 343–4, 346, 368
Desjardins, Paul 323
Di Stefano, Michelangelo 345
Diaz, Armando 61
Disperata (paramilitary *squadra*) 79, 85, *128*
Divisione Affari Generali e Riservati (DAGR) 182
Divisione Polizia Politica *see* Polpol
Dogali, Battle of (1887) 17
Dolci, Gioacchino: appearance and character 207, *224*; background and early life 207; *confino* on Lipari 207, 210, 211; escape plans 222–8; aborted escape attempt 228; pardoned and released 228–9; assistance with other *confinati*'s escape 228–9, 231; involvement in leafleting flight over Milan 256, 257, 258, 294; engagement 322
Dollfuss, Engelbert 315
Donatello, *Marzocco* 22
Donizetti, Gaetano 17
Dopolavoro (national labour agency) 179
Dostoevsky, Fyodor 79, 184; *The Brothers Karamazov* 218
Draper, Ruth 293, 294, 338, 364
Dream V (boat) 229, 231, 232–4, 236
Dumini, Amerigo xiv, 79, 81, 82, 85, 114, 181–2*n*
Duse, Eleonora 24–5, 45

earthquakes 35, 53, 206
Eastbourne, Sussex 361
Ebert, Friedrich 136
Economist (newspaper) 275
Eden, Anthony (*later* 1st Earl of Avon) 304, 333
Edinburgh 121
Edine, Djelal 229
Ehrenburg, Ilya 329
Einaudi, Giulio 310
Einaudi, Luigi 112, 158, 164, 274–5, 310, 340, 373
Eisenstein, Sergei 322
elections, Italian: (1913) 46; (1919) 75; (1921) 80; (1924) xiii, 113–14; (1929) 266
Elena of Montenegro, Queen consort 34, 272, *314*

Elisabeth, Empress of Austria ('Sisi') 14
Emanuele, Santo 344–5, 367–8
Emma Liona (play; Amelia Rosselli) 52, 110
Emmy (nanny) 20
Energie Nuove (magazine) 95
Engels, Friedrich 158; *The Communist Manifesto* 214
Eritrea 17, 315, 316
Erizzo, Francesco 171, 185, 186
Ethiopia 17, 35, 43; Abyssinian War (1935–36) 315–18, 328, 341
Evening Standard (newspaper) 238
Evian, France 323
Exhibition of the Fascist Revolution (1932–34) 303–4

Fabbri, Paolo 209, 226, 232, 234, 241
Fabians 104, 250, 262–3; summer school (London; 1923) 101–2, 104–7, *106*
Facchinetti, Cipriano 249
Facta, Luigi 87, 89
Faenza 154
Farinacci, Roberto 49, 68, 131, 148, 371
fasci movement 49, 68–9, 73, 77, 80, 81–2, 127; overseas branches 103, 121, 253, 304, 363; *see also* Grand Council of Fascism; National Fascist Party; *squadristi*
Fassini, Alberto 339
Fauran, Jacques 346, 349, 368
Favignana 189
Felicità Perduta (novella; Amelia Rosselli) 18
feminism 15, 37–8, 44, 71–2, 110–111, 305
Ferdinand and Isabella, King and Queen of Spain 2
Ferrara 84–5, 148
Ferrero, Gina *see* Lombroso, Gina
Ferrero, Guglielmo 38, 147, 161, 275, 309, 353, 359, 369
Ferrero, Leo 38, 39, 59, 70, 147, 173, 215, 309
Fez, Morocco 13
Fiat (car manufacturer) 99, 103; Fiat 18 BL 77

fiduciari (secret police agents) 251–2
Fiesole 22, 45, 114
Figaro, Le (newspaper) 42
Filippelli, Filippo 126, 134
Filippich (*confinato* on Lipari) 209, 241
Filliol, Jean 344, 346, 349–50, 357, 368
Finzi, Ida (Haydée) 52
First World War: outbreak 47–8; Italian entry 48–50, 51; Italian Front 51–2, 54–8, 61, 63; casualty totals 52, 61, 64, 66; rationing and shortages 59–60; refugees 61–2; end of war 63–4, 66
Fiuggi 237
Fiume 66, 67, 112
Florence: civic pride and characteristics of Florentines 19, 32, 42; post-unification redevelopment 20, 32, 41–2; English-speaking community 21–2, 60; cultural life and clubs 22–3, 25–6, 38, 41–2, 60, 70; strikes and industrial unrest 32; local politics and administration 32–3, 37–8, 46; Jewish community 39–40, 52, 154, 340–41, 367; Red Week riots (1914) 46; during First World War 50, 52, 55, 59–60, 61–2, 63, 64; post-war unrest 66, 69, 72–3, 78–9, 81–2; *fasci* movement 68–9, 78–9, 81–2, 85, 87; first *squadristi* raids 79, 81–2, 99, 109, 127; *seconda ondata* of punitive expeditions 127–30, *128*, *130*, 145–9; St Bartholomew's Night attacks 146–8; subsequent reorganisation of fascist groups 148–9, 153; fascist opponents sent to internal exile 189; cultural and intellectual life under fascists 276–7; remaining anti-fascist networks 280; during Second World War 367; post-war 372
Florence (places and landmarks): Borgo Santi Apostoli 98, 129; British Institute 99, 240; Cemetery delle Porte Sante 123; Liceo Michelangiolo 39, *59*; Lungarni 22, 62, 138, 139; main post office 87, 128; Murate prison 139, 175; National Library 54, 173, 175; Palazzo Frescobaldi 138; Palazzo Vecchio 50, 52, 55, 57, 373; Parco delle Cascine 22–3; Piazza della Signoria 22, 129, 373; Piazza Massimo d'Azeglio 69, 73; Piazza Mentana 125; Piazza Ottaviani 79; Piazza Santa Croce 46; Piazza Santa Maria Novella 128; Piazza Vittorio 49; Ponte Sospeso 81; San Frediano 70, 99, 135; Santa Maria Novella (church) 62; Santa Maria Novella railway station 61, 66; Santa Maria Nuova hospital 120, 147; Teatro della Pergola 79; Teatro Olimpia 68; telephone exchange 87; Trespiano cemetery 373–4; Via Cherubini 20; Via Ferrucci 22; Via Gianbologna 29, 62; Via Giusti 69, 140, 146, 173, 175, 297, 367, 370; Via Jacopo Nardi 124; Via Ricasoli 72; Via San Niccolò 62, 63, 69; Via Tornabuoni 21, 22, 41, 60, 146; *see also* Bagno a Ripoli; Fiesole; Pignone; Rignano sull'Arno; San Domenico; Settignano
Florence university 153, 370, 372; Istituto Cesare Alfieri 65, 84; Istituto di Studi Superiori 34, 62
flying *see* aviation
food shortages and rationing: during First World War 59–60; in penal colonies 196, 218
Forte dei Marmi 309, 334
Forti, Aldo 352, 370
Forti, Francesco 370
Forti, Marco 370
France, Anatole 204
Franco, Francisco 328, 333
Franco, Ramón 292
Franz Ferdinand, Archduke of Austria, assassination 47
Franz Joseph I, Austro-Hungarian Emperor 14
Frassine, Villa Il 25, 48, 75, 140, 141, 306, *307*, 352, 367
Fratelli Minori (novella; Amelia Rosselli) 71
Fratta Polesine 116

Freemasonry 17, 63, 127, 266, 285, 340, 343; fascists' attacks on Freemasons 144–5, 147, 189, 362
Freiburg, Germany 295
Frensham Ponds, Surrey 105
Fresnay, France 322
Freud, Sigmund 15, 30
Frosinone 189; prison 237
Fuchs, Robert 14
Fuga in Quattro Tempi (Carlo Rosselli) 265
Futurist Movement 42–3, 46, 49, 68, 77, 79, 127, 269–70, 304

Garibaldi, Giuseppe 3, 10, 87, 89, 102, 127, 143
Garibaldi Battalion (International Brigades) 336–7
Garosci, Aldo 331, 368
Garvin, J.L. 89
Gasparri, Pietro 261
Gazzetta del Popolo (newspaper) 321
Genoa 11, 76, 114, 152–3
Genoa university, Istituto Superiore di Scienze Economiche e Commerciali 101
Gente Oscura (short-story collection; Amelia Rosselli) 26
Gentile, Giovanni 89, 161–2, 371
Geographical Congress (Venice; 1882) 6
George V, King, state visit to Italy (1923) 92
Gerarchia (magazine) 148
Germani, Giuseppe 305
Ghirlandaio, Domenico 22
Gibson, Violet, assassination attempt on Mussolini 159–60, 303
giellisti see Giustizia e Libertà (anti-fascist resistance movement)
Gillardoni (Milanese doctor) 166
Ginzburg, Leone 309, 310, 311, 312, 366
Giolitti, Giovanni 33–4, 36, 43, 46, 67, 75, 80, 83, 89, 113, 117
Giornale d'Italia, Il (newspaper) 58
Giovanna (maid) 2
Giraudoux, Jean 322
Giustizia, La (newspaper) 123
Giustizia e Libertà (anti-fascist resistance movement): foundation in Paris 248–9, 254; aims, slogan and symbols 249, 282, 326; leafleting flights over Italy 255–8, 292, 294–5; targeted by Italian secret police 282–91, 311–14, 338–9; divisions with other anti-fascist groups 299–301, 318–19, 329; distribution branches in Italy 310; continuation after Rosselli brothers' deaths 356; see also I Quaderni di Giustizia e Libertà
Giustizia e Libertà (newspaper) 320, 321, 323
Goad, Harold 240
Gobetti, Ada (née Prospero) 95, 96, 97, 143, 150, 151
Gobetti, Paolo 150
Gobetti, Piero: appearance and character 94, 94, 95, 96; background and early life 94–5; editorship of Rivoluzione Liberale magazine 95, 96–7, 98, 154; marriage and family 95, 143, 150; arrested for subversion 97–8; on Matteotti's murder and Aventine Secession 117, 118, 119; on Curzio Malaparte 127; attacked by fascists 143, 150; exile and death 150–51, 354; reactions and aftermath 151, 155, 248, 280, 319
Goering, Hermann 304
Goldoni, Carlo 30
Goncourt brothers 21
Gonzales (Milanese lawyer) 171
goose-step march, introduction of 362
Graham, Sir Ronald 90, 118, 121–2
Gramsci, Antonio 93, 95, 238; arrest and trial 162, 192; imprisonment 192, 207, 319; death 341–2
Grand Council of Fascism 91, 148, 315, 366
Grandi, Dino 131
Grañén, Spain 331
Grassini, Emma 5
Grassini, Lina 5
Grassini, Margherita see Sarfatti, Margherita
Great Ormond Street Hospital, London 218

Grenoble 339
Grenoble Centre for Italian Studies, Florence annex 42
Grosseto, *squadristi* raid (June 1921) 82–3
Guadalajara, Battle of (1937) 337–8
Guatelli (*confinato* on Lipari) 209
Guinevere, Queen (legendary figure) 346

Haefner, Viktor 295
Hague Conventions (1899/1907) 42
Haile Selassie, Emperor 318
Halévy, Élie 322
Hamilton, Emma, Lady 52, 110
Hampton Court Palace 261
Harvard University 338
Haydée (Ida Finzi) 52
Heydrich, Reinhard 371
High Commission for Sanctions against Fascism 371
Himmler, Heinrich 371
Hindenburg, Paul von 136
Hindhead, Surrey 104, 105
Hitler, Adolf 181, 262, 340; coming to power 302, 303; visits Italy 302, 314–15, *314*; Nazi involvement in Spanish Civil War 333
Hobhouse, L.T. 102
homosexuality, in penal colonies 196
Huesca, Spain 331–2
Huguet, Louis 345–6, 368

Ibsen, Henrik 27; *The Doll's House* 15, 24
Idea Fissa, L' (play; Amelia Rosselli) 30
Illusione (play; Amelia Rosselli) 26–7
Illustrated London News 262
Impero, L' (newspaper) 143
Impressionism 14
Industrie Femminili (women workers organisation) 26
International Brigades 336; Garibaldi Battalion 336, 337
International Committee of Writers 319
International Geographical Congress (Venice; 1882) 6

interventionist movement (First World War) 48–9
invisible ink, use of 223, 280, 281, 304, 313
Italia Libera (anti-fascist movement) 119–21, 132–3, 281; protests and stunts 123–4, 125, 138–9
Italian American Society 293
Italian Encyclopedia 315
Italian Refugees' Relief Committee (British organisation) 230, 238
Italian Social Republic (Salò) 367

Jaeger gymnastics 4
Jakubiez, Fernand 346, 349–50, 357, 368
James, Henry 21
Jarry, Henri 351
Jewish Youth Convention (Livorno; 1924) 124–5
Jews: Florentine community 39–40, 52, 154, 340–41; Livornese community 9–10; Venetian community 2–3; Viennese community 15; *see also* anti-semitism; racial laws; Zionism
Jones, Lewis 21
Joxe, Françoise and Louis 361
Joyce, James, *Ulysees* 110
Juan-les-Pins, France 310

Kant, Immanuel 225
Keynes, John Maynard, Baron 122; 'A Tract on Monetary Reform' 112
King's College, London 101
Klimt, Gustav 14
Kochnitzky, Léon 68
Konstanz, Germany 294–5; prison 295–6
Ku Klux Klan 343; Italian fascists compared to 90, 276
Kuliscioff, Anna 33, 73, 91–2, *91*, 95–6, 99, 112, 126, 138, 167, 247; death 150, 152, 155, 166

La Spezia 60, 169
Labour Party (British) 101, 107, 115, 121, 122, 262
Lampedusa 189
Lamy, Alice 346, 349

Lancelot (legendary knight) 346
language, fascist reforms of 178
Larchmont, New York 364–6
Lateran Accords (1929) 266–7
Lausanne, Switzerland 264
Lausanne, Treaty of (1923) 90
Laval, Pierre 297
Lawrence, D.H. 6
Lazzarini (*confinato* on Lipari) 209
leafleting flights, anti-fascists' 255–8, 274, 292, 293–5, 296, 338–9
League of Human Rights (France) 245
League of Nations 67, 108, 316, 317, 318
League for the Renewal of National Unity 73
Lear, Edward 21
Leith, Scotland 121
Lenin, Vladmir 89; Leninism 69
Leonardo da Vinci Society 23, 52, 341
Leonardo (magazine) 25–6, 36
Leto, Guido 282
Levi family 5–6
Levi, Alessandro 70–71, 95, 138–9, 154, 170, 175, 184, 264, 275, 276, 353
Levi, Augusto 5
Levi, Carlo 96, 216, 243, 261, 311, 312, 313, 366; attends Fabian summer school in England 104–7, 106; *Christ Stopped at Eboli* 313
Levi, Mario 310, 312
Levi, Nina 5
Levi, Nino 140
Levi, Primo 367
Levi, Sarina 138–9, 154, 211–12, 353
Libertà, La (Italian exiles' newspaper) 237, 247
Libya 148, 315, 337; Libyan War (1911–12) 42–4, 50, 191
Lipari, penal colony 188, 189, 190, 202–14, 218–31, 234–5, 240, 290
Littorio, Il (newspaper) 157
Livorno 9–10, 80, 130; Jewish Youth Convention (1924) 124–5
Lloyd George, David (*later* 1st Earl Lloyd-George of Dwyfor) 122
Lodano, Switzerland 255, 256

Lofting, Hugh, *Dr Doolittle* 322
Lombroso, Gina: appearance and character 38; marriage and family 38; career 38; friendship with Amelia Rosselli 38–9, 212, 359; establishes children's charity with Amelia 60; views on women's suffrage 72; death of son 309; death 369
London: Rosselli family banking interests 9–10; Mazzini's exile 10–11, 102; Joe and Amelia Rosselli's honeymoon (1892) 13; Mussolini visits (1923) 90; Italian community 90, 92, 102–4, 121, 262–3, 304, 317; Marion Cave's early life in 99; Carlo Rosselli visits (1923/24) 101–2, 104–5, 107–8, 121–2; Marion Cave visits with son (1928/29) 218, 230; Carlo's speaking tour (1929) 250; Nello's research trip (1930) 260–66
London School of Economics 250
London, Treaty of (1915) 50, 66
Longanesi, Leo 132
Louisiana 191
Lucca 82, 130
Lucetti, Gino, assassination attempt on Mussolini 160
Luchaire, Fernande *see* Salvemini, Fernande
Luchaire, Jean 59, 70, 139
Luchaire, Julien 42, 59
Luchini, Alberto 100
Lugano, Lake 11, 312
Lugano, Switzerland 165–6, 257, 281–2
Lupi di Toscana (infantry division) 337
Luporini, Giovanni 145–6, 147
Lussu, Emilio: appearance and character 206, 224, 225, 233; background and early life 206, 225; *confino* on Lipari 206–7, 211, 214; escape plans 207, 222–8; aborted first attempt 228; renewed escape planning 228–31; escapes from Lipari 231–5, 233; reaches Tunis 233–4, 236; travels to Paris 236–7, 248; publishes article on imprisonment and

escape 240; early role in exile community in Paris 248, 253, 254, 278–9, 304; director of Giustizia e Libertà movement 249, 277, 282, 303; secret police's surveillance of 151–2, 283–4, 311; life in Paris 299; relationship with Joyce Salvadori 299; leaves Paris for convalescence 319; last meeting with Carlo Rosselli 342; reaction to Rosselli brothers' deaths 353; at their funeral 354; continues work with Giustizia e Libertà 356; in New York during wartime 364, 366; returns to Italy to serve with partisans 366; testifies at trial for Rosselli killings 368; at Carlo and Nello's reburial in Florence 373; later life and career 371

Lussu, Joyce 299

Luzzatti, Vittorio 185, 186

Lyceum Clubs 38; Florentine chapter 38, 44, 45, 52, 72, 110, 111, 276, 341; International Congress (Florence; 1922) 111

McCall's (magazine) 363

MacDonald, Ramsay 115, 122, 262

Machiavelli, Niccolò 3

Macugnaga 47

Madrid 13, 292–3, 333

Maeterlinck, Maurice, *The Blue Bird* 72

Maffi, Cardinal Pietro 130

Mafia 266, 267

Magri, Mario 209–10, 222

Mahler, Gustav 14

Malaparte, Curzio (Kurt Erich Suckert) 127

Malraux, André 322, 329

Manchester Guardian (newspaper) 140, 185, 186, 238, 250, 289

manganelli (weapons) 77, 78, 103; La Madonna del Manganello statue 130

Manifesto of Antifascist Intellectuals 161

Manifesto of Fascist Intellectuals 161

Manifesto of Racial Scientists 362

Manin, Daniele 3

Mann, Thomas 289

Mannin, Ethel 305

Manzoni, Alessandro 95, 143

March on Rome, Mussolini's (1922) 86, 87–8; tenth anniversary commemoration 303–4

Marchetti, Ferruccio 140

Margherita of Savoy, Queen consort (*later* Queen mother) 6, 88

Margulies, Samuel Hirsch 39

Mariani, Teresa 26

Mariapò (maid) 140–41, 146

Marie José of Belgium, Princess 253, 272

Marinetti, Filippo Tommaso 42, 49, 68, 79, 269–70, 316, 371

Marseilles 227, 229, 236, 251

Marx, Karl 158; *The Communist Manifesto* 214

Marxism 11, 33, 80, 96, 214, 278, 279

Mary, Queen consort, state visit to Italy 92

Marzocco, Il (magazine) 22–3, 24, 25–6, 28, 38, 44

Massa 169

Matteotti, Giacomo: appearance and character xiii, 96, *115*; member of parliament 78, 115; expulsion from Socialist Party and establishment of United Socialist Party 93, 119; marriage and family 96; with anti-fascist circle in Turin 96; anti-fascist publications xiii, 96; visits England 115–16; speech to Chamber of Deputies (30 May 1924) xiii–xiv, 116; kidnap and murder xiv, 116, *116*, 126, 134; reactions and aftermath xiv–xv, 116–18, 121, 126, 131, 133, 138–9, 181n, 205–6, 248, 293, 319, 355–6

Matteotti, Isabella xiv, 96, 116, 305

Matteotti, Velia xiv, 96, 116, 205–6, 304–6

Matteotti Battalion (Spanish Civil War militia) 335

Mazzini, Giuseppe: appearance, character and career 3, 10–11, 102, 185, 204; Rosselli family's admiration of xv, 11, 26, 40, 49,

96, 133, 155–6, 164; Nello
Rosselli's writings on 73, 100,
111, 136, 152, 173, 174, 260, 310
Mazzini e Bakunin (Nello Rosselli)
152, 174, 260
Mazzini Society (United States) 366
Meinecke, Friedrich 137
Memmi, Alberto 197–8
Menapace, Ermanno 254
Menelik II, Emperor of Ethiopia 17
Messina 68, 222; earthquake (1908)
35
Messina university 35
Mieli, Virginia 17, 26
Mila, Massimo 298
Milan: foundation of fascist
movement 68; industrial unrest
76; falls to fascists 85, 87;
fascists' suppression of local
opposition 114; establishment of
secret police inspectorate 182,
273, 274; anti-fascists' leafleting
flight over 255–8, 274, 294;
anarchist bombing of trade fair
274, 282, 284; remaining anti-
fascist networks 280–82, 310
Milan (places and landmarks): Alfa
Romeo car plant 76; La Scala
161, 165, 179; Manzoni Theatre
45; Piazza del Duomo xiv, 33, 95;
Piazza Duse 167; Piazza San
Sepolcro 68; San Vittore prison
155, 167; Via Borghetto 159; Via
Silvio Pellico 282; *see also*
Bocconi University; Università
Proletaria
Milazzo 204, 208, 218
Milizia Volontaria per la Sicurezza
Nazionale (MVSN) 91
Milne, A.A., *Winnie the Pooh* 322
Mitterrand, François 344
Mitterrand, Robert 344
Modena 3, 54
Molfetta 34, 109
Moll, Carl 14
monarchy, Italian 34; and fascist
regime 90, 253, 272–3; *see also*
Umberto I, King; Victor
Emmanuel III, King
Mondo, Il (newspaper) 126, 247
Montanelli, Giuseppe 340

Monte Amiato, Siele mercury mine 69
Monte Carlo 13; casino 18, 229
Monte Pelato, Battle of (1936) 332
Montecatini 144
Monteleone, La Madonna del
Manganello 130
Monteverdi, Claudio 7
Montreal 362
Montreux, Switzerland 264, 336, 359
Moral Hygiene, Decalogue of 276
Moravia, Alberto: childhood and
early life 46, 80, 110; suffers
tuberculosis of the bones 46, 110;
treatment in sanatorium 110, 158;
writing and publication of *Gli
indifferenti* 158, 263; visits Nello
and Carlo Rosselli in London and
Paris 263; burns Rosselli letters to
avoid arrest 312; response to
sacking from *Gazzetta del Popolo*
321; silence following Rosselli
brothers' deaths 357, 369; *Le
ambizioni sbagliate* 321; *Il
conformista* 369
Morgan, Thomas B. 240
Mori, Cesare 84
Morpurgo, Giacomo 54, 57, 58, 66
Morzine, France 327
Mosley, Lady Cynthia 304
Mosley, Sir Oswald 304, 344
Mozart, Wolfgang Amadeus 2, 14
Munich 136
Murray, Gilbert 250
Mussolini, Arnaldo xiii, 118, 125,
181, 269
Mussolini, Benito: appearance 36, 68,
86, *113*, *241*, *272*; background
and early life 36; editor of *Avanti!*
36–7, 46; marriage and family 37,
67, 271, 272; mistresses 37, 171,
181, 271; opposition to Libyan
War 43; imprisonment for public
order offences 43; secures
dominance over revolutionary
wing of Socialist Party 46–7;
resigns from *Avanti!* and founds *Il
Popolo d'Italia* 49; adopts
interventionist position on Italian
entry to war 49; foundation of
fascism 67–9, 73, 103; failure in
1919 elections 75; challenges

Gaetano Salvemini to duel 75; elected to parliament 80–81; rise to power 83–7, 99; marches on Rome 86, 87–8; becomes prime minister 87–8; first cabinet and early months of government 89–92, 101, 104, 110–11, *113*, 119–20; suppression of opposition 101, 109, 112–13, 114, 117–18, 125–6, 143–4, 145, 148, 152, 182; Corfu incident 108; Acerbo Law and 1924 election victory xiii, 113–14; murder of Giacomo Matteotti xiii–xv, 116–17, 118, 126, 131, 134; triumphant speech to Chamber of Deputies (3 January 1925) 130–32; new fascist-dominated cabinet 131; development of personality cult 132, 178, 303–4; Zaniboni assassination plot 152; *l'anno Napoleonico* (1926) and establishment of dictatorship 159, 160–64; further assassination attempts 159–61, 303, 310–11; anger at Filippo Turati's escape from Italy 167, 169; development of totalitarian state 177–83, 188–9, 266–76, 302, 304; response to 'Trial of the Professors' verdict 187; agrees to free Nello Rosselli from *confino* 199–200; issuing of *confino* pardons 221; reaction to escape of *confinati* from Lipari 234, 235, 237, 240–41, 250–53; and anti-fascists' leafleting flights 257, 294, 296; moves personal office to Palazzo Venezia 270–71; targeting of anti-fascist exile groups 285, 286, 289, 290, 319; relations with Hitler 302, 314–15, 333; speaks at Exhibition of the Fascist Revolution 303–4; Abyssinian war 315–18; banning of Moravia's new novel 321; ally of Franco in Civil War 328, 333; response to defeat of fascist forces at Battle of Guadalajara 337–8; views on Jews and anti-semitism 340, 362; introduction of race laws 362;

ousted from power 366; Salò Republic 367; death 368
Mussolini, Edda *see* Ciano, Edda
Mussolini, Rachele 37, 67, 271, 272
MVSN (Milizia Volontaria per la Sicurezza Nazionale) 91

Nantes 361
Naples, Capodimonte 41
Napoleon Bonaparte, Emperor 2, 6; Mussolini compared to 122, 240
Nathan family 10, 11
Nathan, Ernesto 11, 17, 193; mayor of Rome 29, 37, 45; military service 53
Nathan, Henrietta *see* Rosselli, Henrietta
Nathan, Mary 57
Nathan, Mayer Moses 11
Nathan, Sarina 10, 11
National Congress of Italian Women 37–8
National Education, Ministry of 269
National Fascist Party: formation 81; rise to power 81–8; first months in power 89–92, 101, 104, 112–13; Acerbo Law and 1924 election victory xiii, 113–14; expulsion of Florentine members following St Bartholomew's Night attacks 148; 'exceptional laws' and establishment of one-party state 160–64, 188–9; consolidation of one-party state 302, 304; *see also* Grand Council of Fascism
National Institute of Fascist Culture 161–2
National Liberal Club, London 107, 250
National Union of Italian Women 72
Nationalist Association, Italian 42–3
Nazi Germany 181, 302, 314–15, 333, 340, 361, 366
Nazione, La (newspaper) 32, 41
Neera (Anna Radius Zuccari) 26
Nenni, Pietro: background and character 154; friendship with Carlo Rosselli 154, 165; their publication of anti-fascist newspaper 154–5; arrest 155,

157; exile 166, 183, 303, 321;
Spanish Civil War 335, 353;
reaction to Carlo's death 353
Nérac, France 246
New Deal (United States) 304
New School for Social Research,
New York 364
New Statesman (magazine) 98
New York 293, 362–6
New York Times 294
Niccoli, Alfredo 75
Nice 135, 169, 339, 344
Nicolson, Sir Harold 66, 108, 262
Night of St Bartholomew (1925)
146–8
Nightingale, Florence 25
Nitti, Antonia 247
Nitti, Francesco Fausto: appearance
and character 205, *224*, *233*;
background and early life 202,
205–6; *confino* on Lipari 202,
206, 211, 214, 220; escape plans
207, 222–8; aborted first attempt
228; renewed escape planning
228–31; escapes from Lipari
231–5, *233*; reaches Tunis 233–4,
236; travels to Paris 236–7, 248;
produces book on imprisonment
and escape 240, 263; exile in
Paris 248, 278–9, 322; director of
Giustizia e Libertà movement 249,
277; secret police's surveillance of
251–2
Nitti, Francesco Saverio 66, 109,
202, 245, 247, 249
Nitti, Luigia 322
Nitti, Vincenzo 249
Noi Giovani (magazine) 59
Non Mollare (underground
newspaper) 132–6, 143, 144–5,
149, 248
North American Review (journal)
240
Nostra Bandiera, La (Jewish
newspaper) 341
Noufflard, André and Berthe 322
Novara 85
Nudi, Francesco 182, 273, 274, 282,
288
Nuova Rivista Storica (journal) 111
Nuovo Giornale (magazine) 129

Observer (newspaper) 81, 89, 98
Odin, René (agent 'Togo') 312
Oeuvre, L' (Paris newspaper) 337
Ojetti, Ugo 57
Olympic Games, Amsterdam (1928)
268
Opera Nazionale Balilla (fascist
youth organisation) 179–80, *179*,
268, 315
Orano, Paolo 341
Orbetello lagoon 269
Ordine Nuovo, L' (newspaper) 93
Orlando, Vittorio 66, 75, 89
Orléans (French ship) 198
Orvieto 204
Orvieto, Adolfo 5–6, 22–3
Orvieto, Angiolo 5–6, 22–5, 45,
52–3, 60, 141, 154, 275, 276, 341
Orvieto, Annalia 23, 52
Orvieto, Laura (*née* Cantoni):
appearance and character 23, 71;
background and early life 23;
marriage and family 23, 45;
friendship with Amelia Rosselli
23, 25, 27, 31, 38–9, 44, 52, 59,
111, 154, 276; and Eleonora Duse
24–5; writings 28, 44, 341
Orvieto, Leonfrancesco 23, 45, 59
Ottoman Empire 42–3, 66, 90;
Libyan War (1911–12) 42–3
Ouida (Maria Louise Ramé) 22
OVRA (secret police) 182, 251,
273–4, 282–4, 339, 371
Oxford 107
Oxilia, Italo 167–8, 183–4, 223, 229,
231, 233, 236, 252

Padua university 2
Pagani, Bruna 225, 227, 228
Paget, Walburga, Lady 21
Palermo 191; Ucciardone prison
176–7, 198
Palestine 362
Pankhurst, Sylvia 238, 305, 318, 319
Pantelleria 189
papacy 8, 9, 50, 88, 267, 268, 273,
275–6; *see also* Catholic Church
Papini, Giovanni 25, 36
Paris: Carlo Rosselli visits as young
man 101; Italian exiles in 142,
150, 153, 184, 245–8, *246*,

278–9, 299–300, 318–19; *fascio* branch 253; Carlo arrives in after escape from Lipari 236–7, 248; Carlo's family establishes home in 249–50, 291, 298, 321–3; surveillance of exile community 251–3, 282–4, 299, 311–12, 316–17, 319, 329–30, 339; Rosselli brothers' funeral 353–5
Paris Commune 111
Parma 3, 85–6, 87
Parri, Esther 184, 186, 212–13, 218, 232
Parri, Ferruccio: appearance and character 97, 164, 185, 213; background and early life 97, 164, 185; editorship of *Il Caffè* magazine 97, 143; distribution of *Non Mollare* underground newspaper 134; role in escape network 164, 165–166, *168*, 169; arrest and imprisonment 169, 170, 182–3, 202, 213; trial 183–7; *confino* on Lipari 187, 212–13, 214, 218, 221, 230–31, 232; arrested for complicity in Carlo Rosselli's escape 234; released from *confino* 280; resumed anti-fascist operations 280–82, 285; caught in secret police trap 285–8; returned to Lipari 290; in New York during wartime 364, 366; post-war prime minister 371; at Rosselli brothers' reburial in Florence 373, *374*
Parri, Giorgio ('Dodo') 212, 232
partisans (Second World War) 366–7, 368, 371
Partito d'Azione 367, 371
Partito Popolare Italiano 261
Peace, Charles 121
Peacock, Mrs (friend of Marion Cave) 226
pellagra (disease) 37
Pellizzi, Camillo 103
penal islands 161, 174, 176, 188–92, 240–42, 371; *see also* Lipari; Ponza; Ustica
Pentecostalists 357
Perpignan 292
Perrone Compagni, Marchese Dino 81

Pertini, Sandro: early life 120, 164; leaves Italy 167–9, *168*; in exile 247, 280; trial of escape accomplices 183–7; arrest and imprisonment on return to Italy 280–81; on Amelia Rosselli 359
Perugia 86, 87
Perugia university 341
Petacci, Clara 368
Petrarch 3
Picasso, Pablo 355–6
Pietre (magazine) 215
Pignone, steelworks 32, 79
Pilati, Bruno 147, 149
Pilati, Gaetano 135; murdered 146–7, 149, 185
Pincherle, Amelia *see* Rosselli, Amelia Pincherle
Pincherle, Anna 2, 4, 29, 309
Pincherle, Carlo 2, 4, 17, 110, 158, 369
Pincherle, Elena 2
Pincherle, Emilia 1–2, 3, 4, 7, 8, 13
Pincherle, Gabriele: appearance and character 2; education 2; legal career 8, 17, 29; relationship with sister Amelia and her sons 29, 45, 80; and Aldo Rosselli's military service and death 57–8; member of Senate 141, 199; visits and assistance to imprisoned nephews 175, 176, 199; death 219–20
Pincherle, Giacomo 1–2, 3, 4, 7, 50
Pincherle, Leone 3
Pini (Milanese doctor) 166
Pinocchio (fictional character) 269
Pinzi, Renzo 135, 136, 139
Pirandello, Luigi 23, 317, 348
Pirelli (tyre manufacturer) 103
Pisa 130
Pisa university 62
Pisacane, Carlo 120, 136, 243, 264; Nello Rosselli's biography 243, 264, 275
Pistoia 144, 211
'Pitigrilli' (spy) *see* Segre, Dino
Pius IX, Pope 8
Pius XI, Pope 88, 267, 268, 273, 275–6
Plath, Sylvia 370
plebiscite (1929) 266

Poggiolino, Villa del 23, 24, 54
Poincaré, Raymond 248
Polpol (Divisione Polizia Politica) 182, 251, 282, 345, 371
Ponte Tresa, Switzerland 312
Pontine Marshes, draining of 266, 271, 304
Ponza, penal colony 198, 241–3
Popolo d'Italia, Il (newspaper) 49, 68, 74, 83, 125, 169, 240, 250, 261, 337
Popp, Adelheid 15
Popular Culture, Ministry of 304
Porcellotti, Maria 211
Portofino 159
Poveromo, Amleto 181–2n
Predappio 37
Prezzolini, Giuseppe 25, 36, 37
Pritchard, Bertha 238, 250, 261, 263, 302
Pro Cultura (Florentine Jewish association) 39
Prospero, Ada see Gobetti, Ada
Pucci, Enrico 273
Puccini, Giacomo, Madama Butterfly 99
Pupeschi, Bice 163
Putnam's (publishing house) 263

Quaderni di Giustizia e Libertà, I (newspaper) 300–301, 302–3, 337, 338, 356
Quainton, Buckinghamshire 360, 361–2
Quarto Stato, Il (magazine) 155, 157–8, 159, 163–4, 248

racial laws 362, 367
radio 180–81
railways 41, 283
Rama VII, King of Siam 304
Rapallo 172
Ravenna 85, 283
Red Cross, International Committee of the 241, 317
Red Week (June 1914) 46–7
Rèfolo, El (play; Amelia Rosselli) 30–31, 38
Reggio Calabria 35
Regina Margherita (vaporetto) 6
Rennell, 1st Baron (previously Sir Rennell Rodd) 103

Restellini, Camilla 296
revolutions of 1848 3
Rey, Captain (spy) 283
Ricci, Renato 85, 128–9
Rignano sull'Arno, Villa Il Frassine 25, 48, 75, 140–41, 306, 307, 352, 367
Rimini 85
Risorgimento 3, 10, 102, 133, 192, 245; unification (1870) 1, 3–4, 8, 11, 16, 93
Rivoluzione Liberale (magazine) 95, 96–7, 98, 154
Robespierre, Maximilien 239
Rocco, Alfredo 254
Roda, Graziella 339
Rodd, Sir Rennell (later 1st Baron Rennell) 103
Rolland, Romain 70
Roma del Popolo, La (newspaper) 11, 17
Rome: becomes capital of unified Italy 8, 11; post-unification development 8; Ernesto Nathan as mayor 29, 37, 45; Red Week riots (1914) 46; Mussolini's march on (1922) 86, 87–8; fascists' suppression of local opposition candidates 114; Mussolini's plans for redevelopment 271–2; anti-fascists' leafleting flight over 292, 293–4; Exhibition of the Fascist Revolution (1932–34) 303–4; liberation (1944) 367
Rome (places and landmarks): Campidoglio 159; Colosseum 272; EUR 272; Foro Mussolini 268; Hotel Savoia 87; Palazzo Chigi 90, 152, 270, 271; Palazzo del Quirinale 8; Palazzo Marignoli 16; Palazzo Torlonia 271; Palazzo Venezia 270, 280, 292, 293; Piazza Navona 8, 333, 370; Piazza San Silvestro 283; Pincio 8; Regina Coeli prison 136, 139, 286, 287, 289; Via Nazionale 8; see also Scuola di Storia Moderna e Contemporanea
Roosevelt, Eleanor 362
Roosevelt, Franklin Delano 304
Rosenwald, Marion 362

Ross, Janet 60

Rosselli, Alberto 341, 342, 348, 352, 359, *360*, 362, *363*, 365, 368, 373

Rosselli, Aldo (Carlo and Nello's brother; 'Topinino'): birth 16; childhood 19–21, 25, 27–30, 39–41; schooling 27, 28, 39, 40; death of father 41; university student 48, 53; pro-interventionist position on Italian entry into War 49, 50, 53; joins up 53; officer training 53–4, *54*; active service 54–7; killed in action 57–8, 62, 64, 72; charities and organisations established in memory 58–9, 60, 64; posthumous award of medal for valour 69; reburial 216

Rosselli, Aldo (Nello's son) 310, 342, 352, *358*, 359, *360*, 362, *363*, 365, 368, 373

Rosselli, Amelia Pincherle: family background 1–4; birth 1; childhood in Venice 1, 2, 4–7, 28, 50; death of father 7; family moves to Rome 7, 8; first meets Giuseppe Rosselli 8–9; their courtship and engagement 9, 12–13; marriage and honeymoon 13; early married life in Vienna 14, 15–16; growing interest in art and culture 14, 15; writes first play (*Anima*) 15–16; birth of first son (Aldo) 16; family returns to Rome 16, 17; first productions and success of *Anima* 17–18, 20, 27, 38; writes first novella (*Felicità Perduta*) 18; birth of second and third sons (Carlo and Nello) 18; breakdown of marriage 18, 19; moves with children to Florence 19–21; writes first children's book (*Topinino*) 20–21; friendship with Laura Orvieto 22–5, 38–9, 44; introduced to Giulio and Giorgina Zabban ('Zio Giù' and 'Zia Gì') 25; growing role in literary and political life of Florence 26–8, 30–31, 37–8, 44–5; raising of children 27–30, 39–41, 44, 47–8, 60, 125; founder member of Lyceum Club Florentine chapter 38, 44, 45, 52; friendship with Gina Lombroso 38–9; death of husband 41, 45; writing and production of new play (*San Marco*) 45; reaction to outbreak of First World War 47–8, 49, 50, 52; wartime work 52–3, 57; and Aldo's military service 53–4, 55; Aldo's death 57–8, 62, 72; establishes charities and organisations in Aldo's memory 58–9, 60, 64; moves to flat in Via San Niccolò 62–3; wealth from inherited mining shares 69; buys house on Via Giusti 69; writing of *Fratelli Minori* 71; gradual resumption of position in cultural and political life of Florence 71–3, 110, 111; reaction to fascist takeover 92; arranges treatment for Nello after motorcycle accident 109, 110; support for young Alberto Moravia 110, 158; reaction to raid on Circolo di Cultura 130; *squadristi* raids on family home 140–42, 146; meets up with sons in Alto Adige 142–3; leaves Florence during St Bartholomew's Night attacks 146; returns to family home after attacks 147–8, 149; reservations about Carlo's proposed engagement to Marion Cave 149, 156; stays with Carlo in Genoa 149–50, 152; returns to Florence and diminishing circle of friends 153–4; disappointment at Carlo's resignation from teaching posts 157; reaction to Carlo's marriage 158, 159; visits Carlo and Marion in Milan 165; Carlo's arrest and imprisonment 169, 170–71, 175; Nello's marriage 173–4; Nello's arrest and imprisonment 176, 177; birth of first grandchild 177; Carlo's trial 184; visits Nello during *confino* on Ustica 195, 196, 198; seeks help for Nello from Gioacchino Volpe at university in Rome 199;

visits Carlo during *confino* on Lipari 211, 219; birth of granddaughter Silvia 215; death of brother Gabriele 219–20; re-arrest and imprisonment of Nello following Carlo's escape 237, 238, 239, 242; visits imprisoned daughter-in-law and grandson in Aosta 238; Nello's release 243; stays with Nello and family at Bagno a Ripoli 243–5; reaction to Carlo's anti-fascist operations in exile 258; life with Nello's family in Florence 260, 297, 306–8, 339; visits Nello during research trip to London 263, 264; resigns from Lyceum club 276, 341; ceases publishing ventures and play-writing 276; birth of grandson Andrea 291; deaths of Leo Ferrero, Giulio Zabban and sister Anna 309–10; Carlo's children visit in Florence 326–7; in Paris while Carlo goes to Civil War in Spain 329; remains in Florence during Carlo and Nello's trip to Normandy 342, 348; learns of their deaths 352; travels to Paris 352; at the wake and funeral 353–4, 355; remains in Paris following funeral 357–9; rents house in Switzerland 359–61; moves to England with daughter-in-law and family 360, 361–2; family leaves Europe for United States following outbreak of war 361–2, *363*; life in New York 364–6; returns to Italy after war 368–70; later life and death 372

Character & characteristics: altruism 5, 23; appearance 8, 9, *12*, 31, *54*, 72, 243–5, *360*, *363*; courage 2; elegance 23, 72; family nicknames 211; handwriting 62; honesty 8; insecurity 8, 72; intelligence 8; Jewishness 39–40, 124, 341; languages spoken 5, 8, 15, 72; letter-writing 12, 13; literary reputation 17–18, 20, 27, 31; motherhood 16, 18, 27–30, 39–41, 44, 47, 60, 125; pets 5, 6, 276; philanthropy 17, 26, 58–9, 60; sadness 31, 58; sense of duty 2, 60; strength of character 8

Writings: *Anima* 15–16, 17–18, 20, 27, 38; *Emma Liona* 52, 110; *Felicità Perduta* 18; *Fratelli Minori* 71; *Gente Oscura* 26; *L'idea Fissa* 30; *Illusione* 26–7; *El Rèfolo* 30–31, 38; *San Marco* 45; *El Socio del Papá* 30; *Topinino* 20–21, 125; *Topinino, Garzone di Bottega* 27–8

Rosselli, Andrea ('Aghi') 291, 299, 322, 323, 326–7, 336, 348, 352, *358*, *363*, 368, 370, 373

Rosselli, Angiolo 9–10

Rosselli, Carlo: birth 18; childhood 19–20, 23, 25, 27–30, 31, 39–41, 45, 47–8, 50, 52; schooling 28, 39; death of father 41; convalescence in Viareggio at time of outbreak of war 47–8; and brother Aldo's military service 54, 55; death of Aldo 57–9; contributions to *Noi Giovani* magazine 59; leaves school 60; called up 60; military training and service 60–61, 62–3, 63–4; nineteenth birthday 63–4; returns home after end of war 64–5, 69–71; university studies 65, 73, 79–80, 84, 100–101; on editorial committee of *Vita* magazine 70; disciple of Gaetano Salvemini 73–5, 93; Circolo di Cultura group meetings 75, 83, 93, 98–9, 100, 111, 129–30; attends Socialist Party National Congress 80; meets Filippo Turati 80, 95; reaction to fascist takeover 85, 92, 93, 100, 108, 114, 122; moves to Turin to complete university studies 93–6, 100–101; meets Piero Gobetti 95, 96; contributions to *Rivoluzione Liberale* magazine 96–7, 98; accepts part-time academic posts in Milan and Genoa 101; travels to England for Fabian summer school 101–2, 104–7, *106*; and brother Nello's motorcycle accident 110; takes up posts in Milan and Genoa 111–12, 138, 149–50, 152; admiration for Giacomo Matteotti 115; reaction to Matteotti's murder 118–19; returns to England to observe first Labour government 121–3; takes part in Italia Libera stunts in Florence 123–4, 125; reaction to raid on Circolo di Cultura 129–30; production of *Non Mollare* underground newspaper 132–6, 143, 144; arrested following wreath-laying in honour of Matteotti 138–9; at Salvemini's trial 139; learns of *squadristi* raid on family home 140–42; meets up with mother and brother in Alto Adige 142–3; leaves Florence during St Bartholomew's Night attacks 146, 148; courtship with Marion Cave 149, 150, 156; closes down *Non Mollare* 149; mother and brother stay with in Genoa 149–50, 152–3; death of Amendola and Gobetti 150–51; collaboration with Pietro Nenni 154–5; publication of *Il Quarto Stato* magazine 155–6; attacked in street 156–7; resigns from teaching posts 157, 158; remains in Milan to continue editing *Il Quarto Stato* 157–8; marriage and honeymoon 158, 172; travels to Stresa and Portofino with Marion 158–9; early married life in Milan 159, 164, 165; *Il Quarto Stato* shut down 163–4; establishment of escape network 164, 165–6; Turati's escape 166–9, *168*, 174, 313; arrest and imprisonment 169, 170–71, 174, 213; transferred to penal island 174–5, 176, 182–3, 190; birth of son Giovanni ('Mirtillino') 177, 184; trial 171, 183–7; Mussolini sends back to internal exile 187, 190; *confino* on Lipari 190, 202–214, 215–16, 218–20; begins writing *Socialismo Liberale* 214,

229, 231; escape plans 207, 220, 221–8, *224*; death of uncle Gabriele 219–20; aborted first escape attempt 228; renewed escape planning 228–31; escapes from Lipari 231–5, *233*, 274; reaches Tunis 233–4, 236; travels to Paris 236–7, 248; successful campaign for release of wife and son 237–9; early role in exile community in Paris 240, 248, 254, 278–80; foundation of Giustizia e Libertà movement 248–9, 254, 282; establishes family home in Paris 249–50, 291; continues work on *Socialismo Liberale* 250; short speaking tour in London 250; secret police's surveillance of 251–2, 265, 277, 283, 299, 311–14, 316–17, 320, 322, 329–30, 371; completion of *Socialismo Liberale* 255; birth of daughter Melina 255; organises leafleting flight over Milan 255–8; friendship with Don Luigi Sturzo 261–2; refused passport to visit Nello in London 262; visited by Alberto Moravia 263; family life in Paris 278, 291, 297–300, 321–3, 326, 341; publication of *Socialismo Liberale* 279–80; Giustizia e Libertà movement targeted by Italian secret police 282–91; birth of son Andrea 291–2; visits Spain following establishment of Second Republic 292–3; plans for further leafleting flight 292, 294–5; capture and imprisonment in Koblenz 295–6; released with fine 296; returns to Paris 297–300, 309–310; reaction to divisions between exile movements 300–301, 318–19; deaths of Turati and Treves 301–2, 318; developing role as leader in exile community 302, 318–21; publication of '*La guerra che torna*' article 302–3; campaigns on behalf of Velia Matteotti 304–5; family holidays

310, 323–7, *324*, *325*; targeted by spy 'Pitigrilli' 311–14, 339; opposition to Abyssinian war 316–18, 328; meets Trotsky 318–19; publishes *Giustizia e Libertà* newspaper 320–21, 323; reviews Moravia's *Le ambizioni sbagliate* 321; reaction to outbreak of Spanish Civil War 328–30; leaves for Spain 330; joint commander of Colonna Francisco Ascaso 330–31; fighting around Huesca 331–2; takes over sole command of unit 332–3, 334–5; under continued surveillance by Italian secret police 334, 338–9, 342; radio broadcast on behalf of Republicans 334, 337; falls ill 335–6; resigns from unit and returns home 335–6; role in recruitment for International Brigades 336–7; writes on Republicans' victory at Battle of Guadalajara 337–8; plans further leafleting flight over Italy 338–9; reaction to death of Antonio Gramsci 341–2; last holiday with Marion 342–3; convalescence trip to Normandy 342, 345, 346–9, *347*; reunited with Nello 347–9, *348*; their murder 349–50; autopsy and identification of body 351–2; news of death reaches Italy 352–4; wake and funeral in Paris 353–5; posthumous tributes 353, 355–6, 373–4; investigations into murders 355–7, 367–8; trial of perpetrators 368; reburial in Florence 373–4
Character & characteristics: analytical mind 218–19; appearance *vi*, 21, 29–30, *29*, 48, 49, 64, *106*, 112, *133*, *168*, *224*, *233*, 259, *324*, *325*, 330, *347*, *348*; argumentative manner 64; childhood illnesses 30, 39, 47, 335; courtesy 298; determination 159, 309–310; dislike of heat 331; eloquence 142; generosity 210, 298; gregariousness 205, 323;

gullibility 284, 313, 339; honesty 100, 259; impatience 100, 159, 259; intelligence 100–101, 112; Jewishness 216; languages spoken 101, 102, 106, 158, 237, 322; modesty 100; musical interests 40, 298; oratory skills 250, 334; rashness 142–3; restlessness 205, 223; self-belief 137, 219; sense of personal responsibility 125, 216; shortsightedness 64; stubborness 30, 298; unpunctuality 138; vanity 112
Writings: *Fuga in Quattro Tempi* 265; '*La guerra che torna*' (article) 302–3; *Socialismo Liberale* 97, 214, 229, 232, 250, 255, 279–80
Rosselli, Gianetta (*née* Nathan) 11, 20
Rosselli, Giovanni ('Mirtillino'): birth 177; names and nickname 177; infancy *183*, 184, 193, 210–11; family joins father during *confino* on Lipari 203, 210–13; visits England with mother 218; treated for amoebic dysentery 218; returns to Lipari 218; leaves Lipari with mother 230; imprisoned with mother following father's escape from *confino* 237, 238; their release 239; family life in Paris 249–50, 278, 322, 326; childhood development 255, 296, 298, *307*, 322, 326; in south of France with recuperating mother 292, 293; family holidays 310, 323, *324*, 336; schooling 322, 348; on father's surveillance by secret police 339; in Paris during parents' trip to Normandy 348; father's death 351, 352, 361; family leaves Europe for United States 361, 362, *363*; life in New York 365; family returns to Italy after war 368–9; university and military service 370; at father's reburial in Florence 373, *374*; death of mother 370
Rosselli, Giuseppe ('Joe'): appearance and character 9, *12*, 15, 18, 19, 40; family background 9–10; birth and childhood 10; education 9,

10; first meets Amelia Pincherle 8–9; their courtship and engagement 9, 12–13; marriage and honeymoon 13; early married life in Vienna 14, 15, 16; musical interests and training 9, 14, 16; birth of first son 16; family returns to Rome 16, 17; birth of second and third sons 18; death of father 18; gambling and financial difficulties 15, 18, 326; breakdown of marriage 18, 19; remains in Rome after wife leaves with children 19–20; subsequent contact with family 21, 41; final illness and death 41, 45; legacy 69

Rosselli, Henrietta (*née* Nathan) 10

Rosselli, Melina: birth 255; childhood 299, 322, 323, 326–7, 336, 337, *358*; father's death 352; family leaves Europe for United States 361–2, *363*; life in New York 365; family returns to Italy after war 368–9, 372; at father's reburial in Florence 373; later life and death 370

Rosselli, Mirtillino *see* Rosselli, Giovanni ('Mirtillino')

Rosselli, Nello *see* Rosselli, Sabatino ('Nello')

Rosselli, Paola: birth 243; infancy *217*, 243; early childhood 276, 277, 297, 306–8, 342, 348, *358*, *359*; father's death 352–3; family stays with grandmother in Switzerland 359–61; family moves to England *360*, 361–2; family leaves Europe for United States 361–2, *363*; life in New York 364–5; family returns to Italy after war 368–9; engagement 370; at father's reburial in Florence 373

Rosselli, Pellegrino 9–10, 11, 20

Rosselli, Raffaelo 9–10

Rosselli, Sabatino (Joe Rosselli's father) 9–10; death 18

Rosselli, Sabatino ('Nello'): birth 18; childhood 19–20, 21, 23, 25, 27–30, 39–41, 45, 47–8, 50; schooling 28, 39, 41; death of father 41; death of brother Aldo 57–8; co-edits *Noi Giovani* magazine 59; leaves school 60; enrols at university 62; volunteers for military service 62; military training 63; returns home after end of war 64–5, 69–71; resumption of university studies 65, 69–70, 73, 79–80; on editorial committee of *Vita* magazine 70; thesis on Mazzini 73, 100, 152, 173; disciple of Gaetano Salvemini 73–5; Circolo di Cultura group meetings 75, 83, 93, 98–9, 100, 111, 129–30; short posting as army reservist 81, 84; reaction to fascist takeover 92, 100, 114; injured in motorcycle accident 109; recuperation 109–110; works part-time for *La Voce* publishing house 111; reaction to Giacomo Matteotti's murder 118–19; role in Italia Libera movement 120–21, 123–4, 125; first meets Maria Todesco 124; their courtship 124, 136, 156; attends Jewish Youth Convention in Livorno 124–5; reaction to raid on Circolo di Cultura 129–30; production of *Non Mollare* underground newspaper 132–6; research trip to Germany 136–8, 140; learns of Salvemini's arrest and *squadristi* raid on family home 137–8, 142; meets up with mother and brother in Alto Adige 142–3; leaves Florence during St Bartholomew's Night attacks 146, 148; stays with brother in Genoa 149–50, 152–3; research and writing of *Mazzini e Bakunin* 152; contributions to *Il Quarto Stato* magazine 155; engagement to Maria 156; attends brother's wedding 158; brother's arrest and imprisonment 169, 174; marriage and honeymoon 169, 172–3, *172*; early married life 173–4, 175; awarded scholarship to Scuola di Storia Moderna e Contemporanea in

Rome 173; publication of *Mazzini e Bakunin* 174; arrest and imprisonment 175–7; sentenced to five years' internal exile 176, 183; *confino* on Ustica 190–201, 216; letter to Senator Boselli 199–200; freed after seven months' confinement 200–201; works on archival research 214–15, 216; visits Benedetto Croce 215; birth of daughter Silvia 215–16; oversees reburial of elder brother's remains 216; family moves to Turin 216, 218; publishes one issue of clandestine newspaper 216; death of uncle Gabriele 219–20; re-arrest and imprisonment following brother's escape from *confino* 237, 238, 239; transferred to Ponza penal colony 241–3; continues research projects during imprisonment 242–3; released from Ponza and charges dropped 243; birth of daughter Paola 243; buys L'Apparita at Bagno a Ripoli 243; research trip to London 260–66; meets up with Maria in Switzerland 264; writing of biography of Pisacane 264, 275; reluctantly returns to Italy 265–6, 267–8, 274; intellectual and social life in Florence under fascists 274–7, 308–9, 310; publication of biography of Pisacane 275; family life in Florence 297, 306–8, 309–310, 339–40; death of Leo Ferrero 309; birth of son Aldo 310; family holidays on French Riviera 310, 323, *325*; secret police's surveillance of 312–13, 339; listens to Carlo's broadcast from Spain 334; further planned literary projects 340; birth of son Alberto 341; travels to Normandy to meet Carlo 342, 345, 347–9, *348*; their murder 349–50; autopsy and identification of body 351–2; news of death reaches Italy 352–4; wake and funeral in Paris 353–5; posthumous tributes

353, 355–6, 373–4; investigations into murders 355–7, 367–8; trial of perpetrators 368; reburial in Florence 373–4
Character & characteristics: appearance *vi*, 29, 30, 64, 73, 80, *132, 172, 176, 217, 259, 325, 348*; determination 259–60; honesty 100, 137, 259; insecurity and self-doubt 137, 259, 340; intelligence 100–101; Jewishness 124–5, 137; languages spoken 136; modesty 100; musical interests 40; philanthropy 70; sense of personal responsibility 125, 216; stubborness 30; studiousness 64; worrying 109; writing style 340
Writings: article on Mazzini, Bakunin and the Paris Commune 111; *Carlo Pisacane nel Risorgimento Italiano* 243, 264, 275; *Mazzini e Bakunin* 152, 174, 260, 261
Rosselli, Silvia: birth 215–16; infancy 216; early childhood *217, 242, 243, 276, 277, 297, 306–8, 310, 342, 358, 359*; father's death 352–3; family stays with grandmother in Switzerland 359–61; family moves to England *360*, 361–2; family leaves Europe for United States 361–2, *363*; life in New York 364–5, 366; family returns to Italy after war 368–9; engagement 370; at father's reburial in Florence 373
Rosselli Brigades (wartime partisans) 367
Rossetti, Raffaele 223, 226–7, 231, 249
Rossi, Ada 281, 286, 287, 290, 291
Rossi, Cesare 114, 126, 134
Rossi, Elide 281, *286*, 289, 290–91
Rossi, Ernesto: family background 74; appearance and character 74, *286*; wounded during First World War 74; disciple of Gaetano Salvemini 74, 92–3, 98; attacked by *squadristi* 83; reaction to fascist takeover 92–3, 114; and Giacomo Matteotti's murder 118; leader of

Italia Libera movement 120, 123, 125, 130; production of *Non Mollare* underground newspaper 132–4, 135; escapes to France fearing arrest 136; on Gaetano Pilati 147; code name for 149; visits Carlo Rosselli in prison 170; resumed anti-fascist operations in Italy and France 280–82, 285; caught in secret police trap 285–6, 288, 289; attempted escape 287; trial and imprisonment 289–91, 319, 340, 353; marriage 291; reaction to Rosselli brothers' deaths 353; released 366; serves with partisans during wartime 366; at Carlo and Nello's reburial in Florence 373; later life and career 371; death 374

Rossi, Paolo 125

Rossi, Serenella 281, 289, 290

Rothermere, Harold Harmsworth, 1st Viscount 122

royal family, Italian *see* monarchy, Italian

Royan, France 323

Ruskin, John 6

Russell, Bertrand, 3rd Earl 121, 122

Russell, Dora, Countess 250, 305

Russian Revolution (1917) 59, 75–6; *see also* Bolshevism

Sagno, Ernesto 209

St Bartholomew's Night (1925) 146–8

St Paul's Girls' School, London 99

Saint-Just, Louis Antoine de 96

Salandra, Antonio 89

Salò Republic 367

salute, Roman, fascists' introduction of 92

Salvadori, Joyce 299

Salvatelli, Florinda 208–9

Salvation Army 357

Salvemini, Emanuela 34

Salvemini, Fernande (*earlier* Luchaire) 139, 196

Salvemini, Gaetano: appearance and character 35–6, 73, 97, *106*, 139, *298*, 364; background and early life 34–5; early academic career 35, 36; loses family in Messina earthquake 35, 53; political engagement 35–6; involvement in *La Voce* magazine 36; opposition to Libyan War 43–4; foundation of *L'Unità* newspaper 44; relations with Rosselli family 44, 45; shot at during Red Week riots 46; views on First World War 48–9, 62, 66; declined military service on health grounds 53; lectures at Anglo-Italian library in Florence 60; post-war resumption of academic position 73; early role in anti-fascist movement 73, 83–4; mentor to Rosselli brothers and their circle 73–5, 83, 92–3, 98–101, 112, 248, 262; elected to parliament 75, 77; challenged to duel by Mussolini 75; reaction to fascist takeover 88, 89, 92–3, 114, 126; lecture tour and Fabian summer school in England 101–2, 104–7, *106*; receives threats on return to Florence 109, 114; protests with Italia Libera movement 120, 123; involvement in *Non Mollare* underground newspaper 134, 135; marriage to Fernande Luchaire 139; arrested in Rome 136, 137–8; imprisonment and trial 139–40; friends and lawyers attacked on his release 140; leaves Italy with incriminating documents against Mussolini 140; in exile in France and England 142, 153, 156, 211, 226, 245, 246, 248; on death of Pietro Gobetti 151; visits Marion Cave's parents in England 156; signatory to *Manifesto of Antifascist Intellectuals* 161; on birth of Carlo Rosselli's first son 177; and Carlo's escape from *confino* 226, 229, 236; campaigns for release of Carlo's wife 237–8; founder member of Giustizia e Libertà movement 249, 282, 285; publication of *The Fascist Dictatorship in Italy* 261; reunited with Nello in London 262, 264;

on fascist propaganda machine 267; on Carlo Rosselli's *Socialismo Liberale* 279; campaigns to save *giellisti* colleagues from death penalty 289; friendship with Lauro de Bosis 293, 294; breaks with Giustizia e Libertà 300; campaigns on behalf of Velia Matteotti 305–6; opposition to Abyssinian war 318; disagreements with Carlo 319, 338; joins Carlo's family on trips 323, 326; on Carlo's departure for Civil War in Spain 330; settles in United States 338, 362, 364, 366; reaction to Carlo and Nello's deaths 353, 356, 368; returns to Italy after war 370; speaks at Marion Cave's memorial service and Carlo and Nello's reburial 370, 373, 374; death 374

Salvemini, Maria 35

Salvemini, Ughetto 35, 53

San Domenico 22, 146

San Marco (play; Amelia Rosselli) 45

San Sebastian, Spain 345

Santa Margherita Ligure 158

Santillán, Diego Abad de 330

Santo Stefano, prison 281

Santoni, Vera 209

Sardinia 206, 267, 280

Sarfatti, Margherita (*née* Grassini) 5, 37, 52, 171, 181, 263

Sarno, Pasquale 186

Savona 85, 114, 167; 'Trial of the Professors' 183–7, 257

Savonarola, Girolamo 143

Sbardelotto, Angelo 311

Scalarini, Giuseppe 193

Schirru, Michele 289

Schnitzler, Arthur 15; *Fräulein Else* 230

schools, under fascists 269, 275

Schulz, Elisabeth 339

Scuola di Storia Moderna e Contemporanea, Rome 173, 199, 260

Second International (socialist) 303

Second World War 361–2, 366–7, 371

Segre, Dino (agent 'Pitigrilli') 311–14, 339

Segre, Sion 310, 311, 312

Serge, Victor 298

Sesto Fiorentino 79

Settignano 22, 23; I Tatti 142, 153

Seville, Spain 13

Sforza, Carlo 245, 257–8

Shaw, George Bernard 104, 289, 305, 319; *St Joan* 122

Sheridan, Clare 89

Siele mercury mine, Rosselli family's income from shares in 69, 98, 134

Siena 82, 140; Collegio Tolomei 40; Palio 77

Sigma N (boat) 226–7, 228, 229

Silvestro (imprisoned journalist) 166, 170, 174

Sinclair, Upton 204

Siusi allo Sciliar 142–3

Smedley, Constance 38

Social Democratic Party (German) 136

Social Democratic Workers Party (Austrian) 15

Socialismo Liberale (Carlo Rosselli) 97, 214, 229, 232, 250, 255, 279–80

Socialist Party (Italian) 33, 46–7, 49, 71, 75, 78, 80, 83, 87, 93; *see also* Aventine Secession; United Socialist Party

Società Leonardo da Vinci 23, 52, 341

Socio del Papá, El (play; Amelia Rosselli) 30

Soir, Le (Brussels newspaper) 294

Somaliland 17, 315, 316, 362

Sorbonne University 361

Sorrento 142

Sortino (penal colony director) 197

Spain: election of 1931 and establishment of Second Republic 292; outbreak of Civil War 328–9; international involvement in war 328, 333; foreign volunteers 330–31, 336–7; fighting in Aragon 331–3, 335; Franco installed as head of state 333; Battle of Guadalajara 337–8; escalation of war 359; *see also* Barcelona; Madrid

Spangano (*confinato* on Lipari) 222

Spanish flu epidemic (1918) 63

Special Tribunal for the Defence of the State 161, 186, 189, 207, 290

Spectator (magazine) 240

sport and exercise, under fascism 179, 180, 268, 304

Sprigge, Sylvia 140

squadristi (paramilitaries): formation and growth 77, 78, 81–2, 86; first punitive raids 77–9, 77, 81–6, 88, 99, 109, 127; attacks on press 77, 82–3, 84, 112–13, 117, 129, 143, 144–5; suppression of attempted general strike 84; reformation into national militia (MVSN) 91; *seconda ondata* of punitive expeditions 124, 126, 127–30, 128, 130, 143–9, 206; raids on Rosselli family home 140–42, 146; St Bartholomew's Night attacks 146–8; reorganisation of Tuscan militia 148, 153; trials 148–9

Stagnetto, Spartaco 197

Stalin, Joseph 181, 333; Stalinism 342

Steed, Henry Wickham 121

Strasbourg 121

Strauss, Johann 14

Stresa 158–9

strikes and industrial unrest 32, 76, 76, 79, 84, 93–4; abolition of right to strike 178

Stromboli 211

Sturzo, Don Luigi 261–2, 267, 293, 319, 321, 364

Suardo, Giacomo 200

Suckert, Kurt Erich (Curzio Malaparte) 127

suffrage, women's 71–2, 110–111

Sunday Times (newspaper) 294

Swarthmore College, Pennsylvania 370

Tablet, The (magazine) 267

Tagli (*confinato* on Lipari) 209

Tamburini, Tullio 81, 82, 87, 128–9, 144, 148

Tarchiani, Alberto: appearance and character 223; career in journalism 223; role in Carlo Rosselli's escape from *confino* 223–4, 226–7, 229–30, 231, 234, 236; founder member of Giustizia e Libertà movement 249, 254, 277, 279, 286, 304; organisation of leafleting flights 255, 256, 257, 258, 295, 296, 338; visits Spain following establishment of Second Republic 292; breaks with Giustizia e Libertà 319; at Rosselli brothers' funeral 354; in New York during wartime 364; returns to Italy to serve with partisans 366; later life and career 371

Tatti, I (villa) 142, 153

Tawney, R.H. 102, 122

Teatro dell'Arte (theatre company) 17

Telegrafo, Il (newspaper) 355

Tellini, Enrico, assassinated 108

Tenaille, Charles 368

Teresa (maid) 4, 6

Térésah (fairy-story writer) 45

Terni 85

Terrassa, Spain 331

Tétouan, Morocco 13

Thorndike, Dame Sibyl 122

Tiberius Gracchus the Elder 211

Timau 64, 216

Times, The (newspaper) 88, 89, 112, 122, 237, 355

Times Educational Supplement 98

Todesco, Gianna 367

Todesco, Luisa 194, 198–9, 306, 352, 367, 369

Todesco, Maria: appearance and character 124, 172, 196, 217, 363; background and early life 124; first meets Nello Rosselli 124; their courtship and engagement 124, 136, 156; marriage and honeymoon 169, 172–3, 172; early married life 173–4, 175; first pregnancy and miscarriage 173, 175; Nello's arrest and imprisonment 'as danger to state' 175–6, 177; joins Nello during *confino* on Ustica 194–201; second pregnancy 195–6, 199; couple leaves Ustica and settles in Rome 200–201, 215; birth of daughter Silvia 215–16; family moves to Turin 216; Nello's re-arrest following brother's escape from *confino* 237; in Florence during Nello's second period of imprisonment 242; Nello's release 243; birth of daughter Paola 243; family buys L'Apparita at Bagno a Ripoli 243; meets up with Nello in Switzerland and London 264; Nello returns to family in Italy 265–6, 266–7; social and family life in Florence 276–7, 297, 306–8, 339–40; birth of son Aldo 310; family holidays on French Riviera 310, 323; birth of son Alberto 339, 341; remains in Florence while Nello travels to Normandy 342; Nello's death 352, 353–4; family stays with mother-in-law in Switzerland 359–61; family moves to England 361–2; family leaves Europe for United States following outbreak of war 361–2, *363*; life in New York 364–6; returns to Italy after war 368–70, 372; at Nello and Carlo's reburial in Florence 373

Todesco, Max 124, 264, 367, 369
Togliatti, Palmiro 356
'Togo' (spy) *see* Odin, René
Tolmezzo 54
Tolstoy, Leo, *War and Peace* 218, 326
Topinino stories (Amelia Rosselli) 20–21, 27–8, 125
Torrigiani, Domizio 147, 208, 213, 231, 234
Toscanini, Arturo 179, 289, 322, 354
totalitarianism 177–83, 188–9, 266–76, 302, 304
Toynbee, Arnold 289
'tragic Sunday' (August 1920) 79
Traina, Egidio 316
Traquandi, Nello 120, 125, 132, 134, 280, 286, 290, 340, 373, 374
trasformismo (coalition-building process) 16, 34
Tremiti Islands 43, 189

Trento 48, 50, 63
Trevelyan, Sir Charles 121
Treves, Claudio 93, *95*, 165; leaves Italy 166; in exile in Paris 245, 248, 280; production of *La Libertà* newspaper 247; death 301–2, 318, 354
'Trial of the Intellectuals' (1931) 289–91
'Trial of the Professors' (1927) 183–7, 257
Trieste 48, 50, 52, 63–4, 280
Tripolitania *see* Libya
Trotsky, Leon 318–19
Tunis 227, 231, 234, 236
Turati, Filippo: appearance and character 33, *91*, *95*, *168*, 245, *300*, *346*; relationship with Anna Kuliscioff 33, 95–6, 150, 167, 247; leader of Italian Socialist Party 33, 46, 75, 78, 80; Carlo Rosselli first meets 80, 95–6; on rise of fascists 84, 88, 113; expulsion from Socialist Party and establishment of United Socialist Party 87, 93; Milan apartment as meeting place for young intellectuals 95–6, 138; reaction to Giacomo Matteotti's murder 116, 117; fascists' threats against 124, 166; death of Anna Kuliscioff 150, 152, 166; views on ineffectiveness of Aventine secessionists 161; escape from Italy 166–9, *168*, 174, 313; in exile in Paris 184, 196, 245, 246, *246*, 247, 299–300; trial of escape accomplices 183–7, 257; greets escaped *confinati* 236–7; support for Fernando de Rosa 254; testifies at anti-fascist leafleters' trial 257; views on Carlo Rosselli's *Socialismo Liberale* 280; description of Camilla Restellini 296; liaison between exile groups 299–300; declining health 301; death 301, 318, 354
Turin: civic pride and characteristics of Piemontese 93; role in Italian unification 3, 93; industry 93–4; strikes and industrial unrest 76,

93–4; falls to fascists 87; anti-fascist movement 94–5; fascists' suppression of opposition 114, 117; remaining anti-fascist networks 280, 310; mass arrests of anti-fascists 312–13
Turin (places and landmarks): Fiat factory 93; theatres 17, 26; Via XX Settembre 96
Turin university 93, 94, 274–5
Two Sicilies, Kingdom of the 3

Udine 55, 114, 216
Umberto I, King 6, 34
Umberto, Crown Prince (*later* King Umberto II) 272; assassination attempt 253
unification of Italy (1870) 1, 3–4, 8, 11, 16, 93
Unità, L (newspaper) 44, 73
United Press (news agency) 240
United Socialist Party (PSU) 93, 118–19
Università Proletaria, Milan 112
universities, under fascists 274–6; *see also* Bocconi University; Florence university; Genoa university; Scuola di Storia Moderna e Contemporanea; Turin university
Urbino 114
Ustica, penal colony 176, 188, 189, 190–201, *194*, 207, 213, 239
Uxbridge, Middlesex 99, 156

Vado Ligure 167
Valentino, Rudolph 364
Valiani, Guido 283
Vanden Heuvel, Maria 263
Vannucci, Dino 120, 123, 135
Varazze 171
Varese 85, 167
Vatican *see* Catholic Church; papacy
Vendée revolt (1793) 160
Venice: Jewish community 2–3; Austrian rule 2–3, 6; siege of 1848–49 3, 4, 45, 50; Risorgimento and Italian unification 3–4; launch of vaporetto service 6; foreign tourism 6, 7; theatrical life 30; *fasci* movement 68; Futurists'

plans for 270
Venice (places and landmarks): Giudecca 3; Grand Canal 1, 6; Lido 7; Murano 7; Palazzo Boldù 1, 4; Piazza San Marco 6; public gardens 5; Veneta Marina 5
Venice Biennale (1934) 314
Vercelli 145
Verdi, Giuseppe 17, 50; *Simon Boccanegra* 340
Verne, Jules 240
Verona 55
Versailles Conference (1919) 66–7
Viareggio 47, 287
Vicién, Spain 331
Victor Emmanuel II, King 8
Victor Emmanuel III, King: appearance and character 34, 43, 90, 272–3, *314*; accession 34; opposition to Libyan War 43; during First World War 64; asks Mussolini to form government 87; refuses call for martial law 88; Mussolini's twice-weekly meetings with 90; welcomes Acerbo Law election revision 113; refuses Mussolini's resignation following murder of Matteotti xiv; approves Mussolini's new cabinet 131; royal visit to Florence (1924) 135–6; during Hitler's visit to Italy *314*; becomes Emperor of Abyssinia 318
Vienna 14–16
Vienna Secession (art movement) 14
Vigevano 63
Villars, Switzerland 359–61
Vita (magazine) 70
Viterbo 85
Vivaldi, Antonio 7
Viviani della Robbia, Maria Bianca 31
Voce, La (magazine) 36, 37, 111
Voce della Donna, La (magazine) 304
volata (sport) 179
Volpe, Gioacchino 173, 199–200, 214–15, 243, 260, 265, 275, 340, 373
Volpi, Albino 79, 114, 181–2*n*
Voltaire 204

Vonin, Paul 231
Vulcano 211, 221

Wagner, Otto 14
Wagner, Richard 7
Wal Wal incident (1934) 315–16
Waterfield, Lina 80–81, 92, 123
Webb, Beatrice 104
Webb, Sidney (*later* Baron Passfield)
  104, 105
West Isleworth, Middlesex 370
West, Dame Rebecca 121
women's suffrage 71–2, 110–11

youth organisations, fascist 179–80,
  179, 180, 266, 268, 315

Zabban, Giorgina ('Zia Gì'):
  appearance and character 25, *307*;
  literary career 25; as honorary
  aunt to Rosselli family 25, 28, 31,
  41, 58, 64, 154, 175, 196, 306;
  circle of female friends 38–9;
  contributions to organisations in
  Aldo Rosselli's memory 59;
  membership of Lyceum Club 111;
  during St Bartholomew's Night
  attacks 146; death of husband
  309; deaths of Carlo and Nello
  Rosselli 352–3; in wartime
  Florence 367
Zabban, Giulio ('Zio Giù'):
  appearance and character 25, *307*;
  career 25; as honorary uncle to
  Rosselli family 25, 31, 58, 60–61,
  154, 175, 306; wartime military
  service 55; death 309
Zamboni, Anteo 160
Zamboni, Assunto 339
Zanata, Giuseppe 317
Zanella, Alfredo 338–9
Zani, Pietro 281–2
Zaniboni, Tito, assassination plot
  against Mussolini 152, 153, 160
Zanotti Bianco, Umberto 140
Zionism 39, 124–5, 341